Collins COBUILD

Key Words for IELTS

Book 1: STARTER

HarperCollins Publishers
Westerhill Road
Bishopbriggs
Glasgow
G64 2QT

First edition 2011

Reprint 10 9 8 7 6 5 4 3 2 1

© HarperCollins Publishers 2011

ISBN 978-0-00-736545-6

Collins ® is a registered trademark of
HarperCollins Publishers Limited

www.collinslanguage.com

A catalogue record for this book is
available from the British Library

Typeset by Davidson Publishing
Solutions, Glasgow

Printed in Great Britain by Clays Ltd,
St Ives plc

Editorial staff

Senior editor
Julie Moore

Project manager
Lisa Sutherland

Contributors
Sandra Anderson
Jamie Flockhart
Lucy Hollingworth
Kate Mohideen
Elizabeth Walter
Kate Wild
Kate Woodford

For the publishers
Lucy Cooper
Kerry Ferguson
Gavin Gray
Elaine Higgleton

Computing support
Thomas Callan

The publishers would like to thank
the following for their invaluable
contribution to the series:
Sharon Chalmers
Rachael Clarke
Jane Cursiter
Patrick Hubbuck
Martin Jenkins

contents

introduction

Collins COBUILD KeyWords for IELTS: Book 1 Starter is the first in a series of three vocabulary books created for learners of English who plan to take the IELTS exam. Book 1: Starter is aimed at students making the move from general English to IELTS preparation and provides a solid grounding in the key words you need to start working towards the IELTS exam.

The first section of the book consists of **word lists** organized by subject and topic area. You can use these lists to help you **revise** sets of vocabulary or when preparing for writing tasks. The words are grouped into **common topics**, such as working life and the environment. The word lists also contain vocabulary organized by **functions**, such as talking about types and groups of people or time expressions, which will help you to express yourself fluently.

The second section of the book contains alphabetically ordered dictionary-style entries for **key words** and **phrases**. The vocabulary items have been chosen to fully prepare you for the kind of language found in the IELTS exam. The words and phrases regularly appear in the most **common IELTS topics**, and are clearly labelled by subject area. More formal vocabulary, including words from the **Academic Word List**, have also been included to introduce you to the style of language used in formal, written contexts. You will find all the basic vocabulary you need to start tackling IELTS-style writing tasks, such as data commentary and basic essays.

Each word is illustrated with **examples** of natural English taken from the Collins corpus and reflects the style of language used in IELTS texts. As well as definitions and examples, entries include additional information about **collocations** and **phrases**, as well as **usage notes** to help you put the vocabulary you have learnt into practice.

There are **synonyms** and **antonyms** at each entry to help you widen your range of vocabulary and create more variety in your writing style. The **Extend your vocabulary** boxes help you understand the differences between sets of similar words, so you can be sure that your English is accurate and natural.

We hope you enjoy preparing for IELTS using Collins COBUILD KeyWords for IELTS. Once you have mastered the vocabulary in Book 1, the words and phrases in Books 2 and 3 will help you to not only achieve the IELTS score you are aiming for, but equip you for success in the future.

We have used the International Phonetic Alphabet (IPA) to show how the words are pronounced.

IPA Symbols

Vowel Sounds

ɑː	calm, ah
æ	act, mass
aɪ	dive, cry
aɪə	fire, tyre
aʊ	out, down
aʊə	flour, sour
e	met, lend, pen
eɪ	say, weight
eə	fair, care
ɪ	fit, win
iː	seem, me
ɪə	near, beard
ɒ	lot, spot
eʊ	note, coat
ɔː	claw, more
ɔɪ	boy, joint
ʊ	could, stood
uː	you, use
ʊə	sure, pure
ɜː	turn, third
ʌ	fund, must
ə	the first vowel in about

Consonant Sounds

b	bed, rub
d	done, red
f	fit, if
g	good, dog
h	hat, horse
j	yellow, you
k	king, pick
l	lip, bill
m	mat, ram
n	not, tin
p	pay, lip
r	run, read
s	soon, bus
t	talk, bet
v	van, love
w	win, wool
x	loch
z	zoo, buzz
ʃ	ship, wish
ʒ	measure, leisure
ŋ	sing, working
tʃ	cheap, witch
θ	thin, myth
ð	then, bathe
dʒ	joy, bridge

Notes

Primary and secondary stress are shown by marks above and below the line, in front of the stressed syllable. For example, in the word *abbreviation*, /əˌbriːviˈeɪʃən/, the second syllable has secondary stress and the fourth syllable has primary stress.

We do not normally show pronunciations for compound words (words which are made up of more than one word). Pronunciations for the words that make up the compounds are usually found at their entries in other parts of the book. However, compound words do have stress markers.

Headwords are organized in alphabetical order.

Labels tell you more about how and when the word is used

Words from the Academic Word List are highlighted

Words from the same root are shown together

at|tain /əˈteɪn/ *(attains, attaining, attained)*   `ACADEMIC WORD`

VERB If you **attain** something, you gain it or achieve it, often after a lot of effort. [FORMAL] ○ *the best way to attain the objectives of our strategy* ○ *Business has yet to attain the social status it has in other countries.*

▶ COLLOCATIONS:
attain **enlightenment/perfection**
attain a **status/rank/goal/objective**

> **EXTEND YOUR VOCABULARY**
>
> You can talk about **reaching** or **achieving** something like a goal or a level. ○ *The temperature reached the required level.* ○ *There are simpler ways of achieving the same result.*
>
> **Attain** is a more formal verb, used especially to talk about getting to a high or respected level. ○ *a book that in time attained the status of a classic*

at|tain|ment /əˈteɪnmənt/ *(attainments)*

NOUN ○ [+ of] *the attainment of independence* ○ *their educational attainments*

▶ COLLOCATIONS:
the attainment **of** something
the attainment of a **goal**
educational/academic attainments
▶ SYNONYMS: achievement, success
▶ ANTONYM: failure

Information boxes help increase your understanding of the word and when to use it

Collocations help you put the word into practice

Synonyms and antonyms help expand your vocabulary

Labels show common grammatical patterns

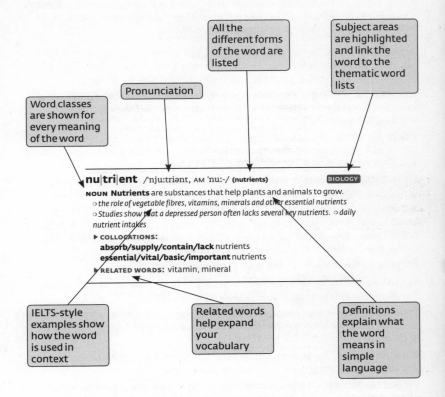

All the different forms of the word are listed

Subject areas are highlighted and link the word to the thematic word lists

Pronunciation

Word classes are shown for every meaning of the word

nu|tri|ent /ˈnjuːtriənt, AM ˈnuː-/ **(nutrients)**   BIOLOGY

NOUN Nutrients are substances that help plants and animals to grow.
  ○ *the role of vegetable fibres, vitamins, minerals and other essential nutrients*
  ○ *Studies show that a depressed person often lacks several key nutrients.* ○ *daily nutrient intakes*
  ▶ **COLLOCATIONS:**
    absorb/supply/contain/lack nutrients
    essential/vital/basic/important nutrients
  ▶ **RELATED WORDS:** vitamin, mineral

IELTS-style examples show how the word is used in context

Related words help expand your vocabulary

Definitions explain what the word means in simple language

All the words in the dictionary section have grammar information given about them. For each word, its word class is shown after the headword. The sections below show more information about each word class.

ADJECTIVE   An adjective is a word that is used for telling you more about a person or thing. You would use an adjective to talk about appearance, colour, size, or other qualities, e.g. *He has been _absent_ from his desk for two weeks*.

ADVERB   An adverb is a word that gives more information about when, how, or where something happens, e.g. *The costs of each part of the process can be measured fairly _accurately_*.

CONJUNCTION   A conjunction is a word such as *and*, *but*, *if*, and *since*. Conjunctions are used for linking two words or two parts of a sentence together, e.g. *Their system worked, _although_ no one was sure how*.

DETERMINER   A determiner is a word that is used at the beginning of a noun group, e.g. *_some_ books, _several_ months*.

NOUN   A noun is a word that refers to a person, a thing, or a quality. In this book, the label *noun* is given to all countable nouns. A countable noun is used for talking about things that can be counted, and that have both singular and plural forms, e.g. *She turned her _head_ away, difficult financial _situations_*.

NUMBER   A number is a word such as *three* and *hundred*.

PHRASAL VERB   A phrasal verb consists of a verb and one or more particles, e.g. *All experiments were _carried out_ by three psychologists*.

PHRASE   Phrases are groups of words which are used together and which have a meaning of their own, e.g. *Most schools are unwilling to cut down on staff _in order to_ cut costs*.

PLURAL NOUN   A plural noun is always plural, and it is used with plural verbs, e.g. *He called the _emergency services_ and they arrived within minutes*.

PREDETERMINER   A predeterminer is used in a noun group before *a*, *the* or another determiner, e.g. *They had only received _half_ the money promised*.

PREPOSITION   A preposition is a word such as *by*, *with*, or *from* which is always followed by a noun group or the *-ing* form of a verb, e.g. *The themes are repeated _throughout_ the film*.

PRONOUN   A pronoun is a word that you use instead of a noun, when you do not need or want to name someone or something directly, e.g. *No one drug will suit everyone and sometimes _several_ may have to be tried*.

QUANTIFIER   A quantifier comes before *of* and a noun group, e.g. *the _bulk_ of the text*.

UNCOUNTABLE NOUN   An uncountable noun is used for talking about things that are not normally counted, or that we do not think of as single items. Uncountable nouns do not have a plural form, and they are used with a singular verb, e.g. *The report has inevitably been greeted with _scepticism_*.

VERB   A verb is a word that is used for saying what someone or something does, or what happens to them, or to give information about them, e.g. *The exhibition _traces_ the history of graphic design*.

Word lists

Pure/general science

chemistry (uncount)
  chemist (noun)
physics (uncount)
  physicist (noun)
science (uncount, noun)
  scientific (adj)
  scientist (noun)

Basic processes
boil (verb)
burn (verb)
cool (verb)
energy (uncount)
freeze (verb)
heat (verb, uncount)
melt (verb)
process (noun)

Basic substances
carbon dioxide (uncount)
chemical (adj, noun)
  chemically (adv)
fuel (noun)
gas (uncount, noun)
liquid (noun, adj)
metal (noun)
  metallic (adj)
oil (uncount)
oxygen (uncount)
substance (noun)

Applied sciences

Engineering
electricity (uncount)
  electric (adj)
  electrical (adj)
electronic (adj)
  electronics (uncount)
engine (noun)
engineering (uncount)
  engineer (noun)
mechanics (uncount)
  mechanical (adj)
  mechanically (adv)
technical (adj)
  technically (adv)
user-friendly (adj)
vehicle (noun)

IT
computer (noun)
  computerized (adj)
computer science (uncount)
  computer scientist (noun)
digital (adj)
  digitally (adv)
electronic (adj)
information technology
(uncount)
online (adj, adv)
technology (noun)
  technological (adj)
  technologically (adv)
user-friendly (adj)

disk (noun)
hardware (uncount)
memory (noun)
wireless (adj)

document (noun)
file (noun)
software (uncount)
store (verb)
  storage (uncount)

Maths & statistics

Maths & calculations
add (verb)
  addition (uncount)
calculate (verb)
  calculation (noun)
divide (verb)
  division (uncount)
double (verb)
equal (adj, verb)
  equally (adv)
even (adj)
mathematics (uncount)
  mathematical (adj)
multiply (verb)
  multiplication (uncount)
odd (adj)
sign (noun)
subtract (verb)
  subtraction (noun)

Numbers & statistics
billion (num, quant)
million (num, quant)
thousand (num, quant, pron)
zero (num, uncount)

amount (noun)
couple (quant, noun)
figure (noun)
number (noun)
several (det, quant, pron)
single (adj)

average (noun, adj)
decimal (adj, noun)
decimal point (noun)
exact (adj)
  exactly (adv)
fraction (noun)
half (noun, predet, adj)
  halve (verb)
level (noun)
per cent (noun, adj, adv)
quarter (noun)
range (noun, verb)
statistic (noun)
  statistical (adj)
third (noun)
total (noun, adj)
twice (adv, predet)

Geography

geography (uncount)
geographical (adj)
geographically (adv)
geographer (noun)

Geographical areas

east (uncount, noun)
eastern (adj)
north (uncount, noun)
northern (adj)
south (uncount, noun)
southern (adj)
west (uncount, noun)
western (adj)

area (noun)
border (noun, verb)
capital (noun)
continent (noun)
continental (adj)
country (noun)
nation (noun)
national (adj)
nationally (adv)
region (noun)
regional (adj)
site (noun)
state (noun)
abroad (adv)
foreign (adj)
international (adj)
internationally (adv)
local (adj)
locally (adv)
located (adj)
location (noun)
worldwide (adv)

Natural world & environment

coast (noun)
coastal (adj)
countryside (uncount)
desert (noun)
environment (noun)
environmental (adj)
environmentally (adv)
environmentalist (noun)
forest (noun)
land (uncount)
landscape (noun)
mountain (noun)
mountainous (adj)
ocean (noun)

air (uncount)
ice (uncount)
oil (uncount)
rock (uncount)
soil (noun)

climate (noun)
global warming (uncount)
greenhouse effect (noun)
greenhouse gas (noun)
season (noun)
drought (noun)
earthquake (noun)
flood (noun)

Man & his environment
discover (verb)
  discovery (noun)

conservation (uncount)
eco-friendly (adj)
pollute (verb)
  pollution (uncount)
recycle (verb)
  recycling (uncount)

congestion (uncount)
crowded (adj)
motorist (noun)
neighbourhood (noun)
traffic (uncount)
transport (uncount, verb)
urban (adj)
vehicle (noun)

agriculture (uncount)
  agricultural (adj)
remote (adj)
rural (adj)

The planet & space
atmosphere (noun)
  atmospheric (adj)
earth (noun)
moon (noun)
ozone layer (noun)
planet (noun)
space (uncount)
universe (noun)

Biology & medicine
biology (uncount)
  biological (adj)
  biologically (adv)
  biologist (noun)

Natural world
conservation (uncount)
endanger (verb)
extinct (adj)
  extinction (uncount)
habitat (noun)
nature (uncount)
  natural (adj)
organic (adj)
season (noun)
wild (adj)
wildlife (uncount)

Plants & animals
creature (noun)
egg (noun)
insect (noun)
nest (noun, verb)
tail (noun)
wing (noun)
young (plural)

native (adj)
native (adj)
species (noun)

leaf (noun)
plant (noun)
root (noun)
seed (noun)
stem (noun)

Human body

bone (noun)
brain (noun)
breathe (verb)
  breath (noun)
heart (noun)
human (adj, noun)
lung (noun)
muscle (noun)
organ (noun)
sense (noun)
sight (uncount, noun, plural)

Health & healthcare

diet (noun)
fit (adj)
  fitness (uncount)
health (uncount)
  healthy (adj)
  healthily (adv)

disease (noun)
heart attack (noun)
injure (verb)
  injured (adj)
  injury (noun)
pain (noun)
  painful (adj)
  painfully (adv)
symptom (noun)
temperature (noun, uncount)

clinic (noun)
cure (verb, noun)
drug (noun)
injection (noun)
medicine (uncount)
  medical (adj)
  medically (adv)
patient (noun)
scan (verb, noun)
treat (verb)
  treatment (noun, uncount)
X-ray (noun, verb)

Society

People & society
charity (noun)
community (noun)
population (noun)
public (noun, adj)
society (uncount, noun)
  social (adj)
  socially (adv)

parent (noun)
  parental (adj)
relationship (noun)
relative (noun)

disability (noun)
  disabled (adj)
equality (uncount)
freedom (uncount)
housing (uncount)
leisure (uncount)
lifestyle (noun)
property (uncount, noun)
resident (noun)
respect (verb, uncount)
right (plural, noun)
way of life (noun)

Age
age (noun, verb)
  aged (adj)
  ageing (adj, uncount)
age group (noun)
generation (noun)
lifetime (noun)

adult (noun, adj)
  adulthood (uncount)
elderly (adj)
middle-aged (adj)
  middle age (uncount)
old age (uncount)
retire (verb)
  retirement (uncount)

childhood (noun)

Society & culture
culture (uncount, noun)
  cultural (adj)
custom (noun)
  customary (adj)
dress (uncount)
habit (noun)
religion (uncount, noun)
  religious (adj)
society (uncount, noun)
  social (adj)
  socially (adv)
tradition (noun)
  traditional (adj)
  traditionally (adv)
Western (adj)
  westernized (adj)
  westernization (uncount)

The state & society
armed forces (plural)
army (noun)
emergency services (plural)
military (adj, noun)
navy (noun)
police (noun)
state (noun)
war (noun)

work & money
pension (noun)
   pensioner (noun)
poor (adj, plural)
   poverty (uncount)
rich (adj)
strike (noun, verb)
   striker (noun)
unemployment (uncount)
   unemployed (adj)
wealth (uncount)
   wealthy (adj)

Politics

council (noun)
   councillor (noun)
government (noun)
party (noun)
politician (noun)
president (noun)
Prime Minister (noun)
protester (noun)
supporter (noun)

campaign (noun, verb)
elect (verb)
   election (noun)
lead (verb)
   leader (noun)
   leadership (noun)
power (uncount)
   powerful (adj)
protest (verb, noun)
represent (verb)
   representative (noun)
support (verb, uncount)
vote (noun)
   voter (noun)

independence (uncount)
peace (uncount)
policy (noun)
politics (plural)
   political (adj)
   politically (adv)
war (noun)

Psychology

The human mind
character (noun)
emotion (noun)
   emotional (adj)
   emotionally (adv)
personality (noun)
violent (adj)
   violently (adv)
   violence (uncount)
willing (adj)

psychology (uncount)

ability (noun)
aware (adj)
   awareness (uncount)
experience (uncount, noun, verb)
intelligent (adj)
   intelligently (adv)
   intelligence (uncount)
knowledge (uncount)
memory (noun)
mind (noun)
skill (noun)
   skilled (adj)
understand (verb)
   understanding (noun)

Business & economics

Working life
assistant (adj, noun)
chief (adj)
client (noun)
colleague (noun)
customer (noun)
director (noun)
lead (verb)
  leader (noun)
  leadership (noun)
manage (verb)
  management (uncount, noun)
  manager (noun)
senior (adj)
staff (noun)
worker (noun)

career (noun)
employ (verb)
  employment (uncount)
  employee (noun)
  employer (noun)
full-time (adj, adv)
hours (plural)
job (noun)
office (noun)
part-time (adj, adv)
pension (noun)
  pensioner (noun)
permanent (adj)
  permanently (adv)
professional (adj, noun)
retire (verb)
  retirement (uncount)
temporary (adj)
  temporarily (adv)
unemployment (uncount)
  unemployed (adj)
earn (verb)

  earnings (plural)
income (noun)
salary (noun)
wage (noun)

apply (verb)
  application (noun)
appointment (noun)
commute (verb)
  commuter (noun)
organize (verb)
  organization (noun, uncount)
responsible (adj)
  responsibility (uncount, plural)
strike (noun, verb)
  striker (noun)
supervise (verb)
  supervision (uncount)
  supervisor (noun)
train (verb)
  training (uncount)
  trainee (noun)

Jobs & professions
armed forces (plural)
army (noun)
composer (noun)
councillor (noun)
emergency services (plural)
journalist (noun)
  journalism (uncount)
lawyer (noun)
musician (noun)
navy (noun)
police (noun)
politician (noun)
teacher (noun)

assistant (adj, noun)
director (noun)
manager (noun)
professional (adj, noun)
supervisor (noun)

Doing business
advertise (verb)
  advertising (uncount)
  advertisement (noun)
association (noun)
brand (noun)
business (uncount, noun)
campaign (noun, verb)
company (noun)
competition (uncount)
  competitive (adj)
factory (noun)
firm (noun)
industry (uncount, noun)
  industrial (adj)
logo (noun)
market (noun, verb)
  marketing (uncount)
modernize (verb)
  artist (noun)
produce (verb)
  product (noun)
  production (uncount)
  producer (noun)
professional (adj, noun)
regulations (plural)
sell (verb)
  sale (noun, plural)
service (noun, plural, uncount)

Finance & economics
budget (noun, verb)
charge (verb, noun)
cost (noun, verb, plural)
finance (uncount)
  financial (adj)
lose (verb)
  loss (noun)
profit (noun, verb)
  profitable (adj)

cost of living (noun)
currency (noun)
economy (noun)
  economic (adj)
income (noun)
lend (verb)
  loan (noun)
tax (noun, verb)
  taxation (uncount)
value (uncount)
  valuable (adj)
wealth (uncount)
  wealthy (adj)

Law

Crime & criminal justice
arrest (verb, noun)
court (noun)
crime (noun)
  criminal (adj)
guilty (adj)
illegal (adj)
  illegally (adv)
innocent (adj)
law (noun, uncount)
legal (adj)
  legally (adv)
trial (noun)

criminal (noun)
judge (noun)
jury (noun)
lawyer (noun)
prisoner (noun)
victim (noun)
witness (noun, verb)

fine (noun, verb)
prison (noun)
punish (verb)
  punishment (noun)

Education

Academic subjects
art (uncount, noun, plural)
  artist (noun)
biology (uncount)
  biologist (noun)
chemistry (uncount)
  chemist (noun)
computer science (uncount)
  computer scientist (noun)
engineering (uncount)
  engineer (noun)
geography (uncount)
  geographer (noun)
history (uncount)
  historian (noun)
law (noun, uncount)
literature (noun, uncount)
mathematics (uncount)
medicine (uncount)
physics (uncount)
  physicist (noun)
politics (plural)
psychology (uncount)
science (uncount, noun)
  scientist (noun)

Educational institutions
college (noun)
high school (noun)
higher education (uncount)
primary school (noun)
secondary school (noun)
university (noun)

Student life
course (noun)
degree (noun)
education (noun)
  educate (verb)
  educational (adj)
graduate (noun, verb)
  graduation (uncount)
learn (verb)
library (noun)
pupil (noun)
qualify (verb)
  qualified (adj)
  qualification (noun)
study (verb, uncount, noun)
  student (noun)
subject (noun)
teach (verb)
  teacher (noun)
  teaching (uncount)
textbook (noun)
timetable (noun)
train (verb)
  training (uncount)
  trainee (noun)

General arts

Arts
culture (uncount, noun)
  cultural (adj)
media (noun)
work (noun)

Art

Performing arts
audience (noun)
perform (verb)
  performance (noun)
  performer (noun)
performing arts (plural)
theatre (noun)

Visual arts
art (uncount, noun, plural)
  artist (noun)
exhibition (noun)
gallery (noun)

Music

compose (verb)
  composer (noun)
music (uncount)
  musical (adj)
  musician (noun)
opera (noun)
orchestra (noun)
  orchestral (adj)

Literature

author (noun)
chapter (noun)
character (noun)
drama (noun, uncount)
fiction (uncount)
literature (noun, uncount)
novel (noun)
passage (noun)
play (noun, verb)
poem (noun)
  poetry (uncount)
  poet (noun)
scene (noun)
text (uncount)
title (noun)

Media

The media
article (noun)
attention (uncount)
audience (noun)
celebrity (noun)
channel (noun)
current affairs (plural)
entertainment (uncount)
journalist (noun)
  journalism (uncount)
media (noun)
popular (adj)
  popularity (uncount)
press (noun)

Language

accent (noun)
alphabet (noun)
  alphabetical (adj)
  alphabetically (adv)
communicate (verb)
  communication (uncount, plural)
fluent (adj)
  fluency (uncount)
  fluently (adv)
formal (adj)
  formally (adv)
  formality (uncount)
grammar (uncount)
  grammatical (adj)
informal (adj)
  informally (adv)
  informality (uncount)
language (noun, uncount)
mean (verb)
  meaning (noun)
native (adj)
pronounce (verb)
  pronunciation (noun)
term (noun)
translate (verb)
  translation (uncount)
  translator (noun)
usage (uncount)
vocabulary (noun)

History

age (noun, verb)
ancient (adj)
century (noun)
date (noun, verb)
decade (noun)
history (uncount)
  historic (adj)
  historical (adj)
  historian (noun)
past (noun, adj)
present-day (adj)

Actions & processes

act (verb, noun)
action (uncount, noun)
active (adj)
  actively (adv)
activity (noun)
behave (verb)
  behaviour (uncount)
effort (noun)
event (noun)
manual (adj)
means (noun)
method (noun)
physical (adj)
  physically (adv)
process (noun)
task (noun)
technique (noun)

arrange (verb)
  arrangement (noun)
calculate (verb)
check (verb)
discover (verb)
  discovery (noun)
explore (verb)
  exploration (noun)
measure (verb)
  measurement (noun)
order (noun, verb)
record (noun, verb)
solve (verb)
  solution (noun)
test (verb, noun)

advance (verb, noun)
  advanced (adj)
build (verb)

create (verb)
  creation (uncount)
design (verb)
develop (verb)
improve (verb)
  improvement (noun)
progress (uncount, noun, verb)
setback (noun)
spread (verb, noun)

attempt (verb, noun)
collect (verb)
  collection (noun, uncount)
enter (verb)
  entrance (noun)
list (noun, verb)
move (verb, noun)
  movement (noun)
online (adj, adv)
operate (verb)
  operation (uncount)
provide (verb)
receive (verb)
repeat (verb)
  repetition (noun, uncount)
  repetitive (adj)
replace (verb)
  replacement (uncount)
update (verb)
use (verb, uncount, noun)
  user (noun)

damage (verb, uncount)
destroy (verb)
  destruction (uncount)
force (verb, uncount)
harm (verb, uncount)
  harmful (adj)
  harmless (adj)
waste (verb, uncount)

choose (verb)
choice (noun)
control (uncount, verb)
correct (adj, verb)
correction (noun)
deal with (ph verb)
decide (verb)
decision (noun)
encourage (verb)
face (verb)
handle (verb)
hesitate (verb)
hesitation (noun)
limit (noun, verb)
manage (verb)
management (uncount, noun)
organize (verb)
organization (noun, uncount)
permit (verb, noun)
permission (uncount)
plan (noun, verb)
planning (uncount)
prepare (verb)
preparation (uncount, plural)
tackle (verb)

avoid (verb)
ban (verb, noun)
barrier (noun)
disappear (verb)
disappearance (noun)
forbid (verb)
forbidden (adj)
ignore (verb)
prevent (verb)
prevention (uncount)
protect (verb)
protection (uncount)
protective (adj)

remove (verb)
removal (uncount)
save (verb)

fail (verb)
failure (noun)
result (noun)
succeed (verb)
success (uncount)
successful (adj)
suffer (verb)

Research

carry out (ph verb)
collect (verb)
collection (noun, uncount)
error (noun)
evidence (uncount)
experiment (noun, verb)
experimental (adj)
find (verb)
findings (plural)
information (uncount)
interview (noun, verb)
invent (verb)
invention (noun)
laboratory (noun)
meter (noun)
method (noun)
prove (verb)
proof (noun)
questionnaire (noun)
research (uncount, verb)
researcher (noun)
result (noun)
show (verb)

States

background (noun)
condition (noun, plural)
exist (verb)
　existence (uncount)
lack (uncount, verb)
own (verb)
　owner (noun)
situation (noun)

Cause & effect

affect (verb)
allow (verb)
benefit (noun, verb)
　beneficial (adj)
cause (noun, verb)
depend (verb)
due to (phrase)
effect (noun)
enable (verb)
factor (noun)
influence (noun, verb)
　influential (adj)
lead to (verb)
prevent (verb)
　prevention (uncount)
problem (noun)
　problematic (adj)
purpose (noun)
reason (noun)
result (noun)
risk (noun)
succeed (verb)
　success (uncount)
　successful (adj)

Compare & contrast

advantage (noun)
alike (adj, adv)
alternative (noun, adj)
　alternatively (adv)
although (conj)
compared with/to (phrase)
despite (prep)
differ (verb)
　different (adj)
　difference (noun)
disadvantage (noun)
drawback (noun)
gap (noun)
however (adv)
opposite (adj)
prefer (verb)
　preference (noun)
similar (adj)
　similarly (adv)
　similarity (noun)

Ideas

area (noun)
case (noun)
example (noun)
fact (noun)
　factual (adj)
　factually (adv)
factor (noun)
idea (noun)
issue (noun)
matter (noun)
point (noun)
topic (noun)

Measurements

centimetre (noun)
foot (noun)
gallon (noun)
gram (noun)
inch (noun)
kilogram (noun)
kilometre (noun)
litre (noun)
metre (noun)
metric system (noun)
mile (noun)
millimetre (noun)
pint (noun)
tonne (noun)
yard (noun)

deep (adj)
  depth (noun)
distance (noun)
  distant (adj)
height (noun)
length (noun)
limit (noun, verb)
long (adv, adj)
measure (verb)
  measurement (noun)
medium-sized (adj)
weight (noun)
  weigh (verb)
wide (adj)
  width (noun)

Physical properties

depth (noun)
height (noun)
length (noun)
speed (noun)
strength (uncount)
temperature (noun, uncount)
weight (noun)

Time

occasion (noun)
period (noun)
programme (noun)
schedule (noun)

current (adj)
  currently (adv)
future (noun, adj)
modern (adj)
  modernize (verb)
  modernization (uncount)
nowadays (adv)
old-fashioned (adj)
present (adj, noun)
recent (adj)
  recently (adv)

annual (adj)
  annually (adv)
constant (adj)
  constantly (adv)
daily (adv, adj)
frequent (adj)
  frequently (adv)
  frequency (uncount)
regular (adj)
  regularly (adv)

eventual (adj)
   eventually (adv)
final (adj)
   finally (adv)
following (prep, adj)
former (adj)
   formerly (adv)
original (adj)
   originally (adv)
previous (adj)
   previously (adv)

Occurrence

available (adj)
   availability (uncount)
common (adj)
   commonly (adv)
everyday (adj)
normal (adj)
   normally (adv)
ordinary (adj)
   ordinarily (adv)
rare (adj)
   rarely (adv)
typical (adj)
   typically (adv)
usual (adj)
   usually (adv)

Shape & position

object (noun)
part (noun)

circle (noun)
   circular (adj)
disc (noun)

rectangle (noun)
   rectangular (adj)
row (noun)
square (noun, adj)
straight (adj, adv)
   straighten (verb)
triangle (noun)
   triangular (adj)

centre (noun)
   central (adj)
   centrally (adv)
direction (noun)
inner (adj)
outdoor (adj)
outer (adj)
position (noun)
surround (verb)
throughout (prep, adv)
upper (adj)

Structures & parts

detail (noun, plural)
group (noun)
ingredient (noun)
item (noun)
kind (noun)
object (noun)
part (noun)
role (noun)
section (noun)
series (noun)
stage (noun)
step (noun)
type (noun)
variety (noun)
   varied (adj)
various (adj)

entire (adj)
  entirely (adv)
general (adj)
overall (adj, adv)
project (noun)
schedule (noun)
structure (uncount, verb)
  structural (adj)
system (noun)
whole (quant)

belong (verb)
combine (verb)
  combination (noun)
complex (adj)
connect (verb)
  connection (noun)
contain (verb)
  container (noun)
  contents (plural)
depend (verb)
form (noun)
include (verb)
  including (prep)
  inclusion (noun)
independent (adj)
  independently (adv)
involve (verb)
  involvement (uncount)
link (noun, verb)
pattern (noun)
separate (adj)
  separately (adv)

Machines & equipment

electric (adj)
  electricity (uncount)
  electrical (adj)
equipment (uncount)
facilities (plural)
machine (noun)
  machinery (uncount)
man-made (adj)
operate (verb)
  operation (uncount)
user-friendly (adj)

code (noun)
computer (noun)
  computerized (adj)
digital (adj)
  digitally (adv)
electronic (adj)
  electronics (uncount)
hardware (uncount)
high-tech (adj)
technology (noun)
wire (noun)
wireless (adj)

engine (noun)
fuel (noun)
mechanics (uncount)
  mechanical (adj)
  mechancially (adv)
meter (noun)

Trends

grow (verb)
  growth (uncount)
increase (verb, noun)
  increasingly (adv)
progress (uncount, noun, verb)
raise (verb)
rise (verb, noun)

cut (verb, noun)
decrease (verb, noun)
drop (verb, noun)
fall (verb, noun)
lower (adj, verb)
worsen (verb)
forecast (noun, verb)
  forecaster (noun)
gradual (adj)
  gradually (adv)
reach (verb)

Travel & tourism

accommodation (uncount)
currency (noun)
tourist (noun)
  tourism (uncount)

commute (verb)
  commuter (noun)
congestion (uncount)
motorist (noun)
passenger (noun)
traffic (uncount)
transport (uncount, verb)
vehicle (noun)

Types of people & groups of people

audience (noun)
community (noun)
crowd (noun)
people (plural, noun)
population (noun)
public (noun, adj)
team (noun)

adult (noun, adj)
  adulthood (uncount)
age group (noun)
generation (noun)
pensioner (noun)
the elderly (plural)
individual (adj, noun)
  individually (adv)
member (noun)
  membership (uncount)

adviser (noun)
assistant (adj, noun)
client (noun)
colleague (noun)
customer (noun)
employee (noun)
expert (noun)
motorist (noun)
owner (noun)
passenger (noun)
patient (noun)
pupil (noun)
resident (noun)
staff (noun)
supporter (noun)
tourist (noun)
user (noun)
worker (noun)

Speech & reporting

account (noun)
advice (uncount)
  advise (verb)
agree (verb)
announce (verb)
  announcement (noun)
answer (verb, noun)
comment (verb, noun)
criticize (verb)
  criticism (noun)
describe (verb)
  description (noun)
disagree (verb)
  disagreement (uncount, noun)
discuss (verb)
  discussion (noun)
explain (verb)
  explanation (noun)
message (noun)
persuade (verb)
  persuasion (uncount)
  persuasive (adj)
question (noun)
recommend (verb)
  recommendation (noun)
record (noun, verb)
refer (verb)
report (noun)
suggest (verb)
  suggestion (noun)
warn (verb)
  warning (noun)

Opinions & beliefs

believe (verb)
  belief (noun)
consider (verb)
doubt (noun, verb)
opinion (noun)
seem (verb)
support (verb, uncount)
  supporter (noun)
view (noun, verb)

Rules

apart from (phrase)
authority (plural, uncount, noun)
code (noun)
except (prep, conj)
  exception (noun)
illegal (adj)
  illegally (adv)
law (noun, uncount)
legal (adj)
  legally (adv)
limit (noun, verb)
necessary (adj)
official (adj, noun)
  officially (adv)
permit (verb, noun)
  permission (uncount)
policy (noun)
regulations (plural)
rule (noun)

General & specific

especially (adv)
highly (adv)
particular (adj)
strict (adj)
thorough (adj)
   thoroughly (adv)

broad (adj)
   broadly (adv)
   broaden (verb)
estimate (verb, noun)
general (adj)
   generally (adv)
rough (adj)
   roughly (adv)

Certain & uncertain

certain (adj)
   certainly (adv)
clear (adj)
   clearly (adv)
likely (adj)
   likelihood (uncount)
obvious (adj)
   obviously (adv)

appear (verb)
expect (verb)
   expectation (plural)
possible (adj)
   possibly (adv)
   possibility (noun)
probable (adj)
   probably (adv)
tend (verb)
   tendency (noun)
unlikely (adj)

Important & unimportant

basic (adj)
   basics (plural)
essential (adj)
important (adj)
   importantly (adv)
   importance (uncount)
key (adj)
main (adj)
   mainly (adv)
major (adj)
necessary (adj)
serious (adj)
   seriously (adv)
significant (adj)
worthwhile (adj)

minor (adj)
unnecessary (adj)
   unnecessarily (adv)

Adverbs of degree

enormously (adv)
entirely (adv)
extremely (adv)
increasingly (adv)
mainly (adv)
slightly (adv)
thoroughly (adv)

Positive qualities

convenient (adj)
  conveniently (adv)
  convenience (uncount)
correct (adj)
  correctly (adv)
effective (adj)
  effectively (adv)
efficient (adj)
  efficiently (adv)
  efficiency (uncount)
fair (adj)
  fairly (adv)
fortunate (adj)
  fortunately (adv)
ideal (adj)
  ideally (adv)
positive (adj, noun)
profitable (adj)
simple (adj)
  simply (adv)
  simplicity (uncount)
suitable (adj)
  suitably (adv)
  suitability (uncount)
useful (adj)
valuable (adj)

Negative qualities

difficult (adj)
  difficulty (noun, uncount)
disadvantage (noun)
drawback (noun)
fragile (adj)
incorrect (adj)
  incorrectly (adv)
negative (adj)
  negatively (adv)
problematic (adj)
repetitive (adj)
unfortunate (adj)
  unfortunately (adv)

Studying

college (noun)
course (noun)
degree (noun)
graduate (noun, verb)
look up (ph verb)
project (noun)
scan (verb, noun)
skim (verb)
study (verb, uncount, noun)
  student (noun)
subject (noun)

Texts

chapter (noun)
essay (noun)
graph (noun)
heading (noun)
note (noun)
paragraph (noun)
table (noun)
textbook (noun)
title (noun)

Academic writing

bracket (noun)
e.g.
etc
term (noun)

accommodation (uncount)
adult (noun, adj)
    adulthood (uncount)
affect (verb)
alternative (noun, adj)
    alternatively (adv)
annual (adj)
    annually (adv)
area (noun)
assistant (adj, noun)
author (noun)
authority (plural, uncount, noun)
available (adj)
    availability (uncount)
aware (adj)
    awareness (uncount)
benefit (noun, verb)
    beneficial (adj)
channel (noun)
chapter (noun)
chemical (adj, noun)
    chemically (adv)
code (noun)
comment (verb, noun)
community (noun)
complex (adj)
computer (noun)
    computerized (adj)
conference (noun)
constant (adj)
    constantly (adv)
couple (quant, noun)
create (verb)
    creation (uncount)
culture (uncount, noun)
    cultural (adj)
currency (noun)
decade (noun)
design (verb)
despite (prep)
document (noun)
drama (noun, uncount)
economy (noun)
    economic (adj)
enable (verb)
energy (uncount)

enormous (adj)
    enormously (adv)
environment (noun)
    environmental (adj)
    environmentally (adv)
    environmentalist (noun)
equipment (uncount)
error (noun)
estimate (verb, noun)
evidence (uncount)
exhibition (noun)
expert (noun)
facilities (plural)
factor (noun)
file (noun)
final (adj)
    finally (adv)
finance (uncount)
    financial (adj)
generation (noun)
ignore (verb)
illegal (adj)
    illegally (adv)
image (noun)
income (noun)
individual (adj, noun)
    individually (adv)
injure (verb)
    injured (adj)
    injury (noun)
intelligent (adj)
    intelligently (adv)
    intelligence (uncount)
involve (verb)
    involvement (uncount)
issue (noun)
item (noun)
job (noun)
legal (adj)
    legally (adv)
link (noun, verb)
located (adj)
    location (noun)
major (adj)
manual (adj)
media (noun)

ACADEMIC WORD LIST

medicine (uncount)
medical (adj)
medically (adv)
method (noun)
military (adj, noun)
minor (adj)
negative (adj)
negatively (adv)
normal (adj)
normally (adv)
obvious (adj)
obviously (adv)
odd (adj)
overall (adj, adv)
paragraph (noun)
per cent (noun, adj, adv)
period (noun)
physical (adj)
physically (adv)
policy (noun)
positive (adj, noun)
previous (adj)
previously (adv)
process (noun)
professional (adj, noun)
project (noun)
psychology (uncount)
range (noun, verb)
region (noun)
regional (adj)
regulations (plural)
remove (verb)
removal (uncount)
research (uncount, verb)
researcher (noun)

resident (noun)
role (noun)
schedule (noun)
section (noun)
security (uncount)
series (noun)
significant (adj)
similar (adj)
similarly (adv)
similarity (noun)
site (noun)
statistic (noun)
statistical (adj)
structure (uncount, verb)
structural (adj)
survive (verb)
survival (uncount)
survivor (noun)
task (noun)
team (noun)
technical (adj)
technically (adv)
technique (noun)
technology (noun)
technological (adj)
technologically (adv)
temporary (adj)
temporarily (adv)
text (uncount)
topic (noun)
tradition (noun)
traditional (adj)
traditionally (adv)
transport (uncount, verb)

Key to grammatical labels used in word lists

adj	adjective	**plural**	plural noun
adv	adverb	**predet**	predeterminer
conj	conjuction	**prep**	preposition
det	determiner	**pron**	pronoun
noun	noun	**quant**	quantifier
num	number	**uncount**	uncountable noun
phrase	phrase	**verb**	verb
ph verb	phrasal verb		

Key Words
A–Z

Aa

abil|ity /ə'bɪlɪti/ (abilities)

NOUN Your **ability to** do something is the fact that you can do it. ○ *The public never had faith in his ability to do the job.* ○ *He has the ability to bring out the best in others.* ○ *[+ of] the ability of an individual to work in a team*

▶ **COLLOCATIONS:**
  the ability **of** *someone*
  have/possess/demonstrate/show/develop an ability
  lack/lose an ability
▶ **PHRASES:**
  skill and ability
  willingness and ability
▶ **SYNONYM:** capability
▶ **ANTONYM:** inability

abroad /ə'brɔːd/

ADVERB If you go **abroad**, you go to a foreign country. ○ *I would love to go abroad this year.* ○ *About 65 per cent of the company's sales come from abroad.*

▶ **COLLOCATIONS:**
  go/travel/work/live/move abroad
  a **trip/holiday** abroad
▶ **SYNONYM:** overseas

ac|cent /'æksənt/ (accents) `LANGUAGE`

NOUN Someone who speaks with a particular **accent** says words in a way that shows which country or part of a country they come from, or which social class they belong to. ○ *He had a slight American accent.*

▶ **COLLOCATIONS:**
  a **Scottish/English/northern** accent
  a **thick/heavy/slight** accent

ac|com|mo|da|tion /ə,kɒmə'deɪʃən/ `ACADEMIC WORD`
(accommodations)

UNCOUNTABLE NOUN **Accommodation** is the buildings or rooms where people live or stay. [BRIT; in AM, use **accommodations**] ○ *The building provides accommodation for 80 students.* ○ *The price includes flights and hotel accommodation.* ○ *Rates are higher for deluxe accommodations.*

a

▶ **COLLOCATIONS:**
  provide/offer/rent/book/find accommodation
  hotel/holiday/temporary/overnight accommodation
  self-catering/B&B/half-board accommodation
  residential/student accommodation
  rented accommodation

---

ac|count /əˈkaʊnt/ (accounts)

NOUN An **account** is a written or spoken report of something that has happened. ○ [+ of] *He gave a detailed account of what happened.* ○ *According to police accounts, Mr and Mrs Hunt were found dead in their kitchen.*
  ▶ **COLLOCATIONS:**
  an account **of** *something*
  give/write/publish an account
  a **full/detailed/brief** account
  a **first-hand/eye-witness/personal** account
  ▶ **PHRASE:** according to accounts
  ▶ **SYNONYMS:** report, description

---

act /ækt/ (acts, acting, acted)

1 VERB When you **act**, you do something for a particular purpose.
  ○ *We must act now to stop climate change.* ○ *The company acted quickly to deal with the problem.* ○ *the duty of doctors to act in the best interest of patients*

2 VERB If someone **acts** in a particular way, they behave in that way.
  ○ *Call the police if you see anyone acting suspiciously.* ○ [+ as if] *He acted as if he hadn't heard any of it.*

3 VERB If someone or something **acts as** a particular thing, they have that role or function. ○ [+ as] *He acted as an advisor to the government.*
  ▶ **COLLOCATIONS:**
  act **as if/like/as** *something*
  act **on behalf of** *someone*
  act **quickly/swiftly/alone/independently**
  act **responsibly/decisively/appropriately**
  act **improperly/illegally/suspiciously**
  ▶ **PHRASES:**
  act in a particular manner/way
  act in the interest of someone/something
  act in self defence
  ▶ **SYNONYMS:** behave, function

4 NOUN An **act** is a thing that someone does. [FORMAL] ○ [+ of] *the act of reading* ○ *He had committed several acts of violence.*

▶ COLLOCATIONS:
the act **of** *doing something*
commit/perform an act
a **criminal/terrorist/illegal** act
an act of **terrorism/violence/vandalism/kindness**
▶ SYNONYMS: action, deed

ac|tion /ˈækʃən/ (actions)

1 UNCOUNTABLE NOUN Action is doing something for a particular purpose. ○ *The government is taking emergency action to deal with the crisis.* ○ *What was needed, he said, was decisive action to halt what he called these savage crimes.* ○ *the only possible course of action*

2 NOUN An **action** is something that you do. ○ *This action has been totally ineffective.* ○ *We are responsible for our own actions.*
▶ COLLOCATIONS:
take action
demand/require/need action
immediate/urgent/further action
decisive/appropriate/direct action
▶ PHRASES:
a plan of action
a course of action
▶ SYNONYMS: measure, step, deed
▶ ANTONYM: inaction

ac|tive /ˈæktɪv/

1 ADJECTIVE Someone who is **active** does a lot of things and has a lot of energy. ○ *Having an active child in the house is very tiring.* ○ *She had a long and active life.*
▶ COLLOCATIONS:
physically active
an active **lifestyle**
keep/remain active
▶ PHRASES:
healthy and active
fit and active
▶ SYNONYMS: energetic, mobile
▶ ANTONYM: inactive

2 ADJECTIVE If someone is **active** in an organization or campaign, they are involved in it, and work hard. ○ *Smith takes an active role in environmental campaigning.* ○ *He is an active member of his local synagogue.*

▶ COLLOCATIONS:
active **in** *something*
active in **politics/the community**
politically active
an active **role/part/member**
▶ SYNONYM: involved
▶ ANTONYM: passive

ac|tive|ly

ADVERB ○ *She actively campaigned for the Democrat Party.* ○ *[+ v-ing] people actively seeking work*
▶ COLLOCATIONS:
be actively **involved**
actively **participate/campaign**
actively **seek/pursue/support** *something*

---

ac|tiv|ity /ækˈtɪvɪti/ (activities)

NOUN An **activity** is something that you spend time doing. ○ *You can take part in activities from canoeing to bird watching.* ○ *leisure activities such as watching television* ○ *The child gets into the family routine for daily activities.* ○ *ideas for classroom activities*
▶ COLLOCATIONS:
take part in/do an activity
a **leisure/recreational/social** activity
a **sporting/outdoor** activity
normal/daily activities
▶ SYNONYMS: pursuit, action, exercise

---

add /æd/ (adds, adding, added)

MATHS

VERB If you **add** numbers or amounts **together**, you calculate their total. ○ *Banks add all the interest and other charges together.* ○ *[+ together] Two and three added together are five.*

• **Add up** means the same as **add**. ○ *More than a quarter of seven year-olds cannot add up properly.*
▶ SYNONYM: total
▶ ANTONYM: subtract

addition /əˈdɪʃən/

UNCOUNTABLE NOUN Addition is the process of calculating the total of two or more numbers. ○ *The children solve maths problems using simple addition and subtraction.*
▶ ANTONYM: subtraction

adult /ˈædʌlt, AM əˈdʌlt/ (adults)

1 NOUN An **adult** is a mature, fully developed person. ○ *Children under 14 must be accompanied by an adult.* ○ *The course is suitable for teenagers and young adults.*

▶ COLLOCATIONS:
  a **young/healthy/responsible** adult
  become an adult
▶ PHRASE: an adult and child
▶ SYNONYM: grown up
▶ RELATED WORDS: child, teenager, adolescent

2 ADJECTIVE Adult means relating to the time when you are an adult, or typical of adult people. ○ *I've lived most of my adult life in London.*

▶ COLLOCATIONS:
  adult **life**
  the adult **population**
  adult **education/learners/literacy**

adult|hood /ˈædʌlthʊd, AM əˈdʌlt-/

UNCOUNTABLE NOUN Adulthood is the state of being an adult. ○ *Most people catch the illness before they reach adulthood.*

▶ COLLOCATIONS:
  early/young adulthood
  reach adulthood
▶ RELATED WORDS: childhood, adolescence

ad|vance /ædˈvɑːns, -ˈvæns/ (advances, advancing, advanced)

1 VERB To **advance** means to make progress, especially in your knowledge of something. ○ *Medical technology has advanced considerably.*

▶ COLLOCATIONS:
  advance **rapidly/greatly/significantly**
  advance **technologically**
▶ SYNONYMS: progress, improve

2 NOUN An **advance** in a particular subject or activity is progress in your knowledge of it. ○ *Scientific advances have transformed our understanding of DNA.* ○ [+ in] *Major advances in microsurgery have been made.*

▶ COLLOCATIONS:
  an advance **in** *something*
  technological/medical/scientific advances
  a **major/significant/great** advance
  make/represent an advance
▶ SYNONYM: development

ad|vanced /æd'vɑːnst, -'vænst/

ADJECTIVE An **advanced** system, method, or design is modern and has been developed from an earlier version of the same thing. ○ *The lamp uses advanced technology to produce a very efficient source of light.* ○ *the most advanced optical telescope in the world*

▶ **COLLOCATIONS:**
  advanced **technology/equipment/techniques**
  technologically/technically advanced
▶ **SYNONYMS:** up-to-date, modern, cutting edge
▶ **ANTONYMS:** basic, elementary, simple

ad|van|tage /æd'vɑːntɪdʒ, -'væn-/ (advantages)

NOUN An **advantage** is a way in which one thing is better than another. ○ [+ of] *The great advantage of this technique is the cost.* ○ [+ over] *These weapons have many advantages over existing ones.*

▶ **COLLOCATIONS:**
  the advantage **of** something
  an advantage **over** something
  a **big/great/major/huge** advantage
  a **distinct/obvious/added** advantage
▶ **SYNONYMS:** benefit, strength, merit, positive
▶ **ANTONYMS:** disadvantage, drawback, negative

ad|ver|tise /'ædvətaɪz/ (advertises, advertising, advertised) `BUSINESS`

VERB If you **advertise** something such as a product, an event, or a job, you tell people about it in newspapers, on television, or on posters. ○ *Companies spend a lot of money advertising new products.* ○ *Religious groups are currently not allowed to advertise on television.*

▶ **COLLOCATIONS:**
  advertise **for** someone
  advertise a **product/property**
  advertise a **job/vacancy/position**
▶ **PHRASES:**
  advertise something on television/the internet
  advertise something in a newspaper
▶ **SYNONYMS:** promote, market

ad|ver|tis|ing /'ædvətaɪzɪŋ/

UNCOUNTABLE NOUN **Advertising** is the activity of creating advertisements and making sure people see them. ○ *The company spends a lot of money on advertising.* ○ *The actor starred in an advertising campaign for Versace.*

▶ **COLLOCATIONS:**
an advertising **campaign/agency**
the advertising **industry**

ad|ver|tise|ment /æd'vɜ:tɪsmənt, AM ,ædvə'taɪz-/ (advertisements)

NOUN An **advertisement** is an announcement in a newspaper, on television, or on a poster about something such as a product, event, or job. [WRITTEN] ○ [+ for] *a television advertisement for cat food*
▶ **COLLOCATIONS:**
an advertisement **for** *something*
place an advertisement
an advertisement **appears** *somewhere*
a **television/newspaper** advertisement
a **full-page** advertisement
▶ **SYNONYM:** commercial

---

ad|vice /æd'vaɪs/

UNCOUNTABLE NOUN If you give someone **advice**, you tell them what you think they should do. ○ *She has given me some good advice.* ○ [+ about] *Don't be afraid to ask for advice about the course.* ○ [+ on] *Your doctor can offer advice on health and fitness.*
▶ **COLLOCATIONS:**
advice **on/about** *something*
advice **from** *someone*
give/offer (*someone*) advice
provide/ask for/seek/get/receive advice
take/follow *someone's* advice
good/sound/bad advice
legal/financial/medical/career advice
professional/independent/expert/practical advice
▶ **SYNONYM:** guidance

ad|vise /æd'vaɪz/ (advises, advising, advised)

1 VERB If you **advise** someone **to** do something, you tell them what you think they should do. ○ [+ to-inf] *Health experts advise us to eat five portions of fruit and vegetables a day.* ○ [+ to-inf] *I strongly advise you to accept the offer.*
▶ **COLLOCATIONS:**
advise **against** *something*
strongly advise
▶ **SYNONYM:** recommend

2 VERB If an expert **advises** people **on** a particular subject, he or she gives them help and information on that subject. ○ [+ on] *She advises*

a

undergraduates on money matters. ○ [+ on] *Your tutor will be able to advise on suitable courses.*

▶ **COLLOCATION:** advise **on** *something*

> **USAGE:** Spelling
>
> **Advice** /æd'vaɪs/ is a noun. Remember, it is an uncountable noun, so you do not talk about 'advices' or 'an advice'. ○ *It is important to get legal advice.* ○ *He has one **piece of advice** for investors.*
>
> **Advise** /æd'vaɪz/ is a verb. Remember, it is always followed by an object - advise + *someone*. ○ *We always advise customers to take out insurance.*

ad|vis|er /æd'vaɪzə/ (advisers) also advisor

NOUN An **adviser** is an expert whose job is to give advice to people.
○ *In Washington, the President and his advisers spent the day in meetings.*
○ *a careers adviser*

▶ **COLLOCATION:** a **financial/legal/economic/political** adviser

af|fect /ə'fekt/ (affects, affecting, affected)   `ACADEMIC WORD`

VERB If something **affects** a person or thing, it influences them or causes them to change in some way. ○ *Nicotine from cigarettes can adversely affect the heart.* ○ *More than seven million people have been affected by drought.* ○ *The new law will directly affect thousands of people.*

▶ **COLLOCATIONS:**
  badly/adversely/directly affect
  seriously/severely/greatly affect
  affect the **outcome/quality/performance of** *something*
  affect **people/everyone**

▶ **SYNONYMS:** influence, impact

> **USAGE: affect** or **effect**?
>
> **Affect** is a verb. The noun that comes from **affect** is **effect**. You can say that something **affects** you, or that it has an **effect** on you.
> ○ *Noise in factories can seriously affect workers' health.* ○ *Noise in factories can have a serious effect on workers' health.*

age /eɪdʒ/ (ages, ageing, aging, aged)   `HISTORY`

1 NOUN Your **age** is the number of years that you have lived. ○ *She has a nephew who is just ten years of age.* ○ [+ of] *At the age of sixteen he qualified for a place at the University of Hamburg.*

▶ COLLOCATIONS:
the age **of** *someone*
at a **young/early** age
in **middle/old** age
the **average/minimum** age
reach the age of *x*
retirement/pension age
an age **group/range/limit**
an age **gap/difference**

▶ PHRASES:
at the age of *x*
x years of age

2 NOUN The **age** of a thing is the number of years since it was made. ○ [+ *of*] *Everything in the room looks suitable for the age of the building.*
▶ COLLOCATION: the age **of** *something*

3 VERB When someone **ages**, or when something **ages** them, they seem much older. ○ *He had always looked so young, but he seemed to have aged in the last few months.* ○ *Worry had aged him.*

4 NOUN An **age** is a period in history. ○ [+ *of*] *the age of steam trains* ○ *We're living in the digital age.*

▶ COLLOCATIONS:
the age **of** *something*
the **digital/internet/information** age
the **modern/Victorian** age

▶ SYNONYM: era

aged /eɪdʒd/

ADJECTIVE You use **aged** followed by a number to say how old someone is. ○ *Alan has two children, aged eleven and nine.*

age|ing /ˈeɪdʒɪŋ/ also aging

The spelling **aging** is also used, mainly in American English.

1 ADJECTIVE Someone or something that is **ageing** is becoming old. ○ *John lives with his ageing mother.* ○ *Ageing aircraft need more frequent safety inspections.*
▶ SYNONYMS: old, elderly
▶ ANTONYMS: young, new

2 UNCOUNTABLE NOUN **Ageing** is the process of becoming old. ○ *Her skin showed signs of ageing.*

a

'age group (age groups) SOCIAL SCIENCE

NOUN An age group is all the people between two particular ages.
- o *The research studied the eating habits of people in the 18-25 age group.*
  - ► COLLOCATIONS:
    in an age group
    the x to y age group
    the over-x/under-x age group
    all/different age groups
    the older/younger age group
  - ► SYNONYMS: generation, peer group

agree /əˈgriː/ (agrees, agreeing, agreed)

VERB If you agree with an action or suggestion, you think it is right.
- o [+ with] *I don't agree with what they're doing.* o [+ with] *Not all scientists agree with this view.*
  - ► COLLOCATIONS:
    agree with something
    generally/broadly/totally agree with something
    agree with a statement/assessment/finding/view
  - ► PHRASE: agree in principle
  - ► ANTONYM: disagree

ag|ri|cul|ture /ˈægrɪkʌltʃə/ GEOGRAPHY

UNCOUNTABLE NOUN Agriculture is farming and the methods that are used to look after crops and animals. o *The Ukraine is strong both in industry and agriculture.*
- ► SYNONYM: farming

ag|ri|cul|tur|al /ˌægrɪˈkʌltʃərəl/

ADJECTIVE o agricultural land o *The price of corn and other agricultural products has increased.*
- ► COLLOCATIONS:
  agricultural land
  an agricultural product/subsidy/worker
  the agricultural industry

air /eə/ SCIENCE GEOGRAPHY

UNCOUNTABLE NOUN Air is the mixture of gases which forms the Earth's atmosphere and which we breathe. o *Every living creature needs air to breathe.* o *She breathed in the cold air.* o *Cars are a major cause of air pollution.*

▶ COLLOCATIONS:
cold/warm/hot air
fresh/clean air
air **pollution/quality**

alike /əˈlaɪk/

1 **ADJECTIVE** If two or more things are **alike**, they are similar. ○ *The two brothers look very alike.*
▶ COLLOCATION: **look/sound** alike
▶ SYNONYM: similar
▶ ANTONYM: different

2 **ADVERB** **Alike** means in a similar way. ○ *They even dressed alike.*
○ *The article makes the false assumption that all men and women think alike.*
▶ COLLOCATION: **dress/think** alike
▶ SYNONYM: similarly
▶ ANTONYM: differently

3 **ADVERB** You use **alike** after mentioning two or more people, groups, or things in order to emphasize that you are referring to both or all of them.
○ *The techniques are being used almost everywhere by big and small companies alike.*
▶ SYNONYM: equally

al∥low /əˈlaʊ/ (allows, allowing, allowed)

1 **VERB** If someone **is allowed to** do something, it is all right for them to do it. ○ [+ to-inf] *The children are not allowed to watch violent TV programmes.*
○ [+ to-inf] *The Government will allow them to advertise on radio and television.*
○ *Smoking will not be allowed.*
▶ SYNONYMS: permit, let
▶ ANTONYM: forbid

2 **VERB** If you **are allowed** something, you are given permission to have it or are given it. ○ *Gifts like chocolates or flowers are allowed.* ○ *He should be allowed the occasional treat.*
▶ SYNONYM: permit
▶ ANTONYMS: forbid, ban

3 **VERB** If you **allow** something **to** happen, you do not prevent it.
○ [+ to-inf] *He won't allow himself to fail.* ○ [+ to-inf] *If the soil is allowed to dry out the tree could die.*
▶ SYNONYMS: permit, let
▶ ANTONYM: prevent

a

al|pha|bet /ˈælfəbet/ (alphabets) `LANGUAGE`

NOUN An **alphabet** is a set of letters in a fixed order which is used for writing the words of a language. ○ *The modern Russian alphabet has 31 letters.* ○ *By the age of six, most children know the alphabet.* ○ *'A' is the first letter of the English alphabet.*
▶ **COLLOCATION:** the **Greek/English/Russian** alphabet
▶ **PHRASE:** a letter of the alphabet

al|pha|beti|cal /ˌælfəˈbetɪkəl/

ADJECTIVE Alphabetical means arranged according to the normal order of the letters in the alphabet. ○ *The names are listed in alphabetical order.*
▶ **COLLOCATION:** an alphabetical **list**
▶ **PHRASE:** in alphabetical order

al|pha|beti|cal|ly /ˌælfəˈbetɪkli/

ADVERB ○ *The catalogue is arranged alphabetically by label name.*
▶ **COLLOCATION:** **list/arrange** something alphabetically

al|ter|na|tive /ɔːlˈtɜːnətɪv/ (alternatives) `ACADEMIC WORD`

1 NOUN An **alternative** is something you can use or do instead of something else. ○ [+ *to*] *New ways to treat arthritis may provide an alternative to painkillers.* ○ *This equipment is very expensive and we need to find a cheaper alternative.*
▶ **COLLOCATIONS:**
  an alternative **to** *something*
  provide/offer an alternative
  seek/consider/find an alternative
  a **good/viable/cheap/safe** alternative

2 ADJECTIVE An **alternative** plan or offer is one that you can use or do instead of the one you already have. ○ *There were alternative methods of travel available.* ○ *They had a right to seek alternative employment.*
▶ **SYNONYMS:** other, alternate, different

al|ter|na|tive|ly /ɔːlˈtɜːnətɪvli/

ADVERB You use **alternatively** to introduce a suggestion or to mention something different to what has just been stated. ○ *Allow about eight hours for the drive from Calais. Alternatively, you can fly to Brive.*

al|though /ɔːlˈðəʊ/

CONJUNCTION You use **although** to introduce a statement which contrasts with something else that you are saying. ○ *Although I was only six, I can remember seeing it on TV.* ○ *Their system worked, although no one was sure how.*
▶ **SYNONYMS:** however, even though

amount /ə'maʊnt/ (amounts)

NOUN The **amount of** something is how much there is, or how much you
have, need, or get. ○ [+ of] *He needs that amount of money to survive.*
○ *apricots contain large amounts of vitamin A* ○ *A certain amount of land is
dedicated to roadways and parks.*

▶ **COLLOCATIONS:**
　an amount **of** something
　a **huge/enormous/large/significant** amount of something
　a **certain/small** amount of something
　increase/reduce the amount of something

▶ **SYNONYMS:** number, quantity, volume

> **USAGE: amount or number?**
>
> You use **amount** with uncountable nouns to talk about how much
> there is of something. ○ *There was only a small amount of water in the glass.*
>
> You use **number** with plural, countable nouns to talk about how
> many there are of something. ○ *She was surprised at the large number of
> students in the class.*

an|cient /'eɪnʃənt/　　　HISTORY

ADJECTIVE Ancient means belonging to the distant past, especially to the
period in history before the end of the Roman Empire. ○ *They believed
ancient Greece and Rome were vital sources of learning.*

▶ **COLLOCATIONS:**
　an ancient **tradition/civilization**
　an ancient **monument/temple/ruin/text**
　ancient **history**
　an ancient **Egyptian/Greek/Chinese** thing

▶ **ANTONYM:** modern

an|nounce /ə'naʊns/ (announces, announcing, announced)

VERB If you **announce** something, you tell people about it publicly
or officially. ○ [+ that] *He will announce tonight that he is resigning from
office.* ○ *The company announced plans to sell music over the Internet.*
○ [+ that] *It was announced that the groups have agreed to a cease-fire.*

▶ **COLLOCATIONS:**
　announce **plans/results/details**
　announce a **deal/agreement/decision**

▶ **SYNONYM:** declare

an|nounce|ment /əˈnaʊnsmənt/ (announcements)

NOUN ○ *Sir Robert made his announcement after talks with the President.*
○ *There has been no formal announcement by either government.*
▶ **COLLOCATIONS:**
  make an announcement
  a **formal/official/public** announcement
  a **surprise** announcement
▶ **SYNONYMS:** declaration, statement

an|nual /ˈænjʊəl/

ACADEMIC WORD

1 ADJECTIVE Annual events happen once every year. ○ *the Labour Party's annual conference* ○ *In its annual report, UNICEF says at least 40,000 children die every day.*

2 ADJECTIVE Annual quantities or rates relate to a period of one year.
○ *The electronic and printing unit has annual sales of about $80 million.*
▶ **COLLOCATIONS:**
  an annual **conference/event**
  an annual **holiday/celebration**
  annual **fees/costs/sales/profits**
  an annual **income/salary/budget**
▶ **SYNONYM:** yearly

an|nual|ly

ADVERB ○ *El Salvador produces 100,000 tons of refined copper annually.*
○ *Companies report to their shareholders annually.*
▶ **SYNONYM:** yearly

an|swer /ˈɑːnsə, ˈæn-/ (answers, answering, answered)

1 VERB When you **answer** someone who has asked you something, you say something back to them. ○ *Just answer the question.* ○ *He paused before answering.* ○ [+ that] *Williams answered that he had no specific proposals yet.*
▶ **COLLOCATIONS:**
  answer a **question/query**
  answer **honestly/directly/immediately**
▶ **SYNONYMS:** reply, respond

2 NOUN An **answer** is something that you say when you answer someone.
○ *Without waiting for an answer, he walked out.* ○ *I asked him a question but I didn't get an answer.*
▶ **COLLOCATIONS:**
  get/give an answer
  a **definite/honest/straight/satisfactory** answer

▶ **PHRASES:**
in answer to someone's question
questions and answers
a question and answer session
▶ **SYNONYMS:** reply, response

3 NOUN An **answer to** a problem is a way of dealing with it or solving it.
○ [+ to] *There are no easy answers to the problems facing the economy.*
○ [+ for] *Prison is not the answer for most young offenders.*
▶ **COLLOCATIONS:**
the answer **to** *something*
the answer **for** *someone*
a **simple/easy/obvious** answer
a **possible** answer
▶ **SYNONYM:** solution

---

apart from /əˈpɑːt frəm/

PHRASE You use **apart from** when you are making an exception to a
general statement. ○ *The room was empty apart from one man seated beside
the fire.* ○ *She was the only British competitor apart from Richard Meade.*
▶ **SYNONYM:** except for

---

ap|pear /əˈpɪə/ (appears, appearing, appeared)

VERB If you say that something **appears to** be the case or **appears to** have
a certain quality, you mean that you have the impression that it is the
case or that it has that quality. ○ *He appeared to be depressed.* ○ *The aircraft
appears to have crashed.* ○ *There appeared to be a problem with the car.*
▶ **SYNONYM:** seem

> **ACADEMIC WRITING: Careful Language**
>
> In academic writing, try not to present something as 100% fact unless
> you have clear evidence. You can use a linking verb like **appear**, **seem**
> or **tend** to show that you believe that something is true or that it is
> often true. ○ *The results appear to show that boys are better at science
> subjects.* (but there may be another explanation) ○ *The system in the
> school seems to work well.* (but it has not been tested/proved) ○ *Older
> people tend to prefer the phone to email.* (but not every older person)

ap|pear|ance /əˈpɪərəns/

NOUN Someone's or something's **appearance** is the way that they look.
○ *She used to be so fussy about her appearance.* ○ [+ of] *He had the appearance of*

a college student. ○ [+ *of*] *A flat-roofed extension will add nothing to the value or appearance of the house.*

▶ **COLLOCATIONS:**
the appearance **of** *someone/something*
something's **physical/external** appearance
improve/enhance *someone's/something's* appearance

▶ **SYNONYM:** look

---

ap|ply /əˈplaɪ/ (applies, applying, applied)   `BUSINESS`

VERB If you **apply for** something such as a job or membership of an organization, you write a letter or fill in a form in order to ask formally for it. ○ [+ *for*] *I am continuing to apply for jobs.* ○ [+ *to-inf*] *They may apply to join the organization.*

▶ **COLLOCATIONS:**
apply **for** *something*
apply for a **job**
apply for a **licence/visa/permit/passport**
apply for a **grant/loan**
apply for **membership**

ap|pli|ca|tion /ˌæplɪˈkeɪʃən/ (applications)

NOUN An **application for** something is a formal written request for it.
○ [+ *for*] *His application for a student loan was rejected.* ○ [+ *to-inf*] *Turkey's application to join the European Community* ○ *Applications should be submitted as early as possible.* ○ *Tickets are available on application.*

▶ **COLLOCATIONS:**
an application **for** *something*
make/submit an application
receive/accept/reject an application
a **job/visa/passport/loan/grant** application
an application **form**

---

ap|point|ment /əˈpɔɪntmənt/ (appointments)

NOUN If you have an **appointment with** someone, you have arranged to see them at a particular time, usually in connection with their work
○ [+ *with*] *She has an appointment with her accountant.* ○ [+ *to-inf*] *I made an appointment to see my tutor.* ○ *a dental appointment*

▶ **COLLOCATIONS:**
an appointment **with** *someone*
have/make/arrange/book an appointment

a

cancel/miss an appointment
a **medical/dental/hospital** appointment
▶ PHRASE: an appointment to see someone

---

area /ˈeəriə/ (areas) `ACADEMIC WORD` `GEOGRAPHY`

1 NOUN An **area** is a particular part of a town, a country, a region, or the world. ○ *the large number of students in the area* ○ *60 years ago half the French population still lived in rural areas.* ○ *All the agricultural areas around this town are completely gone.*
  ▶ COLLOCATIONS:
    in/throughout an area
    the area **around/near/outside** *somewhere*
    a **small/large** area
    a **rural/urban/remote/residential** area
    the **local/surrounding** area
    the **affected/specific/whole/main** area
  ▶ SYNONYMS: region, district

2 NOUN The **area** of a surface such as a piece of land is the amount of flat space or ground that it covers, measured in square units. ○ *The islands cover a total area of 625.6 square kilometers.* ○ *The house was large in area, but it did not have many rooms.*
  ▶ COLLOCATIONS:
    the area **of** *something*
    in area
    the **surface/total** area
    cover an area of *x*
  ▶ SYNONYM: size

3 NOUN You can use **area** to refer to a particular subject or topic, or to a particular part of a larger, more general situation or activity. ○ *Immigration is a politically sensitive area.* ○ *[+ of] Awards were presented to writers in every area of the arts.*
  ▶ COLLOCATIONS:
    an area **of** *something*
    an area of **science/research**
    an area of **interest/concern/disagreement**
    someone's area of **expertise/responsibility**
    a **grey/sensitive** area
  ▶ SYNONYMS: subject, topic, field

a

armed forces /ˌɑːmd ˈfɔːsɪz/

PLURAL NOUN The **armed forces** of a country are its military forces, usually the army, navy, marines, and air force. ○ *He's a captain in the Russian armed forces.*

▶ **PHRASES:**
  a member of the armed forces
  be in the armed forces
▶ **SYNONYM:** the military
▶ **RELATED WORDS:** the army, the navy, the air force

army /ˈɑːmi/ **(armies)**

NOUN An **army** is a large organized group of people who are armed and trained to fight. ○ *He joined the army after leaving school.* ○ *The British and American armies invaded Sicily.* ○ *He's an army officer.*

▶ **COLLOCATIONS:**
  join/leave the army
  an army **officer/chief/commander**
  army **troops/soldiers**
  an army **unit/base/camp/barracks**
  an army **tank/helicopter/truck**
▶ **PHRASE:** be in the armed forces
▶ **RELATED WORDS:** the armed forces, soldier

ar|range /əˈreɪndʒ/ **(arranges, arranging, arranged)**

VERB If you **arrange** an event or meeting, you make plans for it to happen. ○ *She arranged an appointment for Friday afternoon at four-fifteen.* ○ *It is important that meetings are arranged well in advance.* ○ *The Russian leader threw the carefully arranged welcome into chaos.*

▶ **COLLOCATIONS:**
  arrange a **meeting/appointment**
  arrange a **visit/trip/tour/conference**
  carefully/hastily arranged
▶ **SYNONYMS:** organize, plan

ar|range|ment /əˈreɪndʒmənt/ **(arrangements)**

1 NOUN Arrangements are plans and preparations which you make so that something will happen or be possible. ○ *[+ for] The staff is working on final arrangements for the conference.* ○ *[+ to-inf] She telephoned Ellen, but made no arrangements to see her.* ○ *I prefer to make my own travel arrangements.*

▶ **COLLOCATIONS:**
  arrangements **for** *something*

a

    make/discuss/negotiate arrangements
    travel/security arrangements
    ▶ SYNONYM: plans

2 NOUN An **arrangement** is an agreement that you make with someone to do something. ○ *The caves can be visited only by prior arrangement.* ○ [+ to-inf] *Her teacher made a special arrangement to discuss her progress once a month.* ○ *Our policy is to try and come to an arrangement with the owner.*

    ▶ COLLOCATIONS:
    an arrangement **with** *someone*
    come to/make an arrangement
    ▶ PHRASE: by prior arrangement
    ▶ SYNONYM: agreement

---

ar|rest /əˈrest/ (arrests, arresting, arrested)   LAW

VERB If the police **arrest** you, they take you to a police station, because they believe you may have committed a crime. ○ *Police arrested five young men in connection with one of the attacks.* ○ [+ for] *The police say seven people were arrested for minor offences.*

    ▶ COLLOCATION: be arrested **for** *something*
    ▶ PHRASES:
    arrest someone in connection with something
    arrest someone on suspicion of something
    ▶ SYNONYM: detain

● **Arrest** is also a noun. ○ *Police chased the fleeing terrorists and later made two arrests.* ○ *Murder squad detectives approached the man and placed him under arrest.*

    ▶ COLLOCATION: **make** an arrest
    ▶ PHRASE: place someone under arrest

---

art /ɑːt/ (arts)   ARTS

1 UNCOUNTABLE NOUN Art consists of paintings, sculpture, and other pictures or objects which are created for people to look at. ○ *contemporary American art* ○ *Whitechapel Art Gallery*

    ▶ COLLOCATIONS:
    modern/contemporary art
    an art **gallery/exhibition/collection**
    the art **world**
    art **history**

2 NOUN The arts are activities such as music, painting, literature, cinema, and dance. ○ *people working in the arts* ○ [+ of] *the art of cinema*

▶ **COLLOCATIONS:**
the art **of** something
an arts **centre/festival**
visual/performing arts
▶ **PHRASE:** arts and crafts

3 PLURAL NOUN At a university or college, **arts** are subjects such as history, literature, or languages. ○ *arts graduates* ○ *the Faculty of Arts*
▶ **COLLOCATIONS:**
an arts **subject/degree**
an arts **student/graduate**
▶ **RELATED WORDS:** sciences, humanities

art|ist /ˈɑːtɪst/ (artists)

NOUN An **artist** is someone who draws or paints pictures or creates sculptures as a job or a hobby. ○ *Each painting is signed by the artist.* ○ *I'm not a good artist.*
▶ **COLLOCATIONS:**
a **contemporary** artist
a **graphic/visual/conceptual** artist
▶ **SYNONYM:** painter

ar|ti|cle /ˈɑːtɪkəl/ (articles)　　MEDIA

NOUN An **article** is a piece of writing that is published in a newspaper or magazine. ○ *a newspaper article* ○ [+ on] *The magazine published an article on skin cancer.* ○ *According to an article in The Economist the drug could have side effects.*
▶ **COLLOCATIONS:**
an article **about/on** something
a **newspaper/magazine** article
read/write/publish an article
▶ **PHRASE:** according to an article
▶ **SYNONYM:** piece

as|sis|tant /əˈsɪstənt/ (assistants)　　BUSINESS　ACADEMIC WORD

1 ADJECTIVE Assistant is used in front of titles or jobs to indicate a slightly lower rank. For example, an assistant director is one rank lower than a director in an organization. ○ *the Assistant Secretary of Defense* ○ *a young assistant professor at Harvard*
▶ **SYNONYMS:** deputy, junior

2 NOUN Someone's **assistant** is a person who helps them in their work. ○ *Kalan called his assistant, Hashim, to take over while he went out.*

○ *The salesman had been accompanied to the meeting by an assistant.*
▶ SYNONYM: aide

3 NOUN An **assistant** is a person who works in a shop selling things to customers. ○ *The assistant took the book and checked the price on the back cover.* ○ *She got a job as a sales assistant selling handbags.*
▶ COLLOCATION: a **shop/sales** assistant
▶ SYNONYM: sales person

as|so|cia|tion /ə,səʊsi'eɪʃən/ (associations)

NOUN An **association** is an official group of people who have the same job, aim, or interest. ○ *the British Olympic Association* ○ *Research associations are often linked to a particular industry.*
▶ COLLOCATIONS:
a **business/trade/industry/professional** association
a **national/local** association
the **consumers'/residents'/players'** association
▶ SYNONYM: organization

at|mos|phere /'ætməsfɪə/   GEOGRAPHY

NOUN A planet's **atmosphere** is the layer of air or other gases around it.
○ *There are dangerous levels of pollution in the Earth's atmosphere.* ○ *The Partial Test-Ban Treaty bans nuclear testing in the atmosphere.*
▶ COLLOCATION: **in** the atmosphere

at|mos|pher|ic /,ætməs'ferɪk/

ADJECTIVE **Atmospheric** is used to describe something which relates to the Earth's atmosphere. ○ *atmospheric gases* ○ *atmospheric pressure*
▶ COLLOCATION: atmospheric **pressure/conditions/pollution**

at|tempt /ə'tempt/ (attempts, attempting, attempted)

1 VERB If you **attempt to** do something, you try to do it. ○ [+ to-inf] *Scientists are attempting to find a cure for the disease.* ○ *The pilot then attempted an emergency landing.*
▶ SYNONYM: try

2 NOUN If you make an **attempt to** do something, you try to do it, often without success. ○ [+ to-inf] *The statement was a deliberate attempt to deceive people.* ○ *Her first attempt was unsuccessful.* ○ [+ at] *It was one of his rare attempts at humour.*
▶ COLLOCATIONS:
an attempt **at** *something*
make an attempt

a

a **failed/unsuccessful/vain** attempt

a **first/second/last** attempt

a **desperate/deliberate** attempt

> **EXTEND YOUR VOCABULARY**
>
> In general, everyday English the verb **try** is very common. You can use **try** in both informal and more formal written English. ○ *I've been trying to find you all day.* ○ *City officials are trying to find ways to streamline the process.*
>
> **Attempt** is a more formal verb used especially in academic writing. ○ *Many experts have attempted to explain personality development.* As a noun, **try** is only used in informal English. ○ *It might not work, but it's worth a try.*
>
> In more formal writing, you can use the nouns **attempt** or **effort**. ○ *Adults have to make a conscious attempt/effort to learn such skills.*

at|ten|tion /əˈtenʃən/

1 UNCOUNTABLE NOUN Attention is great interest that the public show in someone or something. ○ *The research attracted international attention.* ○ *The conference may help to focus attention on the economy.*

▶ **COLLOCATIONS:**

attract attention

focus attention on *something*

great/considerable attention

public/national/international attention

▶ **SYNONYM:** interest

2 UNCOUNTABLE NOUN If you **bring** something **to** someone's **attention** or **draw** their **attention to** it, you tell them about it or make them notice it. ○ *If we don't keep bringing this issue to people's attention, nothing will be done.* ○ *We need to draw people's attention to what is happening.*

3 PHRASE If you **pay attention to** someone, you watch them, listen to them, or take notice of them. ○ [+ *to*] *The food industry is paying attention to young consumers.* ○ *Other people walk along the beach at night, so I didn't pay any attention at first.*

audi|ence /ˈɔːdiəns/ (audiences)

ARTS MEDIA

1 NOUN The **audience** is the group of people who are watching or listening to a play, concert, film or speech ○ *The entire audience clapped loudly.* ○ [+ *of*] *He was speaking to an audience of students at the Institute for International Affairs.*

▶ **COLLOCATIONS:**

be **in** the audience

an audience **of** *people*
an audience **member**
a **live/receptive/enthusiastic** audience
▶ **PHRASE:** a member of the audience

2 NOUN The **audience** for a television or radio programme consists of all the people who watch or listen to it. ○ [+ *of*] *The series attracted an estimated world-wide audience of 250 million.* ○ [+ *for*] *the highest ever audience for a reality game show*
▶ **COLLOCATIONS:**
  the audience **for** *something*
  an audience **of** *x*
  a **television** audience
  a **wide/broad/large** audience
  the **average/weekly** audience
  a **worldwide/mass/global** audience
  the **target/intended** audience
  attract/appeal to an audience
▶ **SYNONYMS:** viewers, market

---

author /ˈɔːθə/ **(authors)** `ACADEMIC WORD` `LITERATURE`

1 NOUN The **author of** a piece of writing is the person who wrote it.
  ○ [+ *of*] *Jill Phillips, author of the book 'Give Your Child Music'*
  ▶ **COLLOCATION:** the author **of** *something*
  ▶ **SYNONYM:** writer

2 NOUN An **author** is a person whose job is writing books. ○ *Haruki Murakami is Japan's best-selling author.*
  ▶ **COLLOCATIONS:**
    a **best-selling/award-winning** author
    a **famous** author
  ▶ **SYNONYMS:** writer, novelist

---

author|ity /ɔːˈθɒrɪti, AM -ˈtɔːr-/ **(authorities)** `ACADEMIC WORD`

1 PLURAL NOUN The **authorities** are the people who have the power to make decisions and to make sure that laws are obeyed. ○ *The authorities decided to cancel the elections.* ○ *The prison authorities have been criticised for not acting more quickly.*
  ▶ **COLLOCATIONS:**
    prison/airport/immigration/military authorities
    the **Chinese/Russian/French** authorities
  ▶ **SYNONYM:** officials

a

2 UNCOUNTABLE NOUN Authority is the right to command and control other people. ○ *The judge had no authority to order a second trial.* ○ [+ *over*] *The court has no authority over the matter.*

▶ **COLLOCATIONS:**
   authority **over** *something*
   have authority

3 NOUN Someone who is an **authority on** a particular subject knows a lot about it. ○ [+ *on*] *He's universally recognized as an authority on Russian affairs.*

▶ **COLLOCATION:** an authority **on** *something*

▶ **SYNONYM:** expert

---

avail|able /əˈveɪləbəl/

ACADEMIC WORD

ADJECTIVE If something you want or need is **available**, you can get it. ○ *all the available evidence suggests* ○ *There is a lot of information available on this subject.* ○ *The drug is widely available.* ○ [+ *for*] *The studio is available for private use.*

▶ **COLLOCATIONS:**
   available **for** *something*
   available **from/through/via/in** *somewhere*
   widely/freely/readily/easily available
   currently/immediately available
   commercially/publicly/generally available
   the available **information/evidence/space/resources**
   make *something* available

▶ **PHRASE:** available on request

▶ **SYNONYM:** accessible

avail|abil|ity /əˌveɪləˈbɪlɪti/

UNCOUNTABLE NOUN ○ *There is very limited availability of trained and skilled resources.* ○ [+ *of*] *the easy availability of guns*

▶ **COLLOCATIONS:**
   the availability **of** *something*
   easy/limited/widespread availability

---

av|er|age /ˈævərɪdʒ/ (averages, averaging, averaged)

MATHS

1 NOUN An **average** is the result that you get when you add two or more numbers together and divide the total by the number of numbers you added together. ○ [+ *of*] *Take the average of those ratios and multiply by a hundred.* ○ *The school's results are above the national average.*

▶ **COLLOCATIONS:**
   the average **of** *something*

a

    above/below average
    the **national/overall** average
    the **monthly/weekly/annual** average
    ▶ SYNONYM: mean

• **Average** is also an adjective. ○ *The average price of goods rose by just 2.2%.*
○ *The average age for a woman to have her first child was 29.*
    ▶ COLLOCATIONS:
    the average **rate/price/cost**
    the average **age/temperature**
    ▶ SYNONYM: mean

2 ADJECTIVE An **average** person or thing is typical or normal. ○ *The average adult man burns 1,500 to 2,000 calories per day.* ○ *Packaging is about a third of what is found in an average British dustbin.*
    ▶ SYNONYM: typical

3 NOUN An amount or quality that is **the average** is the normal amount or quality. ○ *Most areas suffered more rain than usual, with Northern Ireland getting double the average for the month.*
    ▶ SYNONYM: norm

• **Average** is also an adjective. ○ *£2.20 for a beer is average.* ○ *a woman of average height*

---

avoid /əˈvɔɪd/ **(avoids, avoiding, avoided)**

VERB If you **avoid** something unpleasant that might happen, you do something to stop it from happening. ○ *The pilots had to take emergency action to avoid a disaster.* ○ [+ v-ing] *Lift the table carefully to avoid damaging it.*
    ▶ COLLOCATIONS:
    carefully/narrowly avoid *something*
    avoid **conflict/confrontation/war**
    avoid **confusion/mistakes/embarrassment**
    ▶ SYNONYMS: prevent, stop

---

aware /əˈweə/   ACADEMIC WORD

ADJECTIVE If you are **aware of** something, you know about it. ○ [+ of] *People need to be more aware of the dangers of drug use.* ○ *Staff were not fully aware of his problems.*
    ▶ COLLOCATIONS:
    aware **of** *something*
    fully/well aware
    ▶ ANTONYM: unaware

aware|ness

UNCOUNTABLE NOUN ○ [+ *of/about*] *There has been an increasing awareness of environmental issues.* ○ *We need to raise public awareness of the disease.*

▶ COLLOCATIONS:
awareness **of/about** *something*
increase/raise/promote/heighten awareness
an **increasing/growing/heightened** awareness
public awareness
environmental/political awareness

Bb

back|ground /ˈbækɡraʊnd/ (backgrounds)

NOUN The **background** to an event or situation consists of the facts that explain what caused it. ○ [+ of] *The meeting takes place against a background of continuing political violence.* ○ [+ to] *The background to the experience is important.*

▶ **COLLOCATIONS:**
the background **to/of** something
background **information/knowledge**
background **report/check/material/reading**

▶ **PHRASE:** against a background of something

▶ **SYNONYM:** context

---

ban /bæn/ (bans, banning, banned)

1 VERB To **ban** something means to state officially that it must not be done, shown, or used. ○ *Canada will ban smoking in all offices later this year.* ○ *Last year arms sales were banned.* ○ *a banned substance*

▶ **COLLOCATIONS:**
the **law/legislation** bans something
a **treaty/order/injunction** bans something
ban something **officially/permanently/temporarily**
ban something **altogether/outright**

▶ **SYNONYMS:** prohibit, bar

▶ **ANTONYMS:** permit, legalize

2 NOUN A **ban** is an official ruling that something must not be done, shown, or used. ○ [+ on] *The General also lifted a ban on political parties.* ○ *calls for an outright ban on arms exports*

▶ **COLLOCATIONS:**
a ban **on** something
lift/impose a ban
a **total/outright/temporary** ban
an **import/export/advertising** ban

▶ **SYNONYM:** prohibition

b

bar|ri|er /ˈbæriə/ **(barriers)**

1 **NOUN** A **barrier** is something such as a rule, law, or policy that makes it difficult or impossible for something to happen or be achieved.
○ [+ *to*] *Taxes are the most obvious barrier to free trade.*

2 **NOUN** A **barrier** is a problem that prevents two people or groups from agreeing, communicating, or working with each other. ○ *When you get involved in sports, a lot of the racial barriers are broken down.* ○ *Because of the need to survive, the class barriers were lowered.*

▶ **COLLOCATIONS:**
  a barrier **to/against** *something*
  a barrier **between** *people*
  break down/lower barriers
  a **trade** barrier
  a **language/age/class** barrier
  a **psychological/racial/cultural** barrier

▶ **SYNONYMS:** obstacle, divide

ba|sic /ˈbeɪsɪk/

1 **ADJECTIVE** You use **basic** to describe things, activities, and principles that are the most important or the simplest aspects of something. ○ *the basic skills of reading, writing and communicating* ○ *the basic laws of physics* ○ *Access to justice is a basic right.*

2 **ADJECTIVE** **Basic** goods and services are very simple ones which every human being needs. ○ *shortages of even the most basic foodstuffs* ○ *Hospitals lack even basic drugs for surgical operations.* ○ *the basic needs of food and water*

3 **ADJECTIVE** You can use **basic** to emphasize that you are referring to the most important aspect of a situation, not the less important details. ○ *There are three basic types of tea.* ○ *The basic design has changed little in 100 years.*

▶ **COLLOCATIONS:**
  a basic **principle/rule/idea/right**
  basic **skills/education/understanding/information**
  the basic **problem/question/premise**
  basic **food/foodstuffs/goods**
  basic **services/supplies**
  a basic **need/requirement**

▶ **SYNONYMS:** fundamental, key, essential, main

▶ **ANTONYM:** secondary

ba|sics /'beisiks/

PLURAL NOUN **The basics** of something are its simplest, most important elements, in contrast to more complicated or detailed ones. ○ [+ of] *They will concentrate on teaching the basics of reading, writing and arithmetic.* ○ *A strong community cannot be built until the basics are in place.*

▶ **COLLOCATIONS:**
  the basics **of** something
  learn/teach/cover the basics
  know/understand the basics

▶ **SYNONYM:** fundamentals

bat|tle /'bætəl/ (battles)

1 NOUN A **battle** is a violent fight between groups of people, especially one between military forces during a war. ○ [+ of] *the victory of King William III at the Battle of the Boyne* ○ [+ between] *a gun battle between police and drug traffickers* ○ *men who die in battle*

2 NOUN A **battle** is a conflict in which different people or groups compete in order to achieve success or control. ○ [+ over] *a renewed political battle over Britain's attitude to Europe* ○ [+ between] *the eternal battle between good and evil in the world* ○ [+ for] *a battle for supremacy*

3 NOUN You can use **battle** to refer to someone's efforts to achieve something in spite of very difficult circumstances. ○ [+ against] *the battle against crime* ○ [+ with] *She has fought a constant battle with her weight.* ○ [+ against] *Greg lost his brave battle against cancer two years ago.*

▶ **COLLOCATIONS:**
  the battle **of** something
  a battle **between** two groups
  a battle **with** someone/something
  a battle **against/for/over** something
  a **fierce/bitter** battle
  a **continuing/uphill/long** battle
  a **gun** battle
  a **legal/political/court** battle
  face/fight/win/lose a battle

▶ **PHRASE:** die in battle

▶ **SYNONYMS:** fight, combat, struggle, campaign

be|have /bɪ'heɪv/ (behaves, behaving, behaved)

1 VERB The way that you **behave** is the way that you do and say things, and the things that you do and say. ○ [+ in] *I couldn't believe these people were behaving in this way.* ○ *He'd behaved badly.*

b

2 VERB In science, the way that something **behaves** is the things that it does.
○ *Under certain conditions, electrons can behave like waves rather than particles.*
▶ **COLLOCATIONS:**
behave **in** *a particular way*
behave **like** *something*
behave in a particular **way/manner/fashion**
behave **badly/differently/responsibly**
▶ **SYNONYM:** act

be|hav|iour /bɪˈheɪvjə/

1 UNCOUNTABLE NOUN People's or animals' **behaviour** is the way that they
behave. [in AM, use **behavior**] ○ *Make sure that good behaviour is rewarded.*
○ *He frequently exhibited violent behaviour.* ○ *human sexual behaviour*
▶ **COLLOCATIONS:**
the behaviour **of** *someone*
bad/anti-social/unacceptable/inappropriate behaviour
human/sexual/criminal behaviour
exhibit/display a type of behaviour
▶ **PHRASE:** attitudes and behaviour
▶ **SYNONYM:** conduct

2 UNCOUNTABLE NOUN In science, the **behaviour** of something is the way that
it behaves. [in AM, use **behavior**] ○ *It will be many years before anyone
can predict a hurricane's behavior with much accuracy.* ○ *[+ of] the behaviour of
sub-atomic particles*
▶ **COLLOCATION:** the behaviour **of** *something*

---

be|lieve /bɪˈliːv/ (believes, believing, believed)

VERB If you **believe** that something is true, you think that it is true, but you
are not sure. [FORMAL] ○ *[+ that] Experts believe that the coming drought will
be extensive.* ○ *Sleepiness in drivers is widely believed to be an important cause of
road traffic injuries.* ○ *The main problem, I believe, lies elsewhere.*
→ see note at **consider**
▶ **COLLOCATIONS:**
be **widely** believed
strongly/firmly believe *something*
▶ **SYNONYMS:** think, consider
▶ **ANTONYM:** disbelieve

be|lief /bɪˈliːf/ (beliefs)

NOUN **Belief** is a feeling of certainty that something exists, is true or good,
or is the case. ○ *[+ in] One billion people throughout the world are Muslims,
united by belief in one god.* ○ *[+ in] a belief in personal liberty* ○ *[+ about]
stereotyped attitudes and beliefs about men's and women's roles*

▶ **COLLOCATIONS:**
belief **in** *something*
beliefs **about** *something*
religious/spiritual belief
a **popular/widespread/strong** belief
hold/share a belief
▶ **PHRASES:**
attitudes and beliefs
beliefs and values
contrary to popular belief
▶ **SYNONYMS:** faith, ideology, opinion, view

---

be|long /bɪˈlɒŋ, AM -ˈlɔːŋ/ (belongs, belonging, belonged)

1 VERB If something **belongs to** you, you own it. ○ [+ to] *This handwriting belongs to a male.* ○ *a home he says rightfully belongs to his family*

2 VERB If someone **belongs to** a particular group, they are a member of that group. ○ [+ to] *I used to belong to a youth club.*

3 VERB If something or someone **belongs in** or **to** a particular category, type, or group, they are of that category, type, or group. ○ [+ in/to] *The judges could not decide which category it belonged in.*

▶ **COLLOCATIONS:**
belong **to** *someone/something*
belong **in** *something*
belong in a **category/class/bracket**
rightfully/rightly/legally belong

---

ben|efit /ˈbenɪfɪt/ `ACADEMIC WORD`
(benefits, benefiting or **benefitting, benefited** or **benefitted)**

1 NOUN The **benefit of** something is the help that you get from it or the advantage that results from it. ○ [+ of] *the benefits of this form of therapy* ○ *For maximum benefit, use your treatment every day.* ○ [+ to] *I hope what I have written will be of benefit to someone else.* ○ *This remarkable achievement took place without the benefit of modern telecommunications.*

▶ **COLLOCATIONS:**
the benefit **of** *something*
of benefit **to** *someone*
maximum/potential/additional benefit
health/economic/financial/social benefit
reap the benefit of *something*
bring/provide benefit
▶ **PHRASE:** the benefit of hindsight

b

▶ **SYNONYMS:** advantage, profit
▶ **ANTONYMS:** disadvantage, drawback

2 VERB If you **benefit from** something or if it **benefits** you, it helps you or improves your life. ○ [+ from] *Both sides have benefited from the talks.*
○ *a variety of government programs benefiting children*

▶ **COLLOCATIONS:**
benefit **from** *something*
greatly/directly/personally/financially benefit *someone*
▶ **SYNONYMS:** profit, gain, help

USAGE: benefit or **profit**?

These words both describe something good that you get as a result of something. A **benefit** can be any positive result for an individual or a group of people. ○ *Lowered blood pressure is one benefit of regular exercise.* ○ *Pupils are benefiting from improvements in teaching.*

A **profit** is usually money that a person or a company gets from an activity. ○ *The bank reported a profit of 572 million euros.* ○ *A senior official profited illegally from smuggling.*

---

ben|efi|cial /ˌbenɪˈfɪʃəl/

ADJECTIVE ○ [+ to] *vitamins which are beneficial to our health* ○ *Using computers has a beneficial effect on children's learning.*
▶ **COLLOCATIONS:**
beneficial **to/for** *something/someone*
a beneficial **effect/arrangement**
mutually/hugely/highly/particularly beneficial
▶ **SYNONYMS:** helpful, positive, valuable
▶ **ANTONYMS:** detrimental, negative

bil|lion /ˈbɪljən/ (billions)   `MATHS`

1 NUMBER A **billion** is a thousand million. ○ *3 billion dollars* ○ *This year, almost a billion birds will be processed in the region.*

2 QUANTIFIER If you talk about **billions of** people or things, you mean that there is a very large number of them but you do not know or do not want to say exactly how many. ○ [+ of] *Biological systems have been doing this for billions of years.* ○ [+ of] *He urged U.S. executives to invest billions of dollars in his country.*
▶ **COLLOCATION:** billions **of** *something*

> **USAGE:** Plural forms
>
> For large numbers, the plural form is **billion**, **million**, **thousand** and **hundred** after a number, or after a word or expression referring to a number, such as 'several' or 'a few'. ○ *12/three/several billion dollars*
> ○ *45/six/a few thousand people*
> The plural form of these words is **billions**, **millions**, **thousands** and **hundreds** when you talk more generally about a large number.
> ○ *billions of dollars* ○ *thousands of people*

bi|ol|ogy /baɪˈɒlədʒi/   `SCIENCE` `BIOLOGY`

1 **UNCOUNTABLE NOUN** **Biology** is the science which is concerned with the study of living things. ○ *She studied biology at Sydney University.*
   ▶ **COLLOCATIONS:**
   applied/marine/basic/molecular biology
   a biology **laboratory/teacher/professor/department**
   ▶ **PHRASE:** biology and chemistry

2 **UNCOUNTABLE NOUN** The **biology** of a living thing is the way in which its body or cells behave. ○ [+ *of*] *The biology of these diseases is terribly complicated.* ○ *human biology*
   ▶ **COLLOCATIONS:**
   the biology **of** *something*
   cell/human/reproductive biology

bio|logi|cal /ˌbaɪəˈlɒdʒɪkəl/

ADJECTIVE **Biological** is used to describe processes and states that occur in the bodies and cells of living things. ○ *biological processes* ○ *This is a natural biological response.*
   ▶ **COLLOCATIONS:**
   a biological **system/process/function/activity/effect/agent**
   biological **science**
   a biological **weapon/warfare/attack**
   ▶ **PHRASE:** biological and chemical

bio|logi|cal|ly /ˌbaɪəˈlɒdʒɪkli/

ADVERB ○ *Much of our behaviour is biologically determined.*
   ▶ **COLLOCATIONS:**
   biologically **determined/programmed**
   biologically **active/different**

b

bi|olo|gist /baɪˈɒlədʒɪst/ (biologists)

NOUN A **biologist** is a scientist who studies biology. ○ *biologists studying the fruit fly*
▶ **COLLOCATION:** a **molecular/marine** biologist

boil /bɔɪl/ (boils, boiling, boiled) SCIENCE

VERB When a hot liquid **boils** or when you **boil** it, bubbles appear in it and it starts to change into steam or vapour. ○ *Gold melts at 1,064 degrees centigrade and boils at 2,808 degrees centigrade.* ○ *Boil the water.*
○ [V-ing] *a pot of boiling oil*
▶ **COLLOCATION:** boiling **point**

bone /bəʊn/ (bones) SCIENCE BIOLOGY MEDICINE

NOUN Your **bones** are the hard parts inside your body which together form your skeleton. ○ *Stephen fractured a thigh bone.* ○ *The body is made up primarily of bone, muscle, and fat.*
▶ **COLLOCATIONS:**
   a **broken/fractured** bone
   a **thigh/hip/collar** bone

bor|der /ˈbɔːdə/ (borders, bordering, bordered) GEOGRAPHY

1 NOUN The **border** between two countries or regions is the dividing line between them. Sometimes **the border** also refers to the land close to this line. ○ *They fled across the border.* ○ *the isolated jungle area near the Panamanian border* ○ *the Mexican border town of Tijuana*
▶ **COLLOCATIONS:**
   cross/open/close/control/guard a border
   the border **between** countries
▶ **SYNONYM:** frontier

2 VERB A country that **borders** another country, a sea, or a river is next to it. ○ [V-ing] *the European and Arab countries bordering the Mediterranean* ○ *across Siberia to the Ussuri River bordering China*

brack|et /ˈbrækɪt/ (brackets) ACADEMIC STUDY

NOUN **Brackets** are a pair of written marks that you place round a word, expression, or sentence in order to indicate that you are giving extra information. In British English, curved marks like these are called **brackets**, but in American English, they are called **parentheses**.
○ *The prices in brackets are special rates for the under 18s.* ○ *My annotations appear in square brackets.*

> **COLLOCATIONS:**
> **in** brackets
> **square/curly** brackets
> **SYNONYM:** parenthesis

brain /breɪn/ (brains)　　　SCIENCE BIOLOGY

NOUN Your **brain** is the organ inside your head that controls your body's activities and enables you to think and to feel things such as heat and pain. ○ Her father died of a brain tumour. ○ the development of a child's brain
> **COLLOCATIONS:**
> brain **damage**
> a brain **tumour/cell**
> the **human** brain

brand /brænd/ (brands)　　　BUSINESS

NOUN A **brand** of a product is the version of it that is made by one particular manufacturer. ○ [+ of] another brand of cola ○ I bought one of the leading brands. ○ a supermarket's own brand
> **COLLOCATIONS:**
> a brand **of** something
> **create/build/launch** a brand
> a **leading/own/strong/global** brand
> **SYNONYM:** make

breathe /briːð/　　　SCIENCE BIOLOGY MEDICINE
(breathes, breathing, breathed)

VERB When people or animals **breathe**, they take air into their lungs and let it out again. When they **breathe** smoke or a particular kind of air, they take it into their lungs and let it out again as they breathe.
○ [+ through] Breathe through your nose. ○ [+ in] A thirteen year old girl is being treated after breathing in smoke.
> **COLLOCATIONS:**
> breathe **in/out**
> breathe **through** your *nose/mouth*
> breathe **deeply/heavily/easily**
> breathe **air**
> **SYNONYMS:** inhale, exhale

breath /breθ/ (breaths)

NOUN When you take a **breath**, you breathe in once. ○ He took a deep breath, and began to climb the stairs. ○ Gasping for breath, she leaned against the door.

b

▸ COLLOCATIONS:
take a breath
draw breath
catch your breath
a **long/deep** breath

> USAGE: Spelling
>
> **Breathe** /briːð/ is the verb form and has an 'e' at the end.
> ○ *Breathe slowly.*
>
> **Breath** /breθ/ is the noun form, without an 'e' at the end.
> ○ *a deep breath*

broad /brɔːd/ (broader, broadest)

ADJECTIVE You use **broad** to describe something that includes a large number of different things or people. ○ *A broad range of issues was discussed.* ○ *a broad coalition of workers, peasants, students and middle class professionals*
▸ COLLOCATIONS:
a broad **range/spectrum/category**
broad **support/appeal**
▸ SYNONYM: wide
▸ ANTONYMS: narrow, limited

broad|ly /ˈbrɔːdli/

ADVERB ○ *This gives children a more broadly based education.* ○ *Broadly speaking they divided into two categories.*
▸ PHRASE: broadly speaking

broad|en /ˈbrɔːdən/ (broadens, broadening, broadened)

VERB When you **broaden** something such as your experience or popularity or when it **broadens**, the number of things or people that it includes becomes greater. ○ *We must broaden our appeal.* ○ *The political spectrum has broadened.*
▸ COLLOCATIONS:
broaden *someone's* **appeal/base/horizon**
broaden the **scope/range** of *something*
▸ SYNONYMS: widen, increase, expand
▸ ANTONYMS: narrow, limit

budg|et /ˈbʌdʒɪt/   BUSINESS ECONOMICS
(budgets, budgeting, budgeted)

1 NOUN Your **budget** is the amount of money that you have available to spend. The **budget** for something is the amount of money that a person, organization, or country has available to spend on it. ○ [+ for] *This year's budget for AIDS prevention probably won't be much higher.* ○ *Set goals which you can meet within your budget and resources.* ○ *working on a very tight budget*

▶ **COLLOCATIONS:**
a budget **for** *something*
a **total/annual/overall** budget
a **state/federal** budget
a **marketing/advertising/defence/education** budget
a budget **cut/increase/deficit**
▶ **PHRASES:**
within your budget
a tight budget

2 VERB If you **budget** certain amounts of money for particular things, you decide that you can afford to spend those amounts on those things. ○ [+ for] *The company has budgeted $10 million for advertising.* ○ *I'm learning how to budget.*
▶ **COLLOCATION:** budget **for** *something*

build /bɪld/ (builds, building, built)

VERB If people **build** an organization, a society, or a relationship, they gradually form it. ○ *He and a partner set up on their own and built a successful fashion company.* ○ *Their purpose is to build a fair society and a strong economy.*
▶ **COLLOCATIONS:**
build a **relationship/society/network/reputation**
gradually/slowly build *something*
▶ **SYNONYMS:** create, establish

burn /bɜːn/ (burns, burning, burned, burnt) `SCIENCE`

> The past tense and past participle is **burned** in American English, and **burned** or **burnt** in British English.

1 VERB If there is a fire or a flame somewhere, you say that there is a fire or flame **burning** there. ○ *Fires were burning out of control in the center of the city.* ○ *The furnace has a design that allows the flame to burn at a lower temperature.*

2 VERB If something **is burning**, it is on fire. ○ *One of the vehicles was still burning.* ○ [V-ing] *That boy was rescued from a burning house.*

3 VERB If you **burn** something, you destroy or damage it with fire. ○ *Protesters set cars on fire and burned a building.* ○ *Incineration plants should be built to burn household waste.*

b

4 VERB If you **burn** a fuel or if it **burns**, it is used to produce heat, light, or energy. ○ *The power stations burn coal from the Ruhr region.* ○ *Manufacturers are working with new fuels to find one that burns more cleanly than petrol.*

▶ **COLLOCATIONS:**
burn something **down**
burn **fuel/coal/wood**
burn **brightly/fiercely**
badly/severely burned

busi|ness /ˈbɪznɪs/ (businesses)

`BUSINESS`

1 UNCOUNTABLE NOUN Business is work relating to the production, buying, and selling of goods or services. ○ *young people seeking a career in business* ○ *Jennifer has an impressive academic and business background.* ○ *Harvard Business School*

▶ **COLLOCATIONS:**
a business **school**
conduct business
big/local/global business
a business **model/plan**
a business **leader/partner**

▶ **PHRASE:** do business with someone

2 NOUN A **business** is an organization which produces and sells goods or which provides a service. ○ *The company was a family business.* ○ *The majority of small businesses go broke within the first twenty-four months.*

▶ **COLLOCATIONS:**
a **family/small** business
run/start a business
own/grow/build/operate a business
a **retail/consulting/catering** business

▶ **SYNONYMS:** company, firm

Cc

cal|cu|late /'kælkjʊleɪt/ (calculates, calculating, calculated) MATHS

VERB If you **calculate** a number or amount, you discover it from information that you already have, by using arithmetic, mathematics, or a special machine. ○ *From this you can calculate the total mass in the Galaxy.* ○ [+ that] *We calculate that the average size farm in Lancaster County is 65 acres.* ○ *A computer calculates by switching currents on or off.*

▶ COLLOCATIONS:
a **computer/researcher** calculates *something*
calculate a **rate/cost/amount/value**

▶ SYNONYM: work out

▶ RELATED WORDS: add, subtract, multiply, divide

cal|cu|la|tion /ˌkælkjʊ'leɪʃən/ (calculations)

NOUN ○ *This calculation is made by subtracting the age of death from 65.* ○ [+ of] *the calculation of their assets* ○ *His calculations showed that the price index would go down by half a per cent.*

▶ COLLOCATIONS:
a calculation **of** *something*
perform/make a calculation
a calculation **shows/suggests/indicates** *something*

▶ SYNONYM: sum

cam|paign /ˌkæm'peɪn/ BUSINESS SOCIAL SCIENCE POLITICS
(campaigns, campaigning, campaigned)

1 NOUN A **campaign** is a planned set of activities that people carry out over a period of time in order to achieve something such as social or political change. ○ *During his election campaign he promised to put the economy back on its feet.* ○ [+ to-inf] *Apacs has launched a campaign to improve the training of staff.* ○ [+ against] *the campaign against public smoking*

▶ COLLOCATIONS:
a campaign **on/for/against** *something*
a **presidential/election/advertising** campaign
a **nationwide/political** campaign
launch/run/lead a campaign
a campaign on an **issue**

▶ SYNONYM: protest

c

2 VERB If someone **campaigns for** something, they carry out a planned set of activities over a period of time in order to achieve their aim. ○ [+ for] *We are campaigning for law reform.* ○ [+ for/against] *Mr Burns has actively campaigned against a hostel being set up here.* ○ [+ to-inf] *They have been campaigning to improve the legal status of women.*

▶ **COLLOCATIONS:**
campaign **for/against** *something*
actively/tirelessly campaign
campaign for **independence/reform**

▶ **SYNONYMS:** lobby, protest, advocate, promote

capi|tal /ˈkæpɪtəl/ (capitals) `GEOGRAPHY`

NOUN The **capital** of a country is the city or town where its government or parliament meets. ○ [+ of] *Kathmandu, the capital of Nepal*

▶ **COLLOCATIONS:**
the capital **of** *somewhere*
the capital of a **country/state/province**

car|bon di|ox|ide /ˌkɑːbən daɪˈɒksaɪd/ `SCIENCE`

UNCOUNTABLE NOUN **Carbon dioxide** is a gas. It is produced by animals and people breathing out, and by chemical reactions. The abbreviation CO_2 is also used in written notes and formulae. ○ *The amount of carbon dioxide in the atmosphere has been steadily increasing.* ○ *the level of carbon dioxide in the blood* ○ *carbon dioxide emissions*

ca|reer /kəˈrɪə/ (careers) `BUSINESS`

NOUN A **career** is the job or profession that someone does for a long period of their life. ○ [+ as] *She is now concentrating on a career as a fashion designer.* ○ [+ in] *scientists wishing to pursue a career in medicine* ○ *Staff can choose courses based on their career development plans.*

▶ **COLLOCATIONS:**
a career **in/as** *something*
a career in **politics/industry/law/business**
a career as a **writer/actor/teacher**
a **political/managerial/military/academic** career
have/choose/pursue a career
career **prospects/development**
a career **move/opportunity/path**

▶ **SYNONYMS:** profession, work, employment, vocation

car|ry out /ˌkæri ˈaʊt/ (carries out, carrying out, carried out)

PHRASAL VERB If you **carry out** a task or instruction, you do it or act according to it. ○ *Zuboff carried out case studies in three paper mills.* ○ *The institute is carrying out research into rural health.* ○ *the results of experiments carried out by one or more psychologists*

▶ **COLLOCATIONS:**
carry out **research**
carry out a **survey/experiment/analysis/test/study**

EXTEND YOUR VOCABULARY

Do is a very common verb in everyday English. In academic English, you need to use more specific verbs with different nouns.

carry out/conduct a survey/study/interview/experiment/research
undertake a task/project/study/activity/research/work
perform a task/procedure/operation/experiment

Look out for these verbs when you are reading and notice how they are used.

---

case /keɪs/ (cases)

1 NOUN A particular **case** is a particular situation or incident, especially one that you are using as an individual example or instance of something. ○ [+ *of*] *Surgical training takes at least nine years, or 11 in the case of obstetrics.* ○ *In extreme cases, insurance companies can prosecute for fraud.* ○ [+ *of*] *The Honduran press published reports of eighteen cases of alleged baby snatching.*
→ see note at **occasion**

▶ **COLLOCATIONS:**
a case **of** *something*
a **particular/rare/extreme** case

▶ **PHRASE:** in this/that case
▶ **SYNONYMS:** incident, situation

2 NOUN A **case** is a person or their particular problem that a doctor, social worker, or other professional is dealing with. ○ [+ *of*] *the case of a 57-year-old man who had suffered a stroke* ○ [+ *of*] *Some cases of arthritis respond to a gluten-free diet.* ○ *Child protection workers were meeting to discuss her case.*

▶ **COLLOCATIONS:**
a case **of** *something*
a case of a **disease/illness**
a case of **flu/measles/cancer**

3 NOUN In law, a **case** is a trial or other legal inquiry. ○ *It can be difficult for public figures to win a libel case.* ○ *The case was brought by his family, who say their reputation has been damaged by allegations about him.*

c

▶ COLLOCATIONS:
win/lose a case
bring/continue a case
a **libel/rape/murder** case
a **court** case
▶ SYNONYMS: trial, action

---

cause /kɔːz/ (causes, causing, caused)

1 NOUN The **cause of** an event, usually a bad event, is the thing that makes it happen. ○ [+ of] Smoking is the biggest preventable cause of death and disease. ○ The causes are a complex blend of local and national tensions.
▶ COLLOCATIONS:
a cause **of** something
a **common/probable/major** cause
the **root/underlying** cause of something
the cause of **death**
the cause of a **crash/accident/fire/disease**
determine/investigate/identify/establish/find the cause of something
▶ PHRASE: cause and effect
▶ SYNONYM: reason

2 VERB To **cause** something, usually something bad, means to make it happen. ○ Attempts to limit family size among some minorities are likely to cause problems. ○ The results may cause people concern. ○ [+ to-inf] a protein that gets into animal cells and attacks other proteins, causing disease to spread
▶ COLLOCATIONS:
cause **problems/damage/harm/trouble/delays**
cause **death/injury/pain/disease**
possibly/probably/likely/apparently cause something
▶ SYNONYMS: make, lead to, bring about

---

ce|leb|rity /sɪˈlebrɪti/ (celebrities)   MEDIA

NOUN A **celebrity** is someone who is famous, especially in areas of entertainment such as films, music, writing, or sport. ○ In 1944, at the age of 30, Hersey suddenly became a celebrity. ○ a host of celebrities
▶ COLLOCATIONS:
become a celebrity
celebrity **status**
a celebrity **chef/guest/host**
▶ SYNONYM: star

cen|ti|me|tre /'sentɪmiːtə/ (centimetres)

NOUN A **centimetre** is a unit of length in the metric system equal to ten millimetres or one-hundredth of a metre. The abbreviation **cm** is used in written notes. [in AM, use **centimeter**] ○ *a tiny fossil plant, only a few centimetres high* ○ *Up to 15 centimetres of snow was expected to fall on mainland Nova Scotia.*

▶ **COLLOCATIONS:**
  x centimetres **of** something
  x centimetres **high/tall/long/wide/thick/deep**
  x centimetres **in length/diameter**
  a **square/cubic** centimetre
▶ **RELATED WORDS:** metre, millimetre

ACADEMIC WRITING: Measurements and abbreviations

In notes and diagrams, numbers and abbreviations are often used to show measurements. ○ *Office space: 8m x 12.5m*

However, in essays, such as for the IELTS writing tasks, you should use full words. ○ *The office is eight metres wide by twelve and a half metres long.*

---

cen|tre /'sentə/ (centres)

1 NOUN The **centre** of something is the middle of it. [in AM, use **center**] ○ [+ *of*] *A large wooden table dominates the centre of the room.* ○ *The pain of a heart attack is generally felt in the centre of the chest.*

▶ **COLLOCATION:** the centre **of** something
▶ **SYNONYM:** middle

2 NOUN The **centre** of a town or city is the part where there are the most shops and businesses and where a lot of people come from other areas to work or shop. [in AM, use **center**] ○ *a suburb several miles from the city centre* ○ *a busy street in the town centre*

▶ **COLLOCATION:** the **city/town** centre

cen|tral /'sentrəl/

ADJECTIVE Something that is **central** is in the middle of a place or area. ○ *Central America's Caribbean coast* ○ *a woman living in central London* ○ *a central location in the capital*

▶ **COLLOCATIONS:**
  Central **America/Europe/Asia/London**
  a central **location**

cen|tral|ly

ADVERB ○ *The main cabin has its full-sized double bed centrally placed with plenty*

of room around it. ○ *a centrally located hotel*
▸ **COLLOCATION:** centrally **located**

---

cen|tu|ry /ˈsentʃəri/ (centuries)　　　　　　**HISTORY**

1 NOUN A **century** is a period of a hundred years that is used when stating
a date. For example, the 19th century was the period from 1801 to 1900.
○ *celebrated figures of the late eighteenth century* ○ *a 17th-century merchant's house*

2 NOUN A **century** is any period of a hundred years. ○ *The drought there is
the worst in a century.* ○ *[+ of] This may be ending centuries of tradition.*
▸ **COLLOCATION:** centuries **of** *something*
▸ **RELATED WORDS:** decade, millennium

---

cer|tain /ˈsɜːtən/

1 ADJECTIVE If you say that something is **certain**, you firmly believe that it
is true, or have definite knowledge about it. ○ *One thing is certain, both
have the utmost respect for each other.* ○ *[+ that] It is certain that stammering
becomes more pronounced when the rate of speech is increased.*
▸ **COLLOCATIONS:**
　almost/absolutely/virtually/fairly certain
　look/seem/appear certain
▸ **SYNONYMS:** sure, definite
▸ **ANTONYMS:** uncertain, ambiguous

2 ADJECTIVE You use **certain** to indicate that you are referring to one
particular thing, person, or group, although you are not saying exactly
which it is. ○ *This can create a marked improvement in certain skin conditions.*
○ *Leaflets have been air dropped telling people to leave certain areas.*
▸ **COLLOCATION:** a certain **person/condition/area/type**
▸ **PHRASE:** in certain circumstances/situations
▸ **SYNONYMS:** particular, specific

cer|tain|ly /ˈsɜːtənli/

ADVERB You use **certainly** to emphasize what you are saying when you are
making a statement. ○ *Today's inflation figure is certainly too high.*
○ *Certainly, pets can help children develop friendship skills.*
▸ **COLLOCATION:** certainly **true/possible**
▸ **SYNONYMS:** undoubtedly, definitely

---

chan|nel /ˈtʃænəl/ (channels)　　　**ACADEMIC WORD**　**MEDIA**

NOUN A **channel** is a television station. ○ *the proliferating number of
television channels in America* ○ *the presenter of Channel 4 News*

▶ **COLLOCATIONS:**
a **television/satellite/cable/digital** channel
watch a channel
change channels
▶ **SYNONYM:** station

---

chap|ter /ˈtʃæptə/ ACADEMIC WORD · LITERATURE · ACADEMIC STUDY
(chapters)

NOUN A **chapter** is one of the parts that a book is divided into. Each chapter has a number, and sometimes a title. ○ *Chromium supplements were used successfully in the treatment of diabetes (see Chapter 4).* ○ *the theory proposed in the previous chapter*

▶ **COLLOCATIONS:**
a **new/introductory/opening/closing** chapter
the **next/preceding/previous** chapter

---

char|ac|ter /ˈkærɪktə/ **(characters)** PSYCHOLOGY · LITERATURE

1 NOUN The **character** of a person or place consists of all the qualities they have that make them distinct from other people or places. ○ *a series of interviews that look at clients' character traits and circumstances* ○ *[+ of] The character of this country has been formed by immigration.*

▶ **COLLOCATIONS:**
the character **of** someone/something
the character of a **building/area/society/individual**
a character **flaw/trait**
▶ **SYNONYMS:** nature, personality

2 NOUN The **characters** in a film, book, or play are the people that it is about. ○ *The film is autobiographical and the central character is played by Collard himself.* ○ *He's made the characters believable.*

▶ **COLLOCATIONS:**
a **fictional/main/central** character
a **cartoon/TV** character
portray/play a character

---

charge /tʃɑːdʒ/ **(charges, charging, charged)** BUSINESS

1 VERB If you **charge** someone an amount of money, you ask them to pay that amount for something that you have sold to them or done for them. ○ *Even local nurseries charge £100 a week.* ○ *[+ for] The hospitals charge the patients for every aspirin.* ○ *Some banks charge if you access your account to determine your balance.*

▶ **COLLOCATIONS:**
charge (*someone*) **for** *something*

charge a **fee/rate**
charge **£x**
charge a **client/customer**
charge for a **service/purchase**
▶ ANTONYM: pay

2 NOUN A **charge** is an amount of money that you have to pay for a service. ○ *We can arrange this for a small charge.* ○ [+ of] *Customers who arrange overdrafts will face a monthly charge of £5.*
▶ COLLOCATIONS:
a charge **of** £x
face/pay a charge
a **monthly/annual/additional** charge
▶ SYNONYMS: fee, cost, price, rate

USAGE: **charge**, **cost** or **pay**?

These verbs are all used to talk about exchanging money when you buy something. The seller **charges** someone an amount of money **for** a product or service; they ask for this amount. ○ *The company charges customers £1 a minute for foreign calls.*

A product or service **costs** an amount; this is the price. ○ *Foreign calls cost £1 a minute.*

The customer **pays** an amount **for** a product or service. ○ *Mobile customers pay £1 a minute for foreign calls.*

---

char|ity /'tʃærɪti/ (charities)   SOCIAL SCIENCE

NOUN A **charity** is an organization which raises money in order to help people who are ill, disabled, or very poor. ○ *The National Trust is a registered charity.* ○ *an Aids charity* ○ *The event helps raise money for local charities.*
▶ COLLOCATIONS:
a **health/conservation/wildlife** charity
a **registered/local** charity
support a charity
give/donate money to charity
▶ PHRASE: raise money for charity

---

check /tʃek/ (checks, checking, checked)

VERB If you **check** something such as a piece of information or a document, you make sure that it is correct or satisfactory. ○ *Check the accuracy of everything in your CV.* ○ [+ whether] *officials who inspect new buildings to check whether they conform to safety regulations* ○ [+ that] *Check that the soil mixture is moist.*

▶ **COLLOCATIONS:**
check a **number/date**
check the **details/spelling/accuracy** of *something*
check *something* **thoroughly/carefully**
▶ **PHRASE:** check something for accuracy
▶ **SYNONYMS:** inspect, verify

---

chemi|cal /ˈkemɪkəl/   [ACADEMIC WORD] [SCIENCE] [CHEMISTRY]
(chemicals)

1 ADJECTIVE Chemical means involving or resulting from a reaction between two or more substances, or relating to the substances that something consists of. ○ *chemical reactions that cause ozone destruction* ○ *the chemical composition of the ocean* ○ *soldiers exposed to chemical weapons*
▶ **COLLOCATIONS:**
a chemical **reaction/agent**
the chemical **composition** of *something*
chemical **weapons/warfare**

2 NOUN Chemicals are substances that are used in a chemical process or made by a chemical process. ○ *The whole food chain is affected by the over-use of chemicals in agriculture.* ○ *a spillage from a chemicals factory*
▶ **COLLOCATIONS:**
dangerous/toxic/hazardous chemicals
synthetic/organic chemicals
a chemicals **factory/plant**

chemi|cal|ly /ˈkemɪkli/

ADVERB ○ *chemically-treated foods* ○ *The medicine chemically affects your physiology.*
▶ **COLLOCATION:** chemically **treated/altered/induced**

---

chem|is|try /ˈkemɪstri/   [SCIENCE] [CHEMISTRY]

UNCOUNTABLE NOUN Chemistry is the scientific study of the structure of substances and of the way that they react with other substances. ○ *He studied chemistry at the University of Virginia.* ○ *a world-class chemistry department*
▶ **COLLOCATIONS:**
a chemistry **laboratory/department/textbook**
a chemistry **professor/teacher/lecturer/graduate**
study/teach chemistry
organic chemistry
▶ **PHRASES:**
physics and chemistry
biology and chemistry

chem|ist /ˈkemɪst/ (chemists)

NOUN A **chemist** is a person who does research connected with chemistry or who studies chemistry. ○ *She worked as a research chemist.*

chief /tʃiːf/   BUSINESS

ADJECTIVE **Chief** is used in the job titles of the most senior worker or workers of a particular kind in an organization. ○ *He rose up through the ranks to become chief engineer.*

▶ **COLLOCATIONS:**
   a chief **adviser/correspondent/engineer/economist**
   a chief **executive/officer**

▶ **SYNONYMS:** head, senior

child|hood /ˈtʃaɪldhʊd/ (childhoods)

NOUN A person's **childhood** is the period of their life when they are a child. ○ *She had a happy childhood.* ○ *people who experienced poverty in childhood* ○ *the growing epidemic of childhood obesity*

▶ **COLLOCATIONS:**
   in childhood
   a **happy/idyllic/unhappy/troubled** childhood
   early childhood
   a childhood **memory/experience/illness**
   childhood **asthma/obesity**

▶ **RELATED WORDS:** infancy, adolescence, adulthood

choose /tʃuːz/ (chooses, choosing, chose, chosen)

1 VERB If you **choose** someone or something **from** several people or things that are available, you decide which person or thing you want to have. ○ *They will be able to choose their own leaders in democratic elections.* ○ *[+ from/between] one method chosen from a range of options* ○ *He did well in his chosen profession.*

▶ **COLLOCATIONS:**
   choose **from/between** *things*
   choose *something/someone* **as** *something*
   choose a **path/route/method/option**
   choose **carefully/deliberately/randomly/wisely**

▶ **PHRASE:** pick and choose

▶ **SYNONYMS:** select, opt

▶ **ANTONYM:** reject

2 VERB If you **choose to** do something, you do it because you want to or because you feel that it is right. ○ *[+ to-inf] We chose to focus on white* *middle- and working-class families.* ○ *You can just take out the interest each year, if you choose.*

▶ **COLLOCATIONS:**
choose to **ignore** something
choose to **focus/concentrate on** something
choose to **live/stay** somewhere

▶ **SYNONYMS:** opt, decide

choice /tʃɔɪs/ (choices)

1 NOUN If there is a **choice of** things, there are several of them and you can choose the one you want. ○ [+ *of*] *It's available in a choice of colours.* ○ [+ *between*] *the choice between rapid growth and a stable economy* ○ [+ *of*] *Graduates have a wide choice of career paths.*

2 NOUN Your **choice** is someone or something that you choose from a range of things. ○ [+ *of*] *It is easy to control our choice of words, but more difficult to control our tone of voice.* ○ *the information you need to make informed choices about your diet*

▶ **COLLOCATIONS:**
a choice **of/between** things
a choice of **colours/locations/subjects**
a **wide** choice
have/make a choice
a **career/lifestyle** choice
the **right/obvious/first** choice
an **informed** choice

▶ **SYNONYMS:** selection, option

> **USAGE:** Spelling
>
> Remember, **choose** spelled with two O's is the infinitive and present tense verb form. ○ *If the child is free to choose any food, he usually chooses something sweet.*
>
> **Chose** is the past simple form and **chosen** is the past participle, both spelled with one O. ○ *In the study, 78% of children chose sweet foods.*
>
> **Choice** is the noun form. ○ *Are children's choices based on instinct or experience?*

---

cir|cle /ˈsɜːkəl/ (circles)

NOUN A **circle** is a shape consisting of a curved line completely surrounding an area. Every part of the line is the same distance from the centre of the area. ○ *The flag was red, with a large white circle in the centre.* ○ *I wrote down the number 46 and drew a circle around it.*

▶ **SYNONYM:** ring

cir|cu|lar /ˈsɜːkjʊlə/ **(circulars)**

ADJECTIVE Something that is **circular** is shaped like a circle. ○ *a circular hole twelve feet wide and two feet deep* ○ *Place your hands on your shoulders and move your elbows up, back, and down, in a circular motion.*
▸ **SYNONYM:** round

---

clear /klɪə/ **(clearer, clearest)**

1 ADJECTIVE Something that is **clear** is easy to understand, see, or hear. ○ *The book is clear, readable and adequately illustrated.* ○ *The space telescope has taken the clearest pictures ever of Pluto.* ○ *He repeated his answer, this time in a clear, firm tone of voice.*
▸ **COLLOCATION:** a clear **picture/view/voice**
▸ **ANTONYM:** unclear

2 ADJECTIVE Something that is **clear** is obvious and impossible to be mistaken about. ○ *The clear message of the scientific reports is that there should be a drastic cut in car use.* ○ *A spokesman said the British government's position is perfectly clear.* ○ *It's not clear whether the incident was an accident or deliberate.*
▸ **COLLOCATIONS:**
   a clear **case** of *something*
   clear **evidence**
   a clear **message/signal/indication/idea**
   abundantly/perfectly/absolutely clear
   become clear
   make *something* clear
▸ **PHRASE:** loud and clear
▸ **SYNONYM:** obvious
▸ **ANTONYMS:** unclear, ambiguous, uncertain

clear|ly

ADVERB ○ *Whales journey up the coast of Africa, clearly visible from the beach.* ○ *It was important for children to learn to express themselves clearly.* ○ *Clearly, the police cannot break the law in order to enforce it.* ○ *He was clearly unhappy about the decision.*
▸ **COLLOCATIONS:**
   define/state/demonstrate *something* clearly
   see/speak/communicate clearly
   clearly **visible/audible/evident**
   clearly **delighted/happy/unhappy**
▸ **PHRASE:** clearly and concisely
▸ **SYNONYM:** obviously

cli|ent /ˈklaɪənt/ (clients) `BUSINESS`

NOUN A **client** of a professional person or organization is a person or company that receives a service from them in return for payment. ○ *a solicitor and his client* ○ *The company required clients to pay substantial fees in advance.*

▸ **COLLOCATIONS:**
  a **firm's** clients
  advise/represent a client
  a **prospective** client

▸ **SYNONYM:** customer

> **USAGE: client** or **customer**?
>
> In general, someone who uses a professional service, such as a lawyer or an accountant, is a **client**. Someone who buys goods from a shop or a company is a **customer**.
>
> Doctors and hospitals have **patients**, while hotels have **guests**. People who travel on public transport are referred to as **passengers**.

cli|mate /ˈklaɪmət/ (climates) `GEOGRAPHY`

NOUN The **climate** of a place is the general weather conditions that are typical of it. ○ [+ of] *the hot and humid climate of Cyprus* ○ *Herbs tend to grow in temperate climates.*

▸ **COLLOCATIONS:**
  the climate **of** somewhere
  a **temperate/warm/tropical/humid/mild** climate

▸ **PHRASE:** climate change

▸ **SYNONYM:** weather

> **USAGE: climate** or **weather**?
>
> The **climate** of a place refers to the general weather patterns over a long period of time. The **weather** is used to talk about the conditions at a particular time.

clin|ic /ˈklɪnɪk/ (clinics) `MEDICINE`

NOUN A **clinic** is a building where people go to receive medical advice or treatment. ○ *women who were attending a fertility clinic* ○ *a clinic offering laser eye surgery*

▸ **COLLOCATIONS:**
  a **fertility/family planning/health/abortion** clinic
  attend a clinic
  a clinic **offers** something

▸ **SYNONYMS:** health centre, medical centre

c

---

coast /kəʊst/ (coasts) GEOGRAPHY

NOUN The **coast** is an area of land that is next to the sea. ○ *Campsites are usually situated along the coast, close to beaches.* ○ *[+ of] the west coast of Scotland*

▶ **COLLOCATIONS:**
the coast **of** *somewhere*
on/along/off the coast
the **north/east/south/west** coast
the **Adriatic/Caribbean/Atlantic** coast
a coast **guard**

coast|al /ˈkəʊstəl/

ADJECTIVE ○ *Local radio stations serving coastal areas often broadcast forecasts for yachtsmen.* ○ *The fish are on sale from our own coastal waters.*

▶ **COLLOCATIONS:**
a coastal **area/region/town/city/province**
coastal **waters**

---

code /kəʊd/ (codes) ACADEMIC WORD

1 NOUN A **code** is a set of rules about how people should behave or about how something must be done. ○ *Article 159 of the Turkish penal code* ○ *[+ of] Finance ministers agreed to set up a code of conduct on business taxation.* ○ *local building codes*

▶ **COLLOCATIONS:**
a code **of** *something*
a code of **conduct/practice/ethics/honour/behaviour**
a **dress** code
a **penal/criminal/moral/ethical** code

▶ **SYNONYMS:** rules, laws

2 NOUN A **code** is any system of signs or symbols that has a meaning. ○ *It will need different microchips to reconvert the digital code back into normal TV signals.*

▶ **COLLOCATION:** a **binary/numeric/digital** code

---

col|league /ˈkɒliːg/ (colleagues) BUSINESS

NOUN Your **colleagues** are the people you work with, especially in a professional job. ○ *Female academics are still paid less than their male colleagues.* ○ *In the corporate world, the best sources of business are your former colleagues.*

▶ COLLOCATIONS:
   a **senior/junior** colleague
   a **former/close** colleague
   male/female colleagues
   a **work/professional** colleague
▶ SYNONYM: co-worker

---

col‖lect /kə'lekt/ (collects, collecting, collected)

VERB If you **collect** a number of things, you bring them together from several places or from several people. ○ *They collected rock samples and fossils.* ○ *Data were collected by three methods.* ○ *Fee revenue was collected from four basic sources.*
▶ COLLOCATIONS:
   collect something **from** someone/somewhere
   collect **data/information/evidence**
   collect a **sample/specimen**
   collect **money**
▶ PHRASE: collect and analyze
▶ SYNONYM: gather

col‖lec‖tion /kə'lekʃən/ (collections)

1 NOUN A **collection of** things is a group of similar things that you have deliberately acquired, usually over a period of time. ○ [+ of] *The Art Gallery of Ontario has the world's largest collection of sculptures by Henry Moore.* ○ *a valuable record collection*
▶ COLLOCATIONS:
   a collection **of** things
   a **large/vast/extensive** collection
   a **CD/record/art/stamp** collection
   a collection of **paintings/photographs/sculpture**

2 UNCOUNTABLE NOUN **Collection** is the act of collecting something from a place or from people. ○ *Money can be sent to any one of 22,000 agents worldwide for collection.* ○ [+ of] *computer systems to speed up collection of information* ○ *new guidelines on online data collection*
▶ COLLOCATIONS:
   collection **of** something
   data/tax/debt collection
   collection of **data/information**
▶ SYNONYM: acquisition

col|lege /ˈkɒlɪdʒ/ (colleges) `EDUCATION` `ACADEMIC STUDY`

NOUN A **college** is an institution where students study after they have left school. ○ *She is doing business studies at a local college.* ○ *He is now a professor of economics at Western New England College.* ○ *business programmes offered to college graduates*

▸ **COLLOCATIONS:**
a college **of** *something*
a college of **art/education/commerce**
go to/attend/start/enter/finish college
a **further education/community/sixth-form** college
a **technical/art/agricultural** college
a college **graduate/student/professor**
▸ **PHRASE:** college and university
▸ **RELATED WORD:** university

com|bine /kəmˈbaɪn/ (combines, combining, combined)

1 VERB If you **combine** two or more things or if they **combine**, they exist together. ○ [+ with] *If improved education is combined with other factors dramatic results can be achieved.* ○ [+ to-inf] *Relief workers say it's worse than ever as disease and starvation combine to kill thousands.*

2 VERB If you **combine** two or more things or if they **combine**, they join together to make a single thing. ○ *combine the data from these 19 studies* ○ [+ to-inf] *Carbon, hydrogen and oxygen combine chemically to form carbohydrates and fats.* ○ [+ with] *Combined with other compounds, they created a massive dynamite-type bomb.*

▸ **COLLOCATIONS:**
combine **with** *something*
combine to **form/create/produce** *something*
combine **ingredients/elements**
▸ **SYNONYMS:** join, mix, blend
▸ **ANTONYM:** separate

com|bi|na|tion /ˌkɒmbɪˈneɪʃən/ (combinations)

NOUN A **combination of** things is a mixture of them. ○ [+ of] *A combination of circumstances led to the disaster.* ○ [+ of] *a chemical formed by the combination of elements*

▸ **COLLOCATIONS:**
a combination **of** *things*
a combination of **factors/circumstances/elements/ingredients**
▸ **SYNONYMS:** group, mixture, blend

com|ment /ˈkɒment/

ACADEMIC WORD

(comments, commenting, commented)

1 VERB If you **comment on** something, you give your opinion about it or you give an explanation for it. ○ [+ on] *Stratford police refuse to comment on whether anyone has been arrested.* ○ *'I'm always happy with new developments,' he commented.* ○ [+ that] *Stuart commented that this was very true.*

▶ **COLLOCATIONS:**
comment **on** *something*
comment on a **rumour/allegation/report/matter/incident**
refuse to comment
comment **publicly/directly**

▶ **SYNONYMS:** remark, state, explain

2 NOUN A **comment** is something that you say which expresses your opinion of something or which gives an explanation of it. ○ *He made his comments at a news conference in Amsterdam.* ○ [+ about] *There's been no comment so far from police about the allegations.* ○ [+ on] *A spokesman declined comment on the matter.*

▶ **COLLOCATIONS:**
a comment **on/about** *something*
a comment **from** *someone*
make a comment
a **public/written/brief** comment

▶ **PHRASE:** no comment

▶ **SYNONYM:** statement

com|mon /ˈkɒmən/ (commoner, commonest)

ADJECTIVE If something is **common**, it is found in large numbers or it happens often. ○ [+ in] *His name was Hansen, a common name in Norway.* ○ *Oil pollution is the commonest cause of death for seabirds.* ○ [+ in] *Earthquakes are not common in this part of the world.*

▶ **COLLOCATIONS:**
common **in** *something/somewhere*
common in a **region/area**
common in **women/children/babies**
a common **cause/practice**
increasingly/very/particularly common

▶ **SYNONYMS:** normal, ordinary

▶ **ANTONYMS:** uncommon, rare

> **USAGE: common**, **normal** or **ordinary**?
>
> These words all describe something that exists or happens often and is not unusual.

> You can use **common** to describe things, animals or events, but not usually people. ○ *a common problem*
>
> You can use **normal** and **ordinary** to say that something is what you expect. ○ *a normal/ordinary day*
>
> A **normal** person or thing has nothing wrong with them, no unusual problems. ○ *Being a blood donor does no harm to a normal, healthy person.*
>
> An **ordinary** person or thing is like everyone else, not unusual or special in either a positive or a negative way. ○ *Trams became a means of transport that ordinary people could afford.*

com|mon|ly

ADVERB ○ *Parsley is probably the most commonly used of all herbs.* ○ *Depression occurs most commonly in winter.*
- ▶ **COLLOCATION:** commonly **used/available**
- ▶ **SYNONYM:** widely
- ▶ **ANTONYM:** rarely

com|mu|ni|cate /kəˈmjuːnɪkeɪt/   LANGUAGE
(communicates, communicating, communicated)

VERB If you **communicate with** someone, you share or exchange information with them, for example by speaking, writing, or using equipment. You can also say that two people **communicate**. ○ [+ with] *Officials of the CIA depend heavily on electronic mail to communicate with each other.* ○ [+ by] *Communicating by text can have disadvantages.*
- ▶ **COLLOCATIONS:**
  communicate **with** *someone*
  communicate **by** *something*
  communicate with **others/the public**
  communicate by **email/telephone/letter**
  communicate **verbally/wirelessly/electronically/directly**
- ▶ **SYNONYMS:** converse, correspond

com|mu|ni|ca|tion /kə,mjuːnɪˈkeɪʃən/

1 UNCOUNTABLE NOUN ○ [+ between] *There was a tremendous lack of communication between us.* ○ [+ with] *Good communication with people around you could prove difficult.* ○ *Poor communication skills can be a problem in the workplace.*
- ▶ **COLLOCATIONS:**
  communication **with/between** *people*
  communication **skills**
  written/verbal/direct/electronic/instant communication

2 PLURAL NOUN Communications are the systems and processes that are used to communicate or broadcast information. ○ *In 1962 the USA launched the world's first communications satellite, Telstar.* ○ *advanced communications equipment for emergency workers*

▶ COLLOCATIONS:
wireless/satellite/radio communications
a communications **satellite/device/network**
communications **equipment/technology**

---

com|mu|nity /kə'mjuːnɪti/ [ACADEMIC WORD] [SOCIAL SCIENCE]
(communities)

1 NOUN The community is all the people who live in a particular area or place. ○ *He's well liked by people in the community.* ○ *The growth of such vigilante gangs has worried community leaders, police and politicians.*

▶ COLLOCATIONS:
people **in** the community
a community **leader/group**
community **services**
a community **centre/hall**
▶ PHRASE: individuals and communities
▶ SYNONYMS: neighbourhood, society

2 NOUN A particular **community** is a group of people who are similar in some way. ○ *The police haven't really done anything for the black community in particular.* ○ *Friedmann's work received surprisingly little attention from the scientific community.* ○ *close links to Sao Paulo's business community*

▶ COLLOCATIONS:
the **business/scientific/academic** community
the **black/Asian/Jewish** community

---

com|mute /kə'mjuːt/ **(commutes, commuting, commuted)** [BUSINESS]

VERB If you **commute**, you travel a long distance every day between your home and your place of work. ○ *[+ to/from] Mike commutes to London every day.* ○ *[+ between] McLaren began commuting between Paris and London.* ○ *He's going to commute.*

▶ COLLOCATIONS:
commute **between** *places*
commute **to** *somewhere*
commute **by** *something*
commute to **work**
commute **by train/car/bus**
▶ SYNONYM: travel

com|mut|er (commuters) BUSINESS

NOUN ○ *The number of commuters to London has dropped by 100,000.* ○ *The most desirable properties are in the commuter belt with good transport links.*

▶ COLLOCATIONS:
 a commuter **train/plane/bus**
 a commuter **town/belt**

---

com|pa|ny /ˈkʌmpəni/ (companies)

NOUN A **company** is a business organization that makes money by selling goods or services. ○ *a successful businessman who owned a company that sold coffee machines* ○ *the Ford Motor Company*

▶ COLLOCATIONS:
 a **software/insurance/oil/investment** company
 a **private/public/multinational** company
 own/run/operate a company
 a company **reports/plans/announces/sells/operates** *things*
 a company **executive/director/car**

▶ SYNONYMS: firm, business, corporation, enterprise

---

com|pared /kəmˈpeəd/ BUSINESS

PHRASE If you say, for example, that one thing is large or small **compared with** another or **compared to** another, you mean that it is larger or smaller than the other thing. ○ [+ *with*] *The astronomical unit is large compared with distances on earth.* ○ [+ *to*] *Columbia was a young city compared to venerable Charleston.*

▶ COLLOCATION: compared **with/to** *something*

---

com|pe|ti|tion /ˌkɒmpɪˈtɪʃən/

UNCOUNTABLE NOUN **Competition** is an activity involving two or more firms, in which each firm tries to get people to buy its own goods in preference to the other firms' goods. ○ [+ *in*] *The deal would have reduced competition in the commuter-aircraft market.* ○ *The farmers have been seeking higher prices as better protection from foreign competition.* ○ [+ *from*] *Clothing stores also face heavy competition from factory outlets.*

▶ COLLOCATIONS:
 competition **from** *something*
 competition **for/in** *something*
 competition from a **rival/supplier/producer**
 competition in a **market/marketplace/industry**
 face/increase/reduce competition
 stiff/heavy/intense competition
 international/foreign/domestic competition

com|peti|tive /kəmˈpetɪtɪv/

ADJECTIVE Competitive is used to describe situations or activities in which firms compete with each other. ○ *Only by keeping down costs will America maintain its competitive advantage over other countries.* ○ *Japan is a highly competitive market system.*

▶ COLLOCATIONS:
competitive **in** *something*
competitive in a **market/marketplace**
a competitive **advantage/edge/disadvantage**
a competitive **market/environment**
competitive **pricing**
highly/extremely/globally/internationally competitive

---

com|plex /ˈkɒmpleks, AM kəmˈpleks/ ACADEMIC WORD

ADJECTIVE Something that is **complex** has many different parts, and is therefore often difficult to understand. ○ *in-depth coverage of today's complex issues* ○ *a complex system of voting* ○ *complex machines*

▶ COLLOCATIONS:
a complex **task/calculation/process**
a complex **relationship/system/issue**
▶ SYNONYMS: complicated, intricate
▶ ANTONYM: simple

---

com|pose /kəmˈpəʊz/ **(composes, composing, composed)** ARTS

VERB When someone **composes** a piece of music, they write it. ○ *Vivaldi composed a large number of very fine concertos.* ○ *Cale also uses electronic keyboards to compose.*

▶ COLLOCATIONS:
compose **music**
compose a **symphony/song/score**
▶ SYNONYM: write

com|pos|er /kəmˈpəʊzə/ **(composers)**

NOUN A **composer** is a person who writes music, especially classical music. ○ *an opera written by the German composer Richard Wagner*

▶ COLLOCATIONS:
a **classical/contemporary** composer
a composer **writes** *something*

com|put|er /kəmˈpjuːtə/ (computers) `ACADEMIC WORD` `IT`

NOUN A **computer** is an electronic machine that can store and deal with large amounts of information. ○ *The data are then fed into a computer.* ○ *The company installed a $650,000 computer system.* ○ *The car was designed by computer.*

▶ **COLLOCATIONS:**
by computer
a **personal/laptop/desktop/notebook** computer
computer **software/hardware/technology**
a computer **system/network/screen/game/program**
a computer **user/programmer**
use/access/program a computer

com|put|er|ized /kəmˈpjuːtəraɪzd/

ADJECTIVE A **computerized** system, process, or business is one in which the work is done by computer. [in BRIT, also use **computerised**] ○ *The National Cancer Institute now has a computerized system that can quickly provide information.* ○ *the most highly-computerized businesses*

▶ **COLLOCATIONS:**
a computerized **system/business**
fully/highly computerized

comˈputer science `IT`

UNCOUNTABLE NOUN **Computer science** is the study of computers and their application. ○ *a professor of computer science at MIT* ○ *theoretical work in computer science*

comˈputer ˌscientist

NOUN ○ *Computer scientists have devised a simple system to query these databases.* ○ *a computer scientist at the University of Minnesota*

con|di|tion /kənˈdɪʃən/ (conditions)

1 NOUN The **condition** of someone or something is the state they are in. ○ *He remains in a critical condition in a California hospital.* ○ *The two-bedroom chalet is in good condition.* ○ *Poor physical condition leaves you prone to injury.*

▶ **COLLOCATIONS:**
the condition **of** *something/someone*
in a condition
in a **stable/critical** condition
in **good/excellent/poor** condition
someone's **medical/physical** condition

▶ **SYNONYM:** state

2 PLURAL NOUN The **conditions** in which people live or do things are the factors that affect their comfort, safety, or success. ○ *This change has been timed under laboratory conditions.* ○ *The mild winter has created the ideal conditions for an ant population explosion.* ○ *People are living in appalling conditions.*

▶ **COLLOCATIONS:**
   weather/trading/market conditions
   living/working/employment conditions
   economic/financial conditions
   poor/appalling/favourable/ideal conditions
▶ **SYNONYMS:** circumstances, situation

---

con|fer|ence /ˈkɒnfrəns/ (conferences)   `ACADEMIC WORD`

NOUN A **conference** is a meeting, often lasting a few days, which is organized on a particular subject or to bring together people who have a common interest. ○ [+ on] *The President summoned all the state governors to a conference on education.* ○ *the Conservative Party conference* ○ *Last weekend the Roman Catholic Church in Scotland held a conference, attended by 450 delegates.*

▶ **COLLOCATIONS:**
   a conference **on** something
   attend/hold a conference
   a **peace/party** conference
   a **national/international/annual** conference
   a conference **delegate**
▶ **SYNONYM:** meeting

---

con|ges|tion /kənˈdʒestʃən/

UNCOUNTABLE NOUN If there is **congestion** in a place, the place is extremely crowded and blocked with traffic or people. ○ *The problems of traffic congestion will not disappear in a hurry.* ○ *Energy consumption, congestion and pollution have increased.*

▶ **COLLOCATIONS:**
   traffic/road/airport congestion
   cause/increase congestion
   reduce/ease congestion
   congestion **charge/charging**
▶ **PHRASE:** congestion and pollution
▶ **SYNONYMS:** crowding, overcrowding

---

con|nect /kəˈnekt/ (connects, connecting, connected)

1 VERB If something or someone **connects** one thing **to** another, or if one thing **connects to** another, the two things are joined together. ○ [+ to] *You can connect the machine to your hi-fi.* ○ [+ to] *Two cables connect to each* *corner of the plate.* ○ *a television camera connected to the radio telescope*

2 VERB If a piece of equipment or a place **is connected to** a source of power or water, it is joined to that source so that it has power or water.
○ [+ *to*] *These appliances should not be connected to power supplies.*
○ [+ *to*] *Ischia was now connected to the mainland water supply.*

▶ **COLLOCATIONS:**
connect *something* **to** *something*
be connected **by** *something*
be connected by a **wire/cable**
connect a **computer/device/pipe**
connect **directly/permanently/wirelessly**

▶ **SYNONYM:** attach
▶ **ANTONYM:** disconnect

con|nec|tion /kəˈnekʃən/ (connections)

NOUN [in BRIT, also use **connexion**] ○ *Check all radiators for small leaks, especially round pipework connections.* ○ *a high-speed internet connection*

▶ **COLLOCATIONS:**
a connection **to** *something*
a **cable/wireless/internet/broadband/telephone** connection
a **direct/high-speed/fast** connection
connection **speed**

con|ser|va|tion /ˌkɒnsəˈveɪʃən/ SCIENCE BIOLOGY GEOGRAPHY

UNCOUNTABLE NOUN **Conservation** is saving and protecting the environment. ○ *a four-nation regional meeting on elephant conservation* ○ *tree-planting and other conservation projects*

▶ **COLLOCATIONS:**
wildlife/nature conservation
marine/coastal/urban conservation
a conservation **group/organization/project**
a conservation **area**

▶ **SYNONYM:** ecology
▶ **ANTONYM:** destruction

con|sid|er /kənˈsɪdə/ (considers, considering, considered)

VERB If you **consider** a person or thing **to** be something, you have the opinion that this is what they are. ○ [+ *to-inf*] *We don't consider our customers to be mere consumers; we consider them to be our friends.*
○ *The paper does not explain why foreign ownership should be considered bad.*
○ [+ *as*] *This suggests that we should consider these drugs as addictive.*

▶ COLLOCATIONS:
consider *something* **as** *something*
consider *something* **accurate/acceptable**
consider *something* **suitable/dangerous/safe**

EXTEND YOUR VOCABULARY

Think is a common verb in English. Try to use different verbs in your writing. ○ *Doctors think that the condition may have a genetic basis.* ○ *Experts consider the risk to be very low.* ○ *Some scientists believe that the temperature will continue to rise.*

---

con|stant /ˈkɒnstənt/   ACADEMIC WORD

1 ADJECTIVE You use **constant** to describe something that happens all the time or is always there. ○ *She suggests that women are under constant pressure to be abnormally thin.* ○ *Inflation is a constant threat.*
  ▶ COLLOCATIONS:
  constant **pressure/pain**
  constant **supervision/vigilance/surveillance**
  a constant **companion/threat/reminder/menace**
  ▶ SYNONYMS: continual, ongoing
  ▶ ANTONYM: occasional

2 ADJECTIVE If an amount or level is **constant**, it stays the same over a particular period of time. ○ *The average speed of the winds remained constant.* ○ *The climate is tropical with a fairly constant temperature at 24°C.*
  ▶ COLLOCATIONS:
  remain/stay constant
  fairly/relatively/almost constant
  ▶ SYNONYMS: stable, even
  ▶ ANTONYMS: changeable, uneven

con|stant|ly

ADVERB ○ *The direction of the wind is constantly changing.* ○ *We are constantly being reminded to cut down our fat intake.*
  ▶ COLLOCATIONS:
  constantly **change/evolve/shift**
  constantly **remind/monitor**
  ▶ SYNONYMS: always, continually
  ▶ ANTONYMS: sometimes, occasionally

---

con|tain /kənˈteɪn/ (contains, containing, contained)

1 VERB If something such as a box, bag, room, or place **contains** things, those things are inside it. ○ *Factory shops contain a wide range of cheap*

container | 100

furnishings. ○ The 77,000-acre estate contains five of the highest peaks in Scotland.

2 VERB If a substance **contains** something, that thing is a part of it.
○ preservatives that contain toxic substances ○ Many cars run on petrol which contains lead.

▶ **COLLOCATIONS:**
 a **box/bag/wallet/envelope/file/site** contains things
 contain a **substance/element/ingredient**

▶ **SYNONYMS:** have, include

con|tain|er /kən'teɪnə/ (containers)

NOUN A **container** is something such as a box or bottle that is used to hold or store things in. ○ the plastic containers in which fish are stored and sold

▶ **COLLOCATIONS:**
 a container **of** something
 a container of **milk/water/chemicals**
 a **plastic/glass/metal** container
 fill/load/unload/store a container

▶ **SYNONYMS:** receptacle, vessel

con|tent /'kɒntent/ (contents)

PLURAL NOUN The **contents** of a container such as a bottle, box, or room are the things that are inside it. ○ [+ of] Add the contents of the second jar. ○ Sandon Hall and its contents will be auctioned by Sotheby's on October 6.

▶ **COLLOCATIONS:**
 the contents **of** something
 the contents of a **jar/drawer/folder/suitcase/envelope**
 empty/examine/analyse/inspect the contents of something

con|ti|nent /'kɒntɪnənt/ (continents) GEOGRAPHY

NOUN A **continent** is a very large area of land, such as Africa or Asia, that consists of several countries. ○ Conflicts are taking place in nine out of 52 countries in the African continent. ○ Dinosaurs evolved when most continents were joined in a single land mass.

▶ **COLLOCATIONS:**
 the **Antarctic/African/European/American** continent
 a **whole/entire** continent

con|ti|nen|tal /ˌkɒntɪ'nentəl/

ADJECTIVE Continental is used to refer to something that belongs to or relates to a continent. ○ The most ancient parts of the continental crust are 4000 million years old.

▶ COLLOCATIONS:
continental **drift**
a continental **shelf/crust**

---

con|trol /kən'trəʊl/ **(controls, controlling, controlled)**

1 UNCOUNTABLE NOUN Control of an organization, place, or system is the power to make all the important decisions about the way that it is run.
○ [+ of] *The restructuring involves Mr Ronson giving up control of the company.*
○ [+ over] *The first aim of his government would be to establish control over the republic's territory.* ○ *Nobody knows who is in control of the club.* ○ *All the newspapers were taken under government control.*

2 UNCOUNTABLE NOUN If you have **control** of something or someone, you are able to make them do what you want them to do. ○ [+ of] *He lost control of his car.* ○ [+ over] *Some teachers have more control over pupils than their parents have.*

▶ COLLOCATIONS:
control **of/over** *something*
control of a **situation/territory/city/vehicle**
control over **spending/resources/timing**
have/take/seize/gain/regain control
lose/relinquish/surrender control

▶ PHRASES:
be in control of something
something is under your control

▶ SYNONYMS: power, command

3 VERB The people who **control** an organization or place have the power to take all the important decisions about the way that it is run.
○ *He now controls the largest retail development empire in southern California.*
○ *Almost all of the countries in Latin America were controlled by dictators.*
○ [V-ing] *Minebea sold its controlling interest in both firms.*

▶ COLLOCATIONS:
control a **company/organization/country**
tightly/strictly/carefully controlled

▶ SYNONYMS: manage, direct

---

con|veni|ent /kən'viːniənt/

1 ADJECTIVE If a way of doing something is **convenient**, it is easy, or very useful or suitable for a particular purpose. ○ *a flexible and convenient way of paying for business expenses* ○ [+ to-inf] *Customers find it more convenient to participate online.*

▶ **COLLOCATIONS:**
a convenient **way** of *doing something*
find *something* convenient
▶ **SYNONYM:** handy
▶ **ANTONYM:** inconvenient

2 ADJECTIVE If you describe a place as **convenient**, you are pleased because it is near to where you are, or because you can reach another place from there quickly and easily. ○ [+ *for*] *The town is well placed for easy access to London and convenient for Heathrow Airport.* ○ *the university's convenient city location*

▶ **COLLOCATIONS:**
a convenient **location**
convenient **access**
▶ **ANTONYM:** inconvenient

con|veni|ent|ly

ADVERB ○ *It was very conveniently situated just across the road from the City Reference Library.* ○ *He chose Simi Valley mainly because it was conveniently close to Los Angeles.* ○ *The region falls conveniently into only four main geological areas.*

▶ **COLLOCATIONS:**
conveniently **located/situated**
conveniently **close to** *somewhere*
▶ **ANTONYM:** inconveniently

con|veni|ence /kən'viːniəns/

UNCOUNTABLE NOUN ○ *They may use a credit card for convenience.* ○ *the convenience of a fast non-stop flight* ○ *Internet banking offers greater convenience than telephone banking.*

▶ **COLLOCATIONS:**
the convenience **of** *something*
offer convenience
a convenience **store/shop/meal**
▶ **PHRASE:** comfort and convenience
▶ **ANTONYM:** inconvenience

cool /kuːl/ (cools, cooling, cooled)   SCIENCE

VERB When something **cools** or when you **cool** it, it becomes lower in temperature. ○ *Drain the meat and allow it to cool.* ○ *Huge fans will have to cool the concrete floor to keep it below 150 degrees.* ○ [V-ing] *a cooling breeze*
▶ **ANTONYMS:** warm, heat

cor|rect /kəˈrekt/ (corrects, correcting, corrected)

1 **ADJECTIVE** If something is **correct**, it is in accordance with the facts and has no mistakes. [FORMAL] ○ *The correct answers can be found at the bottom of page 8.* ○ *The following information was correct at time of going to press.* ○ *Doctors examine their patients thoroughly in order to make a correct diagnosis.*

2 **ADJECTIVE** The **correct** thing or method is the thing or method that is required or is most suitable in a particular situation. ○ *The use of the correct materials was crucial.* ○ *the correct way to produce a crop of tomato plants*
▶ **COLLOCATIONS:**
 a correct **procedure/decision/interpretation**
 a correct **answer/diagnosis/theory**
 correct **information/spelling**
 grammatically/factually/technically/absolutely correct
▶ **SYNONYM:** accurate
▶ **ANTONYMS:** incorrect, inaccurate, wrong

> **EXTEND YOUR VOCABULARY**
>
> In everyday English, you often say that something is **right**.
> ○ *What was the right answer?* ○ *You did the right thing.*
>
> You often use **correct** in more formal, written contexts, especially to describe a situation where something is clearly **correct** or **incorrect**.
> ○ *the correct spelling/answer*
>
> You can use **acceptable** or **appropriate** to talk about a situation that involves a judgement or an opinion. ○ *an acceptable/appropriate level of customer service* ○ *Smoking is becoming less socially acceptable.*

3 **VERB** If you **correct** a problem, mistake, or fault, you do something which puts it right. ○ *He may need surgery to correct the problem.* ○ *He has criticised the government for inefficiency and delays in correcting past mistakes.*
▶ **COLLOCATION:** correct a **mistake/error/inaccuracy**
▶ **SYNONYM:** rectify

cor|rect|ly

ADVERB ○ *The report correctly identifies the problems.* ○ *You have to correctly answer each question.* ○ *The software was not installed correctly.*
▶ **COLLOCATION:** **remember/spell/answer/identify** something correctly
▶ **SYNONYM:** properly
▶ **ANTONYM:** incorrectly

cor|rec|tion /kəˈrekʃən/ (corrections)

NOUN ○ [+ of] *legislation to require the correction of factual errors* ○ *We will then make the necessary corrections.*

c

▶ COLLOCATIONS:
the correction **of** something
make a correction

---

cost /kɒst, AM kɔːst/ (costs, costing)   `BUSINESS`

1 NOUN The **cost of** something is the amount of money that is needed in order to buy, do, or make it. ○ [+ of] *The cost of a loaf of bread has increased five-fold.* ○ [+ of] *The price of coffee fell so low that it did not even cover the cost of production.* ○ [+ of] *Badges are also available at a cost of £2.50.*
▶ COLLOCATIONS:
at a cost
the cost **of** something
a cost **of** x
the cost of **petrol/fuel/travel/production**
▶ PHRASE: the cost of living
▶ SYNONYMS: price, value

2 VERB If something **costs** a particular amount of money, you can buy, do, or make it for that amount. ○ *This course is limited to 12 people and costs £50.* ○ *The project was abandoned because it cost too much.* ○ *a scheme which cost taxpayers more than £294 million*
→ see note at **charge**
▶ COLLOCATIONS:
cost **£x**
cost **around/over/about** an amount

3 PLURAL NOUN Your **costs** are the total amount of money that you must spend on running your home or business. ○ *Costs have been cut by 30 to 50 per cent.* ○ *The company admits its costs are still too high.*
▶ COLLOCATIONS:
cut/reduce/increase/estimate/calculate costs
cover/offset costs
costs **rise/soar/increase/vary**
operating/labour/production/additional costs
▶ SYNONYMS: expenses, expenditure
▶ ANTONYMS: profit, earnings

---

cost of liv|ing /ˌkɒst əv ˈlɪvɪŋ, AM ˌkɔːst əv ˈlɪvɪŋ/   `ECONOMICS`

NOUN The **cost of living** is the average amount of money that people in a particular place need in order to be able to afford basic food, housing, and clothing. ○ *The cost of living has increased dramatically.* ○ *Companies are moving jobs to towns with a lower cost of living.*

coun|cil /ˈkaʊnsəl/ (councils) `SOCIAL SCIENCE` `POLITICS`

NOUN A **council** is a group of people who are elected to govern a local area such as a city or, in Britain, a county. ○ *Cheshire County Council* ○ *The city council has voted almost unanimously in favour.* ○ *David Ward, one of just two Liberal Democrats on the council* ○ *reports of local council meetings*

▸ COLLOCATIONS:
  a **county/city/parish/local** council
  a council **member/meeting**
▸ PHRASE: council tax
▸ SYNONYM: local authority

coun|cil|lor /ˈkaʊnsələ/ (councillors)

NOUN A **councillor** is a member of a local council. [in AM, use **councilor**]
  ○ *the first black New York City councillor, Benjamin Davis Jr* ○ *Councillor Michael Poulter*

▸ COLLOCATION: a **parish/city/town/local** councillor
▸ SYNONYM: politician

coun|try /ˈkʌntri/ (countries) `GEOGRAPHY`

NOUN A **country** is one of the political units which the world is divided into, covering a particular area of land. ○ *Indonesia is the fifth most populous country in the world.* ○ *the disputed boundary between the two countries* ○ *the difficult task of running the country*

▸ COLLOCATIONS:
  rule/run/govern a country
  enter/leave/visit/tour a country
  a **developing/developed/industrialized/capitalist** country
  a **rich/poor** country
  a **foreign/communist/capitalist/neighbouring** country
  a **Western/Arab/European/African** country

EXTEND YOUR VOCABULARY

In many contexts, you can use **country**, **nation** or **state** with the same meaning. ○ *Poland became an independent state/nation/country in 1918.*

You can only use **state** to talk about a country as a political unit or its government. You can use **country** and **nation** to talk about the people, culture and life of an area. ○ *the citizens of the poorest nations/countries*

You can only use **country** to talk about a geographical area.
○ *in hot, Mediterranean countries*

---

c

---

country|side /ˈkʌntrisaɪd/ GEOGRAPHY

UNCOUNTABLE NOUN The countryside is land which is away from towns and cities. ○ *Urban areas are often slightly warmer than the surrounding countryside.* ○ *We are surrounded by lots of beautiful countryside.*

▸ **COLLOCATIONS:**
 in the countryside
 open/surrounding/beautiful countryside
▸ **SYNONYM:** landscape
→ see usage note at **nature**

---

cou|ple /ˈkʌpəl/ (couples) ACADEMIC WORD

1 QUANTIFIER If you refer to **a couple of** people or things, you mean two or approximately two of them, although the exact number is not important or you are not sure of it. ○ [+ *of*] *There are a couple of police officers standing guard.* ○ *I think the trouble will clear up in a couple of days.* ○ *a small town in Massachusetts, a couple of hundred miles from New York City*

▸ **COLLOCATIONS:**
 a couple **of** *things*
 a couple of **days/hours/months/weeks/years**
 a couple of **times**
 a couple of **miles/kilometres/metres/inches**
▸ **SYNONYMS:** a few, several

2 NOUN A **couple** is two people who are married, living together, or having a sexual relationship. ○ *The couple have no children.* ○ *after burglars ransacked an elderly couple's home*

▸ **COLLOCATIONS:**
 a **married/divorced/elderly/same-sex/infertile** couple
 a couple **marries/gets married/divorces**

---

course /kɔːs/ (courses) EDUCATION ACADEMIC STUDY

NOUN A **course** is a series of lessons or lectures on a particular subject. ○ [+ *in*] *universities which offer courses in business administration* ○ [+ *on*] *I'm shortly to begin a course on the modern novel.*

▸ **COLLOCATIONS:**
 a course **in/on** *something*
 a **training/refresher/full-time/part-time** course
 a **university/college/degree** course
 take/complete/finish a course
 run/offer a course
 a course **tutor/module/fee**
▸ **SYNONYMS:** class, module, degree

court /kɔːt/ (courts)

LAW

NOUN A **court** is a place where legal matters are decided by a judge and jury or by a magistrate. ○ *a county court judge* ○ *He was deported on a court order following a conviction for armed robbery.* ○ *The 28-year-old striker was in court last week for breaking a rival player's jaw.*

▶ **COLLOCATIONS:**
be **in/at** court
appear in/go to court
a **federal/supreme/county** court
a court **hears/rules/orders** *something*
a court **order/case/hearing/proceeding**

▶ **SYNONYM:** law court

cre|ate /kriˈeɪt/ (creates, creating, created)

ACADEMIC WORD

VERB To **create** something means to cause it to happen or exist. ○ *Tourist companies are creating 45,000 jobs per year.* ○ *Changing interest rates can create problems for home owners.*

▶ **COLLOCATIONS:**
create **jobs/opportunities/chances/problems**
create a **situation/environment/atmosphere**
newly created

▶ **ANTONYM:** destroy

EXTEND YOUR VOCABULARY

Make is a very common verb in everyday English. In more formal and academic writing, you often use more specific verbs with different nouns.

create jobs/problems/opportunities
produce goods/products/a result/an effect
generate revenue/income/profits/electricity/heat

---

crea|tion /kriˈeɪʃən/

UNCOUNTABLE NOUN ○ [+ *of*] *These businesses stimulate the creation of local jobs.* ○ *to the process of wealth creation*

▶ **COLLOCATIONS:**
the creation **of** *something*
the creation of **jobs/wealth**
the creation of a **state/zone/park/database**
job/wealth creation

▶ **SYNONYM:** production
▶ **ANTONYM:** destruction

crea|ture /ˈkriːtʃə/ (creatures) `SCIENCE` `BIOLOGY`

NOUN You can refer to any living thing that is not a plant as a **creature**, especially when it is of an unknown or unfamiliar kind. ○ *Alaskan Eskimos believe that every living creature possesses a spirit.* ○ *After more than a century of study, new marine creatures are still being discovered.*
- ▶ COLLOCATION: a **living/marine/sea** creature
- ▶ SYNONYMS: being, animal

crime /kraɪm/ (crimes) `LAW`

NOUN A **crime** is an illegal action or activity for which a person can be punished by law. ○ *Mr Steele has committed no crime and poses no danger to the public.* ○ *the growing problem of organised crime* ○ *We need a positive programme of crime prevention.*
- ▶ COLLOCATIONS:
  a **violent/serious/petty** crime
  a **war/hate** crime
  organized/juvenile/street/gun crime
  commit/investigate/solve a crime
  tackle/combat/fight crime
  crime **prevention/rate**
  a crime **scene**
  a crime **of violence/passion/murder**
- ▶ SYNONYMS: offence, wrongdoing

crimi|nal /ˈkrɪmɪnəl/ (criminals)

1 NOUN A **criminal** is a person who regularly commits crimes. ○ *A group of gunmen attacked a prison and set free nine criminals in Moroto.* ○ *Thousands of criminals are caught every year using DNA technology.*
- ▶ COLLOCATIONS:
  a **convicted/hardened** criminal
  catch a criminal
- ▶ SYNONYMS: culprit, convict

2 ADJECTIVE Criminal means connected with crime. ○ *Bribery is a criminal offence.* ○ *At 17, he had a criminal record for petty theft.*
- ▶ COLLOCATIONS:
  a criminal **charge/record/offence/investigation/court**
  criminal **justice/proceedings/damage**
  the criminal **system**
- ▶ SYNONYM: illegal
- ▶ ANTONYMS: legal, lawful

---

criti|cize /ˈkrɪtɪsaɪz/ (criticizes, criticizing, criticized)

VERB If you **criticize** someone or something, you express your
disapproval of them by saying what you think is wrong with them. [in
BRIT, also use **criticise**] ○ [+ for] *The minister criticised the police for failing to
come up with any leads.* ○ [+ for] *The regime has been harshly criticized for
serious human rights violations.*

▶ **COLLOCATIONS:**
criticize *someone* **for** *something*
criticize a **government/president**
criticize a **methodology/policy**
sharply/harshly/strongly/widely criticized

▶ **SYNONYMS:** condemn, find fault with
▶ **ANTONYM:** praise

criti|cism /ˈkrɪtɪsɪzəm/ (criticisms)

NOUN Criticism is the action of expressing disapproval of something
or someone. A **criticism** is a statement that expresses disapproval.
○ *The announcement has drawn criticism from analysts.* ○ [+ of] *unfair criticism
of his tactics* ○ [+ that] *The criticism that the English do not truly care about
their children was often voiced.*

▶ **COLLOCATIONS:**
criticism **of** *something/someone*
strong criticism
face/draw criticism

▶ **ANTONYM:** praise

---

crowd /kraʊd/ (crowds)

NOUN A **crowd** is a large group of people who have gathered together,
for example to watch or listen to something interesting, or to protest
about something. ○ *A huge crowd gathered in a square outside the
Kremlin walls.* ○ *The crowd were enormously enthusiastic.* ○ [+ of] *The
explosions took place in shopping centres as crowds of people were shopping
for Mothers' Day.*

▶ **COLLOCATIONS:**
a crowd **of** *people*
a crowd of **people/supporters/onlookers**
attract/draw a crowd
a crowd **gathers/disperses**

▶ **SYNONYMS:** group, mass
▶ **ANTONYM:** individual

crowd|ed /ˈkraʊdɪd/

ADJECTIVE If a place is **crowded**, it is full of people or a lot of people live there. ○ *He peered slowly around the small crowded room.* ○ *The street was crowded and noisy.* ○ [+ with] *The old town square was crowded with people.* ○ *a crowded city of 2 million*

▶ **COLLOCATIONS:**
  crowded **with** people
  a crowded **bus/street/train**

▶ **SYNONYMS:** busy, congested

▶ **ANTONYMS:** empty, quiet

---

cul|ture /ˈkʌltʃə/ (cultures) `ACADEMIC WORD` `ARTS`

1 UNCOUNTABLE NOUN Culture consists of activities such as the arts and philosophy, which are considered to be important for the development of civilization and of people's minds. ○ *aspects of popular culture* ○ *France's Minister of Culture and Education*

▶ **COLLOCATIONS:**
  popular/contemporary culture
  Western/American/Japanese culture

▶ **PHRASES:**
  language and culture
  history and culture

2 NOUN A culture is a particular society or civilization, especially considered in relation to its beliefs, way of life, or art. ○ *people from different cultures* ○ *I was brought up in a culture that said you must put back into the society what you have taken out.*

▶ **COLLOCATION:** a **different/ancient** culture

▶ **SYNONYMS:** tradition, way of life

cul|tur|al /ˈkʌltʃərəl/

ADJECTIVE ○ *a deep sense of personal honour which was part of his cultural heritage* ○ *the Rajiv Gandhi Foundation which promotes cultural and educational exchanges between Britain and India* ○ *the sponsorship of sports and cultural events by tobacco companies*

▶ **COLLOCATIONS:**
  cultural **heritage/identity/diversity**
  cultural **differences**
  a cultural **event/tradition**

▶ **PHRASES:**
  social and cultural
  political and cultural

cure /kjʊə/ (cures, curing, cured)　　　　　　　MEDICINE

1 VERB If doctors or medical treatments **cure** an illness or injury, they cause it to end or disappear. ○ *research that could cure diseases such as Alzheimer's* ○ *Her cancer can only be controlled, not cured.*
▶ **COLLOCATIONS:**
  be cured **of** *something*
  cure a **disease/illness/condition**
  cure **cancer/diabetes**

2 NOUN A **cure for** an illness is a medicine or other treatment that cures the illness. ○ [+ *for*] *There is no known cure for the disease.*
○ [+ *for*] *Doctors hope to find a cure for cancer.*
▶ **COLLOCATIONS:**
  a cure **for** *something*
  a cure for **cancer/insomnia/baldness/diabetes**
  seek/find a cure
  a **known** cure
▶ **SYNONYMS:** remedy, treatment

cur|ren|cy /ˈkʌrənsi, AM ˈkɜːr-/　　ACADEMIC WORD ECONOMICS
(currencies)

NOUN The money used in a particular country is referred to as its **currency**. ○ *Tourism is the country's top earner of foreign currency.*
○ *More people favour a single European currency than oppose it.*
▶ **COLLOCATIONS:**
  European/Asian currencies
  a **single** currency
  a **foreign/local** currency
  currency **exchange**

cur|rent /ˈkʌrənt, AM ˈkɜːr-/

ADJECTIVE Current means happening, being used, or being done at the present time. ○ *The current situation is very different to that in 1990.*
○ *He plans to repeal a number of current policies.*
▶ **COLLOCATIONS:**
  the current **situation/system/crisis**
  the current **level/rate/price**
  the current **owner/president**
▶ **PHRASE:** current affairs
▶ **SYNONYMS:** present, present-day
▶ **ANTONYMS:** past, former, future

c

cur|rent|ly

ADVERB ○ *Twelve potential vaccines are currently being tested on human volunteers.* ○ *He currently has no strong rivals for power.*
▶ **SYNONYMS:** presently, at present

> **EXTEND YOUR VOCABULARY**
>
> In everyday English, you often use words and phrases like **now**, **nowadays** and **at the moment** to talk about things that are happening or are true at the time you are speaking.
>
> In more formal and academic writing, words like **current**, **present** and **currently** are often used. ○ *the current economic crisis* ○ *the present electoral system* ○ *The database currently holds ninety million references.*

cur|rent af|fairs /ˌkʌrənt əˈfeəz, AM ˌkɜːr-/ `MEDIA`

PLURAL NOUN If you refer to **current affairs**, you are referring to political events and problems in society which are discussed in newspapers, and on television and radio. ○ *people who take no interest in politics and current affairs* ○ *the BBC's current affairs programme 'Panorama'*
▶ **COLLOCATION:** a current affairs **programme**

cus|tom /ˈkʌstəm/ (customs) `SOCIAL SCIENCE`

NOUN A **custom** is an activity, a way of behaving, or an event which is usual or traditional in a particular society or in particular circumstances. ○ [+ *of*] *The custom of lighting the Olympic flame goes back centuries.* ○ *Chung has tried to adapt to local customs.*
▶ **COLLOCATIONS:**
   a custom **of** *something*
   a **local/ancient** custom
   a **burial/wedding** custom
▶ **SYNONYMS:** tradition, ritual

cus|tom|ary /ˈkʌstəmri, AM -meri/

ADJECTIVE Customary is used to describe things that people usually do in a particular society or in particular circumstances. [FORMAL] ○ [+ *to-inf*] *It is customary to offer a drink or a snack to guests.* ○ *They interrupted the customary one minute's silence with jeers and shouts.*
▶ **SYNONYMS:** traditional, usual

cus|tom|er /ˈkʌstəmə/ **(customers)** BUSINESS

NOUN A **customer** is someone who buys goods or services, especially from a shop. ○ *Our customers have very tight budgets.* ○ *the quality of customer service* ○ *We also improved our customer satisfaction levels.*
→ see note at **client**

▶ COLLOCATIONS:
a **happy/satisfied/loyal/regular/potential** customer
a **broadband/banking/mortgage** customer
attract/encourage customers
customer **service/care/management**
customer **loyalty/feedback/satisfaction/correspondence**
a customer **base**

▶ SYNONYMS: client, consumer, buyer, shopper

---

cut /kʌt/ **(cuts, cutting)**

> The form **cut** is used in the present tense and is the past tense and past participle.

VERB If you **cut** something, you reduce it. ○ *The first priority is to cut costs.* ○ *[+ by] The U.N. force is to be cut by 90%.* ○ *a deal to cut 50 billion dollars from the federal deficit*

▶ COLLOCATIONS:
cut *x* **from/off** *something*
cut *something* **by** *x*
cut **costs/rates/spending**

▶ SYNONYMS: reduce, decrease
▶ ANTONYM: increase

● **Cut** is also a noun. ○ *[+ in] The economy needs an immediate 2 per cent cut in interest rates.* ○ *the government's plans for tax cuts*

▶ COLLOCATIONS:
a cut **in** *something*
a **tax/pay/budget** cut

▶ SYNONYMS: reduction, cutback
▶ ANTONYM: increase

Dd

dai|ly /ˈdeɪli/

1 **ADVERB** If something happens **daily**, it happens every day. ○ *Cathay Pacific flies daily non-stop to Hong Kong from Heathrow.* ○ *The Visitor Centre is open daily 8.30 a.m. – 4.30 p.m.* ○ *I take aspirin daily to prevent a heart attack.*

● **Daily** is also an adjective. ○ *They held daily press briefings.*

2 **ADJECTIVE** **Daily** quantities or rates relate to a period of one day. ○ *a diet containing adequate daily amounts of fresh fruit* ○ *Our average daily turnover is about £300.*

> ▶ **COLLOCATIONS:**
> **open** daily
> **once/twice** daily
> daily **life**
> a daily **guide/routine/newspaper**
> a daily **intake/dose/allowance/volume** of *something*
> **average/normal/recommended/regular** daily *amount*

> ▶ **PHRASE:** on a daily basis

> ▶ **RELATED WORDS:** weekly, monthly, yearly

dam|age /ˈdæmɪdʒ/ (damages, damaging, damaged)

1 **VERB** To **damage** an object means to break it, spoil it physically, or stop it from working properly. ○ *He maliciously damaged a car with a baseball bat.* ○ *The sun can damage your skin.*

2 **VERB** To **damage** something means to cause it to become less good, pleasant, or successful. ○ *Jackson doesn't want to damage his reputation as a political personality.* ○ *He warned that the action was damaging the economy.*

> ▶ **COLLOCATIONS:**
> damage a **building/vehicle**
> damage **the environment**
> damage someone's **brain/ligaments/knee/ankle**
> damage someone's **prospects/reputation/credibility**
> **badly/severely/seriously/permanently** damage *something*

> ▶ **SYNONYMS:** harm, injure

3 **UNCOUNTABLE NOUN** **Damage** is physical harm that is caused to an object. ○ [+ to] *The blast caused extensive damage to the house.* ○ *Many professional boxers end their careers with brain damage.*

4 **UNCOUNTABLE NOUN** **Damage** consists of the unpleasant effects that
something has on a person, situation, or type of activity. ○ [+ to] *Incidents
of this type cause irreparable damage to relations with the community.*
○ *Adhering to the new rules meant inflicting serious damage on motor racing.*

▶ **COLLOCATIONS:**
  damage **to** *something*
  cause/do/inflict damage
  suffer/sustain damage
  assess/repair damage
  prevent/minimize/avoid/limit damage
  structural/environmental/criminal damage
  brain/ligament/liver/nerve damage
  flood/storm/smoke damage
  bad/severe/serious/extensive/substantial damage
  permanent/irreparable damage

▶ **SYNONYMS:** harm, injury

USAGE: damage, **harm** or **injure**?

You usually talk about **damaging** an object, a situation or a
relationship, but not a person.

  damage a **building/vehicle**
  damage the **environment**
  damage *someone's* **reputation/credibility**

In a medical context, you can talk about **damaging** a part of the body.

  damage a **ligament/tendon/nerve**

You can talk about **harming** a person or an animal, a situation or a
relationship, but not normally an object

  harm a **baby/animal/foetus**
  harm **the environment/wildlife**
  harm **relations/a reputation**

You talk about **injuring** a person or a part of the body.

  injure a **policeman/civilian/soldier**
  injure your **knee/shoulder/ankle**

---

date /deɪt/ (dates, dating, dated)   [HISTORY]

1 **NOUN** A **date** is a specific time that can be named, for example a
particular day or a particular year. ○ *What's the date today?* ○ *You will need
to give the dates you wish to stay and the number of rooms you require.* ○ [+ for]
Closing date for applications is the end of January.

d

▶ COLLOCATIONS:
the date **of/for** *something*
a **delivery/publication/departure/closing** date
a **specific/exact** date
set/fix/schedule/announce/confirm a date
▶ PHRASES:
date of birth
date of purchase
date of publication

2 VERB If you **date** something, you give or discover the date when it was made or when it began. ○ *I think we can date the decline of Western Civilization quite precisely.* ○ [+ from] *The château dates from the fifteenth century* ○ *a long tradition dating back to the early Greeks*
▶ COLLOCATIONS:
date **from/back to** *a time*
date *something* **accurately/precisely**

---

deal with /ˈdiːl wɪð, ˈdiːl wɪθ/ **(deals with, dealing with, dealt with)**

PHRASAL VERB When you **deal with** something or someone that needs attention, you give your attention to them, and often solve a problem or make a decision concerning them. ○ *the way that building societies deal with complaints* ○ *In dealing with suicidal youngsters, our aims should be clear.* ○ *The President said the agreement would allow other vital problems to be dealt with.*
▶ COLLOCATIONS:
deal with a **problem/situation/matter/issue/complaint**
deal with a **crisis/emergency**
deal with *something* **directly/effectively/specifically/adequately**
▶ SYNONYMS: handle, manage, attend to

---

dec|ade /ˈdekeɪd/ **(decades)**　ACADEMIC WORD　HISTORY

NOUN A **decade** is a period of ten years, especially one that begins with a year ending in 0, for example 1980 to 1989. ○ *the last decade of the nineteenth century*
▶ COLLOCATIONS:
the **last/next** decade
recent/past/previous decades
a decade **later/earlier/ago**
decades **of** *something*
decades of **war/conflict/neglect**
▶ RELATED WORD: century

de|cide /dɪ'saɪd/ (decides, deciding, decided)

1 VERB If you **decide** to do something, you choose to do it, usually after you have thought carefully about the other possibilities. ○ [+ to-inf] *She decided to do a secretarial course.* ○ [+ that] *He has decided that he will step down as leader.*

▶ **COLLOCATION:** decide **in favour of/against** *something*

2 VERB If a person or group of people **decides** something, they choose what something should be like or how a particular problem should be solved. ○ *The judge would take her age into account when deciding her sentence.* ○ *This is an issue that should be decided by local and metropolitan government.*

▶ **COLLOCATIONS:**
a **court/judge/jury** decides *something*
a **government/board/committee** decides *something*
decide *someone's* **fate/future**
decide the **matter/issue/outcome**
decide a **case/sentence**

3 VERB If you **decide** that something is true, you form that opinion about it after considering the facts. ○ [+ that] *The government decided that the company represented a security risk.* ○ [+ whether] *The committee has to decide whether the applicant is trustworthy.*

de|ci|sion /dɪ'sɪʒən/ (decisions)

NOUN ○ [+ to-inf] *A decision was taken to discipline Marshall.* ○ *I don't want to make the wrong decision and regret it later.* ○ [+ on] *A final decision on this issue is long overdue.* ○ *The moment of decision cannot be delayed.*

▶ **COLLOCATIONS:**
a decision **about/on** *something*
make/reach/take a decision
a **tough/difficult/hard** decision
a **final/important/major/controversial/unanimous** decision
the **right/wrong** decision
the **government's/court's/judge's** decision

▶ **SYNONYMS:** judgment, conclusion, finding
▶ **ANTONYM:** indecision

deci|mal /'desɪməl/ (decimals) `MATHS`

1 ADJECTIVE A **decimal** system involves counting in units of ten. ○ *the decimal system of metric weights and measures* ○ *In 1971, the 1p and 2p decimal coins were introduced in Britain.* ○ *calculate the result to three decimal places*

▶ **COLLOCATIONS:**
the decimal **system**

decimal **currency/coins**

a decimal **place**

2 NOUN A **decimal** is a fraction that is written in the form of a dot followed by one or more numbers which represent tenths, hundredths, and so on: for example .5, .51, .517. ○ *simple maths concepts, such as decimals and fractions*

▶ **RELATED WORD:** fraction

,deci|mal 'point (decimal points)   MATHS

NOUN A **decimal point** is the dot in front of a decimal fraction.

> **ACADEMIC WRITING: Writing and saying numbers**
>
> In English texts, a decimal point is always written as a dot (.), not a comma (,) as in some other languages. It is pronounced as 'point' when reading the number aloud. ○ 2.5% (two point five per cent)

---

de|crease (decreases, decreasing, decreased)

> The verb is pronounced /dɪˈkriːs/. The noun is pronounced /ˈdiːkriːs/.

1 VERB When something **decreases** or when you **decrease** it, it becomes less in quantity, size, or intensity. ○ [+ by] *Population growth is decreasing by 1.4% each year.* ○ [+ from/to] *The number of independent firms decreased from 198 to 96.* ○ *Gradually decrease the amount of vitamin C you are taking.*

▶ **COLLOCATIONS:**

decrease **in/by** *something*

decrease **from** *x* **to** *y*

significantly/dramatically decrease

slightly/steadily/gradually decrease

decrease the **risk/likelihood/incidence** of *something*

▶ **SYNONYMS:** lower, reduce, fall, drop, decline

▶ **ANTONYMS:** increase, grow, rise

2 NOUN A **decrease in** the quantity, size, or intensity of something is a reduction in it. ○ [+ in] *a decrease in the number of young people out of work* ○ [+ of] *Bank base rates have fallen from 10 per cent to 6 per cent – a decrease of 40 per cent.*

▶ **COLLOCATIONS:**

a decrease **in** *something*

a decrease **of** *x*

a decrease in **size/value**

a **significant/slight/dramatic/sharp/marked** decrease

see/expect/show/report a decrease

▶ **SYNONYMS:** reduction, fall, drop, decline, loss
▶ **ANTONYMS:** increase, growth, rise, gain

EXTEND YOUR VOCABULARY

You use **decrease** and **reduce** to talk about things becoming less or smaller in many different contexts.

decrease/reduce the **amount/risk/likelihood/effectiveness**

You use **fall**, **drop** and **lower** to talk about a number, rate or level becoming less.

the **price/rate** falls/drops
profits/revenues/sales fall/drop
lower the **price/rate/level/cost/limit**

You use **decline** to talk about something becoming less, usually in a way that is negative. ○ *Sales declined by 2.4 % over the month of September.*

---

deep /diːp/ (deeper, deepest)

ADJECTIVE You use **deep** to talk or ask about how much something measures from the surface to the bottom, or from front to back.
○ *I found myself in water only three feet deep.* ○ *How deep did the snow get?*
○ *Dig as deep as you can.*
▶ **COLLOCATIONS:**
  as deep **as** *something*
  deeper **than** *something*
  a **metre/foot/inch** deep

depth /depθ/ (depths)

NOUN The **depth** of something such as a river or hole is the distance downwards from its top surface, or between its upper and lower surfaces. ○ *The smaller lake ranges from five to fourteen feet in depth.*
○ *The depth of the shaft is 520 yards.*
▶ **COLLOCATIONS:**
  the depth **of** *something*
  x metres **in** depth
▶ **RELATED WORDS:** width, height, breadth

---

de|gree /dɪˈgriː/ (degrees) [EDUCATION] [ACADEMIC STUDY]

1 NOUN A **degree** is a unit of measurement that is used to measure temperatures. It is often written as °, for example 23°. ○ *It's over 80 degrees outside.* ○ *Pure water sometimes does not freeze until it reaches minus 40 degrees Celsius.*
▶ **COLLOCATION:** degrees **Celsius/centigrade**

2 NOUN A **degree** is a unit of measurement that is used to measure angles. It is often written as °, for example 23°. ○ *It was pointing outward at an angle of 45 degrees.*

3 NOUN A **degree** at a university or college is a course of study that you take there, or the qualification that you get when you have passed the course. ○ *He took a master's degree in economics at Yale.* ○ *an engineering degree* ○ *the first year of a degree course*

▶ COLLOCATIONS:
a degree **in** something
a degree **from** a university
earn/achieve/obtain/gain a degree
award someone a degree
complete/take a degree
a **first-class/second-class** degree
an **undergraduate/postgraduate** degree
a **university/honours/master's** degree
a **law/science/engineering** degree
a degree **course**
▶ RELATED WORD: diploma

de|lib|er|ate /dɪˈlɪbərət/

ADJECTIVE If you do something that is **deliberate**, you planned or decided to do it beforehand, and so it happens on purpose rather than by chance. ○ *It has a deliberate policy to introduce world art to Britain.* ○ *Witnesses say the firing was deliberate and sustained.*

▶ COLLOCATIONS:
a deliberate **action/attempt/omission/policy**
deliberate **harm/intent**
▶ SYNONYMS: intentional, conscious
▶ ANTONYMS: unintentional, accidental

de|lib|er|ate|ly

ADVERB ○ *It looks as if the blaze was started deliberately.* ○ *Mr Christopher's answer was deliberately vague.*

▶ COLLOCATIONS:
deliberately **ignore/avoid** something
deliberately **choose/target** something
deliberately **mislead** someone
▶ SYNONYMS: intentionally, consciously, knowingly
▶ ANTONYMS: unintentionally, accidentally, inadvertently

de|pend /dɪˈpend/ (depends, depending, depended)

1 VERB If you say that one thing **depends on** another, you mean that the first thing will be affected or determined by the second. ○ [+ on/upon] *The cooking time needed depends on the size of the potato.* ○ *What happened later would depend on his talk with De Solina.* ○ *The value of any tax relief depends upon individual circumstances.*

▶ COLLOCATIONS:
depend **on/upon** something
depend **largely/heavily/entirely/partly/greatly** on something
someone's **life/future/success** depends on something
someone's **livelihood/survival** depends on something
depend on **size/type/outcome**
depend on **circumstances/factors**

2 PHRASE You use **depending on** when you are saying that something varies according to the circumstances mentioned. ○ *Individual vitamin needs vary, depending on size, age and height.* ○ *Cars will be taxed individually depending on when and where and how much they have driven.*

▶ COLLOCATIONS:
depending on **size/type/outcome**
depending on **circumstances/factors**

---

de|scribe /dɪˈskraɪb/ (describes, describing, described)

VERB If you **describe** a person, object, event, or situation, you say what they are like or what happened. ○ [+ what] *We asked her to describe what kind of things she did in her spare time.* ○ *She read a poem by Carver which describes their life together.*

▶ COLLOCATIONS:
describe something/someone **as** something
describe a **scene/situation/incident/process**
describe something/someone **accurately/vividly/briefly**

▶ SYNONYMS: relate, express, depict

USAGE: describe, explain or **show**?

If you **describe** something, you give information or details about it, but not reasons for it. ○ *A witness described the scene.*

If you **explain** something, you give information and reasons to help someone understand it better. ○ *He tried to explain the meaning of the word.* ○ *He explained why birds migrate.*

A person can **describe, explain** or **show** something. ○ *The teacher described/explained/showed how the device worked.*

You can say that facts, research or a graph **show** something, but not **describe** it. ○ *Surveys showed that the numbers of people using the buses had risen.*

de|scrip|tion /dɪ'skrɪpʃən/ (descriptions)

NOUN A **description** of someone or something is an account which explains what they are or what they look like. ○ [+ of] *Police have issued a description of the man who was aged between fifty and sixty.* ○ *a detailed description of the movements and battle plans of Italy's fleet*

▶ **COLLOCATIONS:**
  a description **of** *something/someone*
  provide/give/issue a description
  match/fit a description
  a **detailed/brief/accurate/vivid/full** description
  a **job** description

▶ **SYNONYMS:** account, representation, depiction

---

des|ert /'dezət/ (deserts)   GEOGRAPHY

NOUN A **desert** is a large area of land, usually in a hot region, where there is almost no water, rain, trees, or plants. ○ *the Sahara Desert* ○ *The vehicles have been modified to suit conditions in the desert.*

---

de|sign /dɪ'zaɪn/ (designs, designing, designed)   ACADEMIC WORD

1 VERB When someone **designs** a garment, building, machine, or other object, they plan it and make a detailed drawing of it from which it can be built or made. ○ *They wanted to design a machine that was both attractive and practical.* ○ *men wearing specially designed boots*

▶ **COLLOCATIONS:**
  an **architect/engineer/artist** designs *something*
  design a **machine/product/device/building**

▶ **PHRASES:**
  design and build
  design and manufacture

2 VERB When someone **designs** a survey, policy, or system, they plan and prepare it, and decide on all the details of it. ○ *We may be able to design a course to suit your particular needs.* ○ *A number of very well designed studies have been undertaken.*

▶ **COLLOCATION:** design a **program/system/course/strategy**

▶ **PHRASES:**
  design and develop
  design and implement

3 VERB If something **is designed** for a particular purpose, it is intended for that purpose. ○ [+ to-inf] *This project is designed to help landless people.* ○ [+ for] *It's not designed for anyone under age eighteen.*

▶ **COLLOCATIONS:**
  be designed **for** something/someone
  specifically/specially designed
▶ **SYNONYM:** intended

---

de|spite /dɪ'spaɪt/   `ACADEMIC WORD`

PREPOSITION You use **despite** to introduce a fact which makes the other part of the sentence surprising. ○ *Despite a thorough investigation, no trace of Dr Southwell has been found.* ○ *The National Health Service has visibly deteriorated, despite increased spending.* ○ [+ v-ing] *Despite being the world's richest nation, the USA is also one of the most religious.*
▶ **SYNONYM:** in spite of

---

de|stroy /dɪ'strɔɪ/ (destroys, destroying, destroyed)

VERB To **destroy** something means to cause so much damage to it that it is completely ruined or does not exist any more. ○ *That's a sure recipe for destroying the economy and creating chaos.* ○ *No one was injured in the explosion, but the building was completely destroyed.*
▶ **COLLOCATIONS:**
  destroy a **house/home/building/document**
  destroy **evidence**
  a **fire/earthquake/missile/blast/explosion** destroys something
  completely/totally/nearly destroy something
▶ **SYNONYM:** ruin

de|struc|tion /dɪ'strʌkʃən/

UNCOUNTABLE NOUN **Destruction** is the act of destroying something, or the state of being destroyed. ○ [+ of] *an international agreement aimed at halting the destruction of the ozone layer* ○ *weapons of mass destruction*
▶ **COLLOCATIONS:**
  the destruction **of** something
  cause/prevent the destruction of something
  total/massive/complete/widespread destruction
  environmental/habitat destruction

---

de|tail /'diːteɪl/ (details)

The pronunciation /dɪ'teɪl/ is also used in American English.

1 NOUN The **details of** something are its individual features or elements. ○ [+ of] *The details of the plan are still being worked out.* ○ *I recall every detail of the party.*

2 **PLURAL NOUN** **Details** about someone or something are facts or pieces of information about them. ○ [+ of] *See the bottom of this page for details of how to apply for this exciting offer.* ○ *Full details will be announced soon.*

▶ **COLLOCATIONS:**
details **of/about** *something*
details of a **plan/proposal/agreement**
full/exact/precise/specific details
further/more details
announce/give/provide/release/reveal details

▶ **SYNONYMS:** information, facts, specifics

▶ **ANTONYM:** generalization

---

de|vel|op /dɪˈveləp/ **(develops, developing, developed)**

1 **VERB** When something **develops**, it grows or changes over a period of time and usually becomes more advanced, complete, or severe. ○ *It's hard to say at this stage how the market will develop.* ○ [+ into] *These clashes could develop into open warfare.*

2 **VERB** If you say that a country **develops**, you mean that it changes from being a poor agricultural country to being a rich industrial country. ○ *All countries, it was predicted, would develop and develop fast.*

3 **VERB** If you **develop** a business or industry, or if it **develops**, it becomes bigger and more successful. ○ *She won a grant to develop her own business.* ○ *Over the last few years tourism here has developed considerably.*

4 **VERB** If someone **develops** a new product, idea or theory, they create something new and work on it until it becomes more advanced or detailed. ○ *He claims that several countries have developed nuclear weapons secretly.* ○ *I would like to thank them for allowing me to develop their original idea.* ○ *This point is developed further at the end of this chapter.*

▶ **COLLOCATIONS:**
develop **into** *something*
develop *something* **further**
develop a **technique/strategy/idea**
develop a **business/product**
develop **weapons/technology/software**
a company develops *something*
develop **rapidly/quickly**
newly/fully/highly developed

▶ **PHRASES:**
a developing country
a developed country
develop and design

develop and market
▶ **SYNONYMS:** establish, progress, improve

---

de|vel|op|ment /dɪ'veləpmənt/ (developments)

1 UNCOUNTABLE NOUN Development is the gradual growth or formation of something. ○ [+ of] *an ideal system for studying the development of the embryo* ○ *First he surveys Islam's development.*

2 UNCOUNTABLE NOUN Development is the growth of something such as a business or an industry. ○ *Education is central to a country's economic development.* ○ [+ of] *What are your plans for the development of your company?*

3 NOUN Development is the process or result of making a basic design gradually better and more advanced. ○ *We are spending $850m on research and development.* ○ [+ of] *the development of new and innovative telephone services*

▶ **COLLOCATIONS:**
the development **of** *something*
the development of **capitalism/technology**
the development of a **drug/product/vaccine**
economic/technological/sustainable development
commercial/industrial development
a **technical/new** development
software/product development

▶ **PHRASES:**
growth and development
marketing and development
training and development
research and development

▶ **SYNONYMS:** evolution, advance, progress

---

diet /daɪət/ (diets)   `MEDICINE`

NOUN Your **diet** is the type and range of food that you regularly eat. ○ *It's never too late to improve your diet.* ○ *a healthy diet rich in fruit and vegetables* ○ *Poor diet and excess smoking will seriously damage the health of your hair.*

▶ **COLLOCATIONS:**
a diet **of** *something*
follow/eat a diet
improve *your* diet
feed *someone* a diet
a diet **contains/consists of** *something*
a **poor/healthy/balanced** diet
a **low-fat/vegetarian** diet
your **daily** diet

a diet **high/rich/low/deficient** in *something*

▶ **PHRASES:**
diet and exercise
diet and lifestyle

---

dif|fer /'dɪfə/ (differs, differing, differed)

VERB If two or more things **differ**, they are unlike each other in some way.
○ [+ *from*] *The story he told police differed from the one he told his mother.*
○ *Management styles differ.*

▶ **COLLOCATIONS:**
differ **from** *something*
differ **significantly/considerably/widely/sharply/markedly**
opinions/views differ

▶ **SYNONYMS:** vary, contrast with

dif|fer|ent /'dɪfrənt/

1 ADJECTIVE If two people or things are **different**, they are not like each other in one or more ways. ○ [+ *from*] *London was different from most European capitals.* ○ *We have totally different views.*

2 ADJECTIVE You use **different** to indicate that you are talking about two or more separate and distinct things of the same kind. ○ *Different countries specialised in different products.* ○ *The number of calories in different brands of drinks varies enormously.*

▶ **COLLOCATIONS:**
different **from** *something*
very/completely/totally/entirely different
a different **type/kind/part/thing**
a different **way/approach/view**
be/look/seem/sound/feel different

▶ **SYNONYMS:** contrasting, dissimilar, distinct
▶ **ANTONYMS:** the same, similar, alike, identical

dif|fer|ence /'dɪfrəns/ (differences)

1 NOUN The **difference** between two things is the way in which they are unlike each other. ○ [+ *between*] *That is the fundamental difference between the two societies.* ○ *There is no difference between the sexes.* ○ [+ *in*] *the vast difference in size*

▶ **COLLOCATIONS:**
the difference **between** *things*
a difference **in** *something*
tell/notice the difference
a **significant/big/huge/real/fundamental** difference

the **main/major/only** difference
little/not much/no difference
a difference in **quality/size/attitude/approach**
▶ **SYNONYMS:** contrast, variation, distinction
▶ **ANTONYM:** similarity

2 NOUN A **difference** between two quantities is the amount by which one quantity is less than the other. ○ *The difference between 49 and 100 is 51.*
▶ **COLLOCATION:** the difference **between** *x* and *y*

d

---

dif|fi|cult /ˈdɪfɪkəlt/

ADJECTIVE Something that is **difficult** is not easy to do, understand, or deal with. ○ [+ *for*] *The lack of childcare provisions made it difficult for single mothers to get jobs.* ○ [+ to-inf] *It was a very difficult decision to make.*
▶ **COLLOCATIONS:**
be difficult **for** *someone*
make/find *something* difficult
be/become/prove difficult
very/extremely/increasingly/particularly difficult
a difficult **life/task/time/job**
a difficult **situation/question/position/issue**
a difficult **decision/choice**
▶ **SYNONYMS:** challenging, complex, demanding, hard
▶ **ANTONYMS:** easy, simple, straightforward, undemanding, uncomplicated

dif|fi|cul|ty /ˈdɪfɪkəlti/ (difficulties)

1 NOUN A **difficulty** is a problem. ○ [+ *of*] *the difficulty of getting accurate information* ○ *The country is facing great economic difficulties*

2 UNCOUNTABLE NOUN If you have **difficulty** doing something, you are not able to do it easily. ○ [+ v-ing] *Do you have difficulty getting up?* ○ *The injured man mounted his horse with difficulty.*
▶ **COLLOCATIONS:**
the difficulty **of** *something*
have difficulty **with** *something*
face/experience/encounter difficulties
cause/present/overcome/create a difficulty
economic/financial/technical/practical difficulties
great/severe/considerable/little difficulty
breathing/language difficulties
▶ **SYNONYMS:** trouble, challenge, problem, obstacle
▶ **ANTONYMS:** ease, simplicity

d

digi|tal /ˈdɪdʒɪtəl/ 　　　　　　　　　　　　　IT

ADJECTIVE **Digital** systems record or transmit information in the form of thousands of very small signals. ○ *The new digital technology would allow a rapid expansion in the number of TV channels.*

▸ **COLLOCATIONS:**
　a digital **camera/channel/television/radio/photo**
　digital **technology**
▸ **RELATED WORDS:** terrestrial, analogue

digi|tal|ly

ADVERB ○ *digitally recorded sound*
▸ **COLLOCATION:** digitally **enhanced/recorded**

di|rect /daɪˈrekt, dɪ-/

1 ADJECTIVE **Direct** means moving towards a place or object, without changing direction and without stopping, for example in a journey. ○ *They'd come on a direct flight from Athens.* ○ *the direct route from Amman to Bombay*

• **Direct** is also an adverb. ○ *You can fly direct to Amsterdam from most British airports.*
▸ **COLLOCATION:** a direct **flight/route**
▸ **PHRASE:** have direct access to something
▸ **ANTONYM:** indirect

2 ADJECTIVE You use **direct** to describe an experience, activity, or system which only involves the people, actions, or things that are necessary to make it happen. ○ *He has direct experience of the process of privatisation.* ○ *He seemed to be in direct contact with the Boss.*

• **Direct** is also an adverb. ○ *I can deal direct with your Inspector Kimble.*
▸ **COLLOCATION:** direct **contact/experience**
▸ **PHRASE:** in direct contact with someone
▸ **SYNONYMS:** close, immediate

3 ADJECTIVE You use **direct** to emphasize the closeness of a connection between two things. ○ *They were unable to prove that she died as a direct result of his injection.* ○ *His visit is direct evidence of the improvement in their relationship.*

▸ **COLLOCATIONS:**
　a direct **link/involvement/result**
　a direct **connection/impact/consequence**
▸ **PHRASE:** as a direct result of *something*
▸ **SYNONYMS:** close, immediate
▸ **ANTONYM:** indirect

di|rect|ly /daɪˈrektli, dɪr-/

ADVERB ○ *The jumbo jet is due to fly the hostages directly back to London.*
○ *The British could do nothing directly to help the Austrians.*
▶ **COLLOCATIONS:**
   lead/fly directly *somewhere*
   send *someone* directly *somewhere*
   link directly with *something*
   report/speak/communicate directly
▶ **ANTONYM:** indirectly

---

di|rec|tion /daɪˈrekʃən/ (directions)

1 NOUN A **direction** is the general line that someone or something is moving or pointing in. ○ *St Andrews was ten miles in the opposite direction.*
○ [+ *of*] *He drove off in the direction of Larry's shop.*

2 NOUN A **direction** is the general way in which something develops or progresses. ○ *They threatened to walk out if the party did not change direction.*
▶ **COLLOCATIONS:**
   the **right/opposite/different/wrong** direction
   a **general/future/strategic** direction
   a **clear/new/particular** direction
   change/reverse direction
▶ **PHRASES:**
   change of direction
   in all directions
   in the direction of something
▶ **SYNONYMS:** course, route

---

di|rec|tor /daɪˈrektə, dɪr-/ (directors)   BUSINESS

NOUN The **directors** of a company are its most senior managers, who meet regularly to make important decisions about how it will be run.
○ [+ *of*] *He served on the board of directors of a local bank.* ○ *Karl Uggerholt, the financial director of Braun U.K.*
▶ **COLLOCATIONS:**
   a director **of** something
   a **managing/executive/non-executive** director
   a **deputy/assistant/associate** director
   a **finance/marketing/operations** director
   the **acting** director
   appoint/elect/name a director
   a director **agrees/decides/recommends/approves** something

> **PHRASES:**
  the board of directors
  director and founder
> **SYNONYMS:** manager, executive, CEO

---

disability /ˌdɪsəˈbɪlɪti/ (disabilities)

NOUN A disability is a permanent injury, illness, or physical or mental condition that tends to restrict the way that someone can live their life. ○ *Facilities for people with disabilities are still insufficient.* ○ *athletes who have overcome a physical disability to reach the top of their sport*

> **COLLOCATIONS:**
  cause/suffer/overcome a disability
  a **permanent/severe** disability
  a **mental/learning/physical** disability
  a disability **pension/allowance/benefit/insurance**
> **PHRASE:** people with disabilities
> **SYNONYM:** impairment

dis|abled /dɪˈseɪbəld/

ADJECTIVE Someone who is **disabled** has a disability that tends to restrict the way that they can live their life, especially by making it difficult for them to move about. ○ *practical problems encountered by disabled people in the workplace*

> **COLLOCATIONS:**
  disabled **people**
  physically/mentally/developmentally disabled
  severely disabled
> **PHRASE:** the elderly and disabled

ACADEMIC WRITING: Sensitive issues

When writing about sensitive issues, it is important to choose words carefully and to check that you are using language that people do not find offensive or old-fashioned.

The words **disability** and **disabled** are commonly used to talk about people with physical disabilities. **Handicap** and **handicapped** are now considered old-fashioned and sometimes offensive.

To talk about someone with a mental disability, it is now common to say that they have **learning difficulties**.

dis|ad|vant|age /ˌdɪsəd'vɑːntɪdʒ, -'væn-/ (disadvantages)

NOUN A **disadvantage** is a factor which makes someone or something less useful, acceptable, or successful than other people or things. ○ [+ of] *His two main rivals suffer the disadvantage of having been long-term political exiles.* ○ [+ of] *the advantages and disadvantages of allowing priests to marry*

▶ COLLOCATIONS:
the disadvantages **of** something
suffer/face/experience/overcome a disadvantage
a **distinct/competitive** disadvantage

▶ PHRASE: the advantages and disadvantages of something

▶ SYNONYMS: drawback, inconvenience, downside

▶ ANTONYMS: advantage, benefit

dis|agree /ˌdɪsə'griː/ (disagrees, disagreeing, disagreed)

1 VERB If you **disagree with** someone or **disagree with** what they say, you do not accept that what they say is true or correct. You can also say that two people **disagree**. ○ [+ with] *You must continue to see them no matter how much you may disagree with them.* ○ *They can communicate even when they strongly disagree.*

2 VERB If you **disagree with** a particular action or proposal, you disapprove of it and believe that it is wrong. ○ [+ with] *I respect the president but I disagree with his decision.*

▶ COLLOCATIONS:
disagree **with** someone/something
disagree **on/about** something
disagree with a **statement/assessment/decision/view**
disagree about a **point/issue**
strongly/vehemently/totally/completely/publicly disagree

▶ SYNONYM: differ

▶ ANTONYMS: agree, concur

dis|agree|ment /ˌdɪsə'griːmənt/ (disagreements)

1 UNCOUNTABLE NOUN **Disagreement** means objecting to something such as a proposal. ○ [+ with] *Britain and France have expressed some disagreement with the proposal.*

▶ COLLOCATIONS:
disagreement **with/over/on/about** something
disagreement **continues/remains/exists/arises**
considerable disagreement
express disagreement

▶ SYNONYMS: opposition, dissent

▶ ANTONYM: agreement

d

2 NOUN When there is **disagreement** about something, people disagree
or argue about what should be done. ○ [+ over] *The Congress and the
President are still locked in disagreement over proposals.* ○ *My instructor and I
had a brief disagreement.*
▶ COLLOCATIONS:
   a disagreement **with** someone
   a disagreement **between** people
   disagreement **over/on/about** something
   express/cause disagreement
   resolve/settle a disagreement
   overcome/avoid a disagreement
   a **fundamental/profound/sharp/bitter/serious** disagreement
▶ SYNONYMS: dispute, argument, conflict, dissent
▶ ANTONYM: agreement

dis|ap|pear /ˌdɪsəˈpɪə/ (disappears, disappearing, disappeared)

VERB If something **disappears**, it stops existing or happening.
○ *The immediate security threat has disappeared.* ○ *Symptoms usually
disappear gradually.*
▶ COLLOCATIONS:
   symptoms disappear
   a **species/habitat** disappears
   soon/simply/fast/altogether disappear
   quickly/suddenly/gradually disappear
   entirely/completely/virtually disappear
▶ SYNONYMS: go, vanish
▶ ANTONYMS: appear, emerge

dis|ap|pear|ance /ˌdɪsəˈpɪərəns/ (disappearances)

NOUN ○ [+ of] *the virtual disappearance of the red telephone box* ○ *the
disappearance of animals from the wild*
▶ COLLOCATIONS:
   the disappearance **of** something
   disappearance **from** somewhere
   a **gradual/virtual/sudden/eventual** disappearance
▶ PHRASE: disappearance and destruction
▶ SYNONYM: decline
▶ ANTONYMS: appearance, reappearance

disc /dɪsk/ (discs)

NOUN A **disc** is a flat, circular shape or object. ○ *Most shredding machines are
based on a revolving disc fitted with replaceable blades.* ○ [+ of] *a small disc of metal*

▶ COLLOCATIONS:
a disc **of** *something*
a **revolving/spinning** disc

> **USAGE:** Spelling
>
> In British English, the spelling **disc** is usually used to describe a round, flat object and the spelling **disk** is used to talk about the part of a computer where information is stored.
>
> In American English, the spelling **disk** is used for both.

---

dis|cov|er /dɪsˈkʌvə/ SCIENCE GEOGRAPHY
(discovers, discovering, discovered)

VERB When someone **discovers** a new place, substance, scientific fact, or scientific technique, they are the first person to find it or become aware of it. ○ *the first European to discover America* ○ *In the 19th century, gold was discovered in California.* ○ *[+ how] They discovered how to form the image in a thin layer on the surface.*

▶ COLLOCATIONS:
scientists/researchers/archaeologists discover *things*
discover a **planet/comet/tomb/species/fossil**
discover a **cure** for *something*
discover the **truth** about *something*
soon/first/quickly/finally discover
recently/newly discovered

▶ PHRASES:
discover and develop
discover and explore

dis|cov|ery /dɪsˈkʌvəri/ **(discoveries)**

NOUN If someone makes a **discovery**, they are the first person to find or become aware of a place, substance, or scientific fact that no one knew about before. ○ *In that year, two momentous discoveries were made.* ○ *[+ of] the discovery of the ozone hole over the South Pole*

▶ COLLOCATIONS:
the discovery **of** *something*
make/announce/report a discovery
a **scientific/archaeological** discovery
a **momentous/exciting/remarkable/recent** discovery

▶ PHRASES:
discovery and invention
discovery and exploration

dis|cuss /dɪsˈkʌs/ (discusses, discussing, discussed)

1 VERB If people **discuss** something, they talk about it, often in order to reach a decision. ○ *I will be discussing the situation with colleagues tomorrow.* ○ [+ how] *The cabinet met today to discuss how to respond to the ultimatum.*

2 VERB If you **discuss** something, you write or talk about it in detail. ○ *I will discuss the role of diet in cancer prevention in Chapter 7.*

▶ **COLLOCATIONS:**
discuss *something* **with** *someone*
discuss a **matter/issue/topic/situation**
discuss a **proposal/plan/idea/problem/case**
discuss the **possibility/details** of *something*
openly/publicly discuss *something*
discuss *something* **at length**

▶ **PHRASE:** discuss and debate

▶ **SYNONYMS:** consider, debate, examine

dis|cus|sion /dɪsˈkʌʃən/ (discussions)

1 NOUN If there is **discussion** about something, people talk about it, often in order to reach a decision. ○ [+ of/about/on] *There was a lot of discussion about the wording of the report.* ○ *Council members are due to have informal discussions later on today.*

2 NOUN A **discussion of** a subject is a piece of writing or a lecture in which someone talks about it in detail. ○ [+ of] *For a discussion of biology and sexual politics, see chapter 4.*

▶ **COLLOCATIONS:**
discussion **of/about/on/over** *something*
discussion **with** *someone*
discussion **among/between** *people*
discussion on a **topic/issue/subject/matter**
hold/initiate a discussion
a discussion **concerns/focuses on** *something*
a **detailed/preliminary/frank** discussion
lengthy/further/informal discussions
a discussion **group/paper/forum**

▶ **PHRASES:**
discussion and debate
discussion and negotiation

▶ **SYNONYMS:** debate, argument, examination, analysis

dis|ease /dɪˈziːz/ (diseases)   `MEDICINE`

NOUN A **disease** is an illness which affects people, animals, or plants, for example one which is caused by bacteria or infection. ○ *the rapid spread of disease in the area* ○ *illnesses such as heart disease* ○ *Doctors believe they have cured him of the disease.*

▶ **COLLOCATIONS:**
  a **fatal/deadly/chronic** disease
  heart/lung/kidney disease
  coronary/cardiovascular/respiratory disease
  transmit/contract/develop a disease
  prevent/treat/cure/fight a disease
  diagnose/spread/cause a disease
  a disease **affects/kills** *someone*
  a disease **causes** *something*
▶ **SYNONYMS:** illness, infection, disorder, condition, complaint

disk /dɪsk/ (disks) also disc   `IT`

NOUN In a computer, the **disk** is the part where information is stored. ○ *The program takes up 2.5 megabytes of disk space.*
→ see note at **disc**
▶ **COLLOCATIONS:**
  format/insert/copy a disk
  a disk **holds/stores/contains** *something*
  a **floppy/hard/computer** disk
  disk **space/capacity**

dis|tance /ˈdɪstəns/ (distances)

NOUN The **distance between** two points or places is the amount of space between them. ○ [+ *between*] *the distance between the island and the nearby shore* ○ *Everything is within walking distance.*
▶ **COLLOCATIONS:**
  the distance **between** *x* and *y*
  the distance **from/to** *somewhere*
  a distance **of** *x kilometres*
  walk/travel/cover/drive/measure a distance
  a **short/long/considerable/vast/great** distance
▶ **PHRASE:** within *walking* distance
▶ **SYNONYM:** space

dis|tant /ˈdɪstənt/

ADJECTIVE Distant means very far away. ○ *The mountains rolled away to a distant horizon.* ○ *the war in that distant land*
▶ **COLLOCATIONS:**
  distant **from** *something*
  geographically distant
  a distant **galaxy/object/horizon/land/planet**
  become/grow/seem distant
▶ **SYNONYMS:** far off, remote
▶ **ANTONYMS:** nearby, close

---

di|vide /dɪˈvaɪd/ (divides, dividing, divided)   `MATHS`

1 VERB When people or things **are divided** or **divide into** smaller groups or parts, they become separated into smaller parts. ○ [+ *into*] *The physical benefits of exercise can be divided into three factors.* ○ [+ *into*] *It will be easiest if we divide them into groups.* ○ [+ *in*] *Divide the pastry in half and roll out each piece.*
▶ **COLLOCATIONS:**
  divide *something* **into** *something*
  divide *something* **between** *people*
  divide a **nation/community/society/country**
  divide *something* **evenly/equally/roughly/broadly**
  divide *something* into **categories/sections/segments**
  racially/geographically/politically divided
▶ **SYNONYMS:** split, separate, segregate

2 VERB If you **divide** a larger number **by** a smaller number or **divide** a smaller number **into** a larger number, you calculate how many times the smaller number can fit exactly into the larger number. ○ [+ *by/into*] *Measure the floor area of the greenhouse and divide it by six.*
▶ **COLLOCATION:** divide *something* **by/into** *something*
▶ **RELATED WORDS:** multiply, add, subtract

di|vi|sion /dɪˈvɪʒən/

1 UNCOUNTABLE NOUN The **division of** a large unit **into** two or more distinct parts is the act of separating it into these parts. ○ [+ *into*] *the unification of Germany, after its division into two states at the end of World War Two*
▶ **COLLOCATIONS:**
  the division **of** *something*
  division **into** *something*
▶ **PHRASE:** division and classification
▶ **SYNONYMS:** separation, partition

2 UNCOUNTABLE NOUN Division is the arithmetical process of dividing one number into another number. ○ *I taught my daughter how to do division at the age of six.*
▶ **PHRASE:** division and multiplication
▶ **RELATED WORDS:** multiplication, addition, subtraction

---

docu|ment /ˈdɒkjəmənt/ (documents) `ACADEMIC WORD` `IT`

NOUN A **document** is a piece of text or graphics, for example a letter, that is stored as a file on a computer and that you can access in order to read it or change it. ○ *When you are finished typing, remember to save your document.*
▶ **COLLOCATION: prepare/scan/save/send** a document

---

dou|ble /ˈdʌbəl/ (doubles, doubling, doubled) `MATHS`

VERB When something **doubles** or when you **double** it, it becomes twice as great in number, amount, or size. ○ [+ to] *The number of managers must double to 100 within 3 years.* ○ *The program will double the amount of money available to help pay for child care.*
▶ **COLLOCATIONS:**
 double **in** *something*
 double **to** *x*
 double in **size/value/price**
 double the **size/number/capacity/amount** of *something*

---

doubt /daʊt/ (doubts, doubting, doubted)

1 NOUN If you have **doubt** or **doubts** about something, you feel uncertain about it and do not know whether it is true or possible. If you say you have **no doubt about** it, you mean that you are certain it is true. ○ [+ *about/as to*] *This raises doubts about the point of advertising.* ○ [+ *that*] *There can be little doubt that he will offend again.*
▶ **COLLOCATIONS:**
 doubt **about/over/as to** *something*
 doubts **among** *people*
 grave/serious/considerable/major doubts
 little/much/no doubt
 have/express/raise/voice doubts
 throw/cast doubt on *something*
 doubt the **wisdom/viability/outcome/importance** of *something*
 doubt **surrounds** *something*
▶ **PHRASE:** leave no doubt about something
▶ **SYNONYMS:** uncertainty, indecision, confusion
▶ **ANTONYMS:** certainty, confidence

2 VERB If you **doubt** whether something is true or possible, you believe that it is probably not true or possible. ○ [+ *whether*] *Others doubted whether that would happen.* ○ [+ *if*] *He doubted if he would learn anything new from Marie.*

▶ COLLOCATIONS:
seriously doubt *something*
doubt the **wisdom/authenticity/sincerity** of *something*

▶ SYNONYM: question

dra|ma /ˈdrɑːmə/ (dramas) `ACADEMIC WORD` `LITERATURE`

1 NOUN A **drama** is a serious play for the theatre, television, or radio. ○ *He acted in radio dramas.*

▶ COLLOCATIONS:
be **in** a drama
watch a drama
a drama is **set/filmed** *somewhere*
a drama is **based on** *something*
a drama **continues/begins/unfolds**
a drama **stars/features** *someone*
a **costume/two-part/romantic/historical** drama
a **TV/radio** drama
a **crime/courtroom/comedy** drama
a drama **series**

2 UNCOUNTABLE NOUN You use **drama** to refer to plays in general or to work that is connected with plays and the theatre, such as acting or producing. ○ *He knew nothing of Greek drama.* ○ *She met him when she was at drama school.*

▶ COLLOCATIONS:
study drama
a drama **school/department/student/teacher/critic**

draw|back /ˈdrɔːbæk/ (drawbacks)

NOUN A **drawback** is an aspect of something or someone that makes them less acceptable than they would otherwise be. ○ *He felt the apartment's only drawback was that it was too small.*

▶ COLLOCATIONS:
have drawbacks
outweigh/overcome drawbacks
the **main/only** drawback
a **big/major** drawback

▶ SYNONYMS: disadvantage, difficulty
▶ ANTONYMS: benefit, advantage

dress /dres/

UNCOUNTABLE NOUN You can refer to clothes worn by men or women as
dress. ○ *hundreds of Cambodians in traditional dress*
▶ **COLLOCATIONS:**
  traditional/formal dress
  evening dress
  fancy dress
  a dress **code**
▶ **SYNONYM:** clothes

> **USAGE: dress, clothes** or **costume**?
>
> You use **clothes** or **clothing** to talk generally about things that
> people wear.
>
> You can use **dress** to talk about clothes of a particular style or clothes
> that are worn in a particular context. ○ *traditional African dress of
> dashiki and kofi*
>
> A **costume** is a set of clothes that someone wears especially for a
> performance. ○ *characters dressed in period costume*

drop /drɒp/ (drops, dropping, dropped)

VERB If a level or amount **drops** or if someone or something **drops** it,
it quickly becomes less. ○ [+ *to*] *Temperatures can drop to freezing at night.*
○ *He had dropped the price of his London home by £1.25m.*
→ see note at **decrease**
▶ **COLLOCATIONS:**
  drop **below/from/to** *something*
  drop **by** *x*
  temperature/prices/rates/profits drop
  drop **sharply/dramatically/significantly/slightly**
  drop **suddenly/steadily**
▶ **SYNONYMS:** fall, decline
▶ **ANTONYMS:** rise, increase

● **Drop** is also a noun. ○ [+ *in*] *He was prepared to take a drop in wages.*
○ *The poll indicates a drop in support for the Conservatives.*
▶ **COLLOCATIONS:**
  a drop **in/below** *something*
  a drop in **profits/revenue/earnings/sales/prices**
  a drop in **temperature/demand/numbers**
  a **big/significant/sharp/steep/dramatic** drop
  report/record a drop
  avoid/experience/suffer/show/cause a drop

▶ **SYNONYMS:** fall, decline, decrease, reduction
▶ **ANTONYMS:** rise, increase

---

drought /draʊt/ (droughts)

NOUN A **drought** is a long period of time during which no rain falls.
○ *Drought and famines have killed up to two million people here.*

▶ **COLLOCATIONS:**
  a **prolonged/severe/devastating** drought
  drought **affects/hits/devastates** *somewhere*
  drought **conditions**
▶ **PHRASES:**
  drought and floods
  drought and famine
▶ **RELATED WORD:** flood

---

drug /drʌg/ (drugs)

1 NOUN A **drug** is a chemical which is given to people in order to treat or prevent an illness or disease. ○ *The drug will be useful to hundreds of thousands of infected people.* ○ *the drug companies*

▶ **COLLOCATIONS:**
  prescribe/administer a drug
  buy/sell/market/import a drug
  test/develop a drug
  a drug **causes/affects** *something*
  anti-inflammatory/anti-cancer/prescription drugs
  drug **testing/treatment**
  a drug **company**
▶ **SYNONYMS:** medication, medicine, remedy

2 NOUN **Drugs** are substances that some people take because of their pleasant effects, but which are usually illegal. ○ *His mother was on drugs, on cocaine.* ○ *She was sure Leo was taking drugs.* ○ *the problem of drug abuse*

▶ **COLLOCATIONS:**
  be **on** drugs
  inject/use/take a drug
  supply/smuggle/sell/deal a drug
  a drug **overdose**
  illegal/illicit/recreational/experimental drugs
  performance-enhancing drugs
  a drug **dealer/trafficker/addict/user**
  drug **trafficking/addiction/dealing/smuggling**

drug **use/abuse**
the drug **trade**
▶ **PHRASE:** drugs and alcohol
▶ **SYNONYM:** narcotic

due to

> In British English, pronounced /ˈdjuː tə/ before a consonant and
> /ˈdjuː tʊ/ before a vowel. In American English, pronounced /ˈduː tə/
> before a consonant and /ˈduː tʊ/ before a vowel.

PHRASE If an event is **due to** something, it happens or exists as a direct
result of that thing. ○ *The country's economic problems are largely due to the
weakness of the recovery.*
▶ **COLLOCATIONS:**
  partly/primarily due to *something*
  largely/mainly/mostly due to *something*
▶ **SYNONYMS:** because of, caused by

Ee

earn /ɜːn/ (earns, earning, earned) `BUSINESS`

VERB If you **earn** money, you receive money in return for work that you do. ○ *an unskilled worker earning less than £2.50 an hour* ○ *They moved to Sapa to earn a living in the tourism trade.* ○ *Executive directors can earn between £70,000 and £90,000.*

▶ COLLOCATIONS:
earn **money**
earn £x **a year**
earn a **salary/wage/income/living**

▶ SYNONYM: receive

earn|ings /ˈɜːnɪŋz/

PLURAL NOUN Your **earnings** are the sums of money that you earn by working. ○ *Average weekly earnings rose by 1.5% in July.* ○ *He was satisfied with his earnings as an accountant.*

▶ COLLOCATIONS:
average/net earnings
annual/weekly earnings
earnings **rise/soar/fall/decline**

EXTEND YOUR VOCABULARY

There are many different words to describe money that people get from working. **Income** is the most general word to describe any money a person gets from working, but also from other sources such as investments, a pension, etc. ○ *families on low incomes*

A person's **earnings** are any money they receive from working. ○ *average earnings*

Pay is a general word to describe money that people are paid for a job. It is an uncountable noun and it often refers to the amount paid for a type of job rather than when you talk about an individual. ○ *workers striking over pay and conditions*

You use **wages** to talk about money that people are paid for work in factories, shops, etc. where they are often paid each week, according to the hours they have worked. ○ *the national minimum wage of £5.80 per hour*

You use **salary** to talk about the money earned by someone who works in an office or has a professional job, who is usually paid monthly and earns a fixed amount each year. ○ *an annual salary of £25,000 a year*

---

earth /ɜːθ/ GEOGRAPHY

NOUN Earth or **the Earth** is the planet on which we live. People usually say **Earth** when they are referring to the planet as part of the universe, and **the Earth** when they are talking about the planet as the place where we live. ○ *The space shuttle Atlantis returned safely to Earth today.* ○ *a fault in the Earth's crust*

▶ **COLLOCATIONS:**
  planet Earth
  the Earth's **crust/surface/atmosphere**
▶ **PHRASE:** heaven and earth
▶ **SYNONYM:** world

---

earth|quake /ˈɜːθkweɪk/ (earthquakes) GEOGRAPHY

NOUN An **earthquake** is a shaking of the ground caused by movement of the Earth's crust. ○ *Two powerful earthquakes struck western Japan yesterday.* ○ *Bhuj was hit by an earthquake measuring 7.9 on the Richter scale.*

▶ **COLLOCATIONS:**
  a **devastating/massive/powerful** earthquake
  an earthquake **zone**
  an earthquake **strikes/hits/rocks** *somewhere*
▶ **PHRASES:**
  somewhere is devastated by an earthquake
  an earthquake measuring *x* on the Richter scale
▶ **SYNONYM:** tremor

---

east /iːst/ also **East** GEOGRAPHY

1 UNCOUNTABLE NOUN The east is the direction which you look towards in the morning in order to see the sun rise. ○ *[+ of] the vast swamps which lie to the east of the River Nile* ○ *The canal runs across England from east to west.*

▶ **COLLOCATIONS:**
  east **of** *somewhere*
  to the east of *somewhere*
  a **mile/kilometre** to the east
▶ **PHRASE:** from east to west
▶ **RELATED WORDS:** west, north, south

2 NOUN The east of a place, country, or region is the part which is in
the east. ○ [+ of] *a village in the east of the country*
▶ **COLLOCATIONS:**
the east **of** *somewhere*
in the east of *somewhere*
▶ **RELATED WORDS:** west, north, south

east|ern /ˈiːstən/

ADJECTIVE Eastern means in or from the east of a region, state, or country.
○ *Pakistan's eastern city of Lahore* ○ *France's eastern border with Germany*
▶ **COLLOCATIONS:**
an eastern **shore/coast/border/edge**
an eastern **city/suburb/region/province**
▶ **PHRASE:** Eastern Europe
▶ **RELATED WORDS:** western, northern, southern

---

eco-friendly /ˌiːkəʊˈfrendli/   GEOGRAPHY

ADJECTIVE Eco-friendly products or services are less harmful to the
environment than other similar products or services. ○ *eco-friendly
washing powder* ○ *Tourism must try to be eco-friendly.*
▶ **COLLOCATIONS:**
an eco-friendly **product/vehicle**
eco-friendly **technology/heating/packaging**
▶ **SYNONYMS:** environmentally friendly, green

---

econo|my /ɪˈkɒnəmi/   ACADEMIC WORD BUSINESS ECONOMICS
(economies)

NOUN The economy of a country or region is the system by which money,
industry, and trade are organized. ○ *Zimbabwe boasts Africa's most
industrialised economy.* ○ *The Japanese economy grew at an annual rate of more
than 10 per cent.* ○ *the region's booming service economy*
▶ **COLLOCATIONS:**
the economy **of** *somewhere*
a **modern/industrial/service/market** economy
a **booming/strong/weak** economy
the **global/world/local/domestic** economy
the **American/Canadian/Japanese/British** economy
stimulate/revive/boost the economy
the economy **grows/recovers/shrinks/slows down**

eco|nom|ic /ˌiːkəˈnɒmɪk, ˌek-/

ADJECTIVE Economic means concerned with the organization of the money, industry, and trade of a country, region, or society. ○ *Poland's radical economic reforms* ○ *The pace of economic growth is picking up.* ○ *the current economic crisis*

→ see note at **financial**

---

edu|ca|tion /ˌedʒʊˈkeɪʃən/ EDUCATION

NOUN **Education** involves teaching and learning, usually at a school or college. ○ *a long-term plan to improve the education system* ○ *Paul prolonged his education with six years of advanced study in English.*

▶ **COLLOCATIONS:**
  primary/secondary education
  formal/compulsory/full-time education
  provide/deliver education
  get/receive an education
  an education **system/program**
▶ **PHRASES:**
  adult education
  further education
  higher education
▶ **SYNONYMS:** teaching, learning

edu|cate /ˈedʒʊkeɪt/ (educates, educating, educated)

VERB When someone, especially a child, **is educated**, he or she is taught at a school or college. ○ *He was educated at Haslingden Grammar School.*

▶ **COLLOCATIONS:**
  a **child/student** is educated
  well/poorly educated
▶ **SYNONYM:** teach

edu|ca|tion|al /ˌedʒʊˈkeɪʃənəl/

ADJECTIVE **Educational** matters or institutions are concerned with or relate to education. ○ *the British educational system* ○ *pupils with special educational needs* ○ *The educational backgrounds of health workers range from vocational training to Master's degrees.*

▶ **COLLOCATIONS:**
  an educational **establishment/institution/system**
  an educational **qualification/achievement**
  someone's educational **background**

---

ef|fect /ɪ'fekt/ (effects)

NOUN The **effect of** one thing **on** another is the change that the first thing causes in the second thing. ○ [+ of/on] *The internet could have a significant* effect on trade in the next few years. ○ *The housing market is feeling the effects of the increase in interest rates.* ○ *Even minor head injuries can cause long-lasting psychological effects.*

→ see note at **affect**

▶ COLLOCATIONS:
the effect **of** *something*
the effect **on** *something/someone*
a **profound/dramatic/significant** effect
a **negative/harmful/adverse/devastating** effect
a **positive/beneficial/desired** effect
a **long-term/lasting/immediate** effect
a **psychological/health/knock-on** effect
have an effect on *something/someone*
feel the effects of *something*

▶ PHRASE: cause and effect

▶ SYNONYMS: influence, impact

ef|fec|tive /ɪˈfektɪv/

ADJECTIVE Something that is **effective** works well and produces the results that were intended. ○ [+ *in*] *The project looks at how we could be more effective in encouraging students to enter teacher training.* ○ [+ *against*] *Simple antibiotics are effective against this organism.* ○ *an effective public transport system*

▶ COLLOCATIONS:
effective **in/against** *something*
highly/extremely/particularly effective
an effective **manner/strategy**
an effective **method/means/way**

▶ SYNONYM: successful

▶ ANTONYM: ineffective

ef|fec|tive|ly /ɪˈfektɪvli/

ADVERB ○ *the team roles which you believe to be necessary for the team to function effectively* ○ *Services need to be more effectively organised than they are at present.*

▶ COLLOCATIONS:
function/work/operate effectively
communicate effectively

ef|fi|cient /ɪˈfɪʃənt/

ADJECTIVE If something or someone is **efficient**, they are able to do tasks successfully, without wasting time or energy. ○ *With today's more efficient contraception women can plan their families and careers.* ○ *Technological advances allow more efficient use of labor.* ○ *an efficient way of testing thousands of compounds*

▶ **COLLOCATIONS:**
an efficient **use** of *something*
an efficient **way** of *doing something*
an efficient **manner**
highly/extremely efficient
fuel/energy efficient
▶ **SYNONYMS:** systematic, organized

ef|fi|cient|ly

ADVERB ○ *Enzymes work most efficiently within a narrow temperature range.*
○ *the ability to run a business efficiently*
▶ **COLLOCATIONS:**
function/work/operate/run efficiently
run/manage/organize *something* efficiently

ef|fi|cien|cy /ɪˈfɪʃənsi/

UNCOUNTABLE NOUN ○ *There are many ways to increase agricultural efficiency in the poorer areas of the world.* ○ *Refrigerators have improved energy efficiency by a third in 30 years.*
▶ **COLLOCATIONS:**
energy/fuel efficiency
improve/promote/increase efficiency
efficiency **savings/gains/improvements**

ef|fort /ˈefət/ (efforts)

NOUN If you make an **effort to** do something, you try very hard to do it.
○ [+ to-inf] *Medical schools must make an effort to enrol promising students from minority ethnic groups.* ○ *Finding a cure requires considerable time and effort.*
○ [+ of] *Despite the efforts of the United Nations, the problem of drug traffic continues to grow.*
▶ **COLLOCATIONS:**
the efforts **of** *someone*
make an effort
a **concerted/massive/ongoing** effort
▶ **PHRASE:** time and effort
▶ **SYNONYM:** attempt

e.g. /ˌiː ˈdʒiː/ `ACADEMIC STUDY`

e.g. is an abbreviation that means 'for example'. It is used before a noun, or to introduce another sentence. ○ *We need helpers of all types, engineers, scientists (e.g. geologists) and teachers.* ○ *Or consider how you can acquire these skills, e.g. by taking extra courses.*
▶ **SYNONYMS:** for example, for instance, such as

e

> ### ACADEMIC WRITING: Abbreviations
>
> Although **e.g.** is a common abbreviation in written notes, you should not use it in essays, such as for the IELTS writing task. You can use **for example**, **for instance** or **such as** to introduce an example.
>
> In academic writing, abbreviations are only used in notes, for example, as part of diagrams, tables and graphs. In general, it is better to use full forms rather than abbreviations in essays.

---

egg /eg/ (eggs)   `SCIENCE` `BIOLOGY`

NOUN An **egg** is an oval object that is produced by a female bird and which contains a baby bird. Other animals such as reptiles and fish also lay eggs. ○ *Sea turtles live in the sea but breathe air and lay eggs on the beach.* ○ *Sixty percent of eggs hatched and survived during the breeding season.*

▶ COLLOCATIONS:
  lay/hatch an egg
  an egg **hatches**
  a **chicken/hen/turtle** egg

---

el|der|ly /ˈeldəli/   `SOCIAL SCIENCE`

ADJECTIVE You use **elderly** as a polite way of saying that someone is old. ○ *Typical symptoms of pneumonia may be less prominent in elderly patients.* ○ *Many of those most affected are elderly.*

▶ COLLOCATIONS:
  elderly **people**
  an elderly **man/woman/gentleman/lady/couple**
▶ SYNONYM: old
▶ ANTONYM: young

> ### USAGE: elderly or old?
>
> You use **elderly** as a polite way to talk about people who are old. It is more appropriate to use in written essays.
>
> You can also use **the elderly**, as a noun, to talk about old people as a group. ○ *The elderly and the very young are most at risk.*
>
> You can use **old** when you talk about the process of aging in expressions such as **get older** and **old age**. ○ *Cell renewal slows down as we get older.* ○ *plans for care in old age*
>
> You also use **old** to talk about animals and things. ○ *an old building*

elect /ɪˈlekt/ (elects, electing, elected)   SOCIAL SCIENCE   POLITICS

VERB When people **elect** someone, they choose that person to represent them, by voting for them. ○ *The people of the Philippines have voted to elect a new president.* ○ *[+ as] Pelton was elected as mayor.* ○ *the newly elected prime minister*

▶ COLLOCATIONS:
be elected **as** *something*
elect a **president/leader/government**
democratically/newly/directly elected

▶ SYNONYMS: choose, vote

elec|tion /ɪˈlekʃən/ (elections)

NOUN An **election** is a process in which people vote to choose a person or group of people to hold an official position. ○ *his decision to hold the first general election in Nepal's history* ○ *During his election campaign he promised to increase economic growth.*

▶ COLLOCATIONS:
a **presidential/parliamentary/mayoral** election
a **general/local** election
hold/call/win/lose an election
vote in an election
an election **campaign/manifesto/day/result**

▶ SYNONYMS: vote, poll, ballot

elec|tric|ity /ɪlekˈtrɪsɪti, ˈiːlek-/   SCIENCE   ENGINEERING

UNCOUNTABLE NOUN **Electricity** is a form of energy that can be carried by wires and is used for heating and lighting, and to provide power for machines. ○ *Approximately 40% of the world's electricity is generated using coal.* ○ *infrastructure such as water and electricity supplies*

▶ COLLOCATIONS:
produce/generate/supply electricity
an electricity **supply/supplier/generator**

elec|tric /ɪˈlektrɪk/

ADJECTIVE An **electric** device or machine works by means of electricity, rather than using some other source of power. ○ *The tool is powered by an 1100 watt electric motor.*

▶ COLLOCATIONS:
an electric **motor/heater/guitar**
an electric **current/shock**

elec|tri|cal /ɪˈlektrɪkəl/

ADJECTIVE ○ *shipments of electrical equipment* ○ *The study found that small electrical appliances consume a fifth of the electricity used in a typical American home.*

▶ COLLOCATIONS:
electrical **equipment/appliances/goods**
electrical **engineer/engineering**

elec|tron|ic /ɪlek'trɒnɪk, 'iː-/ SCIENCE ENGINEERING IT

ADJECTIVE An **electronic** device has transistors or silicon chips which
control and change the electric current passing through the device.
○ *cameras, mobile phones and other electronic devices* ○ *the supply, repair and
installation of electronic equipment*
▶ COLLOCATIONS:
electronic **equipment**
an electronic **device/machine/component**
an electronic **system/database**

elec|tron|ics /ɪlek'trɒnɪks/

UNCOUNTABLE NOUN Electronics is the technology of using transistors
and silicon chips, especially in devices such as radios, televisions, and
computers. ○ *Europe's three main electronics companies* ○ *cheaper, better
consumer electronics*
▶ COLLOCATIONS:
consumer electronics
an electronics **company/maker/retailer/manufacturer**

emer|gen|cy /ɪ'mɜːdʒənsi/ (emergencies)

NOUN An **emergency** is an unexpected and difficult or dangerous
situation, especially an accident, which happens suddenly and which
requires quick action to deal with it. ○ *Staff are trained to handle
emergencies.* ○ *The hospital will cater only for emergencies.*
▶ COLLOCATIONS:
in an emergency
a **major/minor** emergency
a **medical/national/family** emergency
an emergency **department/room/exit**
an emergency **supply/worker/vehicle**
▶ PHRASE: a state of emergency
▶ SYNONYM: crisis

e'mer|gen|cy ser|vices

PLURAL NOUN The emergency services are the public organizations
whose job is to take quick action to deal with emergencies when they
occur, especially the fire brigade, the police, and the ambulance service.
○ *The emergency services launched a rescue helicopter.* ○ *He called the emergency
services and within minutes an ambulance arrived.*

emo|tion /ɪ'məʊʃən/ (emotions) `PSYCHOLOGY`

NOUN An **emotion** is a feeling such as happiness, love, fear, anger, or hatred, which can be caused by the situation that you are in or the people you are with. ○ *the different ways that men and women express emotion* ○ *Research has shown that secure children are generally better at dealing with emotions, including sadness and anger.* ○ *Her voice trembled with emotion.*

▶ COLLOCATIONS:
  do something **with** *emotion*
  express/show/convey *emotion*
  strong/intense/raw *emotion*
  mixed/conflicting *emotions*

▶ SYNONYM: feeling

emo|tion|al /ɪ'məʊʃənəl/

1 ADJECTIVE Emotional means concerned with emotions and feelings. ○ *Emotional support is vital during times of difficulty at work.* ○ *Victims are left with emotional problems that can last for life.*

▶ COLLOCATIONS:
  emotional **support**
  emotional **trauma/stress/problems**

▶ SYNONYM: psychological

2 ADJECTIVE An **emotional** situation or issue is one that causes people to have strong feelings. ○ *It's a very emotional issue. How can you advocate selling the ivory from elephants?*

▶ SYNONYM: emotive

emo|tion|al|ly

ADVERB ○ *Play can be used therapeutically with children who are emotionally disturbed.* ○ *an emotionally charged speech*

▶ COLLOCATIONS:
  emotionally **drained/scarred/disturbed/unstable**
  emotionally **charged**

em|ploy /ɪm'plɔɪ/ (employs, employing, employed) `BUSINESS`

VERB If a person or company **employs** you, they pay you to work for them. ○ *The company employs 18 staff.* ○ *[+ in] More than 3,000 local workers are employed in the tourism industry.*

▶ COLLOCATIONS:
  employ someone **as** *something*
  be employed **in** *an industry*
  a **firm/company/corporation** *employs someone*

staff/workers/people are employed
be employed **full-time/part-time**
▶ **SYNONYMS:** hire, recruit

em|ploy|ment /ɪmˈplɔɪmənt/

UNCOUNTABLE NOUN Employment is the fact of having or giving someone
a paid job. ○ *Many graduates are unable to find employment.* ○ *[+ of] the
employment of children under nine* ○ *96% of immigrants are in full-time
employment.* ○ *economic policies designed to secure full employment*
▶ **COLLOCATIONS:**
the employment **of** *someone*
seek/find/provide employment
paid/full-time/part-time employment
employment **opportunities/prospects/law/rights**
an employment **agency**
▶ **SYNONYMS:** work, job, occupation
▶ **ANTONYM:** unemployment

em|ployee /ɪmˈplɔɪiː/ (employees)

NOUN An **employee** is a person who is paid to work for an organization or
for another person. ○ *[+ of] He is an employee of Fuji Bank.* ○ *Many of its
employees are women.*
▶ **COLLOCATIONS:**
an employee **of/at** *something*
hire/recruit/dismiss employees
a **full-time/part-time** employee
a **government/state** employee
an employee of a **company/firm/department**
an employee at a **factory/hospital**
▶ **SYNONYMS:** worker, staff

em|ploy|er /ɪmˈplɔɪə/ (employers)

NOUN Your **employer** is the person or organization that you work for.
○ *employers who hire illegal workers* ○ *The telephone company is the country's
largest employer.*

---

en|able /ɪnˈeɪbəl/ (enables, enabling, enabled) `ACADEMIC WORD`

1 VERB If something **enables** you **to** do a particular thing, it gives you the
opportunity to do it. ○ *[+ to-inf] The new test should enable doctors to detect the
disease early.* ○ *Hypotheses enable scientists to check the accuracy of their theories.*
▶ **SYNONYM:** help

2 VERB To **enable** something **to** happen means to make it possible for it to
happen. ○ *[+ to-inf] The hot sun enables the grapes to reach optimum ripeness.*

○ *The working class is still too small to enable a successful socialist revolution.*
▶ **SYNONYM:** allow
▶ **ANTONYM:** prevent

---

en|cour|age /ɪnˈkʌrɪdʒ, AM -ˈkɜːr-/
(encourages, encouraging, encouraged)

1 VERB If you **encourage** someone **to** do something, you try to persuade them to do it, for example by telling them that it would be a pleasant thing to do, or by trying to make it easier for them to do it. You can also **encourage** an activity. ○ [+ to-inf] *Children should be encouraged to participate in at least one sport.* ○ *Their task is to help encourage private investment in Russia.*

2 VERB If something **encourages** a particular activity or state, it causes it to happen or increase. ○ *a natural substance that encourages cell growth* ○ [+ to-inf] *Slow music encourages supermarket-shoppers to browse longer but spend more.*

▶ **COLLOCATIONS:**
encourage **people/pupils/students/users/participation**
encourage **development/growth/investment**
encourage *someone* to **participate/join/apply/attend**
▶ **ANTONYM:** discourage

---

en|dan|ger /ɪnˈdeɪndʒə/   SCIENCE   BIOLOGY
(endangers, endangering, endangered)

VERB To **endanger** something or someone means to put them in a situation where they might be harmed or destroyed completely. ○ *Plastic bags endanger wildlife.* ○ *endangered species such as lynx and wolf*
▶ **COLLOCATIONS:**
an endangered **species/habitat/animal**
endanger **wildlife**
▶ **SYNONYM:** threaten
▶ **ANTONYMS:** protect, conserve

---

en|er|gy /ˈenədʒi/ **(energies)**   ACADEMIC WORD   SCIENCE

UNCOUNTABLE NOUN Energy is the power from sources such as electricity and coal that makes machines work or provides heat. ○ *a scheme for supporting renewable energy in England and Wales* ○ *Oil shortages have caused an energy crisis.* ○ *The energy efficiency of public transport could be improved.*
▶ **COLLOCATIONS:**
renewable/solar/wind/nuclear energy
energy **efficiency/conservation**

an energy **crisis**
conserve/save/store/consume/generate energy
▶ SYNONYM: power

---

en|gine /ˈendʒɪn/ (engines)   ENGINEERING

NOUN The **engine** of a car or other vehicle is the part that produces the power which makes the vehicle move. ○ *Diesel engines are usually more fuel-efficient than petrol engines.* ○ *an engine failure that forced a jetliner to crash-land in a field*
▶ COLLOCATIONS:
  a **diesel/petrol/steam/jet** engine
  start/switch on/switch off an engine
▶ SYNONYM: motor

---

en|gi|neer|ing /ˌendʒɪˈnɪərɪŋ/   SCIENCE ENGINEERING

UNCOUNTABLE NOUN Engineering is the work involved in designing and constructing engines and machinery, or structures such as roads and bridges. **Engineering** is also the subject studied by people who want to do this work. ○ *the design and engineering of aircraft and space vehicles* ○ *graduates with degrees in mechanical engineering*
▶ COLLOCATIONS:
  chemical/electrical/mechanical engineering
  an engineering **professor/graduate/student/degree**
  an engineering **firm/group**

en|gi|neer /ˌendʒɪˈnɪə/ (engineers)

NOUN An **engineer** is a person who uses scientific knowledge to design, construct, and maintain engines and machines or structures such as roads, railways, and bridges. ○ *Structural engineers assessed the damage to the building.* ○ *one of the engineers who designed the railway*
▶ COLLOCATIONS:
  a **mechanical/electrical/structural** engineer
  an engineer **designs/invents** *something*
  an engineer **surveys/inspects** *something*

---

enor|mous /ɪˈnɔːməs/   ACADEMIC WORD

1 ADJECTIVE Something that is **enormous** is extremely large in size or amount. ○ *The main bedroom is enormous.* ○ *New technology means that it is possible to send enormous amounts of information at once.*
▶ COLLOCATION: an enormous **amount/sum/quantity**
▶ SYNONYMS: vast, tremendous, huge
▶ ANTONYM: tiny

2 ADJECTIVE You can use **enormous** to emphasize the great degree or
extent of something. ○ *This drug holds enormous potential for the treatment
of strokes.*
▶ **COLLOCATIONS:**
  enormous **wealth/potential/influence/success**
  enormous **importance/significance**
  an enormous **task/challenge**
▶ **SYNONYMS:** great, significant

enor|mous|ly

ADVERB ○ *an enormously influential historian* ○ *Blood levels can vary enormously
throughout a 24-hour period.*
▶ **COLLOCATIONS:**
  vary/differ enormously
  grow/expand/improve enormously
  enormously **influential/popular/successful**
▶ **SYNONYMS:** hugely, greatly, incredibly, dramatically, significantly

en|ter /'entə/ (enters, entering, entered)

1 VERB When you **enter** a place such as a building or a country, you go into
it or come into it. [FORMAL] ○ *Anyone without an ID badge is required to sign in
before entering the building.* ○ *the number of illegal immigrants entering the EU*
▶ **COLLOCATIONS:**
  enter a **room/building/country**
  illegally enter *somewhere*
▶ **ANTONYMS:** leave, exit

> **EXTEND YOUR VOCABULARY**
>
> In everyday English, you talk about **going into** a place. ○ *I parked the
> car and went into a shop.*
>
> In more formal writing, you can use the more specific verb **enter**.
> ○ *The thieves entered through a rear door.*

2 VERB If you **enter** a competition, race, or examination, you officially state
that you will compete or take part in it. ○ *Jackie Ballard was the only woman
who entered the race.* ○ *To enter, simply complete the coupon on page 150.*
▶ **COLLOCATION:** enter a **competition/race/contest**

3 VERB To **enter** information **into** a computer or database means to record
it there, for example by typing it on a keyboard. ○ [+ *into*] *Postcodes will be
entered into the statisticians' computers.* ○ *A lot less time is now spent entering
the data.*

▶ **COLLOCATIONS:**
enter *something* **into** *something*
enter *something* into a **computer/database/system**
enter **data/information/username/password**
▶ **SYNONYMS:** key, input

en|trance /ˈentrəns/ (entrances)

NOUN The **entrance to** a place is the way into it, for example a door or
gate. ○ [+ to/into/of] *the entrance to the church* ○ *A marble entrance hall leads
to a sitting room.*
▶ **COLLOCATIONS:**
an entrance **to/into/of** *something*
a **side/main/front/back** entrance
an entrance **hall/gate**
▶ **SYNONYM:** entry
▶ **ANTONYM:** exit

en|ter|tain|ment /ˌentəˈteɪnmənt/ [MEDIA]

UNCOUNTABLE NOUN Entertainment consists of performances of plays
and films, and activities such as reading and watching television, that
give people pleasure. ○ *restaurants that provide entertainment as well as food*
▶ **COLLOCATIONS:**
provide/offer entertainment
live/digital/musical entertainment
▶ **PHRASE:** the entertainment industry

en|tire /ɪnˈtaɪə/

ADJECTIVE You use **entire** when you want to emphasize that you are
referring to the whole of something, for example, the whole of a place,
time, or population. ○ *He had spent his entire life in China as a doctor.* ○ *The
Great Barrier Reef runs almost the entire length of Queensland.* ○ *three per cent
of the entire Scottish population*
▶ **COLLOCATIONS:**
an entire **region/country**
the entire **population/world**
the entire **length** of *something*
someone's entire **life**
▶ **SYNONYMS:** whole, complete, total
▶ **ANTONYMS:** partial, limited

en|tire|ly /ɪnˈtaɪəli/

ADVERB **Entirely** means completely and not just partly. ○ *an entirely new approach* ○ *The two operations achieve entirely different results.* ○ *Their price depended almost entirely on their scarcity.*

▸ **COLLOCATIONS:**
   entirely **new/different**
   entirely **predictable/convincing/understandable**
   consist/depend entirely
   almost entirely
▸ **SYNONYMS:** completely, totally
▸ **ANTONYMS:** partly, partially, slightly

---

en|vi|ron|ment /ɪnˈvaɪərənmənt/ `ACADEMIC WORD` `SCIENCE`
(environments)

1 **NOUN** Someone's **environment** is their surroundings, especially the conditions in which they grow up, live, or work. ○ *Pupils are taught in a safe, secure environment.* ○ *His method is based on observing the animal in its natural environment.*

▸ **COLLOCATIONS:**
   a **safe/secure/supportive** environment
   a **work/business/learning** environment
   a **natural** environment
▸ **SYNONYMS:** surroundings, setting, background

2 **NOUN** **The environment** is the natural world of land, sea, air, plants, and animals. ○ *the need to protect the environment* ○ *Their aim is to increase income from tourism without damaging the environment.*

▸ **COLLOCATIONS:**
   protect/preserve/conserve the environment
   damage/pollute/harm the environment
   an environment **minister/spokesman/department**
▸ **SYNONYMS:** the wild, the natural world, the countryside

> **USAGE: the** + environment
>
> Remember than when you use **the environment** to talk about the natural world, you always need the definite article **the**.

en|vi|ron|men|tal /ɪnˌvaɪərənˈmentəl/

ADJECTIVE ○ *the environmental impact of buildings and transport systems* ○ *It protects against environmental hazards such as wind and sun.*

▸ **COLLOCATIONS:**
   an environmental **group/problem/issue**
   environmental **protection/impact**

en|vi|ron|men|tal|ly

ADVERB ○ *encourage builders to make environmentally sound homes* ○ *the high price of environmentally friendly goods*

▶ **COLLOCATION:** environmentally **friendly/sound**

en|vi|ron|men|tal|ist /ɪnˌvaɪərən'mentəlɪst/ **(environmentalists)**

NOUN An **environmentalist** is a person who is concerned with protecting and preserving the natural environment, for example by preventing pollution. ○ *Environmentalists fear that the mine will destroy the habitats of grizzly bears.*

▶ **SYNONYM:** conservationist

---

equal /'iːkwəl/ **(equals, equalling, equalled)** MATHS
[in AM, use **equaling**, **equaled**]

1 ADJECTIVE If two things are **equal** or if one thing is **equal to** another, they are the same in size, number, standard, or value. ○ [+ *to*] *Investors can borrow an amount equal to the property's purchase price.* ○ *in a population having equal numbers of men and women* ○ *Research and teaching are of equal importance.*

2 ADJECTIVE If people are **equal**, they all have the same rights and are treated in the same way. ○ [+ *in*] *We are equal in every way.* ○ *At any gambling game, everyone is equal.*

▶ **COLLOCATIONS:**
equal **to/in** *something*
an equal **amount/proportion/quantity**
equal **importance/status/value**
equal **pay/treatment/rights**
roughly/approximately/almost equal

▶ **PHRASE:** equal opportunities

▶ **SYNONYMS:** the same, identical, equivalent

▶ **ANTONYMS:** unequal, differing, contrasting

3 VERB If something **equals** a particular number or amount, it is the same as that amount or the equivalent of that amount. ○ *9 percent interest less 7 percent inflation equals 2 percent.* ○ *The average pay rise equalled 1.41 times inflation.*

▶ **COLLOCATION:** equal a **sum/total/amount**

equal|ly /'iːkwəli/

ADVERB ○ *A bank's local market share tends to be divided equally between the local branch and branches located elsewhere.* ○ *All these techniques are equally effective.*

▶ COLLOCATIONS:
   divide/share/distribute *something* equally
   equally **important/valid/effective**
▶ SYNONYM: evenly

equali|ty /ɪˈkwɒlɪti/

UNCOUNTABLE NOUN **Equality** is the same status, rights, and
   responsibilities for all the members of a society, group, or family. ○ [+ *of*]
   equality of the sexes ○ *Women had not achieved full legal and social equality in
   America by the 1930s.*
▶ COLLOCATIONS:
   equality **of** *something*
   racial/sexual/social equality
   equality of **opportunity/status/rights**
▶ SYNONYMS: fairness, equity
▶ ANTONYM: inequality

equip|ment /ɪˈkwɪpmənt/ ACADEMIC WORD

UNCOUNTABLE NOUN **Equipment** consists of the things which are used for
   a particular purpose, for example a hobby or job. ○ *computers, electronic
   equipment and machine tools* ○ *a shortage of medical equipment and medicine*
▶ COLLOCATIONS:
   electrical/electronic/medical/military equipment
   computer/telecoms equipment
   modern/state-of-the-art/high-tech equipment
▶ SYNONYMS: machinery, supplies, tools

> **USAGE:** Uncountable noun
>
> Remember, **equipment** is an uncountable noun, so you do **not** talk
> about 'equipments' or 'an equipment'. ○ *The company supplies schools
> with computer equipment.*
>
> You can talk about a **piece of equipment**. ○ *You can connect up to eight
> pieces of equipment to a single line.*

er|ror /ˈerə/ (errors) ACADEMIC WORD

NOUN An **error** is something you have done which is considered to be
   incorrect or wrong, or which should not have been done. ○ [+ *in*] *NASA
   discovered a mathematical error in its calculations.* ○ [+ *of*] *MPs attacked lax
   management and errors of judgment.* ○ *the risk of making an error in testing a
   hypothesis*

▶ **COLLOCATIONS:**
an error **in/of** *something*
make/discover/correct an error
a **spelling/factual/grammatical/clerical** error
a **basic/common/serious/grave/fatal** error
an error of **judgement/fact**
an error **occurs**
▶ **SYNONYM:** mistake

es|pe|cial|ly /ɪˈspeʃəli/

1 ADVERB You use **especially** to emphasize that what you are saying applies more to one person, thing, or area than to any others. ○ *Vitamin A deficiency is one of the most common causes of blindness in poor countries, especially in small children.* ○ *Regular use of cannabis can damage the respiratory system, especially if it is smoked with tobacco.*
▶ **SYNONYM:** particularly

2 ADVERB You use **especially** to emphasize a characteristic or quality.
○ *Babies lose heat much faster than adults, and are especially vulnerable to the cold in their first month.*
▶ **COLLOCATION:** especially **important/useful/helpful/valuable**
▶ **SYNONYM:** particularly

USAGE: especially or specially?

These adverbs have a similar meaning when they are used before an adjective to emphasize a characteristic or quality. However, **specially** is mostly used in this way in informal English, **especially** is appropriate in more formal writing. ○ *People should be especially careful driving at dawn or dusk.*

In other contexts, the two words have different meanings. You use **especially** to say that something applies more to one person or thing than others. ○ *Later chapters cover marine policy, especially regarding the coastal zone and pollution.*

You use **specially** to say that something is done or made for a particular purpose. ○ *facilities specially designed for disabled users*

---

es|say /ˈeseɪ/ (essays)

NOUN An **essay** is a short piece of writing on one particular subject written by a student. ○ [+ *about*] *Biology pupils were asked to write essays about tree leaves they had collected.*
▶ **COLLOCATIONS:**
an essay **about/on** *something*

write an essay
▶ **SYNONYM:** assignment

---

es|sen|tial /ɪˈsenʃəl/ (essentials)

1 ADJECTIVE Something that is **essential** is extremely important or absolutely necessary to a particular subject, situation, or activity.
○ [+ to-inf] *It was absolutely essential to separate crops from the areas that animals used as pasture.* ○ *Jordan promised to trim the city budget without cutting essential services.*

2 ADJECTIVE The **essential** aspects of something are its most basic or important aspects. ○ *Most authorities agree that play is an essential part of a child's development.* ○ *Tact and diplomacy are two essential ingredients in international relations.*
▶ **COLLOCATIONS:**
  essential **for** *something*
  absolutely essential
  essential **services/information**
  an essential **ingredient/element/part/component**
  an essential **requirement/feature**
▶ **SYNONYMS:** crucial, vital, fundamental, basic
▶ **ANTONYMS:** inessential, unimportant

---

es|ti|mate (estimates, estimating, estimated)   ACADEMIC WORD

> The verb is pronounced /ˈestɪmeɪt/. The noun is pronounced /ˈestɪmət/.

1 VERB If you **estimate** a quantity or value, you make an approximate judgment or calculation of it. ○ [+ that] *The Academy of Sciences currently estimates that there are approximately one million plant varieties in the world.* ○ *He estimated the speed of the winds from the degree of damage.*
▶ **COLLOCATIONS:**
  estimate *something* **at** *x*
  estimate **cost/value/revenue**
  an estimated **percentage/amount**
  originally/previously estimated
▶ **SYNONYMS:** judge, calculate

2 NOUN An **estimate** is an approximate calculation of a quantity or value.
○ [+ of/for] *the official estimate of the election result* ○ *This figure is five times the original estimate.* ○ *a conservative estimate based on previous findings*
▶ **COLLOCATIONS:**
  base an estimate on *something*

estimates **range/vary**
a **conservative/initial/official** estimate

---

etc /et 'setrə/ also **etc.**　　　　　　　`ACADEMIC STUDY`

etc is used at the end of a list to indicate that you have mentioned only some of the items involved and have not given a full list. **etc** is a written abbreviation for 'et cetera'. ○ *Each of the twelve major body systems - stomach, lungs, pancreas, etc - is closely related to certain muscles.*

e

---

even /ˈiːvən/　　　　　　　　　　　　`MATHS`

1 **ADJECTIVE** An **even** measurement or rate stays at about the same level. ○ *The brick-built property keeps the temperature at an even level throughout the year.*
▶ **SYNONYM:** constant

2 **ADJECTIVE** An **even** number can be divided exactly by the number two. ○ *In each capsule there is an even number of particles coloured black or white.*
▶ **ANTONYM:** odd

---

event /ɪˈvent/ **(events)**

NOUN An **event** is something that happens, especially when it is unusual or important. You can use **events** to describe all the things that are happening in a particular situation. ○ [+ *of*] *the events of September 11*
○ *recent events in Europe*
▶ **COLLOCATIONS:**
　the events **of** *something*
　recent/current/historical events
　a **tragic/momentous/significant** event
▶ **SYNONYMS:** occurrence, occasion

---

even|tual /ɪˈventʃʊəl/

ADJECTIVE You use **eventual** to indicate that something happens or is the case at the end of a process or period of time. ○ *There are many who believe that civil war will be the eventual outcome of the racial tension in the country.*
○ *The eventual aim is reunification.*
▶ **COLLOCATIONS:**
　the eventual **winner/champion/outcome**
▶ **SYNONYMS:** ultimate, final

even|tu|al|ly /ɪˈventʃʊəli/

1 **ADVERB** **Eventually** means in the end, especially after a lot of delays, problems, or arguments. ○ *Eventually, the army caught up with him in Latvia.*
○ *The flight eventually got away six hours late.*
▶ **SYNONYM:** finally

2 **ADVERB** **Eventually** means at the end of a situation or process or as the final result of it. ○ *Dehydration eventually leads to death.* ○ *researchers who hope eventually to create insulin-producing cells*
▶ **SYNONYM:** ultimately

---

every|day /ˈevrɪdeɪ/

ADJECTIVE You use **everyday** to describe something which happens or is used every day, or forms a regular and basic part of your life, so it is not especially interesting or unusual. ○ *studies of normal people in everyday life* ○ *the everyday problems of living in the city*
▶ **COLLOCATIONS:**
    everyday **life**
    an everyday **experience/routine/task/occurence**
    an everyday **object/item**
▶ **SYNONYMS:** normal, ordinary

> **USAGE:** Spelling
>
> Remember that **everyday**, written as one word, is an adjective, usually before a noun, to describe something that is a normal part of life. ○ *an everyday occurrence/object/item*
>
> You use **every day**, written as two words, to mean *each day*. ○ *The store is open every day from nine to six, except Sunday.*

---

evi|dence /ˈevɪdəns/   ACADEMIC WORD

UNCOUNTABLE NOUN **Evidence** is anything that you see, experience, read, or are told that causes you to believe that something is true or has really happened. ○ *[+ of/for] a report on the scientific evidence for global warming* ○ *[+ that] There is a lot of evidence that stress is partly responsible for disease.* ○ *[+ to-inf] To date there is no evidence to support this theory.*
▶ **COLLOCATIONS:**
    evidence **of/for** *something*
    find/gather/collect evidence
    present/produce evidence
    evidence **suggests/shows**
    clear/strong/conclusive evidence
    scientific/medical/circumstantial evidence
▶ **PHRASE:** evidence to support something
▶ **SYNONYMS:** proof, support

ex|act /ɪgˈzækt/

ADJECTIVE **Exact** means correct in every detail. For example, an **exact** copy is the same in every detail as the thing it is copied from. ○ *I don't remember the exact words.* ○ *Predicting earth tremors is not an exact science.* ○ *an exact copy of the text*

▶ **COLLOCATIONS:**
exact **words/wording**
an exact **location/date/number**
an exact **replica/copy/science**

▶ **SYNONYMS:** precise, accurate

▶ **ANTONYMS:** approximate, inexact, vague, imprecise

ex|act|ly /ɪgˈzæktli/

ADVERB ○ *No one knows exactly what these substances are.* ○ *The results were exactly as Bohr and Heisenberg predicted.* ○ *Both drugs will be exactly the same.*

▶ **COLLOCATIONS:**
know/remember/determine/explain exactly
almost exactly
exactly **like/the same/the opposite**
exactly **right/alike**

▶ **SYNONYM:** precisely

▶ **ANTONYM:** approximately

ex|am|ple /ɪgˈzɑːmpəl, -ˈzæmp-/ (examples)

1 NOUN An **example of** something is a particular situation, object, or person which shows that what is being claimed is true. ○ [+ *of*] *The doctors gave numerous examples of patients being expelled from hospital.* ○ *The following example illustrates the change that took place.*

▶ **COLLOCATIONS:**
an example **of** something
cite/provide/give an example
an example **illustrates** something
a **good/classic/perfect** example
a **specific/typical/concrete** example

2 PHRASE You use **for example** to introduce and emphasize something which shows that something is true. The abbreviation **e.g.** is used in written notes. ○ *'educational toys' that are designed to promote the development of, for example, children's spatial ability* ○ *A few simple precautions can be taken, for example ensuring that desks are the right height.*

→ see note at **e.g.**

▶ **SYNONYMS:** for instance, such as

ex|cept /ɪkˈsept/

1 **PREPOSITION** You use **except** to introduce the only thing or person that a statement does not apply to, or a fact that prevents a statement from being completely true. ○ *No illness, except malaria, has caused as much death as smallpox.*

● **Except** is also a conjunction. ○ *Physical examination was normal, except that her blood pressure was high.*

2 **PHRASE** You use **except for** to introduce the only thing or person that prevents a statement from being completely true. ○ *Elephant shrew are found over most of Africa, except for the west.*

▶ **SYNONYMS:** apart from, excluding

ex|cep|tion /ɪkˈsepʃən/ (exceptions)

NOUN An **exception** is a particular thing, person, or situation that is not included in a general statement, judgment, or rule. ○ [+ *of*] *The trees there are older than any other trees in the world, with the exception of the Californian redwoods.* ○ *The law makes no exceptions.*

▶ **COLLOCATIONS:**
  make an exception
  a **notable/obvious/possible/rare** exception
  the **sole/only** exception
▶ **PHRASE:** with the exception of

ex|hi|bi|tion /ˌeksɪˈbɪʃən/ (exhibitions) ACADEMIC WORD ARTS

NOUN An **exhibition** is a public event at which pictures, sculptures, or other objects of interest are displayed, for example at a museum or art gallery. ○ [+ *of*] *an exhibition of expressionist art*

▶ **COLLOCATIONS:**
  an exhibition **of** *something*
  an exhibition of **paintings/photographs/art**

ex|ist /ɪgˈzɪst/ (exists, existing, existed)

VERB If something **exists**, it is present in the world as a real thing.
  ○ *animals that no longer exist* ○ *Research opportunities exist in a wide range of pure and applied areas of entomology.*

▶ **SYNONYMS:** occur, be found, be present

ex|ist|ence /ɪgˈzɪstəns/ (existences)

UNCOUNTABLE NOUN The **existence** of something is the fact that it is present in the world as a real thing. ○ [+*of*] *the existence of other galaxies* ○ *The Congress of People's Deputies voted itself out of existence.* ○ [+*of*] *Public worries about accidents are threatening the very existence of the nuclear power industry.*

▶ **COLLOCATIONS:**
the existence **of** *something*
the **very/mere/continued** existence of *something*
acknowledge/deny/prove/confirm the existence of *something*
▶ **SYNONYMS:** presence, occurrence

---

ex|pect /ɪkˈspekt/ **(expects, expecting, expected)**

1 VERB If you **expect** something **to** happen, you believe that it will happen. ○ [+ to-inf] *a council workman who expects to lose his job in the next few weeks* ○ [+ to-inf] *The talks are expected to continue until tomorrow.* ○ *They expect a gradual improvement in sales of new cars.*
▶ **COLLOCATIONS:**
expect **growth/returns/earnings/profits/results**
be **widely** expected
▶ **SYNONYM:** anticipate

2 VERB If you **expect** something, or **expect** a person **to** do something, you believe that it is your right to have that thing, or the person's duty to do it for you. ○ *He wasn't expecting our hospitality.* ○ [+ to-inf] *I do expect to have some time to myself in the evenings.*
▶ **COLLOCATIONS:**
expect *something* **of** *someone*
reasonably/realistically/normally expect *something*

ex|pec|ta|tions /ˌekspekˈteɪʃənz/

PLURAL NOUN Your **expectations** are your strong hopes or beliefs that something will happen or that you will get something that you want. ○ *Students' expectations were as varied as their expertise.* ○ *The car has been General Motors' most visible success story, with sales far exceeding expectations.*
▶ **COLLOCATIONS:**
lower/raise expectations
meet/exceed/surpass expectations
realistic/reasonable/unrealistic/high expectations
▶ **SYNONYMS:** hope, prediction, forecast

---

ex|peri|ence /ɪkˈspɪəriəns/ **(experiences, experiencing, experienced)**

1 UNCOUNTABLE NOUN Experience is knowledge or skill in a particular job or activity, which you have gained because you have done that job or activity for a long time. ○ *He has also had managerial experience on every level.* ○ [+ in/of/with] *three years of relevant experience in stem-cell research*
▶ **COLLOCATIONS:**
experience **of/in/with/as** *something*

have/gain/lack experience
work/office/managerial/professional experience
relevant/previous/essential/valuable experience
▶ ANTONYM: inexperience

2 UNCOUNTABLE NOUN Experience is used to refer to the past events, knowledge, and feelings that make up someone's life or character. ○ I should not be in any danger here, but experience has taught me caution. ○ She had learned from experience to take little rests in between her daily routine.
▶ COLLOCATIONS:
life/past/personal/first-hand experience
learn from experience
experience **teaches/shows** something

3 NOUN An **experience** is something that you do or that happens to you, especially something important that affects you. ○ [+ of] His only experience of gardening so far proved immensely satisfying. ○ Many of his clients are very nervous, usually because of a bad experience in the past.
▶ COLLOCATIONS:
an experience **of/with** something
have/enjoy/describe an experience
a **good/bad/painful/wonderful** experience
the **whole** experience
▶ SYNONYMS: event, incident

USAGE: Countable and uncountable uses

As an uncountable noun, you use **experience** to talk generally about the skills and knowledge that someone has gained over time. You do not talk about 'work experiences' or 'some experiences of dealing with customers'. ○ someone with no previous political experience

As a countable noun, an **experience** is a particular event or situation that you go through. ○ The instructors also make the whole experience a great deal of fun. ○ Traumatic experiences can leave deep emotional scars.

4 VERB If you **experience** a particular situation, you are in that situation or it happens to you. ○ British business is now experiencing a severe recession.
▶ COLLOCATIONS:
experience a **difficulty/problem/loss**
experience **growth/decline**

---

ex|peri|ment (experiments, experimenting, experimented) `SCIENCE`

The noun is pronounced /ɪkˈspɛrɪmənt/. The verb is pronounced /ɪkˈspɛrɪˌment/.

e

1 NOUN An **experiment** is a scientific test which is done in order to discover what happens to something in particular conditions. ○ [+ to-inf] *The astronauts are conducting a series of experiments to learn more about how the body adapts to weightlessness.* ○ *a proposed new law on animal experiments* ○ *This question can be answered only by experiment.*

▶ **COLLOCATIONS:**
conduct/perform an experiment
an experiment **shows/demonstrates/suggests** *something*
a **laboratory/scientific/medical** experiment
animal experiments

2 VERB If you **experiment with** something or **experiment on** it, you do a scientific test on it in order to discover what happens to it in particular conditions. ○ [+ with/on] *In 1857 Mendel started experimenting with peas in his monastery garden.* ○ *The scientists have already experimented at each other's test sites.*

▶ **COLLOCATIONS:**
experiment **with/on** *something*
researchers/scientists experiment

ex|peri|men|tal /ɪkˌsperɪˈmentəl/

1 ADJECTIVE Something that is **experimental** is new or uses new ideas or methods, and might be modified later if it is unsuccessful. ○ *an experimental air conditioning system* ○ *The technique is experimental, but the list of its practitioners is growing.*

▶ **COLLOCATION:** an experimental **vaccine/drug/treatment**

2 ADJECTIVE Experimental means using, used in, or resulting from scientific experiments. ○ *the main techniques of experimental science* ○ *the use of experimental animals* ○ *We have experimental and observational evidence concerning things which happened before and after the origin of life.*

ex|pert /ˈekspɜːt/ **(experts)**   `ACADEMIC WORD`

NOUN An **expert** is a person who is very skilled at doing something or who knows a lot about a particular subject. ○ *Health experts warn that the issue is a global problem.* ○ [+ on] *an expert on trade in that area*

▶ **COLLOCATIONS:**
an expert **in/on** *something*
a **leading/acknowledged** expert
a **legal/medical/health/security** expert
experts **warn/predict/say**

▶ **SYNONYM:** specialist

ex|plain /ɪkˈspleɪn/ (explains, explaining, explained)

1 VERB If you **explain** something, you give details about it or describe it so that it can be understood. ○ *Not every judge, however, has the ability to explain the law in simple terms.* ○ [+ how] *Professor Griffiths explained how the drug appears to work.*

2 VERB If you **explain** something that has happened, you give people reasons for it, especially in an attempt to justify it. ○ [+ why] *Explain why you didn't telephone.* ○ [+ that] *The receptionist apologized for the delay, explaining that it had been a hectic day.*

▶ **COLLOCATIONS:**
    explain the **meaning/significance** of *something*
    explain the **circumstances/situation/reason**
    explain the **difference**
    explain a **phenomenon/concept**
▶ **SYNONYMS:** describe, account for
→ see note at **describe**

ex|pla|na|tion /ˌekspləˈneɪʃən/ (explanations)

NOUN ○ [+of] *The researchers offer two possible explanations of this.* ○ [+ for] *an explanation for the different results*

▶ **COLLOCATIONS:**
    an explanation **of/for** *something*
    give/provide/offer an explanation
    a **plausible/satisfactory** explanation
▶ **SYNONYMS:** reason, description

---

ex|plore /ɪkˈsplɔː/ (explores, exploring, explored)

VERB If you **explore** a place, you travel around it to find out what it is like. ○ *After exploring the old part of town there is a guided tour of the cathedral.* ○ *NASA has launched a spacecraft to explore the planet Mars.*

ex|plo|ra|tion /ˌekspləˈreɪʃən/ (explorations)

NOUN ○ [+ of] *We devote several days to the exploration of the magnificent Maya sites of Copan.*

▶ **COLLOCATIONS:**
    the exploration **of** *somewhere*
    space/polar/undersea exploration

---

ex|tinct /ɪkˈstɪŋkt/

SCIENCE BIOLOGY

ADJECTIVE A species of animal or plant that is **extinct** no longer has any living members, either in the world or in a particular place. ○ *It is 250 years since the wolf became extinct in Britain.* ○ *the bones of extinct animals*

▸ **COLLOCATIONS:**
become extinct
an extinct **species/bird/animal**
▸ **RELATED WORD:** endangered

ex|tinc|tion /ɪkˈstɪŋkʃən/

UNCOUNTABLE NOUN The **extinction** of a species of animal or plant is the death of all its remaining living members. ○ *An operation is beginning to try to save a species of crocodile from extinction.* ○ *Many species have been shot to the verge of extinction.*

▸ **COLLOCATIONS:**
near/close to extinction
the extinction **of** *something*
face extinction
save *something* from extinction
on the **edge/verge/brink** of extinction
▸ **PHRASE:** in danger of extinction

ex|treme /ɪkˈstriːm/

ADJECTIVE Extreme means very great in degree or intensity. ○ *people living in extreme poverty* ○ *the author's extreme reluctance to generalise*

▸ **COLLOCATIONS:**
extreme **poverty/danger/difficulty**
extreme **heat/cold/caution**
▸ **SYNONYM:** great

ex|treme|ly /ɪkˈstriːmli/

ADVERB You use **extremely** in front of adjectives and adverbs to emphasize that the specified quality is present to a very great degree. ○ *These headaches are extremely common.* ○ *Three of them are working extremely well.*

▸ **COLLOCATIONS:**
extremely **difficult/dangerous/important/rare/common**
extremely **useful/helpful/popular/well**
▸ **SYNONYMS:** exceedingly, highly, greatly, very
▸ **ANTONYM:** moderately

Ff

---

face /feɪs/ (faces, facing, faced)

VERB If you **face** something, or **are faced with** something difficult or unpleasant, you have to deal with it. ○ *Williams faces life in prison if convicted of murder.* ○ *[+ with] We are faced with a serious problem.*

▶ COLLOCATIONS:
be faced **with** *something*
face a **challenge/problem/crisis/threat**
face a **fine/trial/sentence**
face **opposition/criticism/competition**

---

fa|cil|ities /fəˈsɪlɪtiz/ ACADEMIC WORD

PLURAL NOUN Facilities are buildings, pieces of equipment, or services that are provided for a particular purpose. ○ *British engineers were disadvantaged by inadequate research facilities.* ○ *Hotel guests can use the leisure facilities free of charge.*

▶ COLLOCATIONS:
sports/leisure/recreational facilities
training/research/conference facilities
medical/health facilities
modern/state-of-the-art facilities
provide/offer/use facilities
improve/upgrade facilities

▶ SYNONYM: amenities

---

fact /fækt/ (facts)

1 NOUN When you refer to something as a **fact** or as **fact**, you mean that you think it is true or correct. ○ *It is a simple scientific fact; humans need food.* ○ *a statement of verifiable historical fact* ○ *He found it difficult to distinguish between fact and fiction.*

2 NOUN Facts are pieces of information that can be discovered. ○ *The aim of the study was to gather basic facts about the performance of the health service.* ○ *His opponent swamped him with facts and figures.*

▶ COLLOCATIONS:
the **basic/bare** facts
a **simple/plain** fact

historical/scientific fact
a **well-known/interesting/fascinating** fact
establish/consider/ignore/hide a fact
a fact **sheet/file**

▶ **PHRASES:**
fact and fiction
facts and figures

▶ **SYNONYMS:** truth, detail, information
▶ **ANTONYM:** fiction

fac|tual /ˈfæktʃʊəl/

ADJECTIVE Something that is **factual** is concerned with facts or contains facts, rather than giving theories or personal opinions. ○ *The editorial contained several factual errors.* ○ *a source of factual information*

▶ **COLLOCATIONS:**
factual **information/evidence**
a factual **account/report/error/inaccuracy**

fac|tu|al|ly

ADVERB ○ *I learned that a number of statements in my talk were factually wrong.* ○ *She told me coolly and factually the story of her life in prison.*

▶ **COLLOCATION:** factually **inaccurate/incorrect/wrong**

---

fac|tor /ˈfæktə/ (factors)   `ACADEMIC WORD`

NOUN A **factor** is one of the things that affects an event, decision, or situation. ○ [+ in] *Physical activity is an important factor in maintaining fitness.* ○ *The relatively cheap price of food may be a contributing factor to the increasing number of overweight people.*

▶ **COLLOCATIONS:**
a factor **in** *something*
a **key/important/major/significant** factor
a **deciding/determining/underlying** factor
a **contributing/complicating** factor
environmental/economic/genetic factors

▶ **SYNONYMS:** element, point

---

fac|to|ry /ˈfæktri/ (factories)   `BUSINESS`

NOUN A **factory** is a large building where machines are used to make large quantities of goods. ○ *He owned furniture factories in New York State.*

▶ **COLLOCATIONS:**
a factory **makes/produces** *something*
a factory **opens/closes**
a **car/chemical/weapons** factory

a factory **worker/owner**
factory **jobs**
▶ SYNONYM: plant

---

fail /feɪl/ (fails, failing, failed)

1 **VERB** If you **fail** to do something that you were trying to do, you do not succeed in doing it. ○ [+ to-inf] *He narrowly failed to qualify.* ○ [+ in] *He failed in his attempt to take control of the company.*

2 **VERB** If an activity, attempt, or plan **fails**, it is not successful. ○ *We tried to develop plans for them to get along, which all failed miserably.* ○ *He was afraid the revolution they had started would fail.* ○ *After a failed military offensive, all government troops and police were withdrawn from the island.*

3 **VERB** If someone or something **fails** to do a particular thing that they should have done, they do not do it. [FORMAL] ○ [+ to-inf] *Some schools fail to set any homework.* ○ [+ to-inf] *The bomb failed to explode.*
▶ COLLOCATIONS:
fail **in** *something*
fail in a **bid/attempt**
narrowly/completely/consistently/repeatedly fail
fail **miserably/dismally**
▶ ANTONYM: succeed

fail|ure /ˈfeɪljə/ (failures)

NOUN **Failure** is a lack of success in doing or achieving something.
○ *Three attempts on the British 200-metre record also ended in failure.*
○ *feelings of failure* ○ *The programme was a complete failure.*
▶ COLLOCATIONS:
a **complete/total** failure
dismal/abject/spectacular failure
▶ PHRASE: end in failure
▶ ANTONYM: success

---

fair /feə/ (fairer, fairest)

ADJECTIVE Something or someone that is **fair** is reasonable and right.
○ *It wasn't fair to blame him.* ○ *Independent observers say the campaign's been much fairer than expected.* ○ *An appeals court had ruled that they could not get a fair trial in Los Angeles.*
▶ COLLOCATIONS:
a fair **trial/election/hearing**
a fair **price/deal/system/society**
fair **treatment**
▶ SYNONYMS: just, reasonable
▶ ANTONYM: unfair

fair|ly /ˈfeəli/

ADVERB ○ *We aim to solve problems quickly and fairly.* ○ *In a society where water was precious, it had to be shared fairly between individuals.*
▶ **COLLOCATION: treat** *someone* fairly
▶ **ANTONYM:** unfairly

fall /fɔːl/ (falls, falling, fell, fallen)

VERB If something **falls**, it becomes less in amount, value, or strength.
○ [+ by] *Output will fall by 6%.* ○ [+ to/from] *The unemployment rate fell to 6.2%.* ○ *Between July and August, oil product prices fell 0.2 per cent.* ○ [V-ing] *It was a time of falling living standards and emerging mass unemployment.*
→ see note at **decrease**
▶ **COLLOCATIONS:**
  fall **by/to/from** x
  fall **sharply/dramatically/slightly**
  a **level/standard/price/rate** falls
▶ **SYNONYMS:** drop, decrease
▶ **ANTONYMS:** rise, increase

● **Fall** is also a noun. ○ [+ in] *There was a sharp fall in the value of the pound.* ○ [+ of] *October figures show a fall of 11.1%.*
▶ **COLLOCATIONS:**
  a fall **in** *something*
  a fall **of** x
  a **sharp/dramatic/steep/sudden** fall
  a **slight** fall
  show/report/predict/expect a fall
▶ **SYNONYMS:** drop, decrease
▶ **ANTONYMS:** rise, increase

fic|tion /ˈfɪkʃən/   `LITERATURE`

UNCOUNTABLE NOUN Fiction refers to books and stories about imaginary people and events, rather than books about real people or events.
○ *Immigrant tales have always been popular themes in fiction.* ○ *Diana is a writer of historical fiction.*
▶ **COLLOCATIONS:**
  write/read fiction
  historical/romantic/crime fiction
  a fiction **book/novel/writer**
▶ **SYNONYMS:** novels, literature
▶ **ANTONYM:** non-fiction

fig|ure /ˈfɪgə, AM -gjər/ (figures) `MATHS`

1 **NOUN** A **figure** is a particular amount expressed as a number, especially a statistic. ○ *Norway is a peaceful place with low crime figures.* ○ *Government figures show that one in three marriages end in divorce.*

▶ **COLLOCATIONS:**
figures **show/reveal/suggest/indicate** *something*
publish/release figures
official/government/crime/unemployment figures
trade/profit/inflation figures
the latest figures
▶ **PHRASE:** facts and figures
▶ **SYNONYM:** statistic

2 **NOUN** A **figure** is any of the ten written symbols from 0 to 9 that are used to represent a number. ○ *In business writing, all numbers over ten are usually written as figures.*

▶ **COLLOCATIONS:**
in/as figures
in single/double figures
▶ **SYNONYMS:** digit, number

file /faɪl/ (files) `ACADEMIC WORD` `IT`

NOUN In computing, a **file** is a set of related data that has its own name. ○ *Now that you have loaded WordPerfect, it's easy to create a file.*

▶ **COLLOCATIONS:**
a **computer/digital** file
a **video/music/audio/image/text** file
a **zip/MP3/PDF** file
create/open/delete a file
send/share/store/retrieve a file
file **format/size/sharing**
▶ **RELATED WORD:** folder

fi|nal /ˈfaɪnəl/ `ACADEMIC WORD`

ADJECTIVE In a series of events, things, or people, the **final** one is the last one. ○ *This was the final stage in the process.* ○ *The third and final day of the conference was different.*

▶ **COLLOCATIONS:**
the final **round/stage/phase/session**
the final **attempt**
the final **day/year/minute**

▸ **PHRASE:** the third/fifth etc. and final ...
▸ **SYNONYM:** last
▸ **ANTONYM:** first

fi|nal|ly /ˈfaɪnəli/

1 ADVERB You use **finally** to indicate that something is last in a series of actions or events. ○ *The action slips from comedy to melodrama and finally to tragedy.*
▸ **SYNONYM:** lastly
▸ **ANTONYM:** firstly

2 ADVERB You use **finally** in speech or writing to introduce a final point, question, or topic. ○ *Finally, and perhaps most importantly, Project Challenge has raised awareness of the issue.*
▸ **SYNONYMS:** in conclusion, lastly
▸ **ANTONYM:** firstly

---

fi|nance /ˈfaɪnæns, fɪˈnæns/ `ACADEMIC WORD` `BUSINESS` `ECONOMICS`

UNCOUNTABLE NOUN Finance is the management of money. ○ *the principles of corporate finance* ○ *We looked at three common problems in international finance.* ○ *A former Finance Minister and five senior civil servants are accused of fraud.*
▸ **COLLOCATIONS:**
   corporate/personal/public/international finance
   a finance **minister/director/committee/department**
▸ **PHRASES:**
   banking and finance
   finance and economics

fi|nan|cial /faɪˈnænʃəl, fɪ-/

ADJECTIVE Financial means relating to or involving money. ○ *The company is in financial difficulties.* ○ *There has been an improvement in the company's financial position.* ○ *the government's financial advisers*
▸ **COLLOCATIONS:**
   a financial **crisis**
   financial **difficulties/problems**
   financial **help/aid/assistance/performance**
   a financial **institution/adviser/officer**
   someone's financial **position**
▸ **SYNONYMS:** monetary, economic

USAGE: financial or **economic**?

You use **financial** to describe things involving the money that a person or an organization has or earns. It also describes organizations that work with money, such as banks. ○ *You should seek independent financial advice.*

You use **economic** to describe things involving the whole economy of a country; the money, business, political policies, etc. ○ *policies to promote economic growth*

---

find /faɪnd/ (finds, finding, found)

VERB If you **find** something, you get information or conclusions based on the results of research or an investigation. ○ [+ *that*] *Scientists found that both groups of birds survived equally well.* ○ *The study found no link between the age of a mother and the risks of cancer in her children.*

▶ COLLOCATIONS:
   a **study/survey/investigation** finds *something*
   research finds *something*
   researchers/investigators/scientists find *something*
▶ SYNONYM: discover

find|ing /ˈfaɪndɪŋ/ (findings)

NOUN Someone's **findings** are the information they get or the conclusions they come to as the result of an investigation or some research. ○ *These findings suggest that as children grow older, socio-cultural factors become more significant.* ○ *We hope that manufacturers will take note of the findings and improve their products accordingly.*

▶ COLLOCATIONS:
   findings **show/suggest/indicate** *something*
   findings **support/confirm** *something*
   publish/report/release findings
   new/recent/the latest findings
   early/initial/preliminary findings
   research/survey findings
▶ SYNONYM: results

---

fine /faɪn/ (fines, fining, fined)   LAW

1 NOUN A **fine** is a punishment in which a person is ordered to pay money because they have done something illegal. ○ [+ *of*] *You can face a fine of up to £2000 for being drunk on an aircraft.* ○ *Police can impose heavy fines or tow away vehicles parked illegally.*

► COLLOCATIONS:
  a fine **for** something
  a fine **of** £x
  face/impose/pay a fine
  a **hefty/heavy/big/on-the-spot** fine
  the **maximum** fine
  a **parking** fine
► SYNONYM: penalty

2 VERB If someone **is fined**, they are punished by being ordered to pay money because they have done something illegal. ○ *She was fined £300 and banned from driving for one month.* ○ *An east London school has set a precedent by fining pupils who break the rules.*
► COLLOCATIONS:
  fine *someone* **£60/£1000**
  fine *someone* **for** *something*
  be **heavily** fined

---

firm /fɜːm/ (firms)   BUSINESS

NOUN A **firm** is an organization which sells or produces something or which provides a service which people pay for. ○ *The firm's employees were expecting large bonuses.* ○ [+ of] *a firm of heating engineers*
► COLLOCATIONS:
  a firm **of** *something*
  a **small/large** firm
  a **law/consulting/accountancy** firm
  a **research/security/computer/software** firm
► SYNONYM: company

---

fit /fɪt/ (fitter, fittest)   MEDICINE

ADJECTIVE Someone who is **fit** is healthy and physically strong. ○ *Firefighters need to be physically fit.* ○ *The players are getting fitter all the time.*
► COLLOCATIONS:
  physically/fully/reasonably fit
  be/get fit
► PHRASE: fit and healthy
► ANTONYM: unfit

fit|ness

UNCOUNTABLE NOUN ○ *Walking lowers blood pressure and improves fitness.* ○ *Swimming is suitable for people of all ages and fitness levels.*

► COLLOCATIONS:
improve/regain fitness
physical/general/full fitness
someone's fitness **level**
a fitness **centre/club/programme/test**
a fitness **instructor/trainer**

---

flood /flʌd/ (floods)   GEOGRAPHY

NOUN If there is a **flood**, a large amount of water covers an area which is usually dry, for example when a river flows over its banks or a pipe bursts.
○ More than 70 people were killed in the floods, caused when a dam burst.
○ Floods hit Bihar state, killing 250 people.
► COLLOCATIONS:
a **bad/devastating/flash** flood
a flood **hits/sweeps** somewhere

---

flu|ent /ˈfluːənt/   LANGUAGE

ADJECTIVE Someone who is **fluent in** a particular language can speak the language easily and correctly. You can also say that someone speaks **fluent** French, Chinese, or some other language. ○ [+ in] She studied eight foreign languages but is fluent in only six of them. ○ He speaks fluent Russian.
► COLLOCATIONS:
fluent **in** something
fluent **English/Japanese/German**
a fluent **speaker** of something

flu|ent|ly

ADVERB ○ He spoke three languages fluently.
► COLLOCATION: **speak** fluently

flu|en|cy

UNCOUNTABLE NOUN ○ [+ in] To work as a translator, you need fluency in at least one foreign language.
► COLLOCATION: fluency **in** something

---

fol|low|ing /ˈfɒləʊɪŋ/

1 PREPOSITION Following a particular event means after that event.
○ In the centuries following Christ's death, Christians genuinely believed the world was about to end. ○ Following a day of medical research, the conference focused on educational practices.
► SYNONYM: after

2 **ADJECTIVE** The **following** day, week, or year is the day, week, or year after the one you have just mentioned. ○ *He had a speech to make the following day.* ○ *The following year she joined the Royal Opera House.*

▶ **SYNONYM:** next

▶ **ANTONYM:** previous

foot /fʊt/ **(feet)**

NOUN A **foot** is a unit for measuring length, height, or depth, and is equal to 12 inches or 30.48 centimetres. When you are giving measurements, the form 'foot' is often used as the plural instead of the plural form 'feet' The abbreviation **ft** is used in written notes. ○ *a shopping and leisure complex of one million square feet* ○ *He was about six foot tall.*

▶ **COLLOCATIONS:**
   x foot **tall/long**
   a **square** foot

▶ **RELATED WORDS:** inch, yard

for|bid /fəˈbɪd/ **(forbids, forbidding, forbade, forbidden)**

VERB If you **forbid** someone **to** do something, or if you **forbid** an activity, you say that it must not be done. ○ [+ to-inf] *The slaves were forbidden to practise their religion.* ○ *Brazil's constitution forbids the military use of nuclear energy.*

▶ **COLLOCATION:** a **law/rule/constitution** forbids *something*

▶ **PHRASE:** forbid the use of something

▶ **SYNONYM:** ban

▶ **ANTONYMS:** permit, allow

for|bid|den /fəˈbɪdən/

ADJECTIVE If something is **forbidden**, you are not allowed to do it or have it. ○ *Smoking was forbidden everywhere.* ○ [+ to-inf] *It is forbidden to drive faster than 20mph.*

▶ **COLLOCATION:** **strictly/expressly** forbidden

force /fɔːs/ **(forces, forcing, forced)**

1 **VERB** If a person, situation, or event **forces** you **to** do something, they make you do it even though you do not want to. ○ [+ to-inf] *He was forced to resign by Russia's conservative parliament.* ○ [+ to-inf] *A back injury forced her to withdraw from the competition.* ○ *They were grabbed by three men who appeared to force them into a car.*

2 **UNCOUNTABLE NOUN** If someone uses **force** to do something, or if it is done by **force**, strong and violent physical action is taken in order to achieve it. ○ [+ to-inf] *The government decided against using force to break-up the demonstrations.* ○ *the guerrillas' efforts to seize power by force*

▶ COLLOCATIONS:
by force
brute/excessive/physical force
use force

---

fore|cast /ˈfɔːkɑːst, -kæst/ **(forecasts, forecasting, forecasted)**

> The forms **forecast** and **forecasted** can both be used for the past tense and past participle.

1 NOUN A **forecast** is a statement of what is expected to happen in the future, especially in relation to a particular event or situation. ○ [+ of] *a forecast of a 2.25 per cent growth in the economy* ○ *He gave his election forecast.* ○ *The weather forecast is better for today.*

▶ COLLOCATIONS:
a forecast **of** something
make/give/revise a forecast
a **growth/economic/earnings/profit** forecast
a **weather/gloomy/optimistic** forecast
▶ SYNONYM: prediction

2 VERB If you **forecast** future events, you say what you think is going to happen in the future. ○ *They forecast a humiliating defeat for the Prime Minister.* ○ [+ that] *He forecasts that average salary increases will remain around 4 per cent.*

▶ COLLOCATIONS:
forecast the **weather**
forecast an **increase**
forecast **growth**
▶ SYNONYM: predict

fore|cast|er /ˈfɔːkɑːstə, -kæst-/ **(forecasters)**

NOUN A **forecaster** is someone who uses detailed knowledge about a particular activity in order to work out what they think will happen in that activity in the future. ○ *Some of the nation's top economic forecasters say the economic recovery is picking up speed.*

▶ COLLOCATIONS:
a **weather/economic** forecaster
a forecaster **says/predicts/warns**

for|eign /ˈfɒrɪn, AM ˈfɔːr-/

1 **ADJECTIVE** Something or someone that is **foreign** comes from or relates to a country that is not your own. ○ *This was his first experience in a foreign country.* ○ *a foreign language* ○ *It is the largest ever foreign investment in the Bolivian mining sector.*

▶ **COLLOCATIONS:**
  a foreign **country/language/currency/holiday**
  foreign **workers/students**
▶ **SYNONYMS:** overseas, international
▶ **ANTONYM:** local

2 **ADJECTIVE** In politics and journalism, **foreign** is used to describe people, jobs, and activities relating to countries that are not the country of the person or government concerned. ○ *the German foreign minister* ○ *the foreign correspondent in Washington of La Tribuna newspaper of Honduras* ○ *the effects of U.S. foreign policy*

▶ **COLLOCATIONS:**
  foreign **policy/aid/debt**
  the foreign **minister/secretary**
  a foreign **correspondent**
▶ **SYNONYMS:** overseas, international
▶ **ANTONYMS:** home, domestic

for|est /ˈfɒrɪst, AM ˈfɔːr-/ **(forests)** `GEOGRAPHY`

NOUN A **forest** is a large area where trees grow close together. ○ *Parts of the forest are still dense and inaccessible.* ○ *25 million hectares of forest*

▶ **COLLOCATIONS:**
  in a forest
  dense/thick forest
  a **tropical/rain** forest
  a forest **fire**

form /fɔːm/ **(forms)**

1 **NOUN** A **form of** something is a type or kind of it. ○ [+ *of*] *He contracted a rare form of cancer.* ○ *I am against hunting in any form.* ○ *In its present form, the law could lead to new injustices.*

▶ **COLLOCATION:** a form **of** something
▶ **SYNONYMS:** type, kind, sort

2 **NOUN** The **form** of something is its shape. ○ *the form of the body*

▶ **SYNONYM:** shape

for|mal /ˈfɔːməl/

1 **ADJECTIVE** **Formal** speech or behaviour is very correct and serious rather than relaxed and friendly, and is used especially in official situations.
○ He wrote a very formal letter of apology to Douglas. ○ Business relationships are necessarily a bit more formal.

2 **ADJECTIVE** A **formal** action, statement, or request is an official one.
○ U.N. officials said a formal request was passed to American authorities.
○ No formal announcement had been made.

▶ **COLLOCATIONS:**
a formal **investigation**
a formal **announcement/statement/agreement**
a formal **offer/request/proposal/complaint**
formal **talks/negotiations**
▶ **SYNONYM:** official
▶ **ANTONYMS:** informal, unofficial

for|mal|ly

ADVERB ○ He spoke formally and politely. ○ Diplomats haven't formally agreed to Anderson's plan.

▶ **COLLOCATIONS:**
formally **announce/declare/launch** something
formally **charge** someone
formally **accept/agree/approve**
▶ **SYNONYM:** officially
▶ **ANTONYMS:** informally, unofficially

for|mal|ity /fɔːˈmælɪti/

UNCOUNTABLE NOUN ○ Lillith's formality and seriousness amused him.
▶ **ANTONYM:** informality

for|mer /ˈfɔːmə/

1 **ADJECTIVE** **Former** is used to describe what someone or something used to be in the past. ○ He pleaded not guilty to murdering his former wife.
○ the former Soviet Union ○ the former home of Sir Christopher Wren

▶ **COLLOCATIONS:**
a former **president**
someone's former **husband/wife/boyfriend/girlfriend**
someone's former **career/home**
▶ **SYNONYM:** ex-
▶ **RELATED WORD:** current

2 **ADJECTIVE** **Former** is used to describe a situation or period of time which came before the present one. [FORMAL] ○ He would want you to remember him as he was in former years.

▶ **PHRASE:** in former times
▶ **SYNONYM:** previous

for|mer|ly /ˈfɔːməli/

ADVERB If something happened or was true **formerly**, it happened or was true in the past. ○ *He had formerly been in the Navy.* ○ *east Germany's formerly state-controlled companies*

for|tu|nate /ˈfɔːtʃʊnɪt/

ADJECTIVE If you say that someone or something is **fortunate**, you mean that they are lucky. ○ [+ to-inf] *He was extremely fortunate to survive.* ○ [+ that] *It was fortunate that the water was shallow.* ○ *She is in the fortunate position of having plenty of choice.*
▶ **SYNONYM:** lucky
▶ **ANTONYMS:** unfortunate, unlucky

for|tu|nate|ly /ˈfɔːtʃʊnɪtli/

ADVERB **Fortunately** is used to introduce or indicate a statement about an event or situation that is good. ○ *Fortunately, the weather that winter was reasonably mild.* ○ *Bombs hit the building but fortunately no one was hurt.*
▶ **SYNONYM:** luckily
▶ **ANTONYM:** unfortunately

frac|tion /ˈfrækʃən/ (fractions)   MATHS

1 NOUN A **fraction of** something is a tiny amount or proportion of it.
○ [+ of] *She hesitated for a fraction of a second before responding.* ○ *The statistics reflect only a tiny fraction of the problem.*
▶ **COLLOCATIONS:**
  a fraction **of** something
  a **small/tiny** fraction
▶ **SYNONYMS:** part, proportion

2 NOUN A **fraction** is a number that can be expressed as a proportion of two whole numbers. For example, ½ and ⅓ are both fractions. ○ *The students had a grasp of decimals, percentages and fractions.*
▶ **RELATED WORD:** decimal

frag|ile /ˈfrædʒaɪl, AM -dʒəl/

1 ADJECTIVE If you describe a situation as **fragile**, you mean that it is weak or uncertain, and unlikely to be able to resist strong pressure or attack.
○ *The fragile economies of several countries could be irreparably damaged.*
○ *The Prime Minister's fragile government was on the brink of collapse.*

▶ **COLLOCATIONS:**
a fragile **economy/government**
a fragile **peace/truce/state/recovery**
▶ **SYNONYMS:** unstable, weak
▶ **ANTONYMS:** strong, stable

2 ADJECTIVE Something that is **fragile** is easily broken or damaged.
○ *He leaned back in his fragile chair.*
▶ **SYNONYM:** weak
▶ **ANTONYMS:** sturdy, strong

---

free|dom /ˈfriːdəm/

UNCOUNTABLE NOUN Freedom is the state of being allowed to do what you want to do. ○ *freedom of speech* ○ *They want greater political freedom.*
○ *Today we have the freedom to decide our own futures.*
▶ **COLLOCATIONS:**
have/enjoy freedom
political/religious/greater freedom
individual/personal/press/media freedom
▶ **PHRASES:**
freedom of speech/expression
freedom of choice
▶ **SYNONYM:** liberty
▶ **ANTONYM:** restriction

---

freeze /friːz/ (freezes, freezing, froze, frozen) `SCIENCE`

VERB If a liquid or a substance containing a liquid **freezes**, or if something **freezes** it, it becomes solid because of low temperatures.
○ *If the temperature drops below 0°C, water freezes.* ○ *The ground froze solid.*
○ *the discovery of how to freeze water at higher temperatures*
▶ **RELATED WORDS:** melt, thaw, boil

---

fre|quent /ˈfriːkwənt/

ADJECTIVE If something is **frequent**, it happens often. ○ *Bordeaux is on the main Paris-Madrid line so there are frequent trains.* ○ *He is a frequent visitor to the house.*
▶ **COLLOCATIONS:**
a frequent **visitor/visit**
a frequent **occurrence**
▶ **SYNONYM:** regular
▶ **ANTONYMS:** infrequent, rare

fre|quent|ly

ADVERB ○ *Iron and folic acid supplements are frequently given to pregnant women.* ○ *the most frequently asked question*

▶ **SYNONYMS:** often, regularly
▶ **ANTONYMS:** infrequently, rarely

fre|quen|cy /ˈfriːkwənsi/

UNCOUNTABLE NOUN The **frequency** of an event is the number of times it happens during a particular period. ○ [+ *of*] *The frequency of Kara's phone calls increased rapidly.* ○ *The tanks broke down with increasing frequency.*

▶ **COLLOCATIONS:**
   the frequency **of** *something*
   great/increasing/alarming/relative frequency

---

fuel /ˈfjuːəl/ (fuels)   SCIENCE

NOUN **Fuel** is a substance such as coal, oil, or petrol that is burned to provide heat or power. ○ *They ran out of fuel.* ○ *industrial research into cleaner fuels* ○ *The country needs to cut its fuel consumption.*

▶ **COLLOCATIONS:**
   use/burn/produce fuel
   fossil/nuclear fuel
   alternative/clean/renewable fuel
   fuel **prices/costs/consumption/efficiency**

---

full-time /ˌfʊlˈtaɪm/ also **full time**   BUSINESS

ADJECTIVE **Full-time** work or study involves working or studying for the whole of each normal working week rather than for part of it. ○ *I have a full-time job.* ○ *full-time staff*

▶ **COLLOCATIONS:**
   a full-time **job/position/student/course**
   full-time **work/employment/education**
   full-time **employees/staff/workers**
▶ **ANTONYM:** part-time

● **Full-time** is also an adverb. ○ *Deirdre works full-time.*
▶ **COLLOCATION:** **work/study** full-time
▶ **ANTONYM:** part-time

---

fur|ther /ˈfɜːðə/

1 ADVERB **Further** means to a greater extent or degree. ○ *Inflation is below 5% and set to fall further.* ○ *The rebellion is expected to further damage the country's image.*

2 ADVERB If you go or get **further with** something, or take something **further**, you make some progress. ○ *They lacked the scientific personnel to develop the equipment much further.*

3 ADJECTIVE A **further** thing, number of things, or amount of something is an additional thing, number of things, or amount. ○ *His speech provides further evidence of his increasingly authoritarian approach.* ○ *They believed there were likely to be further attacks.*

▶ SYNONYM: more

---

fu|ture /ˈfjuːtʃə/ (futures)

1 NOUN The future is the period of time that will come after the present, or the things that will happen then. ○ *The spokesman said no decision on the proposal was likely in the immediate future.* ○ *He was making plans for the future.*

▶ COLLOCATIONS:
   in/for the future
   the **near/foreseeable/immediate/not-too-distant** future
   the **long-term** future

▶ RELATED WORDS: the past, the present

2 ADJECTIVE Future things will happen or exist after the present time. ○ *She said if the world did not act conclusively now, it would only bequeath the problem to future generations.* ○ *Meanwhile, the domestic debate on Denmark's future role in Europe rages on.* ○ *the future King and Queen*

▶ COLLOCATIONS:
   future **generations/plans/prospects**
   future **growth/development/success**
   a future **role**

▶ PHRASES:
   in future years
   at a future date

▶ RELATED WORDS: past, present, current

Gg

---

gal|lery /ˈɡæləri/ (galleries)

NOUN A **gallery** is a place that has permanent exhibitions of works of art in it. ○ *an art gallery* ○ *Check with staff before using a camera in museums or art galleries.* ○ *the National Gallery*

▶ **COLLOCATIONS:**
gallery **space**
a gallery **curator/owner/director/visitor**
a gallery **exhibition/installation**
a **modern-art/art** gallery

---

gal|lon /ˈɡælən/ (gallons)

NOUN A **gallon** is a unit of measurement for liquids that is equal to eight pints. In Britain, it is equal to 4.564 litres. In America, it is equal to 3.785 litres. ○ [+ *of*] *80 million gallons of water a day* ○ *thousands of gallons of fuel*

▶ **COLLOCATION:** a gallon **of** *something*

---

gap /ɡæp/ (gaps)

NOUN A **gap** is a big difference between two things, people, or ideas. ○ *America's trade gap widened.* ○ [+ *between*] *the gap between rich and poor* ○ *The overall pay gap between men and women narrowed slightly.*

▶ **COLLOCATIONS:**
a gap **between** *things*
a **huge/widening** gap
a **gender/generation/pay/age** gap
a gap **widens/narrows/exists/remains**
bridge/close/narrow/reduce the gap

▶ **SYNONYM:** difference

---

gas /ɡæs/ (gases)

1 UNCOUNTABLE NOUN Gas is a substance like air that is neither liquid nor solid and burns easily. It is used as a fuel for cooking and heating. ○ *Coal is actually cheaper than gas.* ○ *Shell signed a contract to develop oil and gas reserves near Archangel.*

▶ COLLOCATIONS:
natural gas
gas **reserves/supply/pipeline**
gas **prices**

2 NOUN A **gas** is any substance that is neither liquid nor solid, for example oxygen or hydrogen. ○ *Helium is a very light gas.* ○ *a huge cloud of gas and dust from the volcanic eruption*

▶ COLLOCATIONS:
a **flammable/non-flammable** gas
hydrogen/chlorine/nitrogen gas
an **atmospheric/inert** gas

---

gen|er|al /ˈdʒenrəl/

1 ADJECTIVE If you talk about the **general** situation somewhere or talk about something in **general** terms, you are describing the situation as a whole rather than considering its details or exceptions. ○ *The figures represent a general decline in employment.* ○ *the general deterioration of English society* ○ *Newton explained his theory in general terms.*

▶ COLLOCATIONS:
a general **decline/improvement/trend**
the general **nature/state/idea/impression** of *something*
a general **description/account/conversation/attitude**
▶ PHRASE: in general terms

2 ADJECTIVE You use **general** to describe something that involves or affects most people, or most people in a particular group. ○ *There was a general feeling of satisfaction.* ○ *a general awareness of the problem*

▶ COLLOCATIONS:
a general **feeling/sense/awareness**
a general **consensus/agreement/observation**
general **advice**
▶ PHRASE: as a general rule
▶ SYNONYMS: common, widespread
▶ ANTONYM: specific

gen|er|al|ly /ˈdʒenrəli/

1 ADVERB You use **generally** to give a summary of a situation, activity, or idea without referring to the particular details of it. ○ *Teachers generally have admitted a lack of enthusiasm.* ○ *Generally speaking, standards have improved.* ○ *a generally positive economic outlook*

▶ COLLOCATIONS:
generally **positive/supportive/upbeat**
generally **unwell/weak/hostile**

▸ **PHRASE:** generally speaking
▸ **SYNONYM:** mainly

2 ADVERB You use **generally** to say that something happens or is used on most occasions but not on every occasion. ○ *As women we generally say and feel too much.* ○ *It is generally true that the darker the fruit the higher its iron content.* ○ *Blood pressure less than 120 over 80 is generally considered ideal.*
▸ **COLLOCATION:** generally **true/accepted/considered/regarded**
▸ **SYNONYMS:** usually, normally, mostly, commonly

---

gen|era|tion /ˌdʒenəˈreɪʃən/ (generations) ACADEMIC WORD

NOUN A **generation** is all the people in a group or country who are of a similar age. ○ *the problems of previous generations* ○ *David Mamet has long been considered the leading American playwright of his generation.* ○ *[+ of] future generations of schoolchildren*
▸ **COLLOCATIONS:**
  a generation **of** *something*
  the **younger/older** generation
  the **current/previous/next/new/future** generation
  our **parent's/grandparent's** generation

---

ge|og|ra|phy /dʒiˈɒɡrəfi/ GEOGRAPHY

UNCOUNTABLE NOUN **Geography** is the study of the countries of the world and of such things as the land, seas, climate, towns, and population. ○ *She studied geography at Cambridge University.* ○ *He teaches geography and history.*
▸ **COLLOCATIONS:**
  a geography **class/lesson/textbook**
  a geography **teacher/professor/lecturer**

geo|graphi|cal /ˌdʒiːəˈɡræfɪkəl/

> The form **geographic** /ˌdʒiːəˈɡræfɪk/ is also used.

ADJECTIVE **Geographical** or **geographic** means concerned with or relating to geography. ○ *Its geographical location stimulated overseas trade.* ○ *a vast geographical area*
▸ **COLLOCATION:** a geographical **location/area/region/boundary**

geo|graphi|cal|ly /ˌdʒiːəˈɡræfɪkli/

ADVERB ○ *It is geographically more diverse than any other continent.*
▸ **COLLOCATIONS:**
  geographically **diverse/widespread**
  geographically **remote/isolated**

ge|og|ra|pher /dʒiˈɒɡrəfə/ (geographers)

NOUN A **geographer** is a person who studies geography or is an expert in it.
▶ **COLLOCATIONS:**
geographers **study/recognize/note** something
a **human/physical/historical** geographer

glob|al warm|ing /ˌɡləʊbəl ˈwɔːmɪŋ/ [SCIENCE]

UNCOUNTABLE NOUN Global warming is the gradual rise in the earth's temperature caused by high levels of carbon dioxide and other gases in the atmosphere. ○ *the impact of global warming* ○ *It may be too late to reverse the effects of global warming.*
▶ **SYNONYMS:** greenhouse effect, climate change

gov|ern|ment /ˈɡʌvənmənt/ [SOCIAL SCIENCE] [POLITICS]
(governments)

NOUN The **government** of a country is the group of people who are responsible for governing it. ○ *The Government has insisted that confidence is needed before the economy can improve.* ○ *[+ of] the governments of 12 European countries* ○ *the government's foreign policy*
▶ **COLLOCATIONS:**
the government **of** a country
the **federal/interim/new** government
a **minority/coalition/power-sharing** government
the **British/Chinese/Canadian** government
a government **official/minister/department/policy**

grad|ual /ˈɡrædʒʊəl/

ADJECTIVE A **gradual** change or process occurs in small stages over a long period of time, rather than suddenly. ○ *Losing weight is a slow, gradual process.* ○ *You can expect her progress at school to be gradual rather than brilliant.*
▶ **COLLOCATION:** a gradual **process/decline/improvement/change**
▶ **SYNONYM:** slow
▶ **ANTONYM:** sudden

gradu|al|ly /ˈɡrædʒʊəli/

ADVERB ○ *The slope gradually decreased.* ○ *Start slowly and gradually increase the number of steps.* ○ *Gradually we learned to cope.*
▶ **COLLOCATIONS:**
gradually **increase/evolve/accumulate**
gradually **decrease/fade/diminish**
▶ **SYNONYMS:** slowly, gently, steadily
▶ **ANTONYMS:** suddenly, sharply

gradu|ate EDUCATION ACADEMIC STUDY
(graduates, graduating, graduated)

> The noun is pronounced /ˈɡrædʒuət/. The verb is pronounced /ˈɡrædʒueɪt/.

1 NOUN In Britain, a **graduate** is a person who has successfully completed a degree at a university or college and has received a certificate that shows this. ○ *In 1973, the first Open University graduates received their degrees.* ○ *[+ from] an Economics graduate from Leeds University*

2 NOUN In the United States, a **graduate** is a student who has successfully completed a course at a high school, college, or university. ○ *The top one-third of all high school graduates are entitled to an education at the California State University.*

▸ COLLOCATIONS:
a graduate **in** something
a graduate **from** somewhere
a **university/college/high-school/recent** graduate
a **science/engineering/sociology** graduate
a **Yale/Harvard/Cambridge** graduate

3 VERB In Britain, when a student **graduates** from university, they have successfully completed a degree course. ○ *[+ in] She graduated in English and Drama from Manchester University.*

4 VERB In the United States, when a student **graduates**, they complete their studies successfully and leave their school or university. You can also say that a school or university **graduates** a student or students. ○ *[+ from] When the boys graduated from high school, Ann moved to a small town in Vermont.* ○ *Last year American universities graduated a record number of students with degrees in computer science.*

▸ COLLOCATIONS:
graduate **in** science/engineering
graduate **from** university/Cambridge

gradua|tion /ˌɡrædʒuˈeɪʃən/

UNCOUNTABLE NOUN Graduation is the successful completion of a course of study at a university, college, or school, for which you receive a degree or diploma. ○ *They asked what his plans were after graduation.*

▸ COLLOCATIONS:
graduation **from** somewhere
a graduation **ceremony/requirement/day**

gram /græm/ (grams)

NOUN A **gram** is a unit of weight. One thousand grams are equal to one kilogram. The abbreviation **g** is used in written notes. [in BRIT, also use **gramme**] ○ *A football weighs about 400 grams.* ○ *[+ of] A single cinnamon roll contains 27 grams of fat.*

→ see note at **centimetre**

▶ **COLLOCATIONS:**
  a gram **of** something
  weigh/contain *x* grams

gram|mar /'græmə/ `LANGUAGE`

UNCOUNTABLE NOUN Grammar is the ways that words can be put together in order to make sentences. ○ *He doesn't have mastery of the basic rules of grammar.* ○ *the difference between Sanskrit and English grammar*

▶ **COLLOCATIONS:**
  grammar **rules**
  English/Latin/Greek/French grammar
  teach/revise/learn/study grammar

▶ **PHRASES:** grammar and spelling/punctuation/vocabulary/syntax

gram|mati|cal /grə'mætɪkəl/

ADJECTIVE Grammatical is used to indicate that something relates to grammar. ○ *Should the teacher present grammatical rules to students?* ○ *grammatical errors*

▶ **COLLOCATIONS:**
  a grammatical **structure/construction**
  a grammatical **error/mistake/correction**
  grammatical **accuracy/complexity/correctness**

graph /grɑːf, græf/ (graphs) `ACADEMIC STUDY`

NOUN A **graph** is a mathematical diagram which shows the relationship between two or more sets of numbers or measurements. ○ *The bar graph opposite shows this.* ○ *As the graph below illustrates, savings peaked at 15.8 percent in September 2008 and have been falling steadily ever since.*

▶ **COLLOCATIONS:**
  a graph **illustrates/shows/represents/indicates** something
  a **bar/line/column** graph
  draw/plot/construct/interpret a graph

green|house ef|fect /ˈgriːnhaʊs ɪfekt/ `SCIENCE`

NOUN The **greenhouse effect** is the problem caused by increased quantities of gases such as carbon dioxide in the air. These gases trap the heat from the sun, and cause a gradual rise in the temperature of the Earth's atmosphere. ○ *Carbon dioxide in the atmosphere is contributing to the greenhouse effect.* ○ *the fight against the greenhouse effect*

▶ COLLOCATIONS:
reduce/offset/slow down/increase the greenhouse effect
cause/contribute to the greenhouse effect

▶ SYNONYMS: global warming, climate change

green|house gas /ˈgriːnhaʊs ˌgæs/ **(greenhouse gases)** `SCIENCE`

NOUN **Greenhouse gases** are the gases which are responsible for causing the greenhouse effect. The main greenhouse gas is carbon dioxide. ○ *Methane is a powerful greenhouse gas.* ○ *carbon dioxide, water vapour and other greenhouse gases*

▶ COLLOCATIONS:
greenhouse gas **emissions**
a **level/source** of greenhouse gases
reduce/tackle/cut/regulate/limit/lower greenhouse gas emissions
produce/emit/release greenhouse gases

group /gruːp/ **(groups)**

NOUN A **group** is a set of people, organizations, or things which are considered together because they have something in common. ○ *She is among the most promising players in her age group.* ○ *As a group, today's old people are still relatively deprived.* ○ *the most vulnerable groups in society*

▶ COLLOCATIONS:
an **age/ethnic/social/peer/minority** group
a **blood** group

grow /grəʊ/ **(grows, growing, grew, grown)**

VERB If an amount, feeling, or problem **grows**, it becomes greater or more intense. ○ [+ by] *The number of unemployed people in Poland has grown by more than a quarter in the last month.* ○ [+ at] *Productivity grew at an annual rate of more than 3 percent.* ○ *Opposition grew and the government agreed to negotiate.* ○ [V-ing] *a growing number of immigrants*

▶ COLLOCATIONS:
grow **by/at** something
continue to grow

grow **longer/bigger/stronger**
grow **rapidly/quickly/steadily/slowly**
▸ SYNONYMS: increase, intensify, strengthen, heighten
▸ ANTONYMS: decrease, lessen, reduce, diminish

growth /grəʊθ/

1 UNCOUNTABLE NOUN The **growth of** something such as an industry, organization, or idea is its development in size, wealth, or importance. ○ [+ of] the growth of nationalism ○ Japan's enormous economic growth ○ high growth rates

2 UNCOUNTABLE NOUN A **growth** in something is an increase in it. ○ [+ in] A steady growth in the popularity of two smaller parties may upset the polls. ○ The area has seen a rapid population growth. ○ [+ of] The market has shown annual growth of 20 per cent for several years.

▸ COLLOCATIONS:
growth **of/in** something
economic/industrial/financial growth
population/sales growth
rapid/strong/steady/slow growth
annual/long-term/sustained/continued growth
▸ PHRASES:
rate of growth
period of growth
▸ SYNONYMS: increase, intensification
▸ ANTONYMS: decrease, reduction

guilty /ˈɡɪlti/ LAW

ADJECTIVE If someone is **guilty of** a crime or offence, they have committed that crime or offence. ○ [+ of] They were found guilty of murder. ○ He pleaded guilty to causing actual bodily harm.

▸ COLLOCATIONS:
guilty **of** something
plead guilty
find someone guilty
a guilty **plea/verdict**
a guilty **defendant/criminal**
▸ ANTONYMS: innocent, not guilty

Hh

hab|it /ˈhæbɪt/ (habits)

NOUN A **habit** is something that you do often or regularly. ○ [+ of] *an estimated 32 million Americans are trying to kick the habit of smoking* ○ *a survey on eating habits in the U.K.* ○ *Good exercise habits should be developed when you are young.*

▶ COLLOCATIONS:
  the habit **of** *doing something*
  have/develop/change a habit
  kick/break a habit
  a **bad/good/annoying** habit
  eating/spending/drinking/viewing/exercise habits

▶ SYNONYM: practice

habi|tat /ˈhæbɪtæt/ (habitats)   SCIENCE BIOLOGY

NOUN The **habitat** of an animal or plant is the natural environment in which it normally lives or grows. ○ *In its natural habitat, the plant will grow up to 25ft.* ○ *It is essential that we protect wildlife habitats.* ○ [+ for] *an ideal habitat for birds*

▶ COLLOCATIONS:
  a habitat **of/for** *something*
  a **natural/native** habitat
  a **wildlife** habitat
  protect/destroy a habitat
  habitat **loss/destruction**

▶ SYNONYM: territory

half /hɑːf, AM hæf/ (halves)   MATHS

NOUN **Half of** an amount or object is one of two equal parts that together make up the whole number, amount, or object. ○ *They need an extra two and a half thousand pounds to complete the project.* ○ [+ of] *More than half of all households have incomes above £35,000.* ○ *The bridge was re-built in two halves.* ○ *400 jobs were cut in the first half of this year.*

• **Half** is also a predeterminer. ○ *We talked for half an hour.* ○ *They had only received half the money promised.* ○ *She's half his age.*

• **Half** is also an adjective. ○ *a half measure of fresh lemon juice* ○ *Steve did not say anything during the first half hour.*

▶ **COLLOCATIONS:**
half **of** *something*
in half
the **first/second/other** half
the **top/bottom** half
half a **mile/hour/century**
a **year/hour/month/minute** and a half
one/two and a half
▶ **PHRASE:** half and half

halve /hɑːv, AM hæv/ (halves, halving, halved)

VERB When you **halve** something or when it **halves**, it is reduced to half its previous size or amount. ○ *men who exercise can halve their risk of cancer* ○ *The work force has been halved in two years.* ○ *Sales of vinyl records halved in 1992 to just 6.7m.*
▶ **COLLOCATIONS:**
halve *something* **in value/size**
halve the **number/deficit**
almost/nearly halve *something*

han|dle /ˈhændəl/ (handles, handling, handled)

VERB If someone handles a problem or situation, they do something to deal with it successfully. ○ *The government was criticised for the way it handled the crisis.* ○ *Pavane might have handled the situation better.* ○ *She cannot handle pressure.*
▶ **COLLOCATIONS:**
handle a **situation/issue/matter/case**
handle a **problem/crisis/complaint/job**
handle **pressure**
handle *something* **badly/well/properly/carefully**
▶ **SYNONYMS:** deal with, manage, cope with
▶ **ANTONYM:** mishandle

hard|ware /ˈhɑːdweə/

UNCOUNTABLE NOUN Hardware is computers and computer equipment but not the programs. ○ *The price of computer hardware has fallen.*
▶ **COLLOCATIONS:**
computer hardware
a hardware **device**
hardware **failure/problems**
install/use hardware
▶ **RELATED WORD:** software

harm /hɑːm/ **(harms, harming, harmed)**

1 VERB To **harm** a person or animal means to injure them. ○ *The hijackers seemed anxious not to harm anyone.*

▶ **COLLOCATIONS:**
   harm **anyone/civilians**
   physically/seriously harm *someone*

▶ **SYNONYMS:** injure, hurt

● **Harm** is also an uncountable noun. ○ [+ *to*] *All dogs are capable of doing harm to human beings.* ○ *High levels of nitrate in the water may cause harm to humans.*

▶ **COLLOCATIONS:**
   harm **to** *someone/something*
   do/cause harm
   serious/great/physical harm

▶ **SYNONYM:** injury

2 VERB To **harm** a thing, means to damage it. ○ *The product may harm the environment.* ○ *Low-priced imports will harm the industry.*

▶ **COLLOCATIONS:**
   seriously/irreparably harm *something*
   deliberately/intentionally harm *something*
   harm the **environment**
   harm **relations**

▶ **SYNONYMS:** damage, ruin

● **Harm** is also an uncountable noun. ○ [+ *to*] *These metals are doing harm to the soil.* ○ *To cut taxes would probably do the economy more harm than good.*

▶ **COLLOCATIONS:**
   harm **to** something
   do/cause harm
   serious/great/real harm
   irreparable harm

▶ **PHRASE:** do more harm than good

▶ **SYNONYM:** damage

→ see note at **damage**

harm|ful /ˈhɑːmfʊl/

ADJECTIVE Something that is **harmful** has a bad effect on something. ○ *the harmful effects of smoking* ○ [+ *to*] *The chemical is potentially harmful to fish.*

▶ **COLLOCATIONS:**
   harmful **to** *someone/something*
   harmful **effects/emissions**
   a harmful **chemical/substance**

potentially harmful
▶ SYNONYM: damaging
▶ ANTONYMS: harmless, safe

harm|less /ˈhɑːmləs/

ADJECTIVE Something that is **harmless** does not have any bad effects.
○ Scientists are trying to develop harmless substitutes for these gases. ○ [+ to]
This experiment was harmless to the animals.
▶ COLLOCATIONS:
harmless **to** someone/something
relatively/essentially/seemingly harmless
▶ SYNONYM: safe
▶ ANTONYM: harmful

head|ing /ˈhedɪŋ/ (headings)

NOUN A **heading** is the title of a piece of writing, which is written or
printed at the top of the page. ○ helpful chapter headings ○ Use headings to
make information easy to find.
▶ COLLOCATION: a **chapter/subject** heading
▶ SYNONYM: title
▶ RELATED WORD: subheading

health /helθ/

UNCOUNTABLE NOUN A person's **health** is the condition of their body and
whether they are ill or not. ○ Salty food is bad for your health. ○ He was 88
and in poor health. ○ [+ of] The clinic aimed to improve the health of the local
population. ○ the effects of pesticides on human health
▶ COLLOCATIONS:
the health **of** someone
good/bad for your health
good/ill/poor/excellent health
mental/sexual/public/human health
health **care/service/system**
a health **professional/worker/expert**
a health **problem/risk**
▶ PHRASES:
health and safety
health and education
be in good/poor health
▶ SYNONYM: well-being
▶ RELATED WORD: fitness

healthy /ˈhelθi/ (healthier, healthiest)

ADJECTIVE ○ *Most of us need to lead more balanced lives to be happy and healthy.* ○ *the glow of healthy skin* ○ *You should have a healthy diet.*

▶ COLLOCATIONS:
be/stay/remain/look/feel healthy
a healthy **appetite/weight/diet/lifestyle**
healthy **skin/hair/food/eating**

▶ PHRASES:
happy and healthy
young and healthy
fit/strong and healthy

▶ ANTONYMS: ill, unhealthy

healthi|ly /ˈhelθɪli/

ADVERB ○ *What I really want is to live healthily for as long as possible.* ○ *You should try to eat healthily.*

▶ COLLOCATION: **eat/live** healthily

---

heart /hɑːt/ (hearts)   SCIENCE BIOLOGY MEDICINE

NOUN Your **heart** is the organ in your chest that pumps the blood around your body. ○ *The bullet had passed less than an inch from Andrea's heart.* ○ *His heart was beating very fast.* ○ *The baby was born with a heart condition.*

▶ COLLOCATIONS:
your heart **beats/pounds/races**
heart **disease/failure/trouble**
a heart **problem/condition/transplant**
heart **surgery**
the heart **muscle**

---

heart at|tack /ˈhɑːt ətæk/ (heart attacks)   MEDICINE

NOUN If someone has a **heart attack**, they have a bad pain in their chest, and their heart stops working. ○ *My grandfather had a heart attack.* ○ *He died of a heart attack.*

▶ COLLOCATIONS:
have/suffer a heart attack
die of a heart attack

▶ SYNONYM: cardiac arrest

heat /hiːt/ (heats, heating, heated)

SCIENCE

1 VERB When you **heat** something, you raise its temperature, for example by using a flame or a special piece of equipment. ○ *Heat the tomatoes and oil in a pan.* ○ *heated swimming pools*
▶ **COLLOCATION:** heat *something* **gently**
▶ **ANTONYM:** cool

2 UNCOUNTABLE NOUN **Heat** is warmth or the quality of being hot. ○ *The seas store heat and release it gradually during cold periods.* ○ *Its leaves drooped a little in the fierce heat of the sun.*
▶ **COLLOCATIONS:**
generate/produce/provide/radiate heat
lose/keep/retain heat
a heat **source**
heat **loss**
intense/sweltering/fierce/gentle/summer heat
▶ **SYNONYM:** warmth

height /haɪt/ (heights)

NOUN The **height** of a person or thing is their size or length from the bottom to the top. ○ *Her weight is about normal for her height.* ○ *I am 5'6" in height.* ○ [+ of] *The tree can grow to a height of 20ft.* ○ *He was a man of medium height.*
▶ **COLLOCATIONS:**
a height **of** x
be x **in** height
be **of** *normal* height
have/reach a height of x
of **medium/normal/average** height
the **maximum/minimum** height
the **average** height
▶ **RELATED WORDS:** length, depth

hesi|tate /ˈhezɪteɪt/ (hesitates, hesitating, hesitated)

1 VERB If you **hesitate**, you do not speak or do something for a short time, usually because you are uncertain or embarrassed. ○ *The telephone rang. Catherine hesitated, debating whether to answer it.* ○ *She hesitated for a while and then she said 'Yes'.*

2 VERB If you **hesitate to** do something, you delay doing it or are unwilling to do it, usually because you are not certain it would be right. If you do not **hesitate to** do something, you do it immediately.

h

○ [+ to-inf] *I hesitate to criticize the referee because I thought he was generally good.* ○ [+ to-inf] *I wouldn't hesitate to talk to them.*

hesi|ta|tion /ˌhezɪˈteɪʃən/ (hesitations)

NOUN ○ *Despite some hesitations, members voted 15-0 to accept the resolution.* ○ *Mirella approached him and, after a brief hesitation, shook his hand.*

▶ COLLOCATIONS:
without hesitation
after hesitation
a **slight/brief** hesitation

▶ SYNONYM: pause

---

high|er edu|ca|tion /ˌhaɪə edʒʊˈkeɪʃən/ [EDUCATION]

UNCOUNTABLE NOUN **Higher education** is education at universities and colleges. ○ *The government wants more young people to go into higher education.* ○ *There has been a cut in higher education funding.*

▶ COLLOCATIONS:
in/into higher education
go into higher education
a higher education **institution/course**
higher education **students/teaching/learning**
higher education **research/funding**
the higher education **sector**

---

high|ly /ˈhaɪli/

ADVERB **Highly** is used before some adjectives to mean 'very'. ○ *It was a highly successful business.* ○ *It's highly unlikely that he'll come.* ○ *the highly controversial nuclear energy programme*

▶ COLLOCATIONS:
highly **successful/effective/popular**
highly **unusual/likely/unlikely**
highly **dangerous/toxic/controversial/intelligent**

▶ SYNONYMS: extremely, very

---

high school /ˈhaɪ skuːl/ (high schools) [EDUCATION]

1 NOUN In Britain, a **high school** is a school for children aged between eleven and eighteen. ○ *Sunderland High School* ○ *My sister's going to high school next year.*

2 NOUN In the United States, a **high school** is a school for children usually aged between fourteen and eighteen. ○ *an 18-year-old kid who dropped out of high school* ○ *the high school football team*

▶ **COLLOCATIONS:**
be **in/at** high school
go to/attend high school
a high school **student/teacher**
▶ **SYNONYM:** secondary school
▶ **RELATED WORDS:** primary school, elementary school

---

high-tech /ˌhaɪˈtek/ also **high tech** or **hi tech**   SCIENCE

ADJECTIVE High-tech activities or equipment use the most modern technology. ○ *Taiwan's high-tech industry* ○ *New high-tech equipment allows doctors to magnify a section of your skin and project it on to a computer screen.*
▶ **COLLOCATIONS:**
a high-tech **company/industry/firm**
high-tech **equipment**
a high-tech **job/system**
▶ **SYNONYMS:** state-of-the-art, cutting edge
▶ **ANTONYM:** low-tech

---

his|to|ry /ˈhɪstəri/   HISTORY

1 UNCOUNTABLE NOUN History is all the events that have happened in the past. ○ *The Catholic Church has played an important role throughout Polish history.* ○ *the most evil mass killer in history* ○ *[+ of] the history of Birmingham* ○ *religious history*
▶ **COLLOCATIONS:**
throughout/in history
the history **of** *something*
British/American history
political/military/social/religious/human history

2 UNCOUNTABLE NOUN History is the subject that deals with events that have happened in the past. ○ *He studied history at university.*
▶ **COLLOCATIONS:**
study/teach history
a history **teacher/professor/student**
a history **lesson**

his|tor|ic /hɪˈstɒrɪk, AM -ˈtɔːr-/

ADJECTIVE Something that is **historic** is important in history or is likely to be important. ○ *The opening of the Scottish Parliament was a historic moment.* ○ *a fourth historic election victory*

▶ **COLLOCATIONS:**
a historic **agreement/decision/victory**
a historic **achievement/opportunity**
a historic **event/occasion/moment**

his|tori|cal /hɪˈstɒrɪkəl, AM -tɔːr-/

1 ADJECTIVE Historical people, situations, or things existed in the past and are considered to be a part of history. ○ *Napoleon Bonaparte was an important historical figure.* ○ *the historical impact of Western capitalism on the world* ○ *In Buda, several historical monuments can be seen.*
▶ **COLLOCATION:** a historical **event/figure/site/monument**
▶ **SYNONYM:** ancient

2 ADJECTIVE Historical information, research, and discussion is related to the study of history. ○ *historical records* ○ *modern historical research*
▶ **COLLOCATIONS:**
historical **facts/records/documents/evidence**
historical **research/studies**
the historical **context/background**
▶ **PHRASE:** of historical interest
▶ **SYNONYM:** ancient

> **USAGE: historic or historical?**
>
> You use **historical** to talk about things from the past or related to history. ○ *a detailed analysis of historical records* ○ *the historical context in which Chaucer wrote*
>
> You use **historic** to describe something that was very important in history or a recent event that was so important that it will be remembered in the future. ○ *a battery of cameras captured the historic moment on film*

his|to|rian /hɪˈstɔːriən/ (historians)

NOUN A **historian** is a person who studies history, and who writes books and articles about it. ○ *Some historians believe the famine continued until 1851.*
▶ **COLLOCATIONS:**
a **music/art/family** historian
a **military/social/architectural** historian
a **leading/distinguished** historian

hours /aʊəz/

BUSINESS

PLURAL NOUN You can refer to the period of time during which something happens or operates each day as the **hours** during which it happens or operates. ○ *I worked quite irregular hours.* ○ *[+ of] the hours of darkness* ○ *Phone us during office hours.* ○ *Peter came home in the early hours of the morning.*
○ *The job was easy; the hours were good.*
  ▶ COLLOCATIONS:
   during x hours
   opening/office/business/working hours
   daylight hours
   the **early** hours
  ▶ PHRASE: the hours of daylight/darkness

hous|ing /ˈhaʊzɪŋ/

UNCOUNTABLE NOUN **Housing** is the buildings which people live in.
○ *There is a shortage of affordable housing.* ○ *Poor housing can affect physical and mental health.*
  ▶ COLLOCATIONS:
   build/provide housing
   good/poor/decent/affordable/low-cost housing
   private/rented/temporary/permanent housing
   the housing **market**
   a housing **development/estate/project/scheme**
  ▶ SYNONYM: accommodation

how|ever /haʊˈevə/

1 **ADVERB** You use **however** when you are adding a comment which is surprising or which contrasts with what has just been said. ○ *This was not an easy decision. It is, however, a decision that we had to make.* ○ *Some of the food crops failed. However, the cotton did quite well.* ○ *Higher sales have not helped profits, however.*

2 **ADVERB** You use **however** before an adjective or adverb to emphasize that the degree or extent of something cannot change a situation.
○ *You should always try to achieve more, however well you have done before.*
○ *However hard she tried, nothing seemed to work.* ○ *However much it hurt, he could do it.*
  ▶ SYNONYM: no matter how

hu|man /ˈhjuːmən/ (humans)

1 **ADJECTIVE** **Human** means relating to people. ○ *the human body*
○ *It was one of the worst disasters in human history.*
  ▶ **COLLOCATIONS:**
  human **life/rights/error**
  the human **body/race**
  ▶ **PHRASE:** a human being

2 **NOUN** You can refer to people as **humans**, especially when you are
comparing them with animals or machines. ○ *The drug was tested on
animals before it was tested on humans.*
  ▶ **SYNONYMS:** person, human being

h

Ii

ice /aɪs/

UNCOUNTABLE NOUN Ice is frozen water. ○ *Glaciers are moving rivers of ice.*
○ *The ice is melting.*

▶ **COLLOCATIONS:**
ice **melts/thaws**
an ice **cube/floe**
thin/dry/black/polar/arctic ice

▶ **PHRASE:** snow and ice

idea /aɪˈdiːə/ (ideas)

1 NOUN An **idea** is a plan, suggestion, or possible course of action. ○ [+ *of*]
I really like the idea of helping people. ○ *She told me she'd had a brilliant idea.*

2 NOUN An **idea** is an opinion or belief about what something is like or
should be like. ○ [+ *about*] *Some of his ideas about democracy are entirely his
own.* ○ [+ *that*] *the idea that reading too many books ruins your eyes*

▶ **COLLOCATIONS:**
someone's idea **of** *something*
an idea **about** *something*
have/get an idea
a **good/bright/brilliant/great/interesting** idea
a **new/original/bad/crazy** idea
the **whole/main** idea

▶ **SYNONYMS:** notion, concept

ideal /aɪˈdiːəl/

ADJECTIVE The **ideal** person or thing for a particular task or purpose is the
best possible person or thing for it. ○ *She decided that I was the ideal person
to take over the job.* ○ *I see this as an ideal place to start my managerial career.*
○ *ideal conditions for growth*

▶ **COLLOCATIONS:**
ideal **for** *something*
an ideal **opportunity/climate/temperature**
ideal **conditions/weather**
an ideal **place/location/situation**

▶ **SYNONYM:** perfect

ideal|ly /aɪˈdiːəli/

1 **ADVERB** If you say that **ideally** a particular thing should happen or be done, you mean that this is what would be best, but you know that this may not be possible or practical. ○ *People should, ideally, eat much less fat.* ○ *The restructuring ideally needs to be completed this year.*
▶ **SYNONYM:** preferably

2 **ADVERB** If you say that someone or something is **ideally** suited or **ideally** located, you mean that they are as well suited or located as possible. ○ *The hotel is ideally situated for country walks.*
▶ **COLLOCATIONS:**
ideally **placed/located/situated/positioned**
ideally **suited/qualified**
▶ **SYNONYM:** perfectly

ig|nore /ɪɡˈnɔː/ (ignores, ignoring, ignored) `ACADEMIC WORD`

1 **VERB** If you **ignore** someone or something, you pay no attention to them. ○ *They had ignored the warning signs.* ○ *She ignored legal advice to drop the case.*

2 **VERB** If you say that an argument or theory **ignores** an important aspect of a situation, you are criticizing it because it fails to consider that aspect or to take it into account. ○ *Such arguments ignore the question of where ultimate responsibility lay.* ○ *His article ignores the fact that the environment can exaggerate small genetic differences.*
▶ **COLLOCATIONS:**
ignore **advice/evidence**
ignore a **warning/sign/order/call/rule**
choose/try to ignore *something*
hard/difficult to ignore
largely/simply/completely/totally/deliberately ignore *something*
▶ **PHRASE:** ignore the fact that …
▶ **SYNONYM:** overlook
▶ **ANTONYM:** notice

il|legal /ɪˈliːɡəl/ `ACADEMIC WORD` `LAW`

ADJECTIVE If something is **illegal**, the law says that it is not allowed.
○ [+ to-inf] *It is illegal to intercept radio messages.* ○ *Birth control was illegal there until 1978.* ○ *illegal drugs*
▶ **COLLOCATIONS:**
become illegal
declare/make/consider *something* illegal
an illegal **drug/activity/weapon/trade**

illegal **immigration/immigrants**
▶ **PHRASE:** be illegal for someone to do something
▶ **SYNONYM:** unlawful
▶ **ANTONYM:** legal

il|legal|ly

ADVERB ○ [+ v-ing] *They were yesterday convicted of illegally using a handgun.*
○ *The previous government had acted illegally.*
▶ **COLLOCATIONS:**
 copy/obtain/import *something* illegally
 act/operate/work/enter illegally
▶ **ANTONYM:** legally

---

im|age /'ımıdʒ/ (images)   `ACADEMIC WORD`

1 NOUN The **image** of a person, group, or organization is the way that they appear to other people. ○ [+ *of*] *He has cultivated the image of an elder statesman.* ○ *The tobacco industry has been trying to improve its image.*
▶ **COLLOCATIONS:**
 create/improve/project an image
 a **public/corporate** image
 your **body/self-** image
 a **negative/positive** image
▶ **SYNONYMS:** impression, reputation

2 NOUN An **image** is a picture of someone or something. [FORMAL] ○ [+ *of*] *photographic images of young children* ○ *A computer in the machine creates an image on the screen.*
▶ **COLLOCATIONS:**
 display an image
 a **full-size/mirror** image
 produce/feature/capture an image
▶ **SYNONYM:** picture

---

im|por|tant /ım'pɔːtənt/

ADJECTIVE Something that is **important** is very significant, is highly valued, or is necessary. ○ *The planned general strike represents an important economic challenge to the government.* ○ [+ to-inf] *It's important to answer her questions as honestly as you can.*
▶ **COLLOCATIONS:**
 an important **role/part/issue/question/decision**
 an important **factor/element/aspect/point**
 extremely/particularly/vitally important
 equally/increasingly important

▶ **PHRASE:** the single most important thing
▶ **SYNONYMS:** significant, critical, essential
▶ **ANTONYMS:** unimportant, insignificant

im|por|tant|ly

ADVERB ○ *I was hungry, and, more importantly, my children were hungry.*
○ *Finally, and perhaps most importantly, the early warning system provides a means of monitoring performance.*

im|por|tance /ɪmˈpɔːtəns/

UNCOUNTABLE NOUN ○ [+ *of*] *We have always stressed the importance of economic reform.* ○ *Safety is of paramount importance.* ○ *Institutions place great importance on symbols of corporate identity.*

▶ **COLLOCATIONS:**
be **of** importance
the importance **of** *something*
place importance **on** *something*
recognize/stress/emphasize the importance of *something*
understand/know the importance of *something*
of **great/critical/enormous/growing/increasing** importance
▶ **SYNONYM:** significance
▶ **ANTONYM:** insignificance

---

im|prove /ɪmˈpruːv/ (improves, improving, improved)

VERB If something **improves** or if you **improve** it, it gets better. ○ *Both the texture and condition of your hair should improve.* ○ *Time won't improve the situation.*

▶ **COLLOCATIONS:**
dramatically/significantly improve
improve **slightly**
continue/expect/need/try to improve
▶ **ANTONYM:** deteriorate

im|prove|ment /ɪmˈpruːvmənt/ (improvements)

NOUN ○ [+ *in*] *the dramatic improvements in organ transplantation in recent years*
○ *There is considerable room for improvement in state facilities for treating the mentally handicapped.*

▶ **COLLOCATIONS:**
improvement **in** *something*
an improvement **over** *time*
an improvement in **relations/quality/performance**
show/see/make an improvement

a **gradual/big/dramatic/marked/significant/slight** improvement
home/self- improvement
▸ **ANTONYM:** deterioration

---

inch /ɪntʃ/ (inches)

NOUN An **inch** is an imperial unit of length, approximately equal to 2.54 centimetres. There are twelve inches in a foot. ○ *18 inches below the surface* ○ *white paper no larger than 8 x 11 inches in size*

▸ **COLLOCATIONS:**
an inch **of/in** something
x inches **above/below** something
an inch in **diameter/size/width/height**
an inch of **snow/rain/space**
x inches **wide/tall/thick/deep**
an inch **apart/long/away**
a **square/cubic** inch
several/a few inches
half an inch
▸ **PHRASE:** feet and inches

---

in|clude /ɪnˈkluːd/ (includes, including, included)

1 VERB If one thing **includes** another thing, it has the other thing as one of its parts. ○ *Cortés found 160,000 had died of smallpox, including the emperor, Montezuma.* ○ *The trip has been extended to include a few other events.*

2 VERB If someone or something **is included in** a large group, system, or area, they become a part of it or are considered a part of it. ○ [+ *in*] *I had worked hard to be included in a project like this.* ○ [+ *in*] *The President is expected to include this idea in his education plan.*

▸ **COLLOCATIONS:**
include *something/someone* **in** *something*
include **information/accommodation**
include a **charge/fee/detail/item**
a **package/activity/facility/collection** includes
▸ **ANTONYM:** exclude

in|clud|ing /ɪnˈkluːdɪŋ/

PREPOSITION You use **including** to introduce examples of people or things that are part of the group of people or things that you are talking about. ○ *The drug will have anything up to a hundred side effects, including death.* ○ *many conditions, including allergies, hyperactivity and tooth decay*

○ *Preparation time (not including chilling): 5 minutes.*
▶ **ANTONYM:** excluding

in|clu|sion /ɪnˈkluːʒən/ (inclusions)

NOUN Inclusion is the act of making a person or thing part of a group or collection. ○ [+ in] *His performance justified his inclusion in the team.*
○ [+ of] *the inclusion of the term 'couplehood' in a Dictionary of New Words*
▶ **COLLOCATIONS:**
inclusion **in/of** something
social/possible/late inclusion
▶ **ANTONYM:** exclusion

in|come /ˈɪnkʌm/ (incomes)   `ACADEMIC WORD` `BUSINESS`

NOUN A person's or organization's **income** is the money that they earn or receive, as opposed to the money that they have to spend or pay out.
○ *Many families on low incomes will be unable to afford to buy their own home.*
○ [+ of] *To cover its costs, the company will need an annual income of £15 million.*
→ see note at **earn**
▶ **COLLOCATIONS:**
an income **of** £x
earn an income
supplement *your* income
a **high/low/average/net/gross/annual** income
a **large/small/fixed/second/steady/taxable** income
a **household/family** income
income **tax/support**
▶ **PHRASES:**
loss of income
a source of income
▶ **SYNONYMS:** earnings, salary, revenue
▶ **ANTONYMS:** costs, expenses

in|cor|rect /ˌɪnkəˈrekt/

1 ADJECTIVE Something that is **incorrect** is wrong and untrue. ○ *He denied that his evidence was incorrect.* ○ *People often have incorrect information about food.*
→ see note at **correct**
▶ **COLLOCATIONS:**
an incorrect **assumption/diagnosis/report/figure**
incorrect **information/details**
totally/factually incorrect

▶ **SYNONYMS:** wrong, inaccurate
▶ **ANTONYMS:** correct, accurate

2 ADJECTIVE Something that is **incorrect** is not the thing that is required or is most suitable in a particular situation. ○ *injuries caused by incorrect posture* ○ *incorrect diet*
▶ **COLLOCATION: politically** incorrect
▶ **SYNONYMS:** inappropriate, bad
▶ **ANTONYMS:** correct, appropriate

in|cor|rect|ly

ADVERB ○ *These substances can, if taken incorrectly, be harmful.* ○ *The magazine suggested incorrectly that he was planning to retire.*
▶ **SYNONYMS:** wrongly, inaccurately
▶ **ANTONYM:** correctly

---

in|crease (increases, increasing, increased)

> The verb is pronounced /ɪn'kriːs/. The noun is pronounced /'ɪnkriːs/.

1 VERB If something **increases** or you **increase** it, it becomes greater in number, level, or amount. ○ *The population continues to increase.*
○ [+ *by/from/to*] *Japan's industrial output increased by 2%.*
▶ **COLLOCATIONS:**
   increase **by/from/to** *x*
   increase **in** *something*
   increase **dramatically/rapidly**
▶ **SYNONYMS:** rise, raise
▶ **ANTONYMS:** decrease, reduce

2 NOUN If there is an **increase in** the number, level, or amount of something, it becomes greater. ○ [+ *in*] *a sharp increase in productivity*
○ *He called for an increase of 1p on income tax.*
▶ **COLLOCATIONS:**
   an increase **of/from/to** *x*
   an increase **in** *something*
   an increase in **crime/demand/spending**
   an increase in **size/temperature/value**
   a **population/price/salary** increase
   a **big/marked/sharp** increase
▶ **SYNONYM:** rise
▶ **ANTONYMS:** decrease, reduction

in|creas|ing|ly /ɪnˈkriːsɪŋli/

ADVERB You can use **increasingly** to indicate that a situation or quality is becoming greater in intensity or more common. ○ *He was finding it increasingly difficult to make decisions.* ○ *The U.S. has increasingly relied on Japanese capital.*

▶ **COLLOCATIONS:**
become increasingly...
increasingly **difficult/popular/important**
increasingly **clear/common/complex**
▶ **SYNONYM:** more

---

in|de|pend|ent /ˌɪndɪˈpendənt/

1 ADJECTIVE If one thing or person is **independent of** another, they are separate and not connected, so the first one is not affected or influenced by the second. ○ [+ *of*] *Your questions should be independent of each other.* ○ *Two independent studies have been carried out.*

2 ADJECTIVE If someone is **independent**, they do not need help or money from anyone else. ○ [+ *of*] *Phil was now much more independent of his parents.* ○ *She would like to be financially independent.*

3 ADJECTIVE Independent countries and states are not ruled by other countries but have their own government. ○ *a fully independent state* ○ [+ *from*] *Papua New Guinea became independent from Australia in 1975.*

▶ **COLLOCATIONS:**
independent **of/from** *someone/something*
fully/financially independent
an independent **adviser/inquiry/state**
▶ **SYNONYMS:** self-reliant, self-supporting, liberated, self-governing
▶ **ANTONYM:** dependent

in|de|pen|dent|ly

ADVERB ○ *several people working independently in different areas of the world* ○ [+ *of*] *The commission will operate independently of ministers.* ○ *We aim to help disabled students to live and study independently.*

▶ **COLLOCATIONS:**
do something independently **of** *something/someone*
function/act/operate independently
live/work independently
independently **verify/confirm/own** *something*
▶ **SYNONYMS:** separately, autonomously

in|de|pend|ence /ˌɪndɪˈpendəns/

1 **UNCOUNTABLE NOUN** If a country has or gains **independence**, it has its own government and is not ruled by any other country. ○ [+ from] In 1816, Argentina declared its independence from Spain. ○ the country's first elections since independence in 1962

2 **UNCOUNTABLE NOUN** Someone's **independence** is the fact that they do not rely on other people. ○ He was afraid of losing his independence.

▶ **COLLOCATIONS:**
  independence **from** something/someone
  declare/gain/fight for independence
  full/economic/financial independence
▶ **SYNONYMS:** freedom, liberty
▶ **ANTONYM:** dependence

---

in|di|vid|ual /ˌɪndɪˈvɪdʒuəl/ (individuals)   `ACADEMIC WORD`

1 **ADJECTIVE** **Individual** means relating to one person or thing, rather than to a large group. ○ They wait for the group to decide rather than making individual decisions. ○ Aid to individual countries is linked to progress towards democracy.

▶ **COLLOCATION:** individual **freedom/responsibility/members**
▶ **SYNONYM:** single
▶ **ANTONYMS:** collective, joint

2 **NOUN** An **individual** is a person. ○ anonymous individuals who are doing good things within our community ○ the rights and responsibilities of the individual

▶ **COLLOCATIONS:**
  a **private/wealthy/healthy** individual
  a **particular/certain** individual
  an individual's **right/need**
▶ **SYNONYMS:** human being, person

EXTEND YOUR VOCABULARY

You can use **people** to refer to a large group or to everyone in a society. You can also talk about **the public** to refer to the ordinary people in a society or country. ○ issues affecting young people ○ He accused the government of misleading the public.

You talk about **individuals** to refer to people when each one is considered separately rather than as a group. ○ the genetic differences between any two individuals

in|di|vid|ual|ly

ADVERB ○ *There are 96 pieces and they are worth, individually and collectively, a lot of money.* ○ *Individually they're weak, but as a group they can be devastating.*
▸ **PHRASE:** individually and collectively
▸ **SYNONYM:** singly
▸ **ANTONYMS:** collectively, jointly

---

in|dus|try /ˈɪndəstri/ (industries) `BUSINESS`

1 UNCOUNTABLE NOUN Industry is the work and processes involved in making things in factories. ○ *the changes will boost jobs and benefit Australian industry* ○ *in countries where industry is developing rapidly*

2 NOUN A particular **industry** consists of all the people and activities involved in making a particular product or providing a particular service. ○ *the motor vehicle and textile industries* ○ *the Scottish tourist industry*
▸ **COLLOCATIONS:**
a **booming/thriving** industry
heavy/high-tech industry
the **pharmaceutical/tourism/airline/oil** industry
▸ **PHRASES:**
trade and industry
industry and commerce
▸ **SYNONYM:** business

in|dus|trial /ɪnˈdʌstriəl/

ADJECTIVE ○ *industrial machinery and equipment* ○ *ministers from leading western industrial countries*

---

in|flu|ence /ˈɪnfluəns/ (influences, influencing, influenced)

1 NOUN To have an **influence on** people or situations means to affect what they do or what happens. ○ [+ *on*] *Van Gogh had a major influence on the development of modern painting.* ○ *Many other medications have an influence on cholesterol levels.*
▸ **COLLOCATIONS:**
the influence **of** *someone/something*
influence **on/over** *someone/something*
the influence of **alcohol/drugs**
have/exert influence on *someone/something*
considerable/powerful/positive/political influence
a **major/important/strong/good/bad** influence
▸ **SYNONYM:** effect

2 VERB If someone or something **influences** a person or situation, they have an effect on that person's behaviour or that situation. ○ *We became the best of friends and he influenced me deeply.* ○ *What you eat may influence your risk of getting cancer.* ○ *Leadership means influencing the organization to follow the leader's vision.*

▶ COLLOCATIONS:
influence **behaviour/opinion/people**
influence a **decision/policy/development**
heavily/strongly influence *someone/something*
▶ SYNONYM: affect

in|flu|en|tial /ˌɪnfluˈenʃəl/

ADJECTIVE Someone or something that is **influential** has a lot of influence over people or events. ○ *the influential position of president of the chamber* ○ [+ in] *He had been influential in shaping economic policy.* ○ *one of the most influential books ever written*

▶ COLLOCATIONS:
influential **in** *something*
an influential **figure/voice/magazine**
an influential **cleric/critic/politician**
▶ SYNONYMS: effective, powerful
▶ ANTONYM: ineffective

in|for|mal /ɪnˈfɔːməl/

ADJECTIVE Informal speech or behaviour is relaxed and friendly rather than serious or official. ○ *She is refreshingly informal.* ○ *This was an informal, unofficial investigation.* ○ *This door leads to the informal living area.*

▶ COLLOCATION: an informal **discussion/meeting/talk**
▶ SYNONYMS: relaxed, casual, unofficial
▶ ANTONYM: formal

in|for|mal|ly

ADVERB ○ *She was always there at half past eight, chatting informally to the children.* ○ *All meetings were held informally, and off the record.*

▶ COLLOCATIONS:
meet/talk/dress informally
discuss/agree/advise informally
▶ SYNONYM: unofficially
▶ ANTONYM: formally

in|for|mal|ity /ɪnfɔːˈmælɪti/

UNCOUNTABLE NOUN ○ *He was overwhelmed by their friendly informality.*
○ *a sign that more informality is gradually coming into the language* ○ [+ *of*] *the informality of the communication process*
▶ **COLLOCATION:** the informality **of** *something*
▶ **ANTONYM:** formality

in|for|ma|tion /ˌɪnfəˈmeɪʃən/

UNCOUNTABLE NOUN Information about someone or something consists of facts about them. ○ [+ *about*] *The tables gave background information about each school.* ○ [+ *on*] *Each centre would provide information on technology and training.* ○ *For further information contact the number below.* ○ *an important piece of information*
▶ **COLLOCATIONS:**
  information **about/on** *something*
  additional/further/detailed/background/personal information
  give/provide information
  gather/collect/obtain information
  contain information
▶ **SYNONYMS:** facts, data, details

> **USAGE:** Uncountable noun
>
> Remember that information is an uncountable noun. You do **not** say 'an information' or 'informations' and it is followed by a singular verb. ○ *The information is stored on a database.*
>
> You can talk about a **piece of information** or an **item of information**. ○ *His article contains several pieces of incorrect information.* You can also talk about a **fact** or a **detail**. ○ *His article contains several incorrect details.*

in|for|ma|tion tech|nol|ogy ⊞

UNCOUNTABLE NOUN Information technology is the theory and practice of using computers to store and analyse information. The abbreviation **IT** is often used. ○ *the information technology industry* ○ *The rapid growth of information technology has transformed the working environment.*
▶ **COLLOCATION: spread/growth/development** of information technology

in|gre|di|ent /ɪnˈɡriːdiənt/ **(ingredients)**

NOUN Ingredients are the things that are used to make something. ○ *They found that the original active ingredient or solute changes the water or solvent.*

○ [+ *of*] *What then are the common ingredients of most of our programmes?*
▶ **COLLOCATIONS:**
the ingredients **of** something
a **common/active/secret** ingredient
a **key/important/essential** ingredient
▶ **SYNONYMS:** part, element

in|jec|tion /ɪnˈdʒekʃən/ (injections) `MEDICINE`

NOUN If you have an **injection**, a doctor or nurse puts a medicine into your body using a device with a needle called a syringe. ○ *They gave me an injection to help me sleep.* ○ *It has to be given by injection, usually twice daily.*
▶ **COLLOCATIONS:**
by injection
receive/require/need an injection
give/administer an injection
a **lethal** injection

in|jure /ˈɪndʒə/ (injures, injuring, injured) `ACADEMIC WORD` `MEDICINE`

VERB If you **injure** a person or animal, you damage some part of their body.
○ *A number of bombs have exploded, seriously injuring at least five people.* ○ *stiff penalties for motorists who kill, maim, and injure*
→ see note at **damage**
▶ **COLLOCATIONS:**
seriously/critically/badly injure someone
a **bomb/explosion/blast/fire** injures people
▶ **SYNONYM:** maim

in|jured /ˈɪndʒəd/

ADJECTIVE ○ *The other injured man had a superficial stomach wound.* ○ *Many of them will have died because they were so badly injured.*
▶ **COLLOCATIONS:**
injured **in/by** something
injured in a **crash/accident/attack**
badly/seriously/critically injured
an injured **passenger/officer/soldier/driver**
an injured **shoulder/knee/ankle**
▶ **PHRASE:** killed or injured
▶ **SYNONYMS:** maimed, wounded

in|ju|ry /ˈɪndʒəri/ (injuries)

NOUN ○ *Four police officers sustained serious injuries in the explosion.* ○ *The two other passengers escaped serious injury.* ○ [+ *to*] *a serious injury to his left leg*

▶ COLLOCATIONS:
  an injury **to** *something*
  suffer/cause/escape injury
  a **bodily/minor/internal/life-threatening** injury
  a **personal/serious/severe** injury
  a **knee/shoulder/ankle** injury
▶ SYNONYM: wound

in|ner /ˈɪnə/

ADJECTIVE The **inner** parts of something are the parts which are contained or are enclosed inside the other parts, and which are closest to the centre. ○ *inhabitants of the inner city* ○ *Wade stepped inside and closed the inner door behind him.*
▶ COLLOCATION: the inner **city/circle**
▶ ANTONYM: outer

in|no|cent /ˈɪnəsənt/ [LAW]

ADJECTIVE If someone is **innocent**, they did not commit a crime which they have been accused of. ○ [+ *of*] *He was sure that the man was innocent of any crime.* ○ *She has pleaded innocent to the charge.*
▶ COLLOCATIONS:
  innocent **of** *something*
  innocent of a **crime/charge**
  completely/totally/entirely/perfectly innocent
  seemingly/apparently innocent
  plead/presumed/proven innocent
  an innocent **civilian/victim/bystander**
▶ PHRASE: innocent or guilty
▶ ANTONYM: guilty

in|sect /ˈɪnsekt/ (insects) [SCIENCE] [BIOLOGY]

NOUN An **insect** is a small animal that has six legs. Most insects have wings. Ants, flies, butterflies, and beetles are all insects. ○ *These bears eat insects, rodents and other small animals.* ○ *blood poisoning from insect bites*
▶ COLLOCATIONS:
  an insect **flies/crawls/attacks/eats**
  attract/eat/repel an insect
  a **biting/harmful/stick** insect
  insect **repellent**
  an insect **bite**
▶ PHRASE: birds and insects

in|tel|li|gent /ɪnˈtelɪdʒənt/ ACADEMIC WORD

ADJECTIVE A person or animal that is **intelligent** has the ability to think, understand, and learn things quickly and well. ○ *Susan's a very bright and intelligent woman.* ○ *lively and intelligent conversation* ○ *the opinion that whales are as intelligent as human beings*

▶ **COLLOCATIONS:**
  an intelligent **reader/audience/class/being**
  highly intelligent
▶ **SYNONYMS:** bright, clever, sharp, smart
▶ **ANTONYM:** stupid

in|tel|li|gent|ly

ADVERB ○ *They are incapable of thinking intelligently about politics.* ○ *voting systems that are intelligently designed*

▶ **COLLOCATIONS:**
  behave/respond/act intelligently
  speak/talk/write intelligently
▶ **SYNONYM:** cleverly
▶ **ANTONYM:** stupidly

in|tel|li|gence /ɪnˈtelɪdʒəns/

UNCOUNTABLE NOUN ○ *She's a woman of exceptional intelligence.* ○ [+ of] *It is designed to make the most of the intelligence of a well trained and motivated workforce.*

▶ **COLLOCATIONS:**
  the intelligence **of** something/someone
  human/artificial/emotional intelligence
▶ **SYNONYM:** intellect
▶ **ANTONYMS:** stupidity, ignorance

in|ter|est /ˈɪntrəst, -tərest/ (interests, interesting, interested)

1 NOUN If you have an **interest in** something, you want to learn or hear more about it. ○ [+ in] *There has been a lively interest in the elections in the last two weeks.* ○ [+ in] *His parents tried to discourage his interest in music, but he persisted.* ○ [+ to] *material which was of immense interest to the press*

▶ **COLLOCATIONS:**
  an interest **in** something
  be **of** interest
  of interest **to** someone
  a **level/conflict/place** of interest
  attract/express/lose interest
  great/little/strong/self interest

2 VERB If something **interests** you, it attracts your attention so that you want to learn or hear more about it or continue doing it. ○ *a collection of documents they seem to think might interest us* ○ [+ to-inf] *It may interest you to know that Miss Woods, the housekeeper, witnessed the attack.*

▶ **COLLOCATIONS:**
interest *someone* **in** *something*
interest a **reader/buyer**

in|ter|est|ed /ˈɪntrestɪd/

ADJECTIVE If you are **interested in** something, you think it is important and want to learn more about it or spend time doing it. ○ [+ in] *I thought she might be interested in our proposal.* ○ [+ to-inf] *I'd be interested to meet her.*

▶ **COLLOCATIONS:**
interested **in** *something*
become/get interested
greatly/particularly/mildly/not remotely interested

▶ **SYNONYM:** curious

in|ter|est|ing /ˈɪntrestɪŋ/

ADJECTIVE If you find something **interesting**, it attracts your attention, for example because you think it is exciting or unusual. ○ [+ to-inf] *It was interesting to be in a different environment.* ○ *The research has yielded some interesting findings.*

▶ **COLLOCATIONS:**
interesting **to** *someone*
an interesting **thing/idea/question/fact**
interesting **findings**
find/do/hear/see/read/watch *something* interesting
sound/prove/become/get/look interesting

▶ **PHRASE:** interesting and informative
▶ **SYNONYM:** fascinating
▶ **ANTONYM:** boring

---

inter|na|tion|al /ˌɪntəˈnæʃənəl/

ADJECTIVE **International** means between or involving different countries. ○ *an international agreement against exporting arms to that country* ○ *Kuwait International Airport* ○ *emergency aid from the international community*

▶ **COLLOCATION:** international **community/law/pressure/effort**
▶ **ANTONYM:** domestic

inter|na|tion|al|ly

ADVERB ○ *There are only two internationally recognised certificates in Teaching English as a Foreign Language.* ○ *I am one of the few young women who has made it as a writer financially and internationally.*

▶ **COLLOCATIONS:**
internationally **renowned/acclaimed/famous/recognized**
compete internationally

inter|view /ˈɪntəvjuː/ (interviews, interviewing, interviewed)

1 NOUN An **interview** is a formal meeting at which someone is asked questions in order to find out information about them. ○ *Not everyone who writes in can be invited for interview.* ○ *[+ with] The three-year study is based on interviews with judges, solicitors, parents, counsellors and written judgements.*

▶ **COLLOCATIONS:**
an interview **with** *someone*
a **job** interview
a **telephone/phone** interview
conduct an interview

2 VERB If you **are interviewed**, someone asks you questions about yourself to find out information about you. ○ *[+ for] He was among the three candidates interviewed for the job.* ○ *The junior doctor interviewed her and prepared a case history.*

▶ **COLLOCATIONS:**
interview *someone* **for** *something*
interview *someone* for a **story/article/job**
interview a **witness/candidate/sample**
police/investigators/detectives/researchers interview *someone*
interviewed by a **reporter/journalist/researcher**

in|vent /ɪnˈvent/ (invents, inventing, invented) SCIENCE

VERB If you **invent** something such as a machine or process, you are the first person to think of it or make it. ○ *He invented the first electric clock.* ○ *Writing had not been invented then.*

▶ **SYNONYMS:** come up with, devise

in|ven|tion /ɪnˈvenʃən/ (inventions)

NOUN ○ *The spinning wheel was a Chinese invention.* ○ *[+ of] the invention of the telephone*

▶ **COLLOCATIONS:**
the invention **of** *something*

technological/computer-assisted invention
develop/patent an invention
a **mechanical/revolutionary** invention

---

in|volve /ɪnˈvɒlv/ **(involves, involving, involved)**   ACADEMIC WORD

1 VERB If a situation or activity **involves** something, that thing is a necessary part or consequence of it. ○ [+ v-ing] *Nicky's job as a public relations director involves spending quite a lot of time with other people.* ○ *the risks involved in the procedure*
▶ **COLLOCATION:** involve **risk/work/money**
▶ **SYNONYM:** entail

2 VERB If a situation or activity **involves** someone, they are taking part in it. ○ *If there was a cover-up, it involved people at the very highest levels of government.* ○ *a riot involving a hundred inmates*
▶ **COLLOCATIONS:**
be involved **in** *something*
be **actively/directly/heavily** involved
deeply/emotionally involved
▶ **SYNONYM:** include

in|volve|ment /ɪnˈvɒlvmənt/

UNCOUNTABLE NOUN Your **involvement in** something is the fact that you are taking part in it. ○ [+ in] *There was a strong popular feeling for human involvement in space travel.* ○ [+ with] *She disliked his involvement with the group.*
▶ **COLLOCATIONS:**
someone's involvement **in/with** *something*
active/direct/heavy involvement
deep/emotional/romantic involvement

---

is|sue /ˈɪsjuː, ˈɪʃuː/ **(issues)**   ACADEMIC WORD

NOUN An **issue** is an important subject that people are arguing about or discussing. ○ *A key issue for higher education in the 1990's is the need for greater diversity of courses.* ○ *Is it right for the Church to express a view on political issues?*
▶ **COLLOCATIONS:**
become/debate/address an issue
raise/discuss/resolve an issue
a **complicated/controversial/sensitive** issue
a **legal/political/serious/unresolved** issue
a **key/important/difficult/critical** issue
a **money/safety/election/security** issue
▶ **SYNONYMS:** subject, matter

item /ˈaɪtəm/ (items)

ACADEMIC WORD

NOUN An **item** is one of a collection or list of objects. ○ *The most valuable item on show will be a Picasso drawing.* ○ [+ *of*] *Only one item of hand luggage is permitted.* ○ *a recent news item in a magazine*

▶ **COLLOCATIONS:**
  an item **of/on/in** *something*
  an item of **clothing/equipment/furniture**
  an item of **interest/value**
  an item on a **list/agenda/menu**
  a **news/newspaper** item
  a **luxury/household/food** item

EXTEND YOUR VOCABULARY

In everyday English, you talk about **things** to refer to objects, ideas, events, etc. In more formal writing, you use more specific nouns where possible. You can use **object** to talk about physical things that you can touch. ○ *a heavy metal object*

An **item** can be a physical thing or a piece of information. You use **item** particularly to refer to a single thing that is part of a collection or a list. ○ *the next item on the list*

You can often use **an item of ...** or **a piece of ...** before an uncountable noun to refer to one thing of that type. ○ *The average brain stores about a million items/pieces of information.*

Jj

job /dʒɒb/ (jobs)

ACADEMIC WORD · BUSINESS

1 NOUN A **job** is the work that someone does to earn money. ○ *A healthy person usually has a better chance of getting a job than someone in poor health.* ○ *Thousands have lost their jobs.* ○ *overseas job vacancies*

▶ **COLLOCATIONS:**
  get/find/have/lose a job
  create/cut jobs
  a **full-time/part-time/permanent/temporary** job
  a **good/new/top/well-paid** job
  a **teaching/factory/construction** job
  a job **vacancy**
  job **creation/cuts/losses/satisfaction**
  the job **market**
▶ **SYNONYMS:** work, employment, occupation, position, post

2 NOUN A **job** is a particular task. ○ [+ *of*] *the job of putting together a coalition* ○ *Save major painting jobs for the spring or summer.*

▶ **COLLOCATIONS:**
  the job **of** *something*
  do/start/finish a job
▶ **SYNONYMS:** task, assignment

USAGE: job or **work**?

Job is a countable noun that you use to talk about the set of duties that a person is employed to do. ○ *a part-time job at the local library*
Work is an uncountable noun that you use more generally to talk about what someone does to earn money. ○ *Many people go to the cities to find work.*

You can also use the noun **work** to talk about the place where someone works. When you use it in this way, you do not use a determiner (his, my, the, etc.) in front of it. ○ *She wasn't at work yesterday.* ○ *She came into work as usual this morning.*

You can also refer to a particular thing that needs to be done as a **job** or a **piece of work**. ○ *We've got a very important piece of work/job coming up, so I can't take time off.*

jour|nal|ist /ˈdʒɜːnəlɪst/ (journalists)   `MEDIA`

NOUN A **journalist** is a person whose job is to collect news and write about it for newspapers, magazines, television, or radio. ○ *Journalists reported that residents were in shock.*

▶ **COLLOCATIONS:**
a journalist **interviews** *someone*
a journalist **reports/writes about** *something*
a **television/tabloid/investigative** journalist

▶ **SYNONYMS:** reporter, correspondent

jour|nal|ism /ˈdʒɜːnəlɪzəm/

UNCOUNTABLE NOUN **Journalism** is the job of collecting news and writing about it for newspapers, magazines, television, or radio. ○ *He began a career in journalism, working for the North London Press Group.* ○ *It was an accomplished piece of investigative journalism.*

▶ **COLLOCATIONS:**
work **in** journalism
a **piece of** journalism
investigative/tabloid/literary journalism

▶ **SYNONYMS:** reporting, the press

judge /dʒʌdʒ/ (judges)   `LAW`

NOUN A **judge** is the person in a court of law who decides how the law should be applied, for example how criminals should be punished. ○ *The judge adjourned the hearing until next Tuesday.* ○ *Judge Mr Justice Schiemann jailed him for life.*

▶ **COLLOCATIONS:**
a **federal/district/high court** judge
a judge **rules/orders/decides/grants** *something*
a judge **convicts/jails/sentences** *someone*
someone **appoints** a judge
the **presiding** judge

▶ **PHRASE:** judge and jury

jury /ˈdʒʊəri/ (juries)   `LAW`

NOUN In a court of law, the **jury** is the group of people who have been chosen from the general public to listen to the facts about a crime and to decide whether the person accused is guilty or not. ○ *The jury convicted Mr Hampson of all offences.* ○ *the tradition of trial by jury*

▶ **COLLOCATIONS:**
 be **on** a jury
 a jury's **verdict**
 a jury **convicts/acquits** *someone*
 a jury **hears** *evidence*
 serve on a jury
 convince/tell the jury
 a **grand/hung/unbiased** jury
▶ **PHRASES:**
 jury service
 trial by jury

Kk

key /kiː/

ADJECTIVE The **key** person or thing in a group or situation is the most important one. ○ He is expected to be the key witness at the trial. ○ Education is likely to be a key issue in the next election. ○ an area of the brain that plays a key role in voluntary movement

▶ **COLLOCATIONS:**
a key **issue/factor/element/role**
a key **stage/area**
a key **player/figure/witness**

▶ **SYNONYMS:** essential, vital, crucial

▶ **ANTONYMS:** minor, unimportant

kilo|gram /ˈkɪləgræm/ (kilograms) also **kilogramme**

NOUN A **kilogram** is a metric unit of weight. One kilogram is a thousand grams, or a thousandth of a metric ton, and is equal to 2.2 pounds. The abbreviations **kilo** and **kg** are also used in informal English and in written notes. ○ a parcel weighing around 4.5 kilograms ○ [+ of] a kilogram of butter
→ see note at **centimetre**

▶ **COLLOCATIONS:**
a kilogram **of** something
weigh x kilograms

▶ **RELATED WORD:** gram

kilo|metre /ˈkɪləmiːtə, kɪˈlɒmɪtə/ (kilometres)

NOUN A **kilometre** is a metric unit of distance or length. One kilometre is a thousand metres and is equal to 0.62 miles. The abbreviation **km** is also used in written notes. [in AM, use **kilometer**] ○ [+ from] about twenty kilometres from the border ○ [+ of] The fire destroyed some 40,000 square kilometres of forest. ○ vehicles travelling at up to 300 kilometres per hour
→ see note at **centimetre**

▶ **COLLOCATIONS:**
x kilometres **from** somewhere
x kilometres **of** something
x **square/cubic** kilometres of something

▶ **PHRASE:** x kilometres per hour
▶ **RELATED WORDS:** metre, mile

---

kind /kaɪnd/ (kinds)

NOUN If you talk about a particular **kind of** thing, you are talking about one of the types or sorts of that thing. ○ [+ of] *Each method is designed to obtain a particular kind of information.* ○ *the kind of person who takes advice well* ○ *This is the biggest project of its kind in the world.* ○ *Ear pain of any kind must never be ignored.*

▶ COLLOCATIONS:
a kind **of** *person/thing*
a **different/similar/particular/certain/new/special** kind
the **same/other/right/wrong** kind
various kinds

> **EXTEND YOUR VOCABULARY**
>
> You use **kind of**, **type of** and **sort of** to talk about a class of people or things. **Kind of** is the most common and is used in both speech and writing. **Type of** is slightly more formal and is used especially to talk about things which can be divided into clear categories, such as in academic writing. **Sort of** is more informal and is used mostly in spoken English.
>
> These are all countable nouns and after words like **all** and **many**, you use the plural form **kinds/types of**. After these phrases, you can use either a plural or a singular noun. ○ *Worms feed on many different kinds of plants/plant.* ○ *The survey covered all types of employees/employee.*
>
> If you use a number in front of **kinds/types of**, you should use a singular noun after it. ○ *There are four main types of volcano.*
>
> After **kind/type of** you use a singular noun. ○ *two people with the same kind/type of personality*

---

knowl|edge /ˈnɒlɪdʒ/

UNCOUNTABLE NOUN Knowledge is information and understanding about a subject which a person has, or which all people have. ○ [+ of] *Our ancestors had a detailed knowledge of wildlife.* ○ *the quest for scientific knowledge*

▶ COLLOCATIONS:
knowledge **of/about** *something*
knowledge of a **language/subject**
basic/in-depth/detailed/first-hand/prior knowledge

scientific/technical/specialized knowledge
have/possess/gain/lack knowledge
▶ **SYNONYMS:** awareness, understanding, expertise
▶ **ANTONYM:** ignorance

Ll

la|bora|tory /ləˈbɒrətri, AM ˈlæbrətɔːri/ (laboratories) `SCIENCE`

NOUN A **laboratory** is a building or a room where scientific experiments and research are carried out. **Lab** is also used in informal and spoken English. ○ *The two scientists tested the idea in laboratory experiments.* ○ *a medical research laboratory*

▶ COLLOCATIONS:
a laboratory **conducts** *experiments*
equip a laboratory
laboratory **conditions/equipment**
a laboratory **test/experiment/technician**
a **well-equipped/mobile/testing** laboratory
a **forensic/biological/clinical/research** laboratory

---

lack /læk/ (lacks, lacking, lacked)

1 UNCOUNTABLE NOUN If there is a **lack of** something, there is not enough of it or it does not exist at all. ○ [+ *of*] *Despite his lack of experience, he got the job.* ○ [+ *of*] *The charges were dropped for lack of evidence.*

▶ COLLOCATIONS:
a lack **of** *something*
a lack of **experience/interest/knowledge**
a lack of **resources/support/evidence/progress**
a lack of **sleep/confidence**
show/cite/perceive a lack
a **complete/total/distinct** lack
a **relative/apparent** lack

▶ SYNONYMS: shortage, absence, deficiency
▶ ANTONYM: abundance

2 VERB If you say that someone or something **lacks** a particular quality or that a particular quality **is lacking** in them, you mean that they do not have any or enough of it. ○ *It lacked the power of the Italian cars.* ○ *Certain vital information is lacking in the report.*

▶ COLLOCATIONS:
be lacking **in** *something*
lacking in **confidence**
lack **resources/skills/credibility**

lack **confidence/courage/ability**
sorely/sadly/totally/often lacking

ACADEMIC WRITING: Avoiding negatives

In formal, academic writing, you need to be as clear and accurate as possible. Sometimes, it is better to avoid complicated negative constructions by using words like **lack** that have a negative meaning. For example, the sentences: *Almost a third of students aged 14 lacked basic reading skills.* and *Inspectors criticized the lack of adult supervision of children.* are clearer and simpler than: *Almost of third of students aged 14 did not have basic reading skills.* and *Inspectors criticized the fact that there was not enough adult supervision of children.*

---

land /lænd/ GEOGRAPHY

1 UNCOUNTABLE NOUN Land is an area of ground, especially one that is used for a particular purpose such as farming or building. ○ *Good agricultural land is in short supply.* ○ *160 acres of land* ○ *a small piece of grazing land*

▶ COLLOCATIONS:
an amount **of** land
buy/sell/acquire land
clear/occupy/own land
public/private land
fertile/dry/arable/agricultural land
grazing/farm/desert/forest land
a **piece/acre of** land

2 UNCOUNTABLE NOUN Land is the part of the world that consists of ground, rather than sea or air. ○ *It isn't clear whether the plane went down over land or sea.* ○ *a stretch of sandy beach that was almost inaccessible from the land*

▶ COLLOCATION: land **surrounds** *something*
▶ PHRASE: land or sea

---

land|scape /ˈlændskeɪp/ (landscapes) GEOGRAPHY

NOUN The **landscape** is everything you can see when you look across an area of land, including hills, rivers, buildings, trees, and plants. ○ *Arizona's desert landscape* ○ [+ of] *We moved to Northamptonshire and a new landscape of hedges and fields.*

▶ COLLOCATIONS:
a landscape **of** *something*
change/transform/alter the landscape
a **rural/urban** landscape
a **beautiful/bleak/barren/desert** landscape

▶ **SYNONYM:** scenery
▶ **RELATED WORD:** seascape

---

lan|guage /ˈlæŋgwɪdʒ/ (languages)   `LANGUAGE`

1 NOUN A **language** is a system of communication which is used by the people of a particular country or region for talking or writing. ○ *the English language* ○ *Students are expected to master a second language.*

2 UNCOUNTABLE NOUN Language is the use of a system of communication which consists of a set of sounds or written symbols. ○ *Students examined how children acquire language.*

▶ **COLLOCATIONS:**
speak/learn/use/master/understand a language
study/teach a language
acquire language
language **learning/skills/teaching/acquisition**
a language **barrier**
the **English/French** language
modern languages
a **different/common/official/foreign** language
someone's **own/native/first/second** language
abusive/foul language

▶ **PHRASES:**
language and culture
language and literature

---

law /lɔː/ (laws)   `LAW`

1 NOUN The **law** is a system of rules that a society or government develops in order to deal with crime, business agreements, and social relationships. You can also use the **law** to refer to the people who work in this system. ○ *Obscene and threatening phone calls are against the law.* ○ *[+ on] breaking the law on financing political parties* ○ *The book analyses why women kill and how the law treats them.*

2 NOUN A **law** is one of the rules in a system of law which deals with a particular type of agreement, relationship, or crime. ○ *the country's liberal political asylum law* ○ *The law was passed on a second vote.*

3 UNCOUNTABLE NOUN Law is the study of systems of law and how laws work. ○ *He came to Oxford and studied law.* ○ *He holds a law degree from Bristol University.*

▶ **COLLOCATIONS:**
a law **against/on** something
violate a law

break/obey/uphold the law
pass/enforce/introduce/change/propose a law
study/practise law
the law **prohibits/bans/forbids/prevents** *something*
the law **requires/permits/allows** *something*
the laws **governing** *something*
federal/international/criminal/European law
copyright/immigration/privacy/employment law
new/current/existing/strict/tough laws
law **enforcement/school**
a law **degree/student/professor**
▶ **PHRASES:**
against the law
law and order
laws and regulations
changes in the law
▶ **SYNONYMS:** rule, regulation

---

law|yer /ˈlɔɪə/ (lawyers) `LAW`

NOUN A **lawyer** is a person who is qualified to advise people about the law and represent them in court. ○ *Prosecution and defence lawyers are expected to deliver closing arguments next week.*
▶ **COLLOCATIONS:**
hire/consult/appoint a lawyer
a lawyer **argues/claims** *something*
a lawyer **represents/acts for/advises/defends** *someone*
a **defence/divorce/immigration** lawyer
a **human rights/civil rights/criminal/corporate** lawyer
a **prominent/top** lawyer
▶ **SYNONYMS:** attorney, barrister

---

lead /liːd/ (leads, leading, led) · `SOCIAL SCIENCE` `POLITICS` `BUSINESS`

VERB If you **lead** a group of people, an organization, or an activity, you are in control or in charge of the people or the activity. ○ *He led the country between 1949 and 1984.* ○ *Mr Mendes was leading a campaign to save Brazil's rainforest from exploitation.*
▶ **COLLOCATIONS:**
lead a **campaign/investigation**
lead a **team/coalition/group/delegation/country**
▶ **SYNONYMS:** control, manage, direct

lead|er /ˈliːdə/ (leaders)

NOUN The **leader** of a group of people or an organization is the person who is in control of it or in charge of it. ○ *We are going to hold a rally next month to elect a new leader.*

▶ **COLLOCATIONS:**
the leader **of** *something*
elect/choose a leader
a **business/community/church** leader
a **party/union/opposition** leader
a **world/religious/political** leader
a **deputy** leader
the leader of a **republic/nation/country**
the leader of a **party/movement/group**
the leader of the **opposition**
▶ **SYNONYM:** head

lead|er|ship /ˈliːdəʃɪp/ (leaderships)

NOUN You refer to people who are in control of a group or organization as the **leadership**. ○ *He is expected to hold talks with both the Croatian and Slovenian leaderships.* ○ [+ *of*] *the Labour leadership of Haringey council in north London*

▶ **COLLOCATIONS:**
the leadership **of** *something*
liberal/communist leadership
union/party/church leadership
the leadership **decides/agrees/rejects** *something*

---

lead to (leads to, leading to, led to)

Pronounced /liːd tə/ before a consonant and /liːd tʊ/ before a vowel.

PHRASAL VERB If something **leads to** a situation or event, usually an unpleasant one, it begins a process which causes that situation or event to happen. ○ *Ethnic tensions among the republics could lead to civil war.* ○ *He warned yesterday that a pay rise for teachers would lead to job cuts.*

▶ **COLLOCATION: eventually/ultimately/inevitably/often/** lead to *something*
▶ **SYNONYMS:** result in, bring about, give rise to, prompt

---

leaf /liːf/ (leaves)   SCIENCE BIOLOGY

NOUN The **leaves** of a tree or plant are the parts that are flat, thin, and usually green. Many trees and plants lose their leaves in the winter and grow new leaves in the spring. ○ [+ *of*] *In the garden, the leaves of the horse* *chestnut had already fallen.* ○ *The Japanese maple that stands across the drive had just come into leaf.*

▸ **COLLOCATIONS:**
the leaves **of** *something*
leaves **fall/drop**
a tree **loses** *its leaves*

▸ **PHRASE:** come into leaf

---

learn /lɜːn/ **(learns, learning, learned, learnt)** `EDUCATION`

> American English uses the form **learned** as the past tense and past participle. British English uses either **learned** or **learnt**.

1 VERB If you **learn** something, you obtain knowledge or a skill through studying or training. ○ *Their children were going to learn English.* ○ [+ to-inf] *He is learning to play the piano.* ○ [+ how] *learning how to use new computer systems*

▸ **COLLOCATIONS:**
learn **about** *something*
learn about **history/culture/money**
learn to **read/swim/cook/drive**
learn a **skill/language/technique**
learn **quickly/fast/early**

▸ **SYNONYMS:** master, grasp

> **USAGE: learn, study** or **teach**?
>
> If you **study** something, you read and listen to information in order to **learn** about it. **Studying** describes the activities involved in education. **Learning** is the process of gaining new knowledge or skills. ○ *I studied German at school, but I only learnt a few basic words.* If you **teach** someone a subject or a skill, you give them information or instructions to help them to **learn.** ○ *He teaches History at the university.* ○ *My grandfather taught me to swim.*

2 VERB If you **learn** of something, you find out about it. ○ [+ of] *The zoological world learned of two new species of lizard.* ○ [+ that] *It didn't come as a shock to learn that the fuel and cooling systems are the most common causes of breakdown.*

▸ **COLLOCATION:** learn **of** *something*

▸ **SYNONYM:** discover

---

le|gal /ˈliːɡəl/ `ACADEMIC WORD` `LAW`

1 ADJECTIVE Legal is used to describe things that relate to the law. ○ *He vowed to take legal action.* ○ *the British legal system* ○ *I sought legal advice on this.*

▶ COLLOCATIONS:
 legal **action/advice/fees/costs**
 a legal **battle/challenge/expert/adviser**
 legal **rights/proceedings**
 the legal **profession/system**

2 ADJECTIVE An action or situation that is **legal** is allowed or required by law. ○ *What I did was perfectly legal.* ○ *drivers who have more than the legal limit of alcohol*

▶ COLLOCATIONS:
 perfectly/entirely legal
 the legal **limit**
 a legal **requirement**
▶ SYNONYMS: lawful, permissible
▶ ANTONYMS: illegal, unlawful

le|gal|ly

ADVERB ○ *It could be a bit problematic, legally speaking.* ○ *A lorry driver can legally work eighty-two hours a week.*

▶ COLLOCATIONS:
 legally **binding/enforceable/liable**
 legally **oblige/entitle/require** *someone to do something*
 legally **recognise** *something*
 legally **married**
 act/operate/work legally
▶ PHRASE: morally or legally
▶ ANTONYMS: illegally, unlawfully

---

lei|sure /ˈleʒə, AM ˈliːʒ-/

UNCOUNTABLE NOUN **Leisure** is the time when you are not working and you can relax and do things that you enjoy. ○ *a relaxing way to fill my leisure time* ○ *one of Britain's most popular leisure activities*

▶ COLLOCATIONS:
 leisure **time**
 a leisure **centre/facility/complex/activity/pursuit**
 the leisure **industry**
 leisure **travel**
▶ SYNONYMS: recreation, free time
▶ ANTONYM: work

lend /lend/ (lends, lending, lent)

BUSINESS ECONOMICS

VERB When people or organizations such as banks **lend** you money, they give it to you and you agree to pay it back at a future date, often with an extra amount as interest. ○ *The bank is reassessing its criteria for lending money.* ○ [+ to] *financial de-regulation that led to institutions being more willing to lend* ○ [+ to] *the bank's policy on lending money to political parties*

▶ COLLOCATIONS:
  lend something **to** someone
  lend **money/£x**
  lend a **sum**
  a **bank/building society** lends *money*

▶ SYNONYMS: loan, advance

▶ ANTONYM: borrow

loan /ləʊn/ (loans)

NOUN A **loan** is a sum of money that you borrow. ○ *The president wants to make it easier for small businesses to get bank loans.* ○ *loan repayments*

▶ COLLOCATIONS:
  a loan **from** somewhere
  a loan **of** x
  a loan **at** a particular rate
  offer/approve/guarantee a loan
  obtain/secure/get/repay a loan
  a **personal/bank/student** loan
  a **fixed-rate/interest-free/low-interest** loan
  a **short-term/cheap/outstanding** loan
  a **secured/unsecured** loan
  a **home/housing/mortgage** loan
  a loan **rate/agreement/guarantee/repayment**
  a loan **totals** x

▶ SYNONYMS: advance, credit

▶ RELATED WORDS: overdraft, grant, mortgage

length /leŋθ/ (lengths)

1 **NOUN** The **length** of something is the amount that it measures from one end to the other along the longest side. ○ *It is about a metre in length.* ○ [+ of] *the length of the field* ○ [+ of] *The plane had a wing span of 34ft and a length of 22ft.*

2 **NOUN** The **length** of something such as a piece of writing is the amount of writing that is contained in it. ○ *a book of at least 100 pages in length* ○ [+ of] *The length of a paragraph depends on the information it conveys.*

3 NOUN The **length** of an event, activity, or situation is the period of time from beginning to end for which something lasts or during which something happens. ○ [+ *of*] *The exact length of each period may vary.* ○ *His film, over two hours in length, is a subtle study of family life.*

▶ **COLLOCATIONS:**
be *x* **in** length
the length **of** *something*
the length of a **prison sentence/stay**
something **stretches/extends** the length of *something*
have a length of *x*
measure/run/walk/travel the length of *something*
a **considerable/exact/average/short/maximum** length
the **entire/full/whole/total/overall** length of *something*

▶ **PHRASES:**
length of time
of varying lengths
the length and breadth of something
at arm's length
focal length

▶ **RELATED WORDS:** breadth, width, height, depth

lev|el /ˈlevəl/ (levels)

NOUN A **level** is a point on a scale, for example a scale of amount, quality, or difficulty. ○ *If you don't know your cholesterol level, it's a good idea to have it checked.* ○ [+ *of*] *We do have the lowest level of inflation for some years.*

▶ **COLLOCATIONS:**
a level **of** *something*
a level of **risk/activity/support/violence/income**
reduce/lower/increase/raise a level
reach/maintain/achieve a level
a level **drops/falls/rises/increase/remains**
a **high/low/minimum/average/normal** level of *something*
cholesterol/sea/blood/water level
a **record** level
energy levels

▶ **SYNONYMS:** position, degree, stage

li|brary /ˈlaɪbrəri, AM -breri/ (libraries)   EDUCATION

NOUN A **library** is a building where people can study and where things such as books, newspapers, videos, and music are kept for people to read, use, or borrow. ○ *the local library* ○ *She issued them library cards.* ○ *a manuscript held in the university library*

▶ COLLOCATIONS:
a **public/local/central/lending/reference/university** library
a library **lends/contains/holds** something
a library **card/book**

life|style /ˈlaɪfstaɪl/ (lifestyles) also **life style**, **life-style**

NOUN The **lifestyle** of a particular person or group of people is the living conditions, behaviour, and habits that are typical of them or are chosen by them. ○ *They enjoyed an income and lifestyle that many people would envy.* ○ *the change of lifestyle occasioned by the baby's arrival*

▶ COLLOCATIONS:
adopt/enjoy/live/maintain/promote/lead a lifestyle
a **healthy/active/sedentary** lifestyle
a **lavish/alternative/extravagant/comfortable** lifestyle

▶ PHRASES:
diet and lifestyle
lifestyle and culture

▶ SYNONYM: way of life

life|time /ˈlaɪftaɪm/ (lifetimes)

NOUN A **lifetime** is the length of time that someone is alive. ○ *During my lifetime I haven't got around to much travelling.* ○ [+ of] *an extraordinary lifetime of achievement*

▶ COLLOCATIONS:
a lifetime **of** something
a lifetime of **experience/achievement**
spend/last a lifetime
a lifetime **award/achievement/ban/guarantee**
lifetime **employment**
a **whole/entire** lifetime

▶ PHRASE: during your lifetime

like|ly /ˈlaɪkli/ (likelier, likeliest)

1 ADJECTIVE You use **likely** to indicate that something is probably the case or will probably happen in a particular situation. ○ *Experts say a 'yes' vote is still the likely outcome.* ○ [+ that] *If this is your first baby, it's far more likely that you'll get to the hospital too early.*

2 ADJECTIVE If someone or something is **likely to** do a particular thing, they will very probably do it. ○ [+ to-inf] *In the meantime the war of nerves seems likely to continue.* ○ *Once people have seen that something actually works, they are much more likely to accept change.*

▶ **COLLOCATIONS:**
likely to **become/remain/continue/happen/cause**
be/seem/look/appear/become likely
more/most/very/highly/increasingly likely
less/as/not/also/quite likely
a likely **target/explanation/outcome/candidate**
▶ **SYNONYMS:** probable, apt, expected, liable, anticipated
▶ **ANTONYM:** unlikely
→ see note at **possible**

like|li|hood /ˈlaɪklihʊd/

UNCOUNTABLE NOUN The **likelihood of** something happening is how likely it is to happen. ○ [+ of] *The likelihood of infection is minimal.* ○ [+ of] *concerns that these changes would increase the likelihood of wrongful conviction*

▶ **COLLOCATIONS:**
the likelihood **of** something
lessen/decrease/reduce the likelihood of something
a **strong/great/high/reasonable/substantial** likelihood
little/less likelihood
▶ **SYNONYMS:** probability, possibility, chance

lim|it /ˈlɪmɪt/ (limits, limiting, limited)

1 NOUN A **limit** is the greatest amount, extent, or degree of something that is possible. ○ *warnings that hospitals are being stretched to the limit* ○ [+ to] *There is no limit to how much fresh fruit you can eat in a day.*

▶ **COLLOCATIONS:**
to the limit
a limit **to** something
the limits **of** something
the limits of **endurance/tolerance**
push/stretch/test something to the limit
put a limit on something
▶ **PHRASE:** there is no limit to something
▶ **SYNONYM:** utmost

2 NOUN A **limit** of a particular kind is the largest or smallest amount of something such as time or money that is allowed because of a rule, law, or decision. ○ *The three month time limit will be up in mid-June.* ○ [+ on] *The economic affairs minister announced limits on petrol sales.*

▶ **COLLOCATIONS:**
a limit **on** something
a limit **of** x
impose/set/place/put a limit on something

reach/exceed/break/raise/reduce a limit
a limit on a **number/amount**
a limit on **emissions/size/spending/investment**
a **speed/credit/age/time** limit
a **strict/legal/daily/reasonable/absolute** limit
a **maximum/upper/minimum** limit
a **spending/alcohol** limit
▶ SYNONYM: restriction

3 VERB If you **limit** something, you prevent it from becoming greater than a particular amount or degree. ○ *He limited payments on the country's foreign debt.* ○ [+ to] *The view was that the economy would grow by 2.25 per cent. This would limit unemployment to around 2.5 million.*

▶ COLLOCATIONS:
limit something **to** x
limit the **amount/number/size** of something
limit the **use** of something
limit **damage**
severely/strictly limit something
▶ SYNONYM: restrict

---

link /lɪŋk/ (links, linking, linked)   ACADEMIC WORD

1 NOUN If there is a **link between** two things or situations, there is a relationship between them, for example because one thing causes or affects the other. ○ [+ between] *the link between smoking and lung cancer* ○ [+ with] *Police are investigating potential links with the bombing of a car on Monday.*

▶ COLLOCATIONS:
a link **between** things
a link **with** something
uncover/investigate a link
a **direct/close/possible/strong** link
▶ SYNONYMS: connection, relationship, association

2 VERB If someone or something **links** two things or situations, there is a relationship between them, for example because one thing causes or affects the other. ○ [+ with] *The study further strengthens the evidence linking smoking with early death.* ○ *The detention raised two distinct but closely linked questions.*

▶ COLLOCATIONS:
link something **with/to** something
closely/directly/inextricably/intimately/allegedly linked
evidence/speculation/rumour links things
a **study** links things
link a **death/murder/incident/suspect/group** to something

liq|uid /ˈlɪkwɪd/ (liquids)　　　SCIENCE

1 NOUN A **liquid** is a substance which is not solid but which flows and can be poured, for example water. ○ *Drink plenty of liquid.* ○ *a container filled with a flammable liquid*

▶ **COLLOCATIONS:**
　drink/pour/absorb a liquid
　a liquid **evaporates/reduces/flows/cools**
　a **flammable/colourless** liquid

▶ **PHRASES:**
　solids and liquids
　liquids and gases

▶ **SYNONYM:** fluid

▶ **ANTONYM:** solid

2 ADJECTIVE A **liquid** substance is in the form of a liquid rather than being solid or a gas. ○ *Wash in warm water with liquid detergent.* ○ *Fats are solid at room temperature, and oil is liquid at room temperature.*

▶ **COLLOCATIONS:**
　liquid **fertiliser/feed/detergent**
　liquid **nitrogen/hydrogen**

▶ **ANTONYM:** solid

list /lɪst/ (lists, listing, listed)

1 NOUN A list is a set of things which all belong to a particular category, written down one below the other, sometimes in a particular order. ○ *There were six names on the list.* ○ *I would have thought if they were looking for redundancies I would be last on the list.* ○ *[+ of] 'First City' joined a long list of failed banks.*

▶ **COLLOCATIONS:**
　be **on** a list
　a list **of** *things*
　a list of **priorities/names/items/candidates/demands**
　make/provide/release/publish/compile a list
　top/head/join a list
　a list **includes/contains/shows** *something*
　a **short/growing/long/endless/lengthy** list
　a **detailed/extensive/full/comprehensive/impressive** list
　a **mailing/shopping/waiting/reading** list
　a **wine/wish/price** list
　last/first/high on a list

2 VERB To **list** several things means to write or say them one after another, usually in a particular order. ○ *Manufacturers must list ingredients in order of the amount used.* ○ *Results are listed alphabetically.*

▶ **COLLOCATIONS:**
 list *something* **under** *something*
 list **ingredients/items/names/numbers**
 list *something* **publicly/officially/separately/alphabetically**
 list *something* under **a heading/category**
▶ **SYNONYMS:** itemize, record

---

lit|era|ture /ˈlɪtrətʃə, AM -tərətʃʊr/ (literatures)   `LITERATURE`

1 **NOUN** Novels, plays, and poetry are referred to as **literature**, especially when they are considered to be good or important. ○ *classic works of literature* ○ *a Professor of English Literature*

2 **UNCOUNTABLE NOUN** The **literature** on a particular subject of study is all the books and articles that have been published about it. ○ [+ *on*] *The literature on immigration policy is extremely critical of the state.* ○ *This work is documented in the scientific literature.*

▶ **COLLOCATIONS:**
 literature **on/about** *something*
 teach/study/review/read literature
 publish/produce literature
 contemporary/English/comparative/classical/modern literature
 scientific/medical literature
 a literature **course/class/student/teacher/professor**
 a literature **review**

▶ **PHRASES:**
 a work of literature
 language and literature
 art and literature

---

li|tre /ˈliːtə/ (litres)

NOUN A **litre** is a metric unit of volume that is a thousand cubic centimetres. It is equal to 1.76 British pints or 2.11 American pints. The abbreviation **l** is used in written notes. [in AM, use **liter**] ○ [+ *of*] *15 litres of water* ○ *This tax would raise petrol prices by about 3.5p per litre.* ○ *a Ford Escort with a 1.9-litre engine*

→ see note at **centimetre**

▶ **COLLOCATIONS:**
 cost *x* **per** litre
 a litre **of** *something*
 a litre of **milk/water/wine/beer/fuel/petrol**
 a *x* litre **engine**

▶ **RELATED WORDS:** pint, centilitre, millilitre

lo|cal /ˈləʊkəl/

ADJECTIVE Local means existing in or belonging to the area where you live, or to the area that you are talking about. ○ *a copy of the local newspaper* ○ *Some local residents joined the students' protest.* ○ *encouraging children to use the local library*

▶ COLLOCATIONS:
  a local **school/shop/hospital/newspaper/pub/library**
  a local **resident/community/population**
▶ SYNONYMS: regional, provincial
▶ ANTONYMS: national, international, foreign

lo|cal|ly

ADVERB ○ *We've got cards which are drawn and printed and designed by someone locally.* ○ *the importance of buying locally produced food*

▶ COLLOCATIONS:
  live/shop locally
  locally **grown/produced/owned/based**
▶ SYNONYM: regionally
▶ ANTONYMS: nationally, internationally

lo|cat|ed /ləʊˈkeɪtɪd, AM ˈləʊkeɪt-/ `ACADEMIC WORD`

ADJECTIVE If something is **located** in a particular place, it is present or has been built there. [FORMAL] ○ *The restaurant is located near the cathedral.* ○ [+ within] *A boutique and beauty salon are conveniently located within the grounds.*

▶ COLLOCATIONS:
  located **in/near/within** *a place*
  conveniently/centrally located
▶ SYNONYM: situated

lo|ca|tion /ləʊˈkeɪʃən/ (locations)

NOUN A **location** is the place where something happens or is situated. ○ *The first thing he looked at was his office's location.* ○ *Macau's newest small luxury hotel has a beautiful location.* ○ [+ of] *finding the exact location of the church*

▶ COLLOCATIONS:
  the location **of** *something*
  a location **for** *something*
  reveal/identify/pinpoint/determine the location of *something*
  a **different/specific/exact/remote/geographical** location
  a **prime/central/ideal/exotic** location
  a **secret/undisclosed/seaside/waterfront** location

▶ **PHRASES:**
location and size
location and name
location and date
locations around the world
locations across the country
▶ **SYNONYMS:** setting, place, situation

---

logo /ˈləʊɡəʊ/ (logos) `BUSINESS`

NOUN The **logo** of a company or organization is the special design or way of writing its name that it puts on all its products, notepaper, or advertisements. ○ *Staff should wear uniforms, and vehicles should bear company logos.* ○ *a red T-shirt with a logo on the front*

▶ **COLLOCATIONS:**
a logo **on** *something*
design/feature/display/bear a logo
a **corporate/company/famous/new** logo
a logo **appears** *somewhere*
a logo **features** *something*
a logo on the **front/back/side/cover** of *something*

▶ **PHRASE:** name and logo
▶ **SYNONYM:** emblem

---

long /lɒŋ, AM lɔːŋ/ (longer, longest)

1 ADVERB You use **long** to ask or talk about amounts of time. ○ *How long have you lived around here?* ○ *He has been on a diet for as long as any of his friends can remember.*

● **Long** is also an adjective. ○ *The average commuter journey there is five hours long.* ○ *Camels can survive for long periods without drinking.*

▶ **COLLOCATIONS:**
last/wait/stay/live/take long
a long **time/period/wait/while**

▶ **PHRASES:**
as long as
how long

2 ADJECTIVE You use **long** to talk or ask about the distance something measures from one end to the other. ○ *An eight-week-old embryo is only an inch long.* ○ *How long is the tunnel?* ○ *In the roots of the olives, you could find centipedes as long as a pencil.*

▶ **COLLOCATIONS:**
x **miles/metres/feet/inches** long

long **nails/hair**
a long **list/report/line**
extremely/relatively/fairly/unusually/very long
a long **distance/way**
▶ ANTONYM: short

---

look up /lʊk ˈʌp/ (looks up, looking up, looked up)   ACADEMIC STUDY

PHRASAL VERB If you **look up** a fact or a piece of information, you find it
out by looking in something such as a reference book, a list, or a website.
○ [+ in] *I looked your address up in the personnel file.* ○ *Many people have to look
up the meaning of this word in the dictionary.*
▶ COLLOCATIONS:
look *something* up **in/on** *something*
look up a **word/fact/meaning**
look up **information**
▶ SYNONYM: research

---

lose /luːz/ (loses, losing, lost)   BUSINESS

1 VERB You say that you **lose** something when you no longer have it
because it has been taken away from you or destroyed. ○ *I lost my job when
the company moved to another state.* ○ *He lost his licence for six months.* ○ *She
was terrified they'd lose their home.*

2 VERB If a business **loses** money, it earns less money than it spends, and is
therefore in debt. ○ *His shops stand to lose millions of pounds.* ○ *$1 billion a
year may be lost.*
▶ COLLOCATIONS:
lose your **job/licence/home**
nearly/completely/almost lose *something*
lose **money/£x/$x**
▶ ANTONYMS: gain, make

loss /lɒs, AM lɔːs/ (losses)

1 NOUN Loss is the fact of no longer having something or having less of it
than before. ○ [+ of] *Wildlife is under threat from hunting, pollution and loss of
habitat.* ○ *The job losses will reduce the total workforce to 7,000.*

2 NOUN If a business makes a **loss**, it earns less than it spends. ○ [+ of] *In
1986 Rover made a loss of nine hundred million pounds.* ○ *Both firms reported
pre-tax losses in the first half.*
▶ COLLOCATIONS:
the loss **of** *something*
the loss of **jobs/earnings/income/revenue/£x**

make/incur/post/report a loss
suffer/sustain/cause a loss
a **net/pre-tax/full-year/quarterly** loss
a **heavy/significant/total/huge** loss
a **financial/annual/operating** loss
job losses

▶ PHRASES:
profit and loss
losses and gains

▶ ANTONYMS: profit, gain

USAGE: **lose**, **loss** or **loose**?

Lose is a verb and it has the irregular past tense form **lost**.
○ *The project began to lose money.* ○ *300 workers lost their jobs when the factory closed.*

Loss is a noun. ○ *The factory closed with the loss of 300 jobs.*

Loose is an adjective to describe something that is not tight or firm. It has no connection with the two words above. ○ *Wear loose, comfortable clothing.*

---

low|er /ˈləʊə/ (lowers, lowering, lowered)

1 **ADJECTIVE** You can use **lower** to refer to the bottom one of a pair of things. ○ *She bit her lower lip.* ○ *the lower deck of the bus* ○ *the lower of the two holes*

▶ COLLOCATIONS:
the lower **of** things
a lower **level/layer/lip/deck**

▶ ANTONYM: upper

2 **ADJECTIVE** You can use **lower** to refer to the bottom part of something. ○ *Use a small cushion to help give support to the lower back.* ○ *fires which started in the lower part of a tower block*

▶ COLLOCATION: the lower **back/part**

▶ ANTONYM: upper

3 **VERB** If you **lower** something, you make it less in amount, degree, value, or quality. ○ *The Central Bank has lowered interest rates by 2 percent.* ○ *This drug lowers cholesterol levels by binding fats in the intestine.*

→ see note at **decrease**

▶ COLLOCATIONS:
lower a **tariff/rate/cost**
lower the **temperature/level** of something

lower **standards/expectations**
dramatically/slowly/significantly lower *something*
▶ **SYNONYMS:** drop, reduce, decrease, lessen, diminish
▶ **ANTONYM:** raise

---

lung /lʌŋ/ (lungs) SCIENCE BIOLOGY MEDICINE

NOUN Your **lungs** are the two organs inside your chest which fill with air when you breathe in. ○ *a patient suffering from a collapsed lung* ○ *X-rays indicated that her lungs were filled with fluid.*
▶ **COLLOCATIONS:**
puncture/damage/penetrate a lung
burn/irritate/blacken/bruise/fill the lungs
lungs **burst/collapse/fill**
a **left/right/collapsed/diseased/damaged** lung
a **healthy/weak** lung
a lung **transplant/infection/disease/disorder**
lung **tissue/function/capacity**
lung **cancer/damage/surgery**

Mm

ma|chine /məˈʃiːn/ (machines)

NOUN A **machine** is a piece of equipment which uses electricity or an engine in order to do a particular kind of work. ○ *The machine can be remotely operated and monitored.* ○ *machines designed to detect hazardous gases* ○ *an electrically operated machine*

▶ **COLLOCATIONS:**
  by machine
  a **washing/gaming/milking** machine
  a **vending/ATM/cash/answering/fax** machine
  a **powerful/modern/reliable/efficient** machine
  a **faulty/unreliable/defective** machine
  operate/use/run/start/stop a machine
  design/build/make a machine
▶ **SYNONYMS:** device, gadget, appliance

ma|chin|ery /məˈʃiːnəri/

UNCOUNTABLE NOUN You can use **machinery** to refer to machines in general, or machines that are used in a factory or on a farm. ○ *quality tools and machinery* ○ *hi-tech packaging machinery*

▶ **COLLOCATIONS:**
  agricultural/industrial machinery
  farm/factory/garden/textile machinery
  mining/printing/manufacturing/harvesting machinery
  electrical/solar-powered/hydraulic machinery
  state-of-the-art/high-tech machinery
  lubricate/oil/repair machinery
  install/operate/manufacture/supply machinery
▶ **PHRASE:** machinery and equipment
▶ **SYNONYMS:** equipment, hardware, technology

main /meɪn/

ADJECTIVE The **main** thing is the most important one of several similar things in a particular situation. ○ *one of the main tourist areas of Amsterdam* ○ *Our main objective was to improve safety.* ○ *What are the main differences and similarities between them?*

▶ **COLLOCATIONS:**
the main **concern/issue/subject/focus/aim/objective**
the main **source/cause/reason**
the main **difference/character/attraction**
the main **bedroom/bathroom/street/road/entrance**
▶ **SYNONYMS:** primary, principal, major, chief

main|ly /ˈmeɪnli/

1 ADVERB You use **mainly** when mentioning the main reason or thing involved in something. ○ *I don't play golf, mainly because I'm no good at it.* ○ *The birds live mainly on nectar.*

2 ADVERB You use **mainly** when you are referring to a group and stating something that is true of most of it. ○ *The staff were mainly Russian.* ○ *the mainly Muslim country* ○ *a mainly elderly population*

▶ **COLLOCATIONS:**
consist/be composed mainly of *something*
mainly **focus on/comprise** *something*
▶ **SYNONYMS:** primarily, principally, chiefly, predominantly, largely

ma|jor /ˈmeɪdʒə/ ACADEMIC WORD

ADJECTIVE You use **major** when you want to describe something that is more important, serious, or significant than other things in a group or situation. ○ *The major factor in the decision to stay or to leave was usually professional.* ○ *Drug abuse is a major problem in the city.* ○ *Exercise has a major part to play in preventing disease.*

▶ **COLLOCATIONS:**
a major **event/concern/project**
a major **problem/factor/change**
▶ **PHRASE:** play a major part in *something*
▶ **SYNONYMS:** key, crucial, central, primary
▶ **ANTONYM:** minor

man|age /ˈmænɪdʒ/ (manages, managing, managed) BUSINESS

1 VERB If someone **manages** an organization, business, or system, they are responsible for controlling it. ○ *Within two years he was managing the store.* ○ *The factory was badly managed.* ○ *the government's ability to manage the economy*

2 VERB If you **manage** time, money, or other resources, you deal with them carefully and do not waste them. ○ *In a busy world, managing your time is increasingly important.* ○ *We are trying to manage water resources effectively.*

m

▶ **COLLOCATIONS:**
manage a **business/system/organization**
manage **time/money/resources**
manage *something* **badly/poorly/aggressively**
manage *something* **successfully/well/carefully/effectively**

▶ **SYNONYMS:** organize, run, direct
▶ **ANTONYMS:** mismanage, waste

man|age|ment /ˈmænɪdʒmənt/ (managements)

1 UNCOUNTABLE NOUN Management is the control and organizing of a business or other organization. ○ *The zoo needs better management.* ○ [+ *of*] *the management of the mining industry* ○ *the responsibility for its day-to-day management*

▶ **COLLOCATIONS:**
the management **of** *something*
business/fiscal/economic management
day-to-day/operational/sustainable management
a management **consultant/structure/system/style**

▶ **PHRASE:** management and administration
▶ **SYNONYMS:** organization, control, directorship

2 NOUN You can refer to the people who control and organize a business or other organization as the **management**. ○ *The management is doing its best to improve the situation.* ○ *We need to get more women into top management.*

▶ **COLLOCATION:** **top/senior/middle** management
▶ **SYNONYM:** staff

man|ag|er /ˈmænɪdʒə/ (managers)

NOUN A **manager** is a person who is responsible for running part of or the whole of a business organization. ○ *The chef, staff and managers are all Chinese.* ○ *a retired bank manager*

▶ **COLLOCATIONS:**
a **bank/business/accounts/general** manager
appoint/recruit/hire/sack/fire a manager

▶ **SYNONYMS:** director, head, executive, leader

---

man-made /ˌmænˈmeɪd/

ADJECTIVE Man-made things are created or caused by people, rather than occurring naturally. ○ *Man-made and natural disasters have disrupted the Government's economic plans.* ○ *man-made lakes* ○ *a variety of materials, both natural and man-made*

▶ **COLLOCATIONS:**
a man-made **lake/waterway**

m

man-made **fibres/fabrics/chemicals**
▶ **SYNONYMS:** artificial, synthetic
▶ **ANTONYM:** natural

---

manu|al /ˈmænjʊəl/ ACADEMIC WORD

ADJECTIVE Manual work is work in which you use your hands or your physical strength rather than your mind. ○ *skilled manual workers* ○ *They work in factory or manual jobs.*
▶ **COLLOCATIONS:**
manual **work/labour**
a manual **job/worker/labourer**
▶ **SYNONYMS:** blue-collar, physical
▶ **ANTONYMS:** clerical, white-collar

---

mar|ket /ˈmɑːkɪt/ (markets, marketing, marketed) BUSINESS

1 NOUN The **market** for a particular type of thing is the number of people who want to buy it, or the area of the world in which it is sold. ○ *the markets targeted by global chains* ○ [+ *for*] *the Russian market for personal computers* ○ [+ *in*] *There is no youth market in cars.*
▶ **COLLOCATIONS:**
a market **for/in** *something*
the **stock/currency/housing/labour/property** market
a **volatile/booming/buoyant/competitive** market
market **share/value/research**
penetrate/manipulate/target/test a market

2 VERB To **market** a product means to organize its sale, by deciding on its price, where it should be sold, and how it should be advertised. ○ *the company that markets the drug* ○ *The devices are being marketed in America this year.* ○ [+ *as*] *The soap is marketed as an anti-acne product.*
▶ **COLLOCATIONS:**
market *something* **as** *something*
market *something* **to** *someone*
market a **product/brand/drug/device**
▶ **SYNONYMS:** advertise, promote, sell

mar|ket|ing /ˈmɑːkɪtɪŋ/

UNCOUNTABLE NOUN Marketing is the organization of the sale of a product, for example, deciding on its price, the areas it should be supplied to, and how it should be advertised. ○ *expert advice on production and marketing* ○ *a marketing campaign* ○ *their sales and marketing director*
▶ **COLLOCATIONS:**
a marketing **company/director/department**

a marketing **plan/strategy**
▶ **PHRASES:**
marketing and advertising
marketing and promotion
sales and marketing
branding and marketing
▶ **SYNONYMS:** advertising, promotion

math|emat|ics /ˌmæθəˈmætɪks/ `MATHS`

UNCOUNTABLE NOUN Mathematics is the study of numbers, quantities, or shapes. The abbreviation **maths** is used in informal and spoken English. ○ *Elizabeth studied mathematics and classics.* ○ *a professor of mathematics at Boston College*
▶ **COLLOCATIONS:**
a mathematics **professor/teacher/graduate/textbook**
teach/study/apply/use mathematics
▶ **SYNONYM:** arithmetic

math|emati|cal /ˌmæθəˈmætɪkəl/

ADJECTIVE Something that is **mathematical** involves numbers and calculations. ○ *mathematical calculations* ○ *It's a mathematical certainty that there is life on other planets.*
▶ **COLLOCATIONS:**
a mathematical **concept/formula**
a mathematical **calculation/equation**

mat|ter /ˈmætə/ **(matters)**

1 NOUN A **matter** is a task, situation, or event which you have to deal with or think about, especially one that involves problems. ○ *It was clear that she wanted to discuss some private matter.* ○ *Until the matter is resolved the athletes will be unable to compete.* ○ *[+ for] Don't you think this is now a matter for the police?* ○ *Business matters drew him to Paris.*
▶ **COLLOCATIONS:**
a matter **for** *someone*
resolve/discuss/settle/investigate/handle a matter
a **personal/private/delicate** matter
a **serious/important/urgent** matter
▶ **SYNONYMS:** affair, issue, concern

2 NOUN If you say that a situation is **a matter of** a particular thing, you mean that that is the most important thing to be done or considered when you are involved in the situation or explaining it. ○ *[+ of] History is always a matter of interpretation.* ○ *[+ of] Observance of the law is a matter of*

m

principle for us. ○ [+ of] *Jack had attended these meetings as a matter of routine for years.*

▶ COLLOCATIONS:
  a matter **of** *something*
  a matter of **urgency/importance**
  a matter of **opinion/debate/principle**
▶ SYNONYM: question

---

mean /miːn/ **(means, meaning, meant)**   LANGUAGE

1 VERB If you want to know what a word, code, signal, or gesture **means**, you want to know what it refers to or what its message is. ○ *In modern Welsh, 'glas' means 'blue'.* ○ *What does 'evidence' mean?* ○ [+ that] *The red signal means you have to stop.* ○ [+ by] *What do you think he means by that?*
▶ COLLOCATIONS:
  mean *something* **by** *something*
  a **word/code/signal/gesture** means *something*

2 VERB If one thing **means** another, it shows that the second thing exists or is true. ○ *An enlarged prostate does not necessarily mean cancer.* ○ [+ that] *If they didn't see him it doesn't necessarily mean he wasn't there.*

3 VERB If one thing **means** another, the first thing leads to the second thing happening. ○ *It would almost certainly mean the end of NATO.* ○ *Trade and product discounts can also mean big savings.* ○ [+ that] *The change will mean that the country no longer has full diplomatic relations with other states.*
▶ COLLOCATIONS:
  generally/usually/basically/simply mean *something*
  necessarily/probably/automatically mean *something*
  literally/effectively/essentially mean *something*
  mean the start/beginning/arrival/end of *something*
▶ PHRASE: almost certainly mean something
▶ SYNONYMS: signify, denote, lead to

mean|ing /ˈmiːnɪŋ/ **(meanings)**

NOUN The **meaning** of something such as a word, symbol, or gesture is the thing that it refers to or the message that it conveys. ○ *the dictionary meaning of the word* ○ [+ of] *They should look up the meaning of the word in the dictionary.* ○ *I became more aware of the symbols and their meanings.*
▶ COLLOCATIONS:
  the meaning **of** *something*
  know/understand/recognize the meaning of *something*
  give/look up the meaning of *something*
▶ SYNONYMS: significance, sense

m

means /miːnz/

NOUN A **means** of doing something is a method, instrument, or process which can be used to do it. **Means** is both the singular and the plural form for this use. ○ [+ to-inf] *The move is a means to fight crime.* ○ [+ of] *They didn't provide me with any means of transport.* ○ [+ of] *Mobile phones will overtake landline phones as the primary means of voice communication.*

▶ COLLOCATIONS:
a means **of/for** *doing something*
a means of **transport/production/survival/communication**
a **convenient/effective/necessary** means of *something*
the **only/sole/primary** means of *something*

▶ PHRASE: by any means available

▶ SYNONYMS: way, method

---

meas|ure /ˈmeʒə/ (measures, measuring, measured)

1 VERB If you **measure** the quality, value, or effect of something, you discover or judge how great it is. ○ *The college measures student progress against national standards.* ○ *The school's success was measured in terms of the number of pupils who got into university.* ○ *It was difficult to measure the impact of the war.*

▶ COLLOCATIONS:
measure *something* **in terms of/against** *something*
measure the **success/progress/impact/quality** of *something*

2 VERB If you **measure** a quantity that can be expressed in numbers, such as the length of something, you discover it using a particular instrument or device, for example a ruler. ○ *Measure the length and width of the gap.* ○ *He measured the speed at which ultrasonic waves travel along the bone.*

▶ COLLOCATIONS:
measure the **length/width/height/temperature** of *something*
measure *something* **carefully/accurately**

▶ PHRASE: weigh and measure

3 VERB If something **measures** a particular length, width, or amount, that is its size or intensity, expressed in numbers. ○ *The house is twenty metres long and measures six metres in width.* ○ *This dinner plate measures 30cm across.*

▶ COLLOCATIONS:
measure *x* in **width/length/height**
measure *x* **across**

▶ SYNONYM: be

meas|ure|ment /ˈmeʒəmənt/ (measurements)

NOUN ○ *We took lots of measurements.* ○ *The measurements are very accurate.* ○ [+ of] *Measurement of blood pressure can be undertaken by nurses.* ○ [+ of] *the measurement of output in the non-market sector*

▶ COLLOCATIONS:

a measurement **of** *something*

the measurement of **pressure/distance/temperature**

the measurement of **output/productivity/effectiveness**

take a measurement

a **precise/accurate/exact** measurement

---

me|chan|ics /mɪˈkænɪks/ `SCIENCE` `PHYSICS` `ENGINEERING`

UNCOUNTABLE NOUN **Mechanics** is the part of physics that deals with the natural forces that act on moving or stationary objects. ○ *the theory of quantum mechanics* ○ *He has not studied mechanics or engineering.*

me|chani|cal /mɪˈkænɪkəl/

1 ADJECTIVE A **mechanical** device has moving parts and uses power in order to do a particular task. ○ *a small mechanical device* ○ *the oldest working mechanical clock in the world*

2 ADJECTIVE **Mechanical** means relating to machines and engines and the way they work. ○ *mechanical engineering* ○ *The train had stopped due to a mechanical problem.*

▶ COLLOCATIONS:

a mechanical **device/digger/pump/engineer**

mechanical **engineering**

a mechanical **problem/failure/fault**

▶ RELATED WORDS: electrical, electronic

me|chani|cal|ly /mɪˈkænɪkli/

ADVERB ○ *The air was circulated mechanically.*

▶ COLLOCATION: mechanically **engineered/operated/controled**

---

me|dia /ˈmiːdiə/ `ACADEMIC WORD` `ARTS` `MEDIA`

NOUN You can refer to television, radio, newspapers, and magazines as **the media**. ○ *It is hard work and not a glamorous job as portrayed by the media.* ○ *bias in the news media* ○ *the intensive media coverage of the issue*

▶ COLLOCATIONS:

in the media

the **foreign/local/international** media

the **mass/mainstream/news** media

the **Western/American/British** media

the media **report/cover/portray** *something*

media **attention/coverage/reports**

a media **correspondent/mogul/analyst**

▶ PHRASE: in/under the media spotlight

▶ SYNONYM: press

USAGE: the media

You use **the media** to refer to television, radio and newspapers generally. It is often followed by a singular verb, but a plural verb is considered correct in more formal writing. ○ *The way in which the media report health issues has come under scrutiny.*

You can also use **media** before another noun to talk about things connected with **the media**. ○ *There was huge media coverage of the event.*

---

medi|cine /ˈmedsən, AM ˈmedɪsɪn/ `ACADEMIC WORD` `MEDICINE`

UNCOUNTABLE NOUN Medicine is the treatment of illness and injuries by doctors and nurses. ○ *He pursued a career in medicine.* ○ *I was interested in alternative medicine and becoming an aromatherapist.* ○ *Psychiatry is an accepted branch of medicine.*

▶ COLLOCATIONS:
  alternative/complementary/herbal medicine
  veterinary/homeopathic/forensic medicine
  conventional/orthodox medicine
  practise/study medicine
  a **branch/field/area** of medicine
▶ SYNONYM: health care

medi|cal /ˈmedɪkəl/

ADJECTIVE Medical means relating to illness and injuries and to their treatment or prevention. ○ *Several police officers received medical treatment for cuts and bruises.* ○ *the medical profession*

▶ COLLOCATIONS:
  the medical **profession/establishment**
  medical **attention/treatment/care**
  medical **staff/students/examiners/experts**

medi|cal|ly /ˈmedɪkli/

ADVERB ○ *I am not medically qualified.* ○ *She was deemed medically fit to travel.*

▶ COLLOCATIONS:
  medically **qualified/trained/certified**
  medically **fit/unfit**

---

medium-sized /ˈmiːdiəmsaɪzd/ also **medium size**

ADJECTIVE Medium-sized means neither large nor small, but approximately half way between the two. ○ *a medium-sized saucepan* ○ *small and medium-sized businesses*

▶ COLLOCATIONS:
a medium-sized **business/organization/firm**
a medium-sized **car/town/venue**
▶ SYNONYMS: average-sized, middle-sized, mid-sized
▶ RELATED WORDS: large, small

---

melt /melt/ (melts, melting, melted)   `SCIENCE`

VERB When a solid substance **melts** or when you **melt** it, it changes to a liquid, usually because it has been heated. ○ *The snow had melted.* ○ *The world's glaciers are melting away.* ○ *Add the melted butter.*

▶ COLLOCATIONS:
melt **away/down**
melt *something* **over/in** *something*
melt **into** *something*
melted **butter/chocolate/wax/cheese**
a **glacier/icecap** melts
snow/ice melts
▶ SYNONYM: dissolve
▶ ANTONYMS: freeze, solidify

---

mem|ber /ˈmembə/ (members)

1 NOUN A **member** of a group is one of the people, animals, or things belonging to that group. ○ [+ *of*] *He refused to name the members of staff involved.* ○ *a sunflower or a similar member of the daisy family* ○ *the brightest members of a dense cluster of stars*

2 NOUN A **member** of an organization such as a club or a political party is a person who has officially joined the organization. ○ *The support of our members is of great importance to the Association.* ○ *Britain is a full member of NATO.* ○ [+ *of*] *He was a member of the British parliament.*

▶ COLLOCATIONS:
a member **of** *something*
a **family/crew/staff/gang** member
a **club/party** member
a **permanent/prominent/key/full** member
members **approve/refuse/support/oppose** *something*
▶ PHRASES:
a member of the public
a member of staff
a member of parliament

mem|ber|ship /'membəʃɪp/ (memberships)

UNCOUNTABLE NOUN Membership of an organization is the state of being a member of it. ○ [+ of] *The country has been granted membership of the World Trade Organisation.* ○ *He sent me a membership form.*

▶ COLLOCATIONS:
membership **of** *something*
a membership **form/card/fee/application**
permanent/full/voluntary membership
expand/increase/limit/restrict membership
award/grant/deny *someone* membership

---

memo|ry /'meməri/   PSYCHOLOGY IT

1 NOUN Your **memory** is your ability to remember things. ○ *All the details of the meeting are fresh in my memory.* ○ [+ for] *He had a good memory for faces.* ○ *He suffers from poor memory and concentration.*

▶ COLLOCATIONS:
in *someone's* memory
a memory **for** *something*
a **good/bad/poor** memory for *something*
a **short/long** memory

▶ SYNONYM: recollection

2 NOUN A computer's **memory** is the part of the computer where information is stored, especially for a short time before it is transferred to disks or magnetic tapes. ○ *The device has 32GB of built-in memory.* ○ *Flash memory is used in digital cameras.* ○ *You can upgrade your computer's memory.*

▶ COLLOCATIONS:
a memory **card/chip**
built-in/on-board/internal/flash memory
a **computer's/device's** memory

---

mes|sage /'mesɪdʒ/ (messages)

NOUN The **message** that someone is trying to communicate, for example in a book or play, is the idea or point that they are trying to communicate. ○ *The film has a very powerful anti-war message.* ○ *The clear message from this research is that children do not benefit from this.*

▶ COLLOCATIONS:
get/understand/send/convey/deliver a message
the **main/general** message of *something*
a **clear/powerful/strong/positive** message

▶ SYNONYMS: idea, point

met|al /ˈmetəl/ (metals)

SCIENCE CHEMISTRY

NOUN Metal is a hard substance such as iron, steel, gold, or lead. ○ *furniture made of wood, metal and glass* ○ *The roof is made of corrugated sheet metal.* ○ *deposits of precious metals*

▶ COLLOCATIONS:
   a metal **detector/rod/plate/bar**
   precious/base/scrap/sheet/corrugated metal
   alkali/ferrous/non-ferrous/heavy metal
   molten/red-hot/liquid metal
   extract/smelt/brush metal

me|tal|lic /məˈtælɪk/

ADJECTIVE Metallic means consisting entirely or partly of metal. ○ *metallic objects such as a nail file or cigarette lighter* ○ *What is the symbol for the metallic element cobalt?*

▶ COLLOCATION: a metallic **element/object**
▶ SYNONYM: metal

me|ter /ˈmiːtə/ (meters)

SCIENCE

NOUN A **meter** is a device that measures and records the amount or level of something. ○ *Light in the ocean can be measured by light meters.* ○ *The meter shows the amount of carbon dioxide released in the emissions.*

▶ COLLOCATIONS:
   a **gas/electricity/water/light** meter
   a **moisture/decibel/pH** meter
   read/check/use a meter
   a meter **measures/shows**
   a meter **reading**
▶ SYNONYM: device

> USAGE: **meter** or **metre**?
>
> In British English, a **meter** is a measuring device and a **metre** is a unit of length (= 100 centimetres).
>
> In American English, the spelling **meter** is used for both meanings.

meth|od /ˈmeθəd/ (methods)

ACADEMIC WORD

NOUN A **method** is a particular way of doing something. ○ [+ of] *The pill is the most efficient method of birth control.* ○ *new teaching methods* ○ *Experts will use a variety of scientific methods to measure fatigue levels.*

▶ COLLOCATIONS:
   a method **of** *something*

a method of **teaching/execution/calculation/communication**
a **scientific/proven/statistical/efficient** method
a **preferred/usual/conventional/traditional** method
devise/employ/adopt/test a method
a **teaching/cooking/testing/detection** method
▶ **SYNONYMS:** manner, procedure

---

me|tre /'miːtə/ (metres)

NOUN A **metre** is a metric unit of length equal to 100 centimetres. The abbreviation **m** is used in written notes. [in AM, use **meter**] ○ *He won the 400 metres freestyle.* ○ *The tunnel is 10 metres wide and 600 metres long.*
→ see note at **centimetre** and **meter**
▶ **COLLOCATIONS:**
x metres **of** *something*
x metres **above/below/behind/from** *something*
x metres **long/wide/high/deep**
x metres in **height/length/diameter**
x **square/cubic/linear** metres
▶ **RELATED WORDS:** kilometre, centimetre

---

met|ric sys|tem /'metrɪk sɪstəm/

NOUN The **metric system** is the system of measurement that uses metres, grams, and litres. ○ *The country has adopted the metric system.*
▶ **COLLOCATION:** **use/adopt/introduce** the metric system
▶ **ANTONYM:** imperial system

---

middle-aged /ˌmɪdəl'eɪdʒd/

ADJECTIVE If you describe someone as **middle-aged**, you mean that they are neither young nor old. People between the ages of 40 and 60 are usually considered to be middle-aged. ○ *More and more middle-aged adults have to care for older parents.* ○ *She was middle-aged and single.*
▶ **COLLOCATION:** a middle-aged **woman/man/couple**
▶ **PHRASES:**
middle-aged and middle-class
middle-aged and married
▶ **ANTONYMS:** young, elderly

mid|dle age /ˌmɪdəl 'eɪdʒ/ also **middle-age**

UNCOUNTABLE NOUN ○ *Men tend to put on weight in middle age.* ○ *When we reach middle age we often need more sleep.*
▶ **COLLOCATIONS:**
in/into/of middle age

reach/arrive at/enter/approach middle age
obesity/fertility/disease in middle age
late/early/advancing middle age
▶ SYNONYM: midlife
▶ ANTONYMS: youth, old age

---

mile /maɪl/ (miles)

NOUN A **mile** is a unit of distance equal to 1760 yards or approximately 1.6 kilometres. The abbreviation **mi** is used in written notes. ○ *They drove 600 miles across the desert.* ○ *The hurricane is moving at about 18 miles per hour.* ○ *She lives just half a mile away.* ○ *The lake is about ten miles long.* ○ *a 50-mile bike ride*

▶ COLLOCATIONS:
x miles **above/below/outside** from *something*
x miles **long/wide/high/deep**
x miles in **circumference/length/diameter**
x **square/cubic/nautical** miles
x miles **per** *something*
x miles per **gallon/day/hour**
x miles **north/south/east/west** of *something*
travel/run/walk/cycle/drive x miles
x miles **away**

▶ RELATED WORD: kilometre

---

mili|tary /ˈmɪlɪtri, AM -teri/ (militaries)   `ACADEMIC WORD`

1 ADJECTIVE Military means relating to the armed forces of a country. ○ *Military action may become necessary.* ○ *Military personnel will help with the relief efforts.* ○ *last year's military coup*

▶ COLLOCATIONS:
a military **commander/base/force/presence**
military **personnel/action/intelligence/intervention**
a military **operation/offensive/coup**

▶ SYNONYMS: armed forces, army
▶ ANTONYM: civilian

2 NOUN The military are the armed forces of a country, especially officers of high rank. ○ *The military has overthrown the government.* ○ *Did you serve in the military?*

▶ COLLOCATIONS:
in the military
serve in the military
involve/equip/deploy the military
the **British/American/Israeli/Turkish** military

m

the military **oust/overthrow** *a government*
the military **invade/enter** *a country*
▶ SYNONYM: army
▶ RELATED WORDS: navy, air force

mil|li|metre /ˈmɪlɪmiːtə/ (millimetres)

NOUN A **millimetre** is a metric unit of length that is equal to a tenth of a centimetre or a thousandth of a metre. The abbreviation **mm** is used in written notes. [in AM, use **millimeter**] ○ *a tiny pill, about 20 millimetres long* ○ *It measures just one millimetre in diameter.*
→ see note at **centimetre**
▶ COLLOCATIONS:
  x millimetres **of** *something*
  x millimetres **from** *something*
  x millimetres of **rain/precipitation**
  x millimetres **thick/wide/short/deep**
  x millimetres in **size/length/diameter**
  x **square/cubic** millimetres
▶ RELATED WORDS: metre, centimetre

mil|lion /ˈmɪlɪən/ (millions)   MATHS

1 NUMBER A **million** or one **million** is the number 1,000,000. ○ *Up to five million people a year visit the county.* ○ *Profits for 1999 topped £100 million.*
▶ COLLOCATIONS:
  x million **things/people**
  spend/invest/save/waste £/$*x* million

2 QUANTIFIER If you talk about **millions of** people or things, you mean that there is a very large number of them but you do not know or do not want to say exactly how many. ○ *The programme was viewed on television in millions of homes.* ○ [+ of] *The rain forest is millions of years old.*
▶ COLLOCATION: millions **of** *something*
▶ SYNONYMS: a lot of, many
→ see note at **billion**

mind /maɪnd/ (minds)   PSYCHOLOGY

NOUN Your **mind** is your ability to think and reason. ○ *You have a sharp mind.* ○ *Studying stretched my mind.*
▶ COLLOCATIONS:
  stretch/broaden/sharpen *someone's* mind
  cloud/muddle/warp *someone's* mind
  a **creative/brilliant/sharp** mind

▶ **PHRASES:**
of sound mind
of unsound mind
mind, body and soul
mind over matter
▶ **SYNONYMS:** intellect, brain
▶ **ANTONYM:** body

---

mi|nor /'maɪnə/ ACADEMIC WORD

ADJECTIVE You use **minor** when you want to describe something that is less important, serious, or significant than other things in a group or situation. ○ *She had a minor role in the film.* ○ *Officials say the problem is minor, and should be quickly overcome.*

▶ **COLLOCATIONS:**
a minor **problem/matter/incident/setback**
minor **things/details/surgery/damage**
a minor **ailment/injury/wound/accident**
a minor **road/league/role**
▶ **SYNONYMS:** unimportant, small
▶ **ANTONYMS:** major, important

---

mod|ern /'mɒdən/

1 ADJECTIVE Modern means relating to the present time, for example the present decade or present century. ○ *the problem of materialism in modern society* ○ *the alienation of the modern world*

2 ADJECTIVE Something that is **modern** is new and involves the latest ideas or equipment. ○ *Modern technology has opened our eyes to many things.* ○ *It was a very modern school for its time.*

▶ **COLLOCATIONS:**
modern **society/living**
fairly/quite/relatively modern
very/thoroughly/strikingly modern
modern **technology/design/medicine**
a modern **kitchen/bathroom/house/appliance**
▶ **PHRASE:** the modern world
▶ **SYNONYMS:** contemporary, current, present, advanced, up-to-date, state-of-the-art
▶ **ANTONYMS:** old-fashioned, historical, ancient, primitive, out-of-date, outdated

mod|ern|ize /ˈmɒdənaɪz/ (modernizes, modernizing, modernized)

VERB To **modernize** something such as a system or a factory means to change it by replacing old equipment or methods with new ones. [in BRIT, also use **modernise**] ○ *plans to modernize the curriculum* ○ *We need to modernise our electoral system.* ○ *the cost of modernizing the economy*

▶ COLLOCATIONS:
rapidly/radically/extensively modernize
modernize the **economy/military/curriculum**
modernize **infrastructure/agriculture/production**

▶ SYNONYM: update

mod|erni|za|tion /ˌmɒdənaɪˈzeɪʃən/

UNCOUNTABLE NOUN ○ *the modernization of the region* ○ *a five-year modernization programme*

▶ COLLOCATIONS:
the modernization **of** something
a modernization **programme/project/plan**
technological/industrial/agricultural modernization
rapid/extensive/massive modernization
undergo/introduce/encourage modernization

---

moon /muːn/ (moons) `GEOGRAPHY`

NOUN **The moon** is the object that you can often see in the sky at night. It goes round the Earth once every four weeks, and as it does so its appearance changes from a circle to part of a circle. ○ *the first man on the moon* ○ *the light of a full moon* ○ *The moon orbits the earth approximately once each month.*

▶ COLLOCATIONS:
on the moon
a **full/new/half/quarter** moon
eclipse/obscure/darken the moon
the moon **orbits** *the earth*
land on the moon

---

mo|tor|ist /ˈməʊtərɪst/ (motorists)

NOUN A **motorist** is a person who drives a car. [mainly BRIT; in AM, use **driver**] ○ *Two-thirds (66.3%) of motorists were driving at, or above, the speed limit.* ○ *a scene witnessed by a passing motorist*

▶ COLLOCATIONS:
urge/advise/warn motorists
a **passing/speeding** motorist

▶ ANTONYM: pedestrian

EXTEND YOUR VOCABULARY

You can talk about a person who drives a car as a **driver**. You use the word particularly to talk about individuals or about types of driver.
○ *Both drivers were unhurt in the accident.* ○ *a taxi/bus/lorry driver*

When you talk about people using the roads in general, you often talk about **motorists**. ○ *A police spokesman warned motorists to avoid the area if possible.*

---

moun|tain /ˈmaʊntɪn, AM -tən/ (mountains) GEOGRAPHY

NOUN A **mountain** is a very high area of land with steep sides. ○ *Ben Nevis, in Scotland, is Britain's highest mountain.* ○ *the rugged mountains of Wales*
  ▶ COLLOCATIONS:
   climb/scale/ascend/descend a mountain
   a **snow-capped/forested/steep** mountain
   a mountain **valley/village/resort**
   a mountain **goat/lion/gorilla**
   mountain **rescue**
  ▶ RELATED WORD: hill

moun|tain|ous /ˈmaʊntɪnəs/

ADJECTIVE A **mountainous** place has a lot of mountains. ○ *the mountainous region of Campania* ○ *the more mountainous terrain of New Hampshire*
  ▶ COLLOCATIONS:
   a mountainous **region/area/landscape**
   mountainous **terrain/scenery**
  ▶ SYNONYM: hilly
  ▶ ANTONYM: flat

---

move /muːv/ (moves, moving, moved)

1 VERB When you **move** something or when it **moves**, its position changes and it does not remain still. ○ *She moved the sheaf of papers into position.* ○ *You can move the camera both vertically and horizontally.* ○ *A traffic warden asked him to move his car.* ○ *I could see the branches of the trees moving back and forth.* ○ *The train began to move.*

2 VERB When you **move**, you change your position or go to a different place. ○ *She waited for him to get up, but he didn't move.* ○ *He moved around the room, putting his possessions together.* ○ *She moved away from the window.*
  ▶ COLLOCATIONS:
   move **from/away from/into/to** something
   move **around/towards/in front of** something

move into **position/place**
move **vertically/horizontally/diagonally**
move **up/down/left/right/back/forward**
hardly/barely move
move **slightly/a little**
move **slowly/gradually/cautiously**
move **quickly/swiftly/rapidly**
▶ **PHRASE:** move back and forth
▶ **SYNONYMS:** shift, go, proceed
▶ **ANTONYMS:** stop, halt, remain still

● **Move** is also a noun. ○ *The doctor made a move towards the door.* ○ *Daniel's eyes followed her every move.*
▶ **COLLOCATIONS:**
a move **towards/away from** *something*
a **slow/gradual** move
a **fast/sudden** move
someone's **every** move
▶ **SYNONYMS:** movement, motion, shift

move|ment /ˈmuːvmənt/ (movements)

1 **NOUN Movement** involves changing position or going from one place to another. ○ *They monitor the movement of the fish going up river.* ○ *There was movement behind the window.* ○ [+ of] *the movements of a large removal van* ○ *Her hand movements are becoming more animated.*
▶ **COLLOCATIONS:**
the movement **of** *something*
a **sudden/quick/jerky/animated** movement
a **slow/sluggish/painful** movement
a **fluid/graceful/smooth** movement
track/follow/monitor *someone's* movements
restrict/control/detect *someone's* movements
▶ **SYNONYM:** motion

2 **NOUN Movement** is a gradual development or change of an attitude, opinion, or policy. ○ [+ towards/away from] *the movement towards democracy in Latin America* ○ *Participants at the peace talks believed movement forward was possible.*
▶ **COLLOCATIONS:**
a movement **towards/away from/from/to** *something*
a **slow/gradual/rapid/sudden** movement
movement **forward**
▶ **SYNONYMS:** shift, change, development, progress

multi|ply /'mʌltɪplaɪ/ (multiplies, multiplying, multiplied) `MATHS`

VERB If you **multiply** one number by another, you add the first number to itself as many times as is indicated by the second number. For example 2 multiplied by 3 is equal to 6. ○ [+ by] *What do you get if you multiply six by nine?* ○ *The frequency was multiplied by the distance to find the speed of sound at each temperature.*

▶ **COLLOCATIONS:**
multiply *x* **by** *y*
multiply *x* **tenfold/exponentially**

multi|pli|ca|tion /ˌmʌltɪplɪˈkeɪʃən/

UNCOUNTABLE NOUN ○ *There will be simple tests in addition, subtraction, multiplication and division.* ○ *formulas that help children learn multiplication tables*

▶ **COLLOCATION:** a multiplication **table/sum/test**

mus|cle /'mʌsəl/ (muscles) `SCIENCE` `BIOLOGY`

NOUN A **muscle** is a piece of tissue inside your body which connects two bones and which you use when you make a movement. ○ *He is suffering from a strained thigh muscle.* ○ *There are three types of muscle in the body.*

▶ **COLLOCATIONS:**
strain/pull/tear a muscle
flex/exercise/tone/build muscles
contract/relax muscles
abdominal/pelvic/cardiac/skeletal muscles
calf/thigh/neck/stomach muscles
a muscle **spasm/relaxant/contraction**
muscle **cramp/strain/fatigue/strength**

mu|sic /'mjuːzɪk/ `ARTS`

1 UNCOUNTABLE NOUN **Music** is the pattern of sounds produced by people singing or playing instruments. ○ *classical music* ○ [+ of] *the music of George Gershwin*

▶ **COLLOCATIONS:**
the music **of** *someone/something*
hear/listen to music
compose/play/perform/write/make music
download/distribute/record music
live/recorded/downloaded music
classical/orchestral/rock/jazz music
a **piece** of music

▶ **PHRASES:**
music and dance
the music business

2 UNCOUNTABLE NOUN Music is the art of creating or performing music.
○ *He went on to study music, specialising in the clarinet.* ○ *a music lesson*

▶ **COLLOCATIONS:**
study/teach music
a music **teacher/student/class/lesson**

mu|si|cal /ˈmjuːzɪkəl/

ADJECTIVE ○ *We have a wealth of musical talent in this region.* ○ *Stan Getz's musical career spanned five decades.*

▶ **COLLOCATIONS:**
a musical **career/instrument/genre/composition**
musical **talent/genius/tradition**

mu|si|cian /mjuːˈzɪʃən/ (musicians)

NOUN A **musician** is a person who plays a musical instrument as their job or hobby. ○ *He was a brilliant musician.* ○ *one of Britain's best known rock musicians*

▶ **COLLOCATIONS:**
a **brilliant/talented/gifted** musician
a **legendary/well-known/renowned** musician
a **classical/jazz/rock/folk/blues** musician
a musician **plays/performs/composes/records** *something*

m

Nn

na|tion /ˈneɪʃən/ (nations) GEOGRAPHY

NOUN A **nation** is an individual country. ○ *Such policies require cooperation between nations.* ○ *The Arab nations agreed to meet in Baghdad.*

→ see note at **country**

▶ **COLLOCATIONS:**
  a **leading/wealthy/powerful/independent** nation
  a **developed/industrialized** nation
  a **poor/developing** nation
  a nation **state**
  nation **building**
  a nation's **capital/economy/history**

▶ **PHRASE:** the nations of the world
▶ **SYNONYM:** country

na|tion|al /ˈnæʃənəl/

ADJECTIVE **National** means relating to the whole of a country or nation rather than to part of it or to other nations. ○ *national and local elections* ○ *major national and international issues* ○ *a member of the U.S. national team*

▶ **COLLOCATIONS:**
  a national **park/treasure/anthem**
  a national **champion/championship/hero/team/stadium**
  national **unity/interest/identity/security**
  a national **newspaper/assembly/election**

▶ **PHRASES:**
  local and national
  national and international

▶ **ANTONYMS:** local, international

na|tion|al|ly

ADVERB ○ *a nationally televised speech* ○ *Duncan Campbell is nationally known for his investigative work.*

▶ **COLLOCATIONS:**
  known nationally
  broadcast/recognized/distributed nationally

▶ **RELATED WORD:** internationally

na|tion|al|ity /ˌnæʃəˈnælɪti/ (nationalities)

NOUN If you have the **nationality** of a particular country, you were born there or have the legal right to be a citizen. ○ *The crew are of different nationalities and have no common language.* ○ *a resident who held dual Iranian-Canadian nationality*

▶ **COLLOCATIONS:**
  dual nationality
  different/other nationalities
▶ **SYNONYMS:** ethnicity, background, origin

---

na|tive /ˈneɪtɪv/ LANGUAGE SCIENCE BIOLOGY

1 ADJECTIVE Your **native** language or tongue is the first language that you learned to speak when you were a child. ○ *She spoke not only her native language, Swedish, but also English and French.* ○ *French is not my native tongue.*

▶ **COLLOCATION:** a native **speaker/language/tongue**
▶ **SYNONYM:** mother
▶ **ANTONYM:** non-native

2 ADJECTIVE Plants or animals that are **native to** a particular region live or grow there naturally and were not brought there. ○ *a project to create a 50 acre forest of native Caledonian pines* ○ [+ to] *Many of the plants are native to Brazil.*

▶ **COLLOCATIONS:**
  native **to** *somewhere*
  native **trees/vegetation/forest**
  a native **species/bird/animal/plant**
  native **land/habitat/flora/fauna**
  native **population/culture**
▶ **SYNONYM:** indigenous
▶ **ANTONYM:** non-native

---

na|ture /ˈneɪtʃə/ SCIENCE BIOLOGY

UNCOUNTABLE NOUN **Nature** is all the animals, plants, and other things in the world that are not made by people, and all the events and processes that are not caused by people. ○ *The most amazing thing about nature is its infinite variety.* ○ *grasses that grow wild in nature* ○ *the ecological balance of nature*

▶ **COLLOCATIONS:**
  in nature
  understand/reflect/explain nature
  change/explore/examine nature

love/preserve nature
mother nature
a nature **reserve/trail**
nature **conservation**
▶ SYNONYM: the environment

natu|ral /ˈnætʃərəl/

ADJECTIVE **Natural** things exist or occur in nature and are not made or caused by people. ○ *The typhoon was the worst natural disaster in South Korea in many years.* ○ *a gigantic natural harbour*
▶ COLLOCATIONS:
perfectly/completely natural
a natural **disaster/resource**
natural **light/gas/beauty**
▶ ANTONYMS: artificial, man-made, synthetic

navy /ˈneɪvi/

NOUN A country's **navy** consists of the people it employs to fight at sea, and the ships they use. ○ *The government announced an order for three Type 23 frigates for the Royal Navy yesterday.* ○ *Her own son was also in the Navy.* ○ *a United States navy ship*
▶ COLLOCATIONS:
in the navy
serve in the navy
join the navy
the **Royal/merchant** Navy
▶ PHRASE: army and navy
▶ RELATED WORDS: army, military

nec|es|sary /ˈnesɪsəri/

ADJECTIVE Something that is **necessary** is needed in order for something else to happen. ○ [+ to-inf] *I kept the engine running because it might be necessary to leave fast.* ○ *We will do whatever is necessary to stop them.* ○ [+ for] *the skills necessary for writing*
▶ COLLOCATIONS:
necessary **for** something
a necessary **action/step/measure/change**
necessary **skills/equipment/precautions**
find/feel/think something is necessary
absolutely/wholly/medically necessary
▶ SYNONYMS: essential, obligatory, required
▶ ANTONYM: unnecessary

nega|tive /ˈnegətɪv/ `ACADEMIC WORD`

ADJECTIVE A fact, situation, or experience that is **negative** is unpleasant, depressing, or harmful. ○ *The news from overseas is overwhelmingly negative.* ○ *All this had an extremely negative effect on the criminal justice system.*
▸ **COLLOCATIONS:**
  a negative **effect/impact/reaction/feeling/attitude**
  a negative **image/experience/comment**
  a negative **reaction/response**
  negative **publicity/thoughts**
  overwhelmingly/wholly/predominantly negative
▸ **SYNONYM:** adverse
▸ **ANTONYM:** positive

nega|tive|ly

ADVERB ○ *This will negatively affect the result over the first half of the year.*
▸ **COLLOCATIONS:**
  negatively **affect/impact/influence** something
  negatively **view/portray** something
▸ **SYNONYM:** adversely
▸ **ANTONYM:** positively

neigh|bour|hood /ˈneɪbəhʊd/ (neighbourhoods) `GEOGRAPHY`

NOUN A **neighbourhood** is one of the parts of a town where people live.
  ○ [+ to-inf] *It seemed like a good neighbourhood to raise my children.* [in AM, use **neighborhood**] ○ [+ of] *He was born and grew up in the Flatbush neighbourhood of Brooklyn.*
▸ **COLLOCATIONS:**
  a **safe/good/bad/poor/quiet** neighbourhood
  a **residential/run-down** neighbourhood
▸ **SYNONYMS:** area, district

nest /nest/ (nests, nesting, nested) `SCIENCE` `BIOLOGY`

1 NOUN A bird's **nest** is the home that it makes to lay its eggs in. ○ *I can see an eagle's nest on the rocks.* ○ *These birds build nests of twigs and leaves in hollows and clefts.*
▸ **COLLOCATIONS:**
  a **bird's/crow's/eagle's** nest
  build a nest
2 VERB When a bird **nests** somewhere, it builds a nest and settles there to lay its eggs. ○ *Some species may nest in close proximity to each other.* ○ [V-ing] *nesting sites*

► COLLOCATIONS:

nest **on/in** something

a nesting **site/box/bird**

3 NOUN A **nest** is a home that a group of insects or other creatures make in order to live in and give birth to their young in. ○ *Some solitary bees make their nests in burrows in the soil.* ○ *a rat's nest*

► COLLOCATION: a **wasp's/ant's/rat's** nest

---

nor|mal /ˈnɔːməl/

ADJECTIVE Something that is **normal** is usual and ordinary, and is what people expect. ○ *The two countries resumed normal diplomatic relations.* ○ [+ for] *Some of the shops were closed but that's quite normal for a Thursday afternoon.* ○ *In November, Clean's bakery produced 50 percent more bread than normal.*

→ see note at **common**

► COLLOCATIONS:

normal **for** something

normal **conditions/development/behaviour/practice**

a normal **pressure/level/feeling/situation/life**

a normal **procedure/routine/cell**

seem/look/appear normal

perfectly/quite/relatively/completely normal

► PHRASES:

as normal

return to normal

back to normal

► SYNONYM: usual

► ANTONYMS: unusual, abnormal

nor|mal|ly /ˈnɔːməli/

ADVERB If you say that something **normally** happens or that you **normally** do a particular thing, you mean that it is what usually happens or what you usually do. ○ *All airports in the country are working normally today.* ○ *Social progress is normally a matter of struggles and conflicts.* ○ *Normally, the transportation system in Paris carries 950,000 passengers a day.*

► COLLOCATIONS:

function/behave/operate/develop normally

eat/breathe/act normally

► SYNONYMS: as normal, as usual

► ANTONYM: abnormally

north /nɔːθ/ also **North**

GEOGRAPHY

1 UNCOUNTABLE NOUN The **north** is the direction which is on your left when you are looking towards the direction where the sun rises. ○ *In the north the ground becomes very cold in the winter.* ○ *Birds usually migrate from north to south.*

2 NOUN The **north** of a place, country, or region is the part which is in the north. ○ *The scheme mostly benefits people in the North and Midlands.* ○ [+ of] *a tiny house in a village in the north of France*

▶ **COLLOCATIONS:**
  north **of** something
  to/in the north
  north of the **border/country/city/capital**
  the north of a **country/city/region**

▶ **PHRASE:** north, south, east and west

▶ **RELATED WORDS:** south, east, west

north|ern /ˈnɔːðən/ also **Northern**

ADJECTIVE Northern means in or from the north of a region, state, or country. ○ *Their two children were immigrants to Northern Ireland from Pennsylvania.* ○ *Prices at three-star hotels fell furthest in several northern cities.*

▶ **COLLOCATIONS:**
  a northern **city/town/region**
  the northern **hemisphere/lights**

▶ **RELATED WORDS:** southern, eastern, western

note /nəʊt/ (notes)

ACADEMIC WORD

1 NOUN A **note** is something that you write down to remind yourself of something. ○ *I knew that if I didn't make a note I would lose the thought.* ○ *Take notes during the consultation.*

▶ **COLLOCATIONS:**
  a note **of** something
  write/take/leave/make a note
  scribble/jot down a note
  a **handwritten** note
  a note **pad/book**

▶ **SYNONYM:** reminder

2 NOUN In a book or article, a **note** is a short piece of additional information. ○ *See Note 16 on page p. 223.* ○ *'Exiles' by James Joyce, edited with an Introduction and notes by J C C Mays*

▶ **COLLOCATIONS:**
a note **about/on** something
add a note
a **brief/detailed** note
▶ **SYNONYMS:** footnote, endnote
▶ **RELATED WORD:** bibliography

---

nov|el /ˈnɒvəl/ (novels) LITERATURE

NOUN A **novel** is a long written story about imaginary people and events.
○ [+ by] a novel by Herman Hesse ○ historical novels set in the time of the Pharaohs
▶ **COLLOCATIONS:**
a novel **about** something/someone
a novel **by** someone
a novel by a **writer/author**
write/publish/read a novel
a **first/late/unfinished/best-selling** novel
a **graphic/classic/literary** novel
a **historical/autobiographical/romantic** novel
▶ **SYNONYMS:** story, book, narrative

---

nowa|days /ˈnaʊədeɪz/

ADVERB Nowadays means at the present time, in contrast with the past.
○ Nowadays it's acceptable for women to be ambitious. But it wasn't then. ○ This method is seldom used nowadays.
→ see note at **current**
▶ **SYNONYMS:** at the present time, currently, these days

---

num|ber /ˈnʌmbə/ (numbers)

1 NOUN A **number** is a word such as 'two', 'nine', or 'twelve', or a symbol such as 1, 3, or 47. You use numbers to say how many things you are referring to or where something comes in a series. ○ No, I don't know the room number. ○ Stan Laurel was born at number 3, Argyll Street. ○ The number 47 bus leaves in 10 minutes.
▶ **COLLOCATIONS:**
a **phone/telephone/account/card/room** number
a **registration/identification** number
▶ **SYNONYM:** figure
2 NOUN You use **number** with words such as 'large' or 'small' to say approximately how many things or people there are. ○ [+ of] Quite a

considerable number of interviews are going on. ○ [+ *of*] *I have had an enormous number of letters from single parents.* ○ [+ *of*] *growing numbers of people*

→ see note at **amount**

▶ **COLLOCATIONS:**
   a number **of** *things*
   a number of **people/cases/patients**
   a **rising/growing/increasing/falling** number
   a **high/large/great/small/low/significant** number

▶ **SYNONYMS:** amount, quantity

Oo

---

ob|ject /ˈɒbdʒɪkt/ **(objects)**

NOUN An **object** is anything that has a fixed shape or form, that you can touch or see, and that is not alive. ○ *an object the shape of a coconut* ○ *In the cosy consulting room the children are surrounded by familiar objects.* ○ *household objects such as lamps and ornaments*

→ see note at **item**

▶ COLLOCATIONS:
  an object **such as**...
  a **heavy/metal/small/sharp/solid** object
  a **familiar/everyday** object
  an **inanimate object**

▶ SYNONYM: thing

---

ob|vi|ous /ˈɒbviəs/   `ACADEMIC WORD`

ADJECTIVE If something is **obvious**, it is easy to see or understand. ○ *the need to rectify what is an obvious injustice* ○ *More and more healthy troops were dying for no obvious reason.* ○ *The answer is obvious.*

▶ COLLOCATIONS:
  an obvious **choice/answer/question/solution**
  an obvious **flaw/danger**
  obvious **reasons/differences**
  blindingly/glaringly/painfully/patently obvious

▶ SYNONYMS: clear, plain

▶ ANTONYMS: unclear, obscure

ob|vi|ous|ly /ˈɒbviəsli/

ADVERB ○ *As a private hospital it obviously needs to balance its budget each year.* ○ *They were obviously disappointed about the decision.*

▶ COLLOCATION: obviously **disappointed/pleased/upset**

▶ SYNONYMS: clearly, of course

---

oc|ca|sion /əˈkeɪʒən/ **(occasions)**

NOUN An **occasion** is a time when something happens, or a case of it happening. ○ *The team repeated the experiment on three separate occasions, with the same results.* ○ *Mr Davis has been asked on a number of occasions.*

▶ COLLOCATIONS:
on an occasion
a **number of** occasions
numerous/several/many occasions
a **previous/separate** occasion

EXTEND YOUR VOCABULARY

In everyday English, you often talk about a **time** when something happens. ○ *I've met him several times and each time, he forgot my name.*

In more formal writing, you can use **occasion** to talk about something that happens at a particular time. You say that something happened on **several occasions** to refer to similar events that happened at different times. ○ *The charges were dropped on each occasion.* ○ *The site was visited on several occasions.*

You can also use **case** to talk about something that happens. You talk about **several cases** to refer to different examples of the same type of event, when the time is not important. ○ *In many cases, the solution is relatively simple.*

---

ocean /ˈəʊʃən/ (oceans) `GEOGRAPHY`

1 NOUN The ocean is the sea. ○ *new technology used to explore the deep ocean* ○ *a fish's habitat on the ocean floor*
  ▶ COLLOCATIONS:
    the **vast/deep/open** ocean
    an ocean **current/wave**
    the ocean **floor**
  ▶ SYNONYM: the sea

2 NOUN An ocean is one of the five very large areas of sea on the Earth's surface. ○ *a small island in the Indian ocean*
  ▶ COLLOCATION: the **Indian/Pacific/Atlantic/Antarctic/Arctic** Ocean
  ▶ SYNONYM: a sea

---

odd /ɒd/ `ACADEMIC WORD` `MATHS`

ADJECTIVE Odd numbers, such as 3 and 17, are those which cannot be divided exactly by the number two. ○ *Multiplying an odd number by an odd number always gives an odd number.* ○ *There's an odd number of candidates.*
  ▶ COLLOCATION: an odd **number**
  ▶ ANTONYM: even

of|fice /ˈɒfɪs, AM ˈɔːf-/ (offices) `BUSINESS`

1 NOUN An **office** is a room or a part of a building where people work sitting at desks. ○ *He had an office big enough for his desk and chair, plus his VDU.* ○ *At about 4.30 p.m. Audrey arrived at the office.* ○ *Telephone their head office for more details.*

▶ **COLLOCATIONS:**
  be **at** the office
  leave the office
  a **head/branch/regional** office
  an office **block/building/complex/worker**
  office **equipment/hours/space**

2 NOUN An **office** is a department of an organization, especially the government, where people deal with a particular kind of administrative work. ○ *Thousands have registered with unemployment offices.* ○ *Downing Street's press office* ○ *the Congressional Budget Office*

▶ **COLLOCATION:** a **press** office
▶ **SYNONYM:** department

of|fi|cial /əˈfɪʃəl/ (officials)

1 ADJECTIVE **Official** means approved by the government or by someone in authority. ○ *According to the official figures, over one thousand people died during the revolution.* ○ *A report in the official police newspaper gave no reason for the move.*

▶ **COLLOCATIONS:**
  official **figures/statistics**
  an official **announcement/statement/policy/visit**
▶ **SYNONYM:** authorized
▶ **ANTONYMS:** unofficial, informal

2 NOUN An **official** is a person who holds a position of authority in an organization. ○ *A senior U.N. official hopes to visit Baghdad this month.* ○ *Local officials say the shortage of water restricts the kind of businesses they can attract.*

▶ **COLLOCATIONS:**
  a **senior/government/military/health** official
  officials **say/warn/confirm** *things*

of|fi|cial|ly

ADVERB ○ *The election results have still not been officially announced.* ○ *The nine-year civil war is officially over.*

▶ **COLLOCATIONS:**
  officially **announce/declare/recognize** *something*

officially **opened/launched**
- ▶ SYNONYM: ceremoniously
- ▶ ANTONYMS: unofficially, informally

oil /ɔɪl/ `SCIENCE` `GEOGRAPHY`

UNCOUNTABLE NOUN **Oil** is a smooth, thick liquid that is used as a fuel and for making the parts of machines move smoothly. Oil is found underground. ○ *The company buys and sells about 600,000 barrels of oil a day.* ○ *the rapid rise in prices for oil and petrol* ○ *The Iraqi economy is almost totally dependent on oil production.*

- ▶ COLLOCATIONS:
  oil **prices/supplies/production**
  an oil **refinery/pipeline/well/rig/spill**
  pump/extract/import/export oil
- ▶ PHRASES:
  gas and oil
  barrels of oil

old age /ˌəʊld ˈeɪdʒ/

UNCOUNTABLE NOUN Your **old age** is the period of years towards the end of your life. ○ *They worry about how they will support themselves in their old age.* ○ *increased risk of Alzheimer's in old age*

- ▶ COLLOCATION: **in** old age
- ▶ ANTONYM: youth

old-fashioned /ˌəʊldˈfæʃənd/

1 ADJECTIVE Something such as a style, method, or device that is **old-fashioned** is no longer used, done, or admired by most people, because it has been replaced by something that is more modern. ○ *The house was dull, old-fashioned and in bad condition.* ○ *There are some traditional farmers left who still make cheese the old-fashioned way.*

2 ADJECTIVE **Old-fashioned** ideas, customs, or values are the ideas, customs, and values of the past. ○ *She has some old-fashioned values and can be a strict disciplinarian.* ○ *good old-fashioned English cooking*

- ▶ COLLOCATIONS:
  an old-fashioned **way/style**
  good old-fashioned...:
  old-fashioned **values/notions**
- ▶ SYNONYM: traditional
- ▶ ANTONYM: modern

on|line /ˌɒnˈlaɪn/ also on-line `IT`

ADJECTIVE Online means available on or connected to the Internet.
○ *an online recruitment service* ○ *Approximately 45 per cent of UK households are now online.*

● **Online** is also an adverb. ○ *The study was published online by the British Medical Journal.*

▶ **COLLOCATIONS:**
an online **retailer/buyer/store/service**
an online **journal/newsletter**
online **banking/shopping/learning/access**
shop/register online
buy/sell/find/access/publish/order *something* online

▶ **SYNONYMS:** on the internet, web-based

▶ **ANTONYM:** offline

op|era /ˈɒpərə/ (operas) `ARTS`

NOUN An **opera** is a play with music in which all the words are sung.
○ [+ about] *a one-act opera about contemporary women in America* ○ *Donizetti's opera 'Lucia di Lammermoor'* ○ *He was also learned in classical music with a great love of opera.*

▶ **COLLOCATIONS:**
an opera **about** *something*
an opera **singer/house**

op|er|ate /ˈɒpəreɪt/ (operates, operating, operated)

1 VERB If you **operate** a business or organization, you work to keep it running properly. If a business or organization **operates**, it carries out its work. ○ *Until his death in 1986 Greenwood owned and operated an enormous pear orchard.* ○ *allowing commercial banks to operate in the country* ○ [V-ing] *Operating costs jumped from £85.3m to £95m.*

2 VERB The way that something **operates** is the way that it works or has a particular effect. ○ *Ceiling and wall lights can operate independently.* ○ *The world of work doesn't operate that way.*

3 VERB When you **operate** a machine or device, or when it **operates**, you make it work. ○ *accidents from driving or operating machinery* ○ *The number of these machines operating around the world has now reached ten million.*

▶ **COLLOCATIONS:**
operating **costs/expenses/profit/loss**
a **company/firm/organization/airline** operates
operate **efficiently/profitably**

operate **machinery**
manually/remotely/independently operated
▶ SYNONYMS: run, work, function

op|era|tion /ˌɒpəˈreɪʃən/

UNCOUNTABLE NOUN ○ [+ *of*] *Company finance is to provide funds for the everyday operation of the business.* ○ *Part-time work is made difficult by the operation of the benefit system.* ○ [+ *of*] *over 1,000 dials monitoring every aspect of the operation of the aeroplane*
▶ COLLOCATIONS:
the operation **of** *something*
the operation of a **vehicle/aircraft/company/system**
oversee/launch/suspend/halt the operation of *something*
manufacturing operations
an operations **manager/director**

opin|ion /əˈpɪnjən/ (opinions)

NOUN Your **opinion** about something is what you think or believe about it.
○ *He held the opinion that a government should think before introducing a tax.*
○ *Most who expressed an opinion spoke favorably of Thomas.*
▶ COLLOCATIONS:
an opinion **about/on** *something*
an opinion about/on a **subject/issue/matter**
have/hold/express/voice/offer/form an opinion
a **personal/strong/favourable** opinion
▶ PHRASE: a matter of opinion
▶ SYNONYMS: feeling, belief, view, point of view

op|por|tu|nity /ˌɒpəˈtjuːnɪti, AM -ˈtuːn-/ (opportunities)

NOUN An **opportunity** is a situation in which it is possible for you to do something that you want to do. ○ [+ *to-inf*] *Participants must have the opportunity to take part in the discussion.* ○ [+ *for*] *I want to see more opportunities for young people.* ○ [+ *in*] *equal opportunities in employment*
▶ COLLOCATIONS:
an opportunity **for** *something/someone*
an opportunity **in** *something*
an opportunity for **growth/advancement/expansion**
take/have/seize/miss/waste an opportunity
give/offer *someone* an opportunity
a **golden/unique/rare/ideal/perfect** opportunity
a **career/business/investment** opportunity
an opportunity **arises**

▶ **PHRASES:**
equal opportunities
the opportunity of a lifetime
▶ **SYNONYM:** chance

---

op|po|site /ˈɒpəzɪt/ (opposites)

ADJECTIVE **Opposite** is used to describe things of the same kind which are completely different in a particular way. For example, north and south are opposite directions, and winning and losing are opposite results in a game. ○ *All the cars driving in the opposite direction had their headlights on.* ○ *Cassiopeia lies on the opposite side of the Pole Star from Ursa Major.* ○ *directly opposite points of view*

▶ **COLLOCATIONS:**
opposite **to** something
the opposite **direction/side/end**
directly/diametrically opposite
▶ **PHRASE:** the opposite sex
▶ **SYNONYMS:** different, other, contrary
▶ **ANTONYMS:** same, identical

---

or|ches|tra /ˈɔːkɪstrə/ (orchestras) `ARTS`

NOUN An **orchestra** is a large group of musicians who play a variety of different instruments together. Orchestras usually play classical music. ○ *the Royal Liverpool Philharmonic Orchestra* ○ *The orchestra played extracts from Beethoven and Brahms.* ○ *an orchestra conducted by Yakov Kreizberg*

▶ **COLLOCATIONS:**
a **chamber/symphony** orchestra
conduct an orchestra
an orchestra **plays/performs** something

or|ches|tral /ɔːˈkestrəl/

ADJECTIVE **Orchestral** means relating to an orchestra and the music it plays. ○ *It was performed in 1901 as an orchestral work.* ○ *an orchestral arrangement of Puccini's score* ○ *recordings of orchestral concerts*

▶ **COLLOCATIONS:**
orchestral **music**
an orchestral **work/piece/arrangement/score/concert**

---

or|der /ˈɔːdə/ (orders, ordering, ordered)

1 PHRASE If you do something **in order to** achieve a particular thing or **in order that** something can happen, you do it because you want to achieve that thing. ○ *Most schools are extremely unwilling to cut down on staff in order to cut costs.* ○ *There are increased funds available in order that these targets are met.*

▶ SYNONYM: so that

2 NOUN If a set of things are arranged or done **in** a particular **order**, they are arranged or done so one thing follows another, often according to a particular factor such as importance. ○ *The table shows the factors ranked in order of importance.* ○ *Sources should be arranged in alphabetical order by the last name of the author.*

▶ COLLOCATIONS:
  in/into order
  in order **of** *something*
  in **alphabetical/chronological/reverse** order
  in order of **importance/priority/preference**

3 VERB The way that something **is ordered** is the way that it is organized and structured. ○ *a society which is ordered by hierarchy* ○ *We know the French order things differently.* ○ *a carefully ordered system in which everyone has his place*

▶ COLLOCATION: be ordered **alphabetically/logically/neatly**
▶ SYNONYMS: organize, structure

---

or|di|nary /ˈɔːdɪnri, AM -neri/

ADJECTIVE Ordinary people or things are normal and not special or different in any way. ○ *the impact that technology will have on ordinary people* ○ *It has 25 calories less than ordinary ice cream.*

→ see note at **common**

▶ COLLOCATIONS:
  ordinary **people/citizens**
  just/perfectly/quite ordinary
▶ SYNONYMS: normal, everyday
▶ ANTONYMS: special, extraordinary

or|di|nari|ly /ˈɔːdɪnərəli, AM -ˈnerɪli/

ADVERB If you say what is **ordinarily** the case, you are saying what is normally the case. ○ *The streets would ordinarily have been full of people. There was no one.* ○ *Similar arrangements apply to students who are ordinarily resident in Scotland.* ○ *places where the patient does not ordinarily go*

▶ SYNONYMS: normally, usually

or|gan /ˈɔːgən/ (organs) `SCIENCE` `BIOLOGY` `MEDICINE`

NOUN An **organ** is a part of your body that has a particular purpose or function, for example your heart or lungs. ○ *damage to the muscles and internal organs* ○ *Fewer than one in ten of donated organs could be used.* ○ *Over 150,000 people in the world need organ transplants.*

▶ COLLOCATIONS:
   a **reproductive/sexual/vital/internal** organ
   an organ **transplant/donor/donation**
   transplant/donate/remove an organ

or|gan|ic /ɔːˈgænɪk/ `SCIENCE` `BIOLOGY`

1 ADJECTIVE Organic methods of farming and gardening use only natural animal and plant products to help the plants or animals grow and be healthy, rather than using chemicals. ○ *Organic farming is expanding everywhere.* ○ *organic fruit and vegetables*

2 ADJECTIVE Organic substances are of the sort produced by or found in living things. ○ *Incorporating organic material into chalky soils will reduce the alkalinity.* ○ *Strong acids tend to destroy organic compounds.*

▶ COLLOCATIONS:
   organic **farming/gardening**
   organic **produce/food/wine/vegetables**
   an organic **molecule/compound/material**
▶ PHRASE: organic chemistry
▶ SYNONYM: natural
▶ ANTONYMS: inorganic, man-made, synthetic

or|gan|ize /ˈɔːgənaɪz/ (organizes, organizing, organized) `BUSINESS`

1 VERB If you **organize** an event or activity, you make sure that the necessary arrangements are made. [in BRIT, also use **organise**] ○ *The Commission will organize a conference on rural development.* ○ *a two-day meeting organized by the United Nations* ○ *The initial mobilization was well organized.*

2 VERB If you **organize** a set of things, you arrange them in an ordered way or give them a structure. [in BRIT, also use **organise**] ○ *a method of organizing a file* ○ *the way in which the Army is organized*

▶ COLLOCATIONS:
   organize *things* **by/into** *something*
   organize *things* by **group/topic**
   organize *things* into **units/sections/chapters**
   organize a **topic/essay**
   organize a **meeting/conference/event/demonstration**

well/poorly/highly organized
neatly/logically/loosely organized
▶ SYNONYMS: plan, arrange, order, structure

or|gani|za|tion /ˌɔːɡənaɪˈzeɪʃən/ (organizations)

1 NOUN An **organization** is an official group of people, for example a political party, a business, a charity, or a club. [in BRIT, also use **organisation**] ○ Most of these specialized schools are provided by voluntary organizations. ○ a report by the International Labour Organization
▶ COLLOCATIONS:
a **charitable/voluntary/non-governmental** organization
a **news** organization
form/join an organization
▶ PHRASE: organizations and individuals
▶ SYNONYM: group

2 UNCOUNTABLE NOUN The **organization** of an event or activity involves making all the necessary arrangements for it. [in BRIT, also use **organisation**] ○ [+ of] the exceptional attention to detail that goes into the organization of this event ○ Several projects have been delayed by poor organization.
▶ COLLOCATIONS:
the organization **of** something
effective/efficient/poor organization
▶ ANTONYM: disorganization

3 UNCOUNTABLE NOUN The **organization of** something is the way in which its different parts are arranged or relate to each other. [in BRIT, also use **organisation**] ○ [+ of] I am aware that the organization of the book leaves something to be desired. ○ The economic organization of a society is critical to the society's success or failure.
▶ COLLOCATIONS:
the organization **of** something
the organization of **society/work/industry**
▶ SYNONYMS: structure, arrangement

origi|nal /əˈrɪdʒɪnəl/ (originals)

ADJECTIVE You use **original** when referring to something that existed at the beginning of a process or activity, or the characteristics that something had when it began or was made. ○ The original plan was to hold an indefinite stoppage. ○ The inhabitants have voted overwhelmingly to restore the city's original name of Chemnitz. ○ the ancient history of Australia's original inhabitants

▸ COLLOCATIONS:
the original **plan/intention/idea/purpose**
original **inhabitants**
▸ SYNONYMS: first, early
▸ ANTONYMS: latest, new

origi|nal|ly /əˈrɪdʒɪnəli/

ADVERB When you say what happened or was the case **originally**, you are saying what happened or was the case when something began or came into existence, often to contrast it with what happened later. ○ *The plane has been kept in service far longer than originally intended.* ○ *The castle was originally surrounded by a triple wall, only one of which remains.*
▸ COLLOCATION: originally **intended/planned/scheduled**
▸ SYNONYM: initially
▸ ANTONYM: subsequently

out|door /ˌaʊtˈdɔː/

ADJECTIVE **Outdoor** activities or things happen or are used outside and not in a building. ○ *sports equipment for outdoor activities such as golf, camping and hiking* ○ *There were outdoor cafes on almost every block.*
▸ COLLOCATIONS:
outdoor **activities/pursuits/recreation**
an outdoor **pool/café/concert/festival**
▸ ANTONYM: indoor

out|er /ˈaʊtə/

ADJECTIVE The **outer** parts of something are the parts which contain or enclose the other parts, and which are furthest from the centre. ○ *burns that damage the outer layer of skin* ○ *the outer suburbs of the city* ○ *an old building with solid outer walls*
▸ COLLOCATIONS:
an outer **layer/edge/surface**
an outer **suburb/wall**
▸ PHRASE: outer space
▸ ANTONYMS: inner, inside

over|all /ˌəʊvərˈɔːl/ `ACADEMIC WORD`

ADJECTIVE You use **overall** to indicate that you are talking about a situation in general or about the whole of something. ○ *the overall rise in unemployment* ○ *A company must have both an overall strategy and local strategies for each unit.* ○ *It is usually the woman who assumes overall care of the baby.*

- **Overall** is also an adverb. ○ *The review omitted some studies. Overall, however, the evidence was persuasive.* ○ *The college has few ways to assess the quality of education overall.*
  - ▶ COLLOCATIONS:
    overall **spending/revenue**
    an overall **impression/strategy/performance**
    an overall **majority/increase**
  - ▶ SYNONYM: general
  - ▶ ANTONYM: specific

---

own /əʊn/ (owns, owning, owned)

VERB If you **own** something, it is your property. ○ *farmers who own land*
○ *At least three British golf courses are now owned by the Japanese.*
  - ▶ COLLOCATIONS:
    own **property/land/shares**
    own a **house/farm/restaurant**
    privately/publicly/jointly owned
  - ▶ SYNONYM: possess

own|er /ˈəʊnə/ (owners)

NOUN The **owner** of something is the person to whom it belongs.
○ [+ of] *Owners of property will lose financially if their property is damaged.*
○ *New owners will have to wait until September before moving in.*
  - ▶ COLLOCATIONS:
    the owner **of** *something*
    the **rightful/previous/original/current owner**
    a **property/home/business/pet** owner

---

oxy|gen /ˈɒksɪdʒən/   SCIENCE

UNCOUNTABLE NOUN **Oxygen** is a colourless gas that exists in large quantities in the air. All plants and animals need oxygen in order to live.
○ *The human brain needs to be without oxygen for only four minutes before permanent damage occurs.* ○ *The baby was put in an incubator with an oxygen mask.* ○ *the ability of the blood to carry oxygen to the heart*
  - ▶ COLLOCATIONS:
    breathe/inhale/carry oxygen
    an oxygen **mask/tank/supply**

ozone lay|er /ˈəʊzəʊn leɪə/

GEOGRAPHY SCIENCE

NOUN **The ozone layer** is the part of the Earth's atmosphere that has the most ozone in it. The ozone layer protects living things from the harmful radiation of the sun. ○ *recent concerns about holes appearing in the ozone layer* ○ *damage to the ozone layer*

o

Pp

pain /peɪn/ (pains)

MEDICINE

NOUN **Pain** is the feeling of great discomfort you have, for example when you have been hurt or when you are ill. ○ *a bone disease that caused excruciating pain* ○ *To help ease the pain, heat can be applied to the area with a hot water bottle.* ○ *[+ in] I felt a sharp pain in my lower back.*

▶ **COLLOCATIONS:**
a pain **in** something
the pain **of** something
ease/soothe/relieve/alleviate pain
feel/endure/cause/reduce pain
pain **persists/worsens/subsides**
back/chest/stomach/muscle pain
excruciating/chronic/severe pain
pain **relief**

▶ **PHRASE:** aches and pains

▶ **SYNONYMS:** suffering, discomfort, agony

pain|ful /'peɪnfʊl/

1 ADJECTIVE If a part of your body is **painful**, it hurts because it is injured or because there is something wrong with it. ○ *Her glands were swollen and painful.* ○ *Sampras awaits the results of a bone scan on a painful left shin.*

2 ADJECTIVE If something such as an illness, injury, or operation is **painful**, it causes you a lot of physical pain. ○ *a painful back injury* ○ *Sunburn is painful and potentially dangerous.*

▶ **COLLOCATIONS:**
a painful **rash/cramp/blister**
excruciatingly/unbearably/extremely painful

▶ **SYNONYM:** sore

pain|ful|ly /'peɪnfʊli/

ADVERB ○ *His tooth had started to throb painfully again.* ○ *He cracked his head painfully against the cupboard.*

P

para|graph /ˈpærəɡrɑːf, -ɡræf/ `ACADEMIC WORD` `ACADEMIC STUDY`
(paragraphs)

NOUN A **paragraph** is a section of a piece of writing. A paragraph always begins on a new line and contains at least one sentence. ○ *The length of a paragraph depends on the information it conveys.* ○ *Paragraph 81 sets out the rules that should apply if a gift is accepted.*
  ▸ **COLLOCATION:** a **brief/opening/introductory/closing** paragraph
  ▸ **SYNONYM:** section

par|ent /ˈpeərənt/ (parents) `SOCIAL SCIENCE`

NOUN Your **parents** are your mother and father. ○ *Children need their parents.* ○ *When you become a parent the things you once cared about seem to have less value.*
  ▸ **COLLOCATIONS:**
    the parents **of** *someone*
    a **foster/adoptive/birth/single/lone** parent

pa|ren|tal /pəˈrentəl/

ADJECTIVE **Parental** is used to describe something that relates to parents in general, or to one or both of the parents of a particular child. ○ *Medical treatment was sometimes given to children without parental consent.* ○ *Parental attitudes vary widely.* ○ *the removal of children from the parental home*
  ▸ **COLLOCATIONS:**
    parental **attitudes/choices/consent**
    parental **responsibilities/rights/involvement**
  ▸ **RELATED WORDS:** maternal, paternal

part /pɑːt/ (parts)

NOUN A **part of** something is one of the pieces, sections, or elements that it consists of. ○ [+ of] *I like that part of Cape Town.* ○ [+ of] *Respect is a very important part of any relationship.*
  ▸ **COLLOCATIONS:**
    part **of** *something*
    part of a **reason/deal/plan/effort**
    a **key/essential/integral/important** part
  ▸ **PHRASE:** part of the world
  ▸ **SYNONYMS:** piece, portion, section, element
  ▸ **ANTONYMS:** whole, entirety

par|ticu|lar /pəˈtɪkjʊlə/

ADJECTIVE You use **particular** to emphasize that you are talking about one thing or one kind of thing rather than other similar ones. ○ *People with a* particular blood type (HLA B27) are much more at risk. ○ I have to know exactly why it is I'm doing a particular job.

▶ **COLLOCATION:** a particular **type/brand/kind/case/problem**
▶ **SYNONYM:** specific
▶ **ANTONYM:** general

par|ticu|lar|ly /pə'tɪkjʊləli/

1 **ADVERB** You use **particularly** to indicate that what you are saying applies especially to one thing or situation. ○ Keep your office space looking good, particularly your desk. ○ More local employment will be created, particularly in service industries.

2 **ADVERB** **Particularly** means more than usual or more than other things. ○ Progress has been particularly disappointing. ○ I particularly liked the wooden chests and chairs.
▶ **COLLOCATIONS:**
  particularly **in/among** something
  particularly **useful/important/interesting/relevant**
  particularly **vulnerable/sensitive/difficult**
  particularly **concerned/pleased/impressed**
▶ **SYNONYM:** especially

part-time /ˌpɑːt'taɪm/ BUSINESS

The adverb is also spelled **part time**.

ADJECTIVE If someone is a **part-time** worker or has a **part-time** job, they work for only part of each day or week. ○ Many businesses are cutting back by employing lower-paid part-time workers. ○ I'm part-time. I work three days a week.

• **Part-time** is also an adverb. ○ I want to work part-time.
▶ **COLLOCATIONS:**
  a part-time **job/worker/employee**
  part-time **employment**
  work/study part-time
▶ **PHRASE:** on a part-time basis
▶ **ANTONYM:** full-time

par|ty /'pɑːti/ (parties) SOCIAL SCIENCE POLITICS

NOUN A **party** is a political organization whose members have similar aims and beliefs. Usually the organization tries to get its members elected to the government of a country. ○ a member of the Labour party ○ India's ruling party ○ her resignation as party leader

▶ COLLOCATIONS:
a **political/opposition/governing/ruling** party
the **Labour/Conservative/Democratic/Republican** party
a party **leader/member/official/conference**
party **leadership**
vote for/support a party

---

pas|sage /ˈpæsɪdʒ/ (passages)   `LITERATURE`

NOUN A **passage** in a book, speech, or piece of music is a section of it that
you are considering separately from the rest. ○ [+ from] He reads a passage
from Milton. ○ the passage in which Blake spoke of the world of imagination
▶ COLLOCATIONS:
a passage **from/in** something
quote/recite/read a passage
a **biblical/lyrical** passage
▶ SYNONYMS: excerpt, extract, section

---

pas|sen|ger /ˈpæsɪndʒə/ (passengers)

NOUN A **passenger** in a vehicle such as a bus, boat, or plane is a person
who is travelling in it, but who is not driving it or working on it. ○ [+ in] Mr
Fullemann was a passenger in the car when it crashed. ○ a flight from Milan with
more than forty passengers on board
▶ COLLOCATIONS:
a passenger **in/on** something
a **front-seat/back-seat** passenger
a **rail/airline/bus** passenger
a passenger **train/bus/plane/ferry/cabin/seat**
take/carry passengers somewhere
passengers **travel/fly/arrive** somewhere
passengers **board** something
▶ SYNONYM: traveller

---

past /pɑːst, pæst/ (pasts)   `HISTORY`

1 NOUN **The past** is the time before the present, and the things that have
happened. ○ In the past, about a third of the babies born to women with
diabetes were lost. ○ He should learn from the mistakes of the past. We have been
here before.

2 NOUN Your **past** consists of all the things that you have done or that have
happened to you. ○ revelations about his past ○ Germany's recent past
▶ COLLOCATIONS:
in the past

the **recent/distant** past

a **country's** past

a **murky/troubled/colourful** past

▶ SYNONYM: history

▶ ANTONYMS: future, present

3 ADJECTIVE Past events and things happened or existed before the present time. ○ *I knew from past experience that alternative therapies could help.* ○ *a return to the turbulence of past centuries*

▶ COLLOCATIONS:

the past **days/weeks/decades/years/centuries**

past **experience/performance**

▶ SYNONYMS: previous, earlier

▶ ANTONYMS: current, future

---

pa|tient /ˈpeɪʃənt/ (patients)   `MEDICINE`

NOUN A **patient** is a person who is receiving medical treatment from a doctor or hospital. A **patient** is also someone who is registered with a particular doctor. ○ *The earlier the treatment is given, the better the patient's chances.* ○ *He specialized in treatment of cancer patients.*

▶ COLLOCATIONS:

a patient **with** an illness

treat/diagnose/cure/help patients

patients **undergo/receive** treatment

a **cancer/MS/cardiac/stroke/mental health** patient

a **sick/ill/elderly** patient

patient **care/records**

▶ SYNONYMS: case, invalid

---

pat|tern /ˈpætən/ (patterns)

NOUN A **pattern** is the repeated or regular way in which something happens or is done. ○ *All three attacks followed the same pattern.* ○ [+ of] *A change in the pattern of his breathing became apparent.*

▶ COLLOCATIONS:

the pattern **of** something

a pattern of **behaviour/activity**

a **clear/familiar/normal/typical/usual** pattern

the **same** pattern

a **behaviour/sleep/eating/weather** pattern

repeat/follow/establish/change a pattern

a pattern **emerges/changes**

▶ SYNONYMS: arrangement, order

peace /piːs/

UNCOUNTABLE NOUN If there is **peace** in a country or in the world, there are no wars or violent conflicts going on. ○ *The President spoke of a shared commitment to world peace and economic development.* ○ *Leaders of some rival factions signed a peace agreement last week.* ○ *They hope the treaty will bring peace and stability to Southeast Asia.*

▶ **COLLOCATIONS:**
  at peace
  peace **in** *a place*
  bring peace **to** *somewhere*
  keep the peace
  peace **talks/negotiations**
  a peace **conference/plan/settlement/agreement/deal**
  world/international/regional peace
  a **lasting/permanent/uneasy** peace

▶ **PHRASES:**
  the Nobel Peace Prize
  peace and stability

▶ **ANTONYM:** war

---

pen|sion /ˈpenʃən/ (pensions)　　BUSINESS

NOUN Someone who has a **pension** receives a regular sum of money from the state or a company because they have retired or because they are widowed or disabled. ○ *struggling by on a pension* ○ *a company pension scheme*

▶ **COLLOCATIONS:**
  on a pension
  receive a pension
  a pension **fund/scheme/plan**
  a **basic/annual/private/state** pension

▶ **SYNONYMS:** allowance, support

pen|sion|er /ˈpenʃənə/ (pensioners)

NOUN A **pensioner** is someone who receives a pension, especially a pension paid by the state to retired people. ○ *Nearly a third of Britain's pensioners live on less than £10,000 a year.*

▶ **COLLOCATIONS:**
  pensioners **receive/live on** £x
  a **poor/frail/disabled/old-age** pensioner
  a pensioner **concession/discount**

▶ **SYNONYM:** OAP

peo|ple /ˈpiːpəl/ (peoples)

1 **PLURAL NOUN** **People** are men, women, and children. ○ *Millions of people have lost their homes.* ○ [+ of] *the people of Angola* ○ *I don't think people should make promises they don't mean to keep.*

→ see note at **individual**

▶ **COLLOCATIONS:**
the people **of/from** *somewhere*
people **throughout/across** *a place*
people of/from a **country/region/culture/background**
most/many/some/other people
young/old/poor/elderly/local people

▶ **PHRASES:**
people and animals
people and places

▶ **SYNONYMS:** humans, human beings, mankind, humankind

2 **NOUN** A **people** is all the men, women, and children of a particular country or race. ○ [+ of] *the native peoples of Central and South America* ○ *It's a triumph for the American people.*

▶ **COLLOCATIONS:**
the people **of** *somewhere*
native/indigenous people

▶ **SYNONYMS:** community, population, race, ethnic group

> **USAGE: people**, **persons** or **peoples**?
>
> The normal plural form of **person** is **people**. ○ *a group four people* ○ *the thinking and attitudes of young people*
>
> The plural form **persons** is used only in very formal official and legal documents.
>
> When you use **people** to talk about a whole population or a race of people, the plural form is **peoples**. ○ *Canada's indigenous peoples, the Amerindians and the Inuit*

per cent /pə ˈsent/ (per cent) also **percent** ACADEMIC WORD MATHS

NOUN You use **per cent** to talk about amounts. For example, if an amount is 10 per cent (10%) of a larger amount, it is equal to 10 hundredths of the larger amount. ○ [+ of] *20 to 40 per cent of the voters are undecided.* ○ *We aim to increase sales by 10 per cent.*

● **Per cent** is also an adjective. ○ *There has been a ten per cent increase in the number of new students arriving at polytechnics this year.*

● **Per cent** is also an adverb. ○ *its prediction that house prices will fall 5 per cent over the year*

▶ **COLLOCATION:** *x* per cent **of** *something*
▶ **SYNONYMS:** percentage, proportion, fraction

ACADEMIC WRITING: Numbers and abbreviations

In written notes, charts, diagrams, etc., you often use numbers (5, 48) and symbols (%, $, =). You also use words and phrases that are not in full sentences. ○ *62% college students = female; 48% college students = male*

In written essays, you can use numbers and some symbols for statistics, but you need to put these into full sentences. All three alternatives below would be acceptable in an IELTS writing task.
○ *62%* **of** *college students are female and 48% are male.* ○ *62 per cent* **of** *college students are female and 48 per cent are male.* ○ *Sixty-two per cent* **of** *college students are female and forty-eight per cent are male.*

It is common to write small numbers in words (four, ten, twelve), but large numbers are usually written in numbers (478, 256).

---

per|form /pəˈfɔːm/ (performs, performing, performed) `ARTS`

VERB If you **perform** a play, a piece of music, or a dance, you do it in front of an audience. ○ *Gardiner has pursued relentlessly high standards in performing classical music.* ○ *This play was first performed in 411 BC.* ○ *He began performing in the early fifties, singing and playing guitar.*

▶ **COLLOCATIONS:**
perform **at** *something*
performed **by** *someone*
perform a **concert/dance/song/play/routine**
perform at a **concert/wedding/reception**
perform **live**
performed by **a musician/orchestra/choir**
▶ **SYNONYMS:** act, present

per|for|mance /pəˈfɔːməns/ (performances)

NOUN A **performance** involves entertaining an audience by doing something such as singing, dancing, or acting. ○ [+ of] *Inside the theatre, they were giving a performance of Bizet's Carmen.* ○ [+ as] *her performance as the betrayed Medea*

▶ **COLLOCATIONS:**
a performance **of** *something*
a performance **as** *someone*
a **live/good/outstanding/poor** performance
give a performance
▶ **SYNONYMS:** production, show

per|form|er /pəˈfɔːmə/ (performers)

NOUN A **performer** is a person who acts, sings, or does other entertainment in front of audiences. ○ *A performer in evening dress plays classical selections on the violin.*

▶ **COLLOCATIONS:**
  a **circus/street/cabaret** performer
  a **star/top/solo** performer

▶ **SYNONYMS:** entertainer, actor, artist

per|ˈform|ing ˌarts   ARTS

PLURAL NOUN Dance, drama, music, and other forms of entertainment that are usually performed live in front of an audience are referred to as **the performing arts**. ○ *funding for museums, galleries and the performing arts*

pe|ri|od /ˈpɪəriəd/ (periods)   ACADEMIC WORD

1 NOUN A **period** is a length of time. ○ [+ *of*] *This crisis might last for a long period of time.* ○ [+ *of*] *a period of a few months* ○ *for a limited period only*

2 NOUN A **period** in the life of a person, organization, or society is a length of time which is remembered for a particular situation or activity. ○ [+ *of*] *a period of economic good health and expansion* ○ [+ *of*] *He went through a period of wanting to be accepted.* ○ *The South African years were his most creative period.*

▶ **COLLOCATIONS:**
  a period **of** *something*
  a period of **transition/uncertainty/calm**
  a **limited/short/long/extended/prolonged** period
  a **holiday/notice/transition** period
  enter/go through/enjoy a period

▶ **PHRASE:** a period of time

▶ **SYNONYMS:** duration, time, spell, while

per|ma|nent /ˈpɜːmənənt/   BUSINESS

1 ADJECTIVE Something that is **permanent** lasts for ever. ○ *Heavy drinking can cause permanent damage to the brain.* ○ *The ban is intended to be permanent.*

2 ADJECTIVE A **permanent** employee is one who is employed for an unlimited length of time. ○ *At the end of the probationary period you will become a permanent employee.* ○ *a permanent job*

▶ **COLLOCATIONS:**
  permanent **residence/status/employment**
  a permanent **job/position/vacancy/employee/worker**

P

permanent **damage/disability**
▶ SYNONYMS: ongoing, lasting
▶ ANTONYMS: temporary, non-permanent, transient

per|ma|nent|ly

ADVERB ○ *His reason had been permanently affected by what he had witnessed.*
○ *permanently employed registered dockers*
▶ COLLOCATIONS:
live/stay/settle *somewhere* permanently
permanently **banned/excluded/damaged/employed**
▶ SYNONYM: forever
▶ ANTONYM: temporarily

---

per|mit (permits, permitting, permitted)

> The verb is pronounced /pə'mɪt/. The noun is pronounced /'pɜːmɪt/.

1 VERB If someone **permits** something, they allow it to happen. If they
permit you **to** do something, they allow you to do it. [FORMAL] ○ *He can
let the court's decision stand and permit the execution.* ○ [+ to-inf] *Employees
are permitted to use the golf course during their free hours.* ○ [+ into] *No outside
journalists have been permitted into the country.*
▶ COLLOCATIONS:
be permitted **into** *somewhere*
be permitted to **visit/enter/travel**
a **law/rule** permits *something*
permit **smoking/access/use**
expressly/legally/knowingly permit
▶ SYNONYMS: allow, let
▶ ANTONYMS: forbid, prohibit

2 NOUN A **permit** is an official document which says that you may do
something. For example you usually need a **permit** to work in a foreign
country. ○ *The majority of foreign nationals working here have work permits.*
▶ COLLOCATIONS:
issue/grant/obtain/require a permit
a **work/residence/building** permit
a **special/temporary/necessary** permit
a permit **holder/application/request/fee**
▶ SYNONYMS: warrant, license

per|mis|sion /pə'mɪʃən/

UNCOUNTABLE NOUN If someone who has authority over you gives you
permission to do something, they say that they will allow you to do it.

○ He asked permission to leave the room. ○ [+ for] Police said permission for the
march had not been granted. ○ They cannot leave the country without
permission.

▶ **COLLOCATIONS:**
  with/without permission
  permission **for** something
  ask/receive permission
  give/grant/refuse permission
  written/special/official/government permission
▶ **SYNONYMS:** authorization, consent
▶ **ANTONYMS:** refusal, denial

---

per|son|al /ˈpɜːsənəl/

1 ADJECTIVE A **personal** opinion, quality, or thing belongs or relates to one
particular person rather than to other people. ○ In addition to being clear
and simple, survey questions should never convey your personal opinions.
○ books, furniture, and other personal belongings ○ an estimated personal
fortune of almost seventy million dollars

2 ADJECTIVE Personal matters relate to your feelings, relationships, and
health. ○ teaching young people about marriage and personal relationships
○ Mr Knight said that he had resigned for personal reasons.

▶ **COLLOCATIONS:**
  a personal **opinion/belief/experience/reason/matter/choice**
  a personal **relationship/life**
  personal **effects/belongings/property/fortune/wealth**
  deeply/intensely/highly/strictly personal
▶ **SYNONYMS:** private, individual
▶ **ANTONYM:** public

---

per|son|al|ity /ˌpɜːsəˈnælɪti/ (personalities)   `PSYCHOLOGY`

NOUN Your **personality** is your whole character and nature. ○ She has such
a kind, friendly personality. ○ Through sheer force of personality Hugh Trenchard
had got his way. ○ These personality traits get passed on from generation to
generation.

▶ **COLLOCATIONS:**
  a **forceful/outgoing/vibrant/bubbly** personality
  a personality **trait/characteristic/flaw/type/disorder**
  have/develop a personality
▶ **SYNONYMS:** temperament, character

per|suade /pə'sweɪd/ (persuades, persuading, persuaded)

VERB If you **persuade** someone **to** do something, you cause them to do it by giving them good reasons for doing it. ○ [+ to-inf] *We're trying to persuade manufacturers to sell them here.* ○ [+ to-inf] *They were eventually persuaded by the police to give themselves up.*

▶ COLLOCATIONS:
   be persuaded **by** *something/someone*
   try/attempt/fail to persuade
   eventually/finally/successfully persuade
   easily persuaded
   persuaded by an **argument**
   persuade *someone* to **stay/reconsider/join**

▶ SYNONYMS: convince, cajole, urge

▶ ANTONYM: dissuade

per|sua|sion /pə'sweɪʒən/

UNCOUNTABLE NOUN Persuasion is the act of persuading someone to do something or to believe that something is true. ○ [+ to-inf] *Mr Gorbachev needed more persuasion to abandon Soviet plans.* ○ *She was using all her powers of persuasion to induce the Griffins to remain in Rollway.*

▶ COLLOCATIONS:
   gentle/friendly persuasion
   use/need/require persuasion

▶ PHRASE: powers of persuasion

▶ SYNONYM: influence

per|sua|sive /pə'sweɪsɪv/

ADJECTIVE Someone or something that is **persuasive** is likely to persuade a person to believe or do a particular thing. ○ *What do you think were some of the more persuasive arguments on the other side?* ○ *I can be very persuasive when I want to be.*

▶ COLLOCATIONS:
   a persuasive **argument/case/essay/manner/tone**
   persuasive **evidence/powers**

▶ SYNONYMS: compelling, convincing, influential

▶ ANTONYMS: ineffective, unconvincing

---

physi|cal /'fɪzɪkəl/   `ACADEMIC WORD`

ADJECTIVE Physical qualities, actions, or things are connected with a person's body, rather than with their mind. ○ *the physical and mental problems caused by the illness* ○ *Physical activity promotes good health.*

▶ **COLLOCATIONS:**
  physical **activities/exercise/exertion**
  physical **strength/fitness**
  a physical **symptom/disability/illness**
  physical **contact/pain/abuse/attraction**
  purely physical
▶ **SYNONYM:** bodily
▶ **ANTONYMS:** mental, emotional, psychological

physi|cal|ly

ADVERB ○ *You may be physically and mentally exhausted after a long flight.*
  ○ *disabled people who cannot physically use a telephone*
▶ **COLLOCATIONS:**
  physically **fit/active/disabled/ill/sick**
  physically **incapable/unable/impossible**
  physically **abused/assaulted/attacked**
  physically **drained/exhausted**
  mature/heal/develop physically
▶ **SYNONYM:** bodily
▶ **ANTONYMS:** mentally, emotionally, psychologically

---

phys|ics /ˈfɪzɪks/   SCIENCE   PHYSICS

UNCOUNTABLE NOUN Physics is the scientific study of forces such as heat, light, sound, pressure, gravity, and electricity, and the way that they affect objects. ○ *the laws of physics* ○ *experiments in particle physics*
▶ **COLLOCATIONS:**
  quantum/particle/nuclear/Newtonian/theoretical physics
  a physics **professor/lecturer/teacher**
  a physics **laboratory/department/experiment**
  study/teach/understand physics
▶ **PHRASE:** physics and chemistry

physi|cist /ˈfɪzɪsɪst/ (physicists)

NOUN A **physicist** is a person who does research connected with physics or who studies physics. ○ *types of sub-atomic particle discovered by physicists*
▶ **COLLOCATIONS:**
  a **quantum/particle/nuclear** physicist
  a **renowned/experimental/distinguished/eminent** physicist
  physicists **invent/devise/study/discover** *things*

pint /paɪnt/ (pints)

NOUN A **pint** is a unit of measurement for liquids. In Britain, it is equal to 568 cubic centimetres or one eighth of an imperial gallon. In America, it is equal to 473 cubic centimetres or one eighth of an American gallon. ○ [+ of] *a pint of milk* ○ [+ of] *The military requested 6,000 pints of blood from the American Red Cross.*

▶ **COLLOCATIONS:**
a pint **of** *something*
a pint of **milk/beer/lager/blood**
a pint **glass/mug**
a **half/quarter** pint

plan /plæn/ (plans, planning, planned)

1 NOUN A **plan** is a method of achieving something that you have worked out in detail beforehand. ○ *The three leaders had worked out a peace plan.* ○ [+ of] *a detailed plan of action for restructuring the group* ○ *He maintains that everything is going according to plan.*

▶ **COLLOCATIONS:**
a plan **for/of** *something*
a plan of **action/attack**
announce/unveil/outline plans
follow/implement a plan
a **long-term/ambitious/detailed/immediate** plan
a **peace/retirement/restructuring** plan
a **master/action** plan
the **original** plan
plans are **underway/in place**
plans **fail/backfire/succeed**

▶ **PHRASE:** go according to plan
▶ **SYNONYMS:** aim, procedure, strategy

2 VERB If you **plan** what you are going to do, you decide in detail what you are going to do, and you intend to do it. ○ [+ for] *It would be difficult for schools to plan for the future.* ○ *I had been planning a trip to the West Coast.* ○ *A planned demonstration has been called off by its organisers.*

▶ **COLLOCATIONS:**
plan **for** *something*
plan a **trip/visit/holiday/meeting/wedding/attack/protest**
plan to **launch/build/introduce** *something*
plan **ahead/carefully/accordingly**
originally/carefully/meticulously planned

▶ **PHRASES:**
plan for the future
plan for every eventuality
▶ **SYNONYMS:** prepare, arrange, organize

plan|ning /ˈplænɪŋ/

UNCOUNTABLE NOUN ○ *The trip needs careful planning.* ○ *The new system is still in the planning stages.*

▶ **COLLOCATIONS:**
need/require/begin/start planning
meticulous/careful/strategic/long-term planning
resource/family/retirement/land-use planning
a planning **stage/process**

▶ **SYNONYMS:** preparation, arrangement

---

plan|et /ˈplænɪt/ (planets)   `GEOGRAPHY`

NOUN A **planet** is a large, round object in space that moves around a star. The Earth is a planet. ○ *The picture shows six of the nine planets in the solar system.*

▶ **COLLOCATIONS:**
a planet **revolves/rotates/spins**
a planet **orbits/circles** *something*
a **ringed/outer/distant/rocky/gaseous** planet
a planet's **surface/atmosphere**

▶ **PHRASE:** Planet Earth

---

plant /plɑːnt, plænt/ (plants)   `SCIENCE` `BIOLOGY`

NOUN A **plant** is a living thing that grows in the earth and has a stem, leaves, and roots. ○ *Water each plant as often as required.* ○ *Exotic plants thrive in humid air.*

▶ **COLLOCATIONS:**
a **native/tropical/exotic/rare** plant
a **hardy/flowering/herbaceous/potted** plant
a plant **species/pot/root**
a plant **thrives/grows/flowers/blooms/wilts**
grow/water a plant

▶ **PHRASE:** plants and animals

---

play /pleɪ/ (plays, playing, played)   `LITERATURE`

1 NOUN A **play** is a piece of writing which is performed in a theatre, on the radio, or on television. ○ [+ *about*] *The company put on a play about the*

homeless. ○ *a Shakespeare play* ○ *The play depicts 48 hours in the lives of three teenagers.*
▶ COLLOCATIONS:
  a play **about** *something*
  write/direct/stage/perform a play
  a **nativity/morality/one-act/radio** play
  a play **opens/begins/unfolds**
  a play **revolves around/explores** *something*
▶ SYNONYMS: show, drama, performance

2 VERB If an actor **plays** a role or character in a play or film, he or she performs the part of that character. ○ *Dr Jekyll and Mr Hyde, in which he played Hyde* ○ *His ambition is to play the part of Dracula.*
▶ COLLOCATIONS:
  a **star/actor/actress** plays *something*
  play a **part/role**
▶ SYNONYMS: act, perform, portray

---

poem /ˈpəʊɪm/ (poems)   LITERATURE

NOUN A **poem** is a piece of writing in which the words are chosen for their beauty and sound and are carefully arranged, often in short lines which rhyme. ○ *recite a love poem*
▶ COLLOCATIONS:
  write/compose/publish a poem
  recite/read/quote a poem
  a **narrative/lyrical/epic/love/war** poem
  a poem **describes/expresses/reveals/reflects** *something*
▶ SYNONYMS: ode, verse

po|et|ry /ˈpəʊɪtri/

UNCOUNTABLE NOUN Poems, considered as a form of literature, are referred to as **poetry**. ○ *Russian poetry* ○ *Lawrence Durrell wrote a great deal of poetry.*
▶ COLLOCATIONS:
  write/compose/publish poetry
  recite/read/quote poetry
  English/Persian/twentieth-century/contemporary poetry
  love/lyric/war/epic poetry
  a poetry **reading/recital**
  a poetry **book/anthology**
▶ SYNONYM: verse
▶ ANTONYM: prose

poet /ˈpəʊɪt/ (poets)

NOUN A **poet** is a person who writes poems. ○ *He was a painter and poet.*
○ *a survey of women poets writing in English*

▸ **COLLOCATIONS:**
   a poet **writes/describes/expresses** something
   a **Romantic/metaphysical/English/Irish/woman** poet
▸ **PHRASE:** poet laureate
▸ **SYNONYMS:** bard, lyricist

---

point /pɔɪnt/ (points)

1 NOUN A **point** is an opinion or fact expressed by someone. ○ *We disagree with every point Mr Blunkett makes.* ○ *Dave Hill's article makes the right point about the Taylor Report.* ○ *The following tale will clearly illustrate this point.*

2 NOUN A **point** is a detail, aspect, or quality of something or someone.
○ *The most interesting point about the village was its religion.* ○ *Several key points emerged from the Oxfordshire experiment.*

▸ **COLLOCATIONS:**
   a point **about** something
   make/illustrate/prove a point
   a **key/focal/main/important/interesting** point
▸ **SYNONYMS:** opinion, fact

---

po|lice /pəˈliːs/

NOUN The **police** are the official organization that is responsible for making sure that people obey the law. The men and women who belong to this organization are referred to as **police**. ○ *The police are also looking for a second car.* ○ *Police say they have arrested twenty people following the disturbances.*

▸ **COLLOCATIONS:**
   the police **arrest/question/interview** *someone*
   the police **say/find/believe/investigate** *things*
   call/contact/alert/notify the police
   state/city/riot/traffic police
   local/armed/military police
   a police **car/station/force/officer/chief**
▸ **SYNONYMS:** law enforcement, police officers

---

poli|cy /ˈpɒlɪsi/ (policies) ACADEMIC WORD   SOCIAL SCIENCE   POLITICS

NOUN A **policy** is a set of ideas or plans that is used as a basis for making decisions, especially in politics, economics, or business. ○ *plans which* include changes in foreign policy and economic reforms ○ the U.N.'s policy-making body

▶ **COLLOCATIONS:**
   foreign/monetary/economic/fiscal/social/public policy
   defence/energy/transport/immigration policy
   a **new/official** policy
   policy **making**
   a policy **maker/adviser/committee/analyst**
   a policy **shift/change**

▶ **PHRASE:** policy and procedure

▶ **SYNONYMS:** procedure, approach, protocol

---

poli|tics /ˈpɒlɪtɪks/   `SOCIAL SCIENCE` `POLITICS`

PLURAL NOUN Politics are the actions or activities concerned with achieving and using power in a country or society. The verb that follows **politics** may be either singular or plural. ○ *The key question in British politics was how long the prime minister could survive.* ○ *[+ of] The film takes no position on the politics of Northern Ireland.* ○ *Politics is by no means the only arena in which women are excelling.*

▶ **COLLOCATIONS:**
   the politics **of** *something/somewhere*
   party politics
   domestic/internal/British/American politics
   leave/enter/dominate/influence/shape politics

▶ **SYNONYMS:** domestic affairs, foreign affairs

po|liti|cal /pəˈlɪtɪkəl/

ADJECTIVE ○ *All other political parties there have been completely banned.* ○ *The Canadian government is facing another political crisis.* ○ *a democratic political system*

▶ **COLLOCATIONS:**
   a political **party/system/leader/agenda**
   a political **crisis/issue/solution**
   a political **correspondent/analyst/editor**
   political **reform/power**
   overtly/purely political

▶ **PHRASES:**
   political and economic
   social and political

▶ **SYNONYM:** governmental

po|liti|cal|ly /pəˈlɪtɪkli/

ADVERB ○ *They do not believe the killings were politically motivated.* ○ *Politically and economically this is an extremely difficult question.*

▶ **COLLOCATIONS:**
politically **sensitive/difficult/impossible/unpopular**
politically **motivated/active/powerful/astute/expedient**

▶ **PHRASES:**
politically and economically
politically and socially
politically and militarily

▶ **SYNONYM:** governmentally

poli|ti|cian /ˌpɒlɪˈtɪʃən/ (politicians)

NOUN A **politician** is a person whose job is in politics, especially a member of parliament or congress. ○ *They have arrested a number of leading opposition politicians.*

▶ **COLLOCATIONS:**
a **democratic/conservative/liberal/opposition** politician
a **leading/senior/prominent/local/corrupt** politician
elect a politician
politicians **promise/claim/decide** *things*

▶ **SYNONYMS:** Member of Parliament, MP, statesman

---

pol|lute /pəˈluːt/ (pollutes, polluting, polluted)   GEOGRAPHY

VERB To **pollute** water, air, or land means to make it dirty and dangerous to live in or to use, especially with poisonous chemicals or sewage. ○ *Heavy industry pollutes our rivers with noxious chemicals.* ○ *A number of beaches in the region have been polluted by sewage pumped into the Irish Sea.*

▶ **COLLOCATIONS:**
pollute the **environment/air/atmosphere**
pollute a **river/sea/ocean/city**
highly/heavily polluted
polluting **fuel/emissions/gases**

▶ **SYNONYM:** contaminate
▶ **ANTONYM:** clean

pol|lu|tion /pəˈluːʃən/

1 UNCOUNTABLE NOUN Pollution is the process of polluting water, air, or land, especially with poisonous chemicals. ○ [+ *of*] *The fine was for the company's pollution of the air near its plants.* ○ *Recycling also helps control environmental pollution by reducing the need for waste dumps.*

2 UNCOUNTABLE NOUN Pollution is poisonous or dirty substances that are polluting the water, air, or land somewhere. ○ *The level of pollution in the river was falling.*

▶ COLLOCATIONS:
pollution **of** *something*
pollution of the **ocean/air/environment**
air/noise/water/light pollution
atmospheric/environmental/industrial pollution
curb/cut/reduce/combat/cause pollution
pollution **control**
a pollution **level/problem**
▶ SYNONYMS: emissions, contamination

---

poor /pʊə, pɔː/ (poorer, poorest)

1 ADJECTIVE Someone who is **poor** has very little money and few possessions. ○ *The reason our schools cannot afford better teachers is because people here are poor.* ○ *He was one of thirteen children from a poor family.*

• **The poor** are people who are poor. ○ *Even the poor have their pride.*

2 ADJECTIVE The people in a **poor** country or area have very little money and few possessions. ○ *Many countries in the Third World are as poor as they have ever been.* ○ *a settlement house for children in a poor neighborhood*

▶ COLLOCATIONS:
desperately/relatively/extremely poor
a poor **country/nation/neighbourhood**
a poor **family/background**
▶ PHRASE: rich and poor
▶ SYNONYMS: impoverished, deprived, poverty-stricken
▶ ANTONYMS: rich, affluent, wealthy, well-off

pov|er|ty /ˈpɒvəti/

UNCOUNTABLE NOUN Poverty is the state of being extremely poor. ○ *According to World Bank figures, 41 per cent of Brazilians live in absolute poverty.* ○ *More than 300 million Indians live below the poverty line.*

▶ COLLOCATIONS:
live **in** poverty
alleviate/eradicate/tackle/combat poverty
abject/extreme/dire/absolute poverty
urban/rural/global/world/third-world poverty
child/pensioner poverty
the poverty **rate/gap/level**
▶ PHRASE: below the poverty line

▶ **SYNONYMS:** deprivation, destitution, penury
▶ **ANTONYMS:** wealth, affluence

---

popu|lar /ˈpɒpjʊlə/

ADJECTIVE Something that is **popular** is enjoyed or liked by a lot of people.
  ○ *This is the most popular ball game ever devised.* ○ *These courses have proved very popular with students.*
  ▶ **COLLOCATIONS:**
  popular **among/with** *people*
  popular among/with **tourists/locals/the public/students**
  popular among/with **voters/consumers/users/buyers**
  hugely/wildly/immensely/extremely popular
  a popular **destination/resort/pastime/song/choice**
  prove/become/remain popular
  ▶ **SYNONYMS:** well-liked, sought-after
  ▶ **ANTONYM:** unpopular

popu|lar|ity /ˌpɒpjʊˈlærɪti/

UNCOUNTABLE NOUN ○ [+ *of*] *the growing popularity of Australian wines among consumers* ○ *Walking and golf increased in popularity during the 1980s.*
  ▶ **COLLOCATIONS:**
  the popularity **of** *something*
  popularity **among/with** *people*
  popularity among/with **voters/audiences/the public**
  increase in/gain/enjoy popularity
  growing/enduring/immense/flagging popularity
  a popularity **poll/rating**
  ▶ **SYNONYMS:** acclaim, approval
  ▶ **ANTONYM:** unpopularity

---

popu|la|tion /ˌpɒpjʊˈleɪʃən/ (populations)   `SOCIAL SCIENCE`

1 NOUN The **population** of a country or area is all the people who live in it.
  ○ [+ *of*] *Bangladesh now has a population of about 110 million.* ○ *the annual rate of population growth*
  ▶ **COLLOCATIONS:**
  a population **of** *x*
  population **density/size/growth/increase/decline**
  the **local/entire** population
  population **growth/decline/control**

2 NOUN If you refer to a particular type of **population** in a country or area, you are referring to all the people or animals of that type there. [FORMAL]

○ *75.6 per cent of the male population over sixteen* ○ *areas with a large black population* ○ *[+ of] the elephant populations of Tanzania and Kenya*

▶ COLLOCATIONS:
a **male/female/elderly/ageing/working-age** population
a **black/white/Muslim/Jewish/Asian/minority** population
a **deer/elephant/bird/fox** population

po|si|tion /pəˈzɪʃən/ (positions)

NOUN The **position** of someone or something is the place where they are in relation to other things. ○ *The ship was identified, and its name and position were reported to the coastguard.* ○ *This conservatory enjoys an enviable position overlooking a leafy expanse.*

▶ COLLOCATIONS:
the position **of** something
occupy/hold/enjoy a position
a position **overlooking** something
▶ SYNONYMS: location, setting, place

posi|tive /ˈpɒzɪtɪv/   ACADEMIC WORD

ADJECTIVE A **positive** fact, situation, or experience is pleasant and helpful to you in some way. ○ *The project will have a positive impact on the economy.* ○ *Working abroad should be an exciting and positive experience for all concerned.*

● **The positive** in a situation is the good and pleasant aspects of it. ○ *Work on the positive, creating beautiful, loving and fulfilling relationships.*

▶ COLLOCATIONS:
a positive **experience/outcome/effect/result/influence/impact**
overwhelmingly/extremely/generally positive
▶ SYNONYMS: beneficial, advantageous
▶ ANTONYM: negative

pos|sible /ˈpɒsɪbəl/

1 ADJECTIVE If it is **possible to** do something, it can be done. ○ *[+ to-inf] If it is possible to find out where your brother is, we shall.* ○ *Everything is possible if we want it enough.* ○ *anaesthetics which have made modern surgery possible*

2 ADJECTIVE A **possible** event is one that might happen. ○ *He referred the matter to the Attorney General for possible action against several newspapers.* ○ *Her family is discussing a possible move to America.* ○ *One possible solution, if all else fails, is to take legal action.*

3 ADJECTIVE If you say that it is **possible that** something is true or correct, you mean that although you do not know whether it is true or correct, you accept that it might be. ○ *It is possible that there's an explanation for all this.*

▶ COLLOCATIONS:
   a possible **explanation/cause/link/motive**
   a possible **scenario/outcome/solution/exception**
   make *something* possible
   everything/anything is possible
   possible to **imagine/identify/avoid** *something*
   perfectly/humanly/entirely/remotely possible
   physically/technically possible
▶ SYNONYMS: potential, conceivable, likely
▶ ANTONYMS: impossible, unlikely, inconceivable

pos|sibly /ˈpɒsɪbli/

ADVERB You use **possibly** to indicate that you are not sure whether something is true or might happen. ○ *Exercise will not only lower blood pressure but possibly protect against heart attacks.* ○ *a painful and possibly fatal operation* ○ *Do you think that he could possibly be right?*

▶ COLLOCATIONS:
   quite/just possibly
   possibly **harmful/illegal/fatal**
▶ SYNONYM: perhaps
▶ ANTONYM: definitely

ACADEMIC WRITING: Careful language

In academic writing, try not to present something as 100% fact unless you have clear evidence. You can use words like **possible/possibly**, **probable/probably**, **likely** and **unlikely** to show how certain you are about something. ○ *a move towards a drier climate possibly due to global warming* ○ *the probable/likely cause of the crisis* ○ *Such restrictions seem unlikely to have much effect.*

---

pos|sibil|ity /ˌpɒsɪˈbɪlɪti/ (possibilities)

NOUN If you say there is a **possibility that** something is the case or **that** something will happen, you mean that it might be the case or it might happen. ○ [+ *that*] *We were not in the least worried about the possibility that sweets could rot the teeth.* ○ *Tax on food has become a very real possibility.*

▶ COLLOCATIONS:
   the possibility **of** *something*
   explore/discuss/raise/consider a possibility
   a **distinct/remote/real** possibility
▶ SYNONYMS: chance, likelihood
▶ ANTONYMS: certainty, impossibility

pow|er /ˈpaʊə/

SOCIAL SCIENCE **POLITICS**

UNCOUNTABLE NOUN If someone has **power**, they have a lot of control over people and activities. ○ *In a democracy, power must be divided.* ○ *a political power struggle between the Liberals and National Party*

▶ **COLLOCATIONS:**
power **over** something/someone
power over **people/others/decisions**
political/economic/military power
enormous/great/considerable/absolute/real power
have/exercise/wield power
a power **struggle/play**

▶ **SYNONYMS:** influence, control, command

pow|er|ful /ˈpaʊəfʊl/

ADJECTIVE ○ *Russia and India, two large, powerful countries* ○ *Hong Kong's powerful business community* ○ *He is a powerful figure in the world of animal conservation.*

▶ **COLLOCATIONS:**
immensely/enormously/incredibly powerful
a powerful **influence/force**
a powerful **nation/country/figure/ally**

▶ **SYNONYMS:** strong, influential
▶ **ANTONYMS:** weak, ineffective

---

pre|fer /prɪˈfɜː/ (prefers, preferring, preferred)

VERB If you **prefer** someone or something, you like that person or thing better than another, and so you are more likely to choose them if there is a choice. ○ *Centipedes are nocturnal and generally prefer moist conditions such as forests or woodlands.* ○ [+ to] *I became a teacher because I preferred books and people to politics.* ○ [+ to-inf] *I prefer to go on self-catering holidays.*

▶ **COLLOCATIONS:**
prefer *something* **to** *something*
prefer to **stay/remain** *somewhere*
prefer to **focus/concentrate/rely** on *something*
prefer to **avoid/forget/ignore** *something*
generally/still/much prefer
prefer an **approach**

▶ **SYNONYMS:** favour, choose
▶ **ANTONYMS:** reject, dislike

pref|er|ence /ˈprefərəns/ (preferences)

NOUN If you have a **preference for** something, you would like to have or do that thing rather than something else. ○ [+ for] *Parents can express* *a preference for the school their child attends.* ○ [+ to] *Many of these products were bought in preference to their own.*

▶ **COLLOCATIONS:**

a preference **for** *something*

in preference **to** *something*

a **personal/individual/sexual** preference

a **consumer/customer/voter/patient** preference

express/give/show a preference

▶ **SYNONYMS:** choice, selection

▶ **ANTONYM:** rejection

---

pre|pare /prɪˈpeə/ **(prepares, preparing, prepared)**

1 VERB If you **prepare** something, you make it ready for something that is going to happen. ○ *Two technicians were preparing a videotape recording of last week's programme.* ○ [+ for] *The crew of the Iowa has been preparing the ship for storage.*

2 VERB If you **prepare for** an event or action that will happen soon, you get yourself ready for it or make the necessary arrangements. ○ [+ for] *The Party leadership is using management consultants to help prepare for the next election.* ○ [+ to-inf] *We are preparing to map the entire genetic structure of the human species.* ○ *His doctor had told him to prepare himself for surgery.*

▶ **COLLOCATIONS:**

prepare **for** *something*

prepare for a **possibility/eventuality**

prepare for a **war/fight/election**

prepare to **risk/sacrifice/pay/accept** *something*

prepare a **report/document/statement/plan/speech**

mentally/fully/carefully/well/adequately prepared

▶ **SYNONYMS:** plan, arrange

prepa|ra|tion /ˌprepəˈreɪʃən/ **(preparations)**

1 UNCOUNTABLE NOUN Preparation is the process of getting something ready for use or for a particular purpose or making arrangements for something. ○ [+ for/of] *Rub the surface of the wood in preparation for the varnish.* ○ *Behind any successful event lay months of preparation.*

▶ **COLLOCATIONS:**

preparation **for/of** *something*

be **in** preparation

thorough/careful/meticulous preparation

▶ **SYNONYM:** arrangement

2 PLURAL NOUN **Preparations** are all the arrangements that are made for
a future event. ○ [+ for] *The United States is making preparations for a
large-scale airlift of 1,200 American citizens.* ○ *Final preparations are underway
for celebrations to mark German unification.*

▶ COLLOCATIONS:
preparations **for** *something*
preparations for **war/invasion**
make/finalize preparations
final preparations
preparations are **underway**
preparations **begin/continue**

▶ SYNONYM: arrangements

---

pres|ent /ˈprezənt/

1 ADJECTIVE You use **present** to describe things and people that exist now,
rather than those that existed in the past or those that may exist in the
future. ○ *He has brought much of the present crisis on himself.* ○ *It has been
skilfully renovated by the present owners.* ○ *No statement can be made at the
present time.*

→ see note at **current**

▶ COLLOCATIONS:
present **circumstances/arrangements/difficulties**
the present **crisis/situation/climate/time**
the present **value** of *something*

▶ SYNONYM: current
▶ ANTONYMS: past, future

2 NOUN **The present** is the period of time that we are in now and the
things that are happening now. ○ *his struggle to reconcile the past with the
present* ○ *continuing right up to the present*

▶ ANTONYMS: past, future

---

present-day /ˌprezəntˈdeɪ/ also **present day**　　`HISTORY`

ADJECTIVE **Present-day** things, situations, and people exist at the time in
history we are now in. ○ *Even by present-day standards these were large
aircraft.* ○ *a huge area of northern India, stretching from present-day
Afghanistan to Bengal*

▶ SYNONYMS: contemporary, modern
▶ ANTONYM: historical

---

presi|dent /ˈprezɪdənt/ (presidents)　　`SOCIAL SCIENCE`　`POLITICS`

1 NOUN The **president** of a country that has no king or queen is the person who is the head of state of that country. ○ *President Mubarak* ○ *The White House says the president would veto the bill.*

2 NOUN The **president** of an organization is the person who has the highest position in it. ○ [+ *of*] *Alexandre de Merode, the president of the medical commission.*

▶ **COLLOCATIONS:**
the president **of** something
the president of a **country/republic/company/firm**
elect/name/appoint a president
become president
the **current/former/outgoing/incumbent** president
the **senior/executive/deputy/vice** president
presidents **say/promise/vow/declare** things

▶ **SYNONYMS:** leader, head of state, premier, chief, CEO

---

press /pres/ MEDIA

NOUN Newspapers are referred to as **the press**. ○ *Today the British press is full of articles on India's new prime minister.* ○ *Press reports revealed that ozone levels in the upper atmosphere fell during the past month.*

▶ **COLLOCATIONS:**
the **national/local** press
the **tabloid/mainstream/right-wing/British** press
a press **release/report/briefing/conference/launch**
the press **releases/reports** things

▶ **SYNONYMS:** newspapers, the media

---

pre|vent /prɪˈvent/ (prevents, preventing, prevented)

VERB To **prevent** something means to ensure that it does not happen. ○ *These methods prevent pregnancy.* ○ [+ *from*] *Further treatment will prevent cancer from developing.* ○ [+ *v-ing*] *We recognized the possibility and took steps to prevent it happening.*

▶ **COLLOCATIONS:**
prevent something **from** happening
prevent a **disease/attack/tragedy**
prevent **pregnancy/cancer/damage/abuse/infection/war**
prevent **overheating/swelling/ageing**
prevent **the spread of** something
prevent **a repeat of** something
thereby/thus prevent something

▶ **SYNONYMS:** stop, hinder
▶ **ANTONYMS:** cause, encourage, promote

pre|ven|tion /prɪˈvenʃən/

UNCOUNTABLE NOUN ○ [+ *of*] *the prevention of heart disease* ○ *crime prevention*

▶ **COLLOCATIONS:**
  the prevention **of** *something*
  the prevention of **disease/cancer/crime**
  crime/suicide prevention
  cancer/disease prevention
▶ **PHRASE:** treatment and prevention
▶ **ANTONYMS:** encouragement, promotion

---

pre|vi|ous /ˈpriːviəs/ ACADEMIC WORD

1 ADJECTIVE A **previous** event or thing is one that happened or existed before the one that you are talking about. ○ *She has a teenage daughter from a previous marriage.* ○ *Previous studies have shown that organic farming methods can benefit the wildlife around farms.*

▶ **COLLOCATIONS:**
  a **previous government/marriage/occasion**
  previous **convictions/studies/estimates/experience**
▶ **SYNONYMS:** earlier, former
▶ **ANTONYMS:** current, later, subsequent

2 ADJECTIVE You refer to the period of time or the thing immediately before the one that you are talking about as the **previous** one. ○ *It was a surprisingly dry day after the rain of the previous week.*

▶ **COLLOCATION:** the previous **day/week/month/year**
▶ **SYNONYM:** preceding
▶ **ANTONYM:** following

pre|vi|ous|ly /ˈpriːviəsli/

ADVERB ○ *Guyana's railways were previously owned by private companies.* ○ *a collection of previously unpublished poems* ○ *He had first entered the House 12 years previously.*

▶ **COLLOCATIONS:**
  previously **unknown/unseen/unpublished/undisclosed**
  previously **reported/announced/stated/forecast**
  previously **owned/held**
  x **days/weeks/months/years** previously
▶ **SYNONYMS:** earlier, formerly
▶ **ANTONYMS:** currently, subsequently

pri|ma|ry school /ˈpraɪməri skuːl,

AM ˈpraɪmeri skuːl/ **(primary schools)** EDUCATION

NOUN A **primary school** is a school for children between the ages of 5 and 11. [mainly BRIT; in AM, usually use **elementary school**] ○ *eight-to nine-year-olds in their third year at primary school* ○ *Greenside Primary School*

▶ **COLLOCATIONS:**
  be **at** primary school
  go to/attend primary school
  primary school **teaching**
  a primary school **teacher/pupil/student**
▶ **SYNONYM:** elementary school
▶ **RELATED WORD:** secondary school

Prime Min|is|ter /praɪm ˈmɪnɪstə/ SOCIAL SCIENCE POLITICS

(Prime Ministers)

NOUN The leader of the government in some countries is called **the Prime Minister**. The abbreviation **PM** is also used in writing or in informal speech. ○ [+ *of*] *the former Prime Minister of Pakistan, Miss Benazir Bhutto* ○ *This had been a disastrous week for Prime Minister Major.*

▶ **COLLOCATIONS:**
  the Prime Minister **of** *somewhere*
  elect a prime minister
  become prime minister
  the **current/former** prime minister
▶ **SYNONYMS:** PM, premier

pris|on /ˈprɪzən/ **(prisons)** LAW

NOUN A **prison** is a building where criminals are kept as punishment or where people accused of a crime are kept before their trial. ○ *The prison's inmates are being kept in their cells.* ○ *He was sentenced to life in prison.*

▶ **COLLOCATIONS:**
  be **in** prison
  go to/face prison
  escape/release from prison
  a **high-security/maximum-security/secure/overcrowded** prison
  a **federal/military/state** prison
  a prison **sentence/term**
  a prison **guard/officer/warder/cell/inmate**
  the prison **authorities/system/service**
▶ **SYNONYM:** jail

pris|on|er /ˈprɪzənə/ (prisoners)

NOUN A **prisoner** is a person who is kept in a prison as a punishment for a crime that they have committed. ○ *The committee is concerned about the large number of prisoners sharing cells.*

▸ COLLOCATIONS:
  free/release a prisoner
  hold *someone* prisoner
  a **political** prisoner
  prisoner **abuse/mistreatment**
  a **former/escaped** prisoner
▸ SYNONYMS: inmate, convict, criminal

prob|able /ˈprɒbəbəl/

ADJECTIVE If you say that something is **probable**, you mean that it is likely to be true or likely to happen. ○ [+ *that*] *It is probable that the medication will suppress the symptom without treating the condition.* ○ *An airline official said a bomb was the incident's most probable cause.*

▸ COLLOCATIONS:
  a probable **cause/explanation/case**
  highly/quite/very probable
▸ SYNONYM: likely
▸ ANTONYM: unlikely

prob|ably /ˈprɒbəbli/

ADVERB If you say that something is **probably** the case, you think that it is likely to be the case, although you are not sure. ○ *The White House probably won't make this plan public until July.* ○ *Van Gogh is probably the best-known painter in the world.*

▸ COLLOCATIONS:
  probably **mean/think/need** *something*
  probably **true/right/correct/safe/fair**
▸ SYNONYMS: perhaps, possibly
▸ ANTONYM: certainly
→ see note at **possible**

prob|lem /ˈprɒbləm/ (problems)

NOUN A **problem** is a situation that is unsatisfactory and causes difficulties for people. ○ [+ *of*] *the economic problems of the inner city* ○ *The main problem is unemployment.* ○ *He told Americans that solving the energy problem was very important.*

▸ COLLOCATIONS:
  the problem **of/with** *something*

the problem of **homelessness/poverty/unemployment**
a **major/serious/real** problem
a **health/drug/security/crime** problem
a **financial/economic/medical/environmental** problem
the **main/biggest** problem
cause/have/face a problem
solve/tackle/address/resolve a problem
a problem **arises/occurs/emerges**
a problem **lies in** *something*
▶ **SYNONYMS:** difficulty, concern

prob|lem|at|ic /ˌprɒbləˈmætɪk/

ADJECTIVE ○ *Some places are more problematic than others for women travelling alone.* ○ *the problematic business of running an economy*
▶ **COLLOCATIONS:**
problematic **behaviour**
a problematic **issue/relationship/situation**
morally/ethically problematic
potentially/inherently problematic
▶ **ANTONYM:** unproblematic

---

pro|cess /ˈprəʊses, AM ˈprɑːses/ (processes) `ACADEMIC WORD`

1 NOUN A **process** is a series of actions which are carried out in order to achieve a particular result. ○ *There was total agreement to start the peace process as soon as possible.* ○ [+ of] *The best way to proceed is by a process of elimination.*

2 NOUN A **process** is a series of things which happen naturally and result in a biological or chemical change. ○ *It occurs in elderly men, apparently as part of the ageing process.*
▶ **COLLOCATIONS:**
a process **of** *something*
a process of **elimination/reconciliation/consultation/integration**
a **learning/selection/decision-making** process
the **peace/reform** process
a **political/democratic/legal** process
the **healing/ageing** process
a **gradual/long/slow/complicated** process
start/begin/repeat/accelerate/complete a process
put/have a process **in place**
▶ **SYNONYMS:** course, procedure

---

pro|duce /prəˈdjuːs, AM -ˈduːs/   `BUSINESS`
(produces, producing, produced)

VERB If you **produce** something, you make or create it. ○ *The company produced circuitry for communications systems.* ○ *locally produced vegetables*
→ see note at **create**
▶ **COLLOCATIONS:**
  produce **goods/products/crops/wine/weapons**
  a **factory/plant/manufacturer/company/farmer** produces *things*
  mass/locally/domestically produced
▶ **SYNONYMS:** make, manufacture, create
▶ **ANTONYM:** consume

prod|uct /ˈprɒdʌkt/ **(products)**

NOUN A **product** is something that is produced and sold in large quantities, often as a result of a manufacturing process. ○ *Try to get the best product at the lowest price.* ○ *South Korea's imports of consumer products increased by 33% this year.*
▶ **COLLOCATIONS:**
  a **new/finished/commercial** product
  consumer/dairy/beef/tobacco/food products
  manufacture/produce/develop/market/launch a product
  import/buy/purchase a product
  export/sell/deliver a product
  product **development/marketing**
  a product **line**
▶ **SYNONYM:** goods

pro|duc|tion /prəˈdʌkʃən/

1 UNCOUNTABLE NOUN Production is the process of manufacturing or growing something in large quantities. ○ *That model won't go into production before late 1990.* ○ *[+ of] tax incentives to encourage domestic production of oil*

2 UNCOUNTABLE NOUN Production is the amount of goods manufactured or grown by a company or country. ○ *We needed to increase the volume of production.*
▶ **COLLOCATIONS:**
  in/into production
  production **of** *something*
  production of **goods/commodities**
  go into production
  increase/boost/stimulate production
  industrial/agricultural/commercial/mass production

oil/gas/steel/food/energy production
production **costs/capacity**
▶ **SYNONYMS:** manufacturing, output

pro|duc|er /prəˈdjuːsə, AM -ˈduːs-/ **(producers)**

NOUN A **producer** of a food or material is a company or country that grows or manufactures a large amount of it. ○ *Saudi Arabia, the world's leading oil producer*
▶ **COLLOCATIONS:**
a producer **of** *something*
a **cattle/beef/oil/steel/cocoa/lumber** producer
a **leading/major/domestic** producer
▶ **SYNONYM:** manufacturer

---

pro|fes|sion|al /prəˈfeʃənəl/   `ACADEMIC WORD` `BUSINESS`

1 ADJECTIVE Professional means relating to a person's work, especially work that requires special training. ○ *His professional career started at Liverpool University.*

2 ADJECTIVE Professional people have jobs that require advanced education or training. ○ *highly qualified professional people like doctors and engineers*

● **Professional** is also a noun. ○ *My father wanted me to become a professional and have more stability.*
▶ **COLLOCATIONS:**
a professional **career/qualification**
professional **development/help/advice**
thoroughly/highly professional
▶ **SYNONYM:** qualified
▶ **ANTONYM:** amateur

---

prof|it /ˈprɒfɪt/ **(profits, profiting, profited)**   `BUSINESS` `ECONOMICS`

1 NOUN A **profit** is an amount of money that you gain when you are paid more for something than it cost you to make, get, or do it. ○ *The bank made pre-tax profits of £3.5 million.* ○ *You can improve your chances of profit by sensible planning.*
▶ **COLLOCATIONS:**
a profit **of** *x*
make/earn/turn/earn/yield a profit
maximize/increase profits
report/forecast/expect profits
profits **rise/soar/fall**
pre-tax/net/gross profits

quarterly/annual/corporate profits
a profit **margin**
▶ PHRASE: profit and loss
▶ SYNONYMS: income, takings
▶ ANTONYM: loss

2 VERB If you **profit from** something, you earn a profit from it. ○ [+ from/by] *Footballers are accustomed to profiting handsomely from bonuses.* ○ [+ from/by] *He has profited by selling his holdings to other investors.*
▶ COLLOCATIONS:
profit **from/by** *something*
profit from a **boom/upturn/invention**
profit **handsomely/enormously**
→ see note at **benefit**

prof|it|able /ˈprɒfɪtəbəl/

ADJECTIVE A **profitable** organization or practice makes a profit. ○ *Drug manufacturing is the most profitable business in America.* ○ [+ for] *It was profitable for them to produce large amounts of food.*
▶ COLLOCATIONS:
profitable **for** *someone*
a profitable **business/enterprise/operation/niche/venture**
highly profitable
▶ SYNONYM: lucrative
▶ ANTONYM: unprofitable

pro|gramme /ˈprəʊɡræm/ (programmes)

NOUN A **programme** of actions or events is a series of actions or events that are planned to be done. ○ *The general argued that the nuclear programme should still continue.* ○ [+ of] *The programme of sell-offs has been implemented by the new chief executive.*
▶ COLLOCATIONS:
a programme **of/for** *something*
a programme of/for **reform/modernization/development**
a **nuclear/educational/cost-cutting/economic/aid** programme
a **comprehensive/ambitious/extensive/radical** programme
▶ SYNONYMS: plan, strategy, schedule

> **USAGE:** Spelling
>
> In British English, **programme** is spelled **-mme** at the end when you are talking about a series of events or actions, or something you watch on television. ○ *the training programme for new employees* ○ *a popular television programme*

Computer software can be referred to as a computer **program**.
○ *a computer program to reformat the data*

In American English, **program** is the usual spelling for all of these meanings.

pro|gress (progresses, progressing, progressed)

The noun is pronounced /ˈprəʊɡres, AM ˈprɑː-/. The verb is pronounced /prəˈɡres/.

1 UNCOUNTABLE NOUN Progress is the process of gradually improving or getting nearer to achieving or completing something. ○ [+ in] *The medical community continues to make progress in the fight against cancer.* ○ [+ towards] *The two sides made little if any progress towards agreement.*

2 NOUN The progress of a situation or action is the way in which it develops. ○ [+ of] *The Chancellor is reported to have been delighted with the progress of the first day's talks.*

▶ COLLOCATIONS:
the progress **of** something
progress **on/in/towards** something
progress towards **peace/democracy/unity**
progress towards a **solution/agreement**
economic/academic progress
good/slow/rapid/remarkable/real/steady progress
make progress

▶ SYNONYMS: advancement, development
▶ ANTONYM: setback

3 VERB To **progress** means to move over a period of time to a stronger, more advanced, or more desirable state. ○ *He will visit once a fortnight to see how his new staff are progressing.* ○ [+ to] *He started with sketching and then progressed to painting.* ○ *A company spokesman said that talks were progressing well.*

▶ COLLOCATIONS:
progress **to** something
a **disease/pregnancy/career** progresses
talks/negotiations progress
progress **smoothly/rapidly/satisfactorily/nicely**

▶ ANTONYM: stall

proj|ect /ˈprɒdʒekt/ (projects)   ACADEMIC WORD   ACADEMIC STUDY

NOUN A **project** is a task that requires a lot of time and effort. ○ *Money will also go into local development projects in Vietnam.* ○ *a research project on*

alternative health care
▶ COLLOCATIONS:
a **research/development/construction/conservation** project
a **major/massive/innovative/long-term** project
fund/finance/support a project
approve/launch/start/undertake/complete a project
a project **manager/director**
▶ SYNONYM: scheme

---

pro|nounce /prəˈnaʊns/   LANGUAGE
(pronounces, pronouncing, pronounced)

VERB To **pronounce** a word means to say it using particular sounds. ○ *Have I pronounced your name correctly?* ○ *He pronounced it Per-sha, the way the English do.*
▶ COLLOCATIONS:
pronounce a **word/name/sentence**
pronounce *something* **properly/correctly**

pro|nun|cia|tion /prəˌnʌnsiˈeɪʃən/ **(pronunciations)**

NOUN ○ *She gave the word its French pronunciation.* ○ *the correct pronunciation of 'nuclear'*
▶ COLLOCATIONS:
the pronunciation **of** *something*
the pronunciation of a **word/name**
the **correct/proper/preferred/standard** pronunciation
English/French/American pronunciation

---

prop|er|ty /ˈprɒpəti/ **(properties)**

1 UNCOUNTABLE NOUN Someone's **property** is all the things that belong to them or something that belongs to them. [FORMAL] ○ *Richard could easily destroy her personal property to punish her for walking out on him.* ○ *Security forces searched thousands of homes, confiscating weapons and stolen property.*
▶ COLLOCATIONS:
personal property
stolen/valuable/damaged property
▶ SYNONYMS: belongings, possessions

2 NOUN A **property** is a building and the land belonging to it. [FORMAL] ○ *Cecil inherited a family property near Stamford.* ○ *privately owned properties*
▶ COLLOCATIONS:
private property

a **rental/beachfront/four-bedroom** property
own/buy/purchase/rent/lease a property
a property **developer/owner**
the property **ladder/market**
▶ SYNONYMS: house, building

---

pro|tect /prəˈtekt/ (protects, protecting, protected)

VERB To **protect** someone or something means to prevent them from
being harmed or damaged. ○ [+ from/against] *The contraceptive pill may
protect women against cancer.* ○ *The government is committed to protecting the
interests of tenants.*

▶ COLLOCATIONS:
protect someone **from/against** something
protect someone from/against **cancer/disease/exploitation**
protect someone's **rights/privacy/interest**
protect **children/civilians/wildlife/the environment**
legally/constitutionally/properly protected
▶ PHRASE: protected by law
▶ SYNONYMS: defend, shield, safeguard
▶ ANTONYMS: endanger, risk

pro|tec|tion /prəˈtekʃən/

UNCOUNTABLE NOUN To give or have **protection** against something
unpleasant means to prevent people or things from being harmed or
damaged by it. ○ [+ against] *Such a diet is widely believed to offer protection
against a number of cancers.* ○ [+ for] *It is clear that the primary duty of parents
is to provide protection for our children.*

▶ COLLOCATIONS:
protection **against/from** something
protection **for** someone
protection against **pregnancy/disease/cancer**
protection from the **sun/wind/elements**
provide/offer/give/afford protection
need/seek/enjoy protection
environmental/consumer/child protection
▶ SYNONYM: care

pro|tec|tive /prəˈtektɪv/

ADJECTIVE Protective means designed or intended to protect something
or someone from harm. ○ *Protective gloves reduce the absorption of chemicals
through the skin.* ○ *Protective measures are necessary if the city's monuments
are to be preserved.*

▶ **COLLOCATIONS:**
protective **clothing/gear/gloves/measures**
a protective **mask/shield/suit/layer**
▶ **SYNONYM:** defensive

---

pro|test (protests, protesting, protested)

> The verb is pronounced /prə'test/. The noun is pronounced /'prəʊtest/.

1 VERB If you **protest against** something or **about** something, you say or show publicly that you object to it. In American English, you usually say that you **protest** it. ○ [+ about/against/at] *Groups of women took to the streets to protest against the arrests.* ○ [+ about/against/at] *The students were protesting at overcrowding in the university hostels.* ○ *They were protesting soaring prices.*

▶ **COLLOCATIONS:**
protest **about/against/at** *something*
protest at a **decision/plan/move/arrest**
protest against a **war/injustice/killing**
demonstrators/campaigners/activists protest
students/workers protest
protest **peacefully/publicly/angrily**
▶ **SYNONYMS:** challenge, object, revolt

2 NOUN A **protest** is the act of saying or showing publicly that you object to something. ○ [+ against] *The opposition now seems too weak to stage any serious protests against the government.* ○ [+ at] *The unions called a two-hour strike in protest at the railway authority's announcement.* ○ *a protest march*

▶ **COLLOCATIONS:**
a protest **about/against/at** *something*
in protest at *something*
stage/lodge/organize a protest
a **peaceful/violent/non-violent/organized** protest
a **political/anti-war/anti-government** protest
a protest **march/rally/demonstration**
▶ **SYNONYMS:** demonstration, rally

pro|test|er /prə'testə/ (protesters) also protestor

NOUN Protesters are people who protest publicly about an issue.
○ *The protesters say the government is corrupt and inefficient.* ○ *anti-abortion protesters*
▶ **COLLOCATIONS:**
protesters **march/gather/chant/rally**

an **anti-war/anti-government/anti-abortion** protester
▶ SYNONYMS: demonstrator, dissident

---

prove /pruːv/ (proves, proving, proved, proved or proven)

1 VERB If something **proves to** be true or **to** have a particular quality, it becomes clear after a period of time that it is true or has that quality. ○ [+ to-inf] *We have been accused of exaggerating before, but unfortunately all our reports proved to be true.* ○ *In the past this process of transition has often proven difficult.* ○ *an experiment which was to prove a source of inspiration for many years to come*

▶ COLLOCATIONS:
prove **likely/difficult/impossible**
prove **successful/popular**
prove **costly/fatal/disastrous**
prove a **hit/success/blessing**

2 VERB If you **prove that** something is true, you show by means of argument or evidence that it is definitely true. ○ [+ that] *The results prove that regulation of the salmon farming industry is inadequate.* ○ [+ how] *trying to prove how groups of animals have evolved* ○ *a proven cause of cancer*

▶ COLLOCATIONS:
prove *something/someone* **right/wrong**
prove *someone's* **innocence/guilt**
prove *something* **conclusively/scientifically**
prove **otherwise**
difficult/hard to prove
tests/statistics/studies/results prove *things*

▶ SYNONYMS: show, verify
▶ ANTONYM: disprove

proof /pruːf/ (proofs)

NOUN **Proof** is a fact, argument, or piece of evidence which shows that something is definitely true or definitely exists. ○ [+ of] *You have to have proof of residence in the state of Texas, such as a Texas ID card.* ○ [+ of] *There is no conclusive proof of the Milancovitch theory.* ○ *Economists have been concerned with establishing proofs for their arguments.*

▶ COLLOCATIONS:
proof **of** *something*
proof of **identity/residency**
conclusive/definite/irrefutable/further/concrete proof
need/provide/offer/furnish proof

▶ SYNONYM: evidence

pro|vide /prəˈvaɪd/ (provides, providing, provided)

VERB If you **provide** something that someone needs or wants, or if you **provide** them **with** it, you give it to them or make it available to them.
○ *I'll be glad to provide a copy of this.* ○ *They would not provide any details.*
○ *[+ with] The government was not in a position to provide them with food.*

▶ COLLOCATIONS:
provide *someone* **with** *something*
provide *someone* with **food/accommodation/information**
provide **details/evidence/support/assistance**
provide a **service/answer**

> **EXTEND YOUR VOCABULARY**
>
> **Give** is a very common verb in everyday English. In academic English, you need to use more specific verbs. You can use **provide** with a wide range of nouns; physical objects, services, information, help etc. Remember to use **with** when you mention who something is given to. ○ *Chapter 2 provides information on possible health problems.* ○ *The animals were provided* **with** *food and water.*
>
> You use **supply** especially to talk about products and services that a business gives to a customer. ○ *The company supplies equipment for the oil industry.*

psy|chol|ogy /saɪˈkɒlədʒi/ `ACADEMIC WORD` `PSYCHOLOGY`

UNCOUNTABLE NOUN Psychology is the scientific study of the human mind and the reasons for people's behaviour. ○ *Professor of Psychology at Bedford College*

▶ COLLOCATIONS:
evolutionary/developmental/cognitive/behavioural psychology
Jungian/Freudian psychology
study/teach psychology
a psychology **professor/lecturer/department/degree**

pub|lic /ˈpʌblɪk/ `SOCIAL SCIENCE`

1 NOUN You can refer to people in general, or to all the people in a particular country or community, as **the public**. ○ *Lauderdale House is now open to the public.* ○ *Pure alcohol is not for sale to the general public.* ○ *Trade unions are regarding the poll as a test of the public's confidence in the government.*

→ see note at **individual**

▶ **COLLOCATIONS:**
the **general/British/American** public
the public's **confidence/trust/opinion**
educate/inform/persuade/mislead the public

▶ **PHRASES:**
open to the public
members of the public

▶ **SYNONYMS:** population, community, people

2 ADJECTIVE Public means relating to all the people in a country or community. ○ *The President is attempting to drum up public support for his economic program.* ○ *The dominance of public opinion resulted in tyranny and mediocrity.*

▶ **COLLOCATION:** public **opinion/interest/support**

---

pun|ish /ˈpʌnɪʃ/ **(punishes, punishing, punished)**   `LAW`

VERB To **punish** someone means to make them suffer in some way because they have done something wrong. ○ [+ *with*] *According to present law, the authorities can only punish smugglers with small fines.* ○ [+ *for*] *No one should be punished twice for the same offence.*

▶ **COLLOCATIONS:**
punish *someone* **for/with** *something*
punish *someone* for a **mistake/offence/crime**
punish *someone* with **death/imprisonment/a fine**
punish a **wrongdoer/criminal/offender**
severely/harshly/unfairly punished

▶ **ANTONYMS:** reward, pardon

pun|ish|ment /ˈpʌnɪʃmənt/ **(punishments)**

NOUN ○ [+ *of*] *a group which campaigns against the physical punishment of children* ○ [+ *for*] *The government is proposing tougher punishments for officials convicted of corruption.* ○ *The usual punishment is a fine.*

▶ **COLLOCATIONS:**
punishment **for** *something*
the punishment **of** *someone/something*
punishment for a **crime/offence**
punishment for **murder/adultery**
the punishment of **children/criminals/offenders/crime**
impose/face/escape punishment
corporal/capital punishment
harsh/severe/appropriate punishment

P

▶ **PHRASES:**
reward and punishment
crime and punishment
▶ **ANTONYMS:** reward, leniency

---

pu|pil /ˈpjuːpɪl/ (pupils)   EDUCATION

NOUN The **pupils** of a school are the children who go to it ○ *Over a third of those now at secondary school in Wales attend schools with over 1,000 pupils.*

▶ **COLLOCATIONS:**
a pupil **at/from** a school
a **primary-school/secondary-school** pupil
a **bright/gifted/disruptive** pupil
▶ **SYNONYMS:** schoolchild, schoolboy, schoolgirl
▶ **RELATED WORD:** student

---

pur|pose /ˈpɜːpəs/ (purposes)

NOUN The **purpose** of something is the reason for which it is made or done. ○ [+ of] *The purpose of the occasion was to raise money for medical supplies.* ○ *Various insurance schemes already exist for this purpose.* ○ *the use of nuclear energy for military purposes* ○ *He was asked about casualties, but said it would serve no purpose to count bodies.*

▶ **COLLOCATIONS:**
the purpose **of** *something*
for a purpose
serve/achieve a purpose
the **main/primary/sole/real** purpose of *something*
medicinal/military/educational purposes
tax/identification/research purposes
▶ **SYNONYMS:** reason, objective, aim

Qq

quali|fy /ˈkwɒlɪfaɪ/ (qualifies, qualifying, qualified)

VERB When someone **qualifies**, they pass the examinations that they need to be able to work in a particular profession. ○ *When I'd qualified and started teaching it was a different story.* ○ [+ as/in] *I qualified as a doctor from London University over 30 years ago.*

▶ **COLLOCATIONS:**
  qualify **as/in** something
  qualify as a **doctor/solicitor/accountant**
  fail to qualify

quali|fied /ˈkwɒlɪfaɪd/

ADJECTIVE ○ *Demand has far outstripped supply of qualified teachers.*
○ *The reader should seek the services of a qualified professional for advice.*

▶ **COLLOCATIONS:**
  highly/fully/suitably/well/newly qualified
  a qualified **teacher/nurse/practitioner**
  qualified to **teach/practise**
▶ **SYNONYMS:** skilled, trained
▶ **ANTONYM:** unqualified

quali|fi|ca|tion /ˌkwɒlɪfɪˈkeɪʃən/ (qualifications)

NOUN ○ *Lucy wants to study medicine but needs more qualifications.*
○ *All surgeons who operate on children must obtain a recognized professional qualification for the care of children.* ○ *Following qualification, he worked as a social worker.*

▶ **COLLOCATIONS:**
  a **vocational/academic/professional** qualification
  a **formal/recognised** qualification
  obtain/gain/require a qualification
▶ **PHRASE:** qualifications and experience
▶ **SYNONYMS:** certificate, accreditation

quar|ter /ˈkwɔːtə/ (quarters) `MATHS`

NOUN A **quarter** is one of four equal parts of something. ○ [+ *of*] *A quarter of the residents are over 55 years old.* ○ [+ *of*] *a quarter of an hour* ○ *a unique 'four-in-one' channel that splits your screen into quarters*

▶ **COLLOCATIONS:**
  a quarter **of** *something*
  into quarters
  a quarter of a **century/pound**
  cut/split/fold *something* into quarters
▶ **RELATED WORD:** half

ques|tion /ˈkwestʃən/ (questions)

NOUN A **question** is a problem, matter, or point which needs to be considered. ○ [+ *of*] *But the whole question of aid is a tricky political one.* ○ *That decision raised questions about the secretary of state's powers.*

▶ **COLLOCATIONS:**
  a question **of** *something*
  raise/pose/beg/consider a question
  a **key/simple/real/serious/tough/important** question
  a **fundamental/crucial/basic/further** question
▶ **SYNONYMS:** issue, point

ques|tion|naire /ˌkwestʃəˈneə, ˌkes-/ (questionnaires)

NOUN A **questionnaire** is a written list of questions which are answered by a lot of people in order to provide information for a report or a survey. ○ *Headteachers will be asked to fill in a questionnaire.* ○ *a questionnaire on key issues*

▶ **COLLOCATIONS:**
  a questionnaire **on/about/regarding** *something*
  complete/fill out/fill in a questionnaire
  a **postal/anonymous/detailed/confidential** questionnaire
▶ **SYNONYM:** survey

Rr

raise /reɪz/ (raises, raising, raised)

1 VERB If you **raise** the rate or level of something, you increase it.
○ *The Republic of Ireland is expected to raise interest rates.* ○ *Two incidents in recent days have raised the level of concern.* ○ *a raised body temperature*

▸ **COLLOCATIONS:**
  raise **taxes/fares**
  raise the **rate/level/price** of *something*
▸ **SYNONYM:** increase
▸ **ANTONYM:** lower

2 VERB If an event **raises** a particular emotion or question, it makes people feel the emotion or consider the question. ○ *The agreement has raised hopes that the war may end soon.* ○ *The accident again raises questions about the safety of the building.*

▸ **COLLOCATIONS:**
  raise a **question/issue**
  raise **concern/awareness/hopes/doubts**
▸ **SYNONYM:** highlight

> **USAGE: raise** or **rise**?
>
> You say that *someone* **raises** something - it is a transitive verb and is usually followed by an object. ○ *The government was forced to raise taxes.* ○ *some of the questions raised by the report*
>
> But you say that *something* **rises** - it is an intransitive verb, so it is not followed by an object and cannot be used in the passive. **Rose** is the past tense form of **rise**. ○ *Car sales rose by nearly 10% in October.*

range /reɪndʒ/ (ranges, ranging, ranged) `ACADEMIC WORD`

1 NOUN A **range of** things is a number of different things of the same general kind. ○ [+ *of*] *Office workers face a wide range of health and safety problems.* ○ [+ *of*] *The two men discussed a range of issues.*

▸ **COLLOCATIONS:**
  a range **of** *things*
  a range of **products/services/activities**
  a range of **issues/options/colours**
  a **wide/broad/limited/narrow** range

offer/cover/provide a range
▸ **SYNONYMS:** variety, selection, collection

2 NOUN A **range** is the complete group that is included between two
points on a scale of measurement or quality. ○ *The average age range is
between 35 and 55.* ○ *products available in this price range*
▸ **COLLOCATIONS:**
  a range **between** *x* **and** *y*
  age/price/product range
  the **full/normal/whole** range

3 VERB If things **range between** two points or **range from** one point **to**
another, they vary within these points on a scale of measurement or
quality. ○ *They range in price from $3 to $15.* ○ *The cars were all new models and
ranged from sports cars to Cadillacs.* ○ *[+ between] temperatures ranging
between 5°C and 20°C*
▸ **COLLOCATIONS:**
  range **from** *something* **to** *something*
  range **between** *something* **and** *something*
  things range **widely**
  temperatures/prices/ages/products range widely
▸ **SYNONYM:** vary

---

rare /ɾeə/ **(rarer, rarest)**

1 ADJECTIVE Something that is **rare** is not common and is therefore
interesting or valuable. ○ *the black-necked crane, one of the rarest species in
the world* ○ *She collects rare plants.* ○ *Do you want to know about a particular
rare stamp or rare stamps in general?*

2 ADJECTIVE An event or situation that is **rare** does not occur very often.
  ○ *those rare occasions when he ate alone* ○ *Heart attacks were extremely rare in
babies, he said.* ○ *I think it's very rare to have big families nowadays.*
▸ **COLLOCATIONS:**
  rare **for** *someone to do something*
  rare **in** *people*
  rare in **humans/adults/babies**
  extremely/relatively/increasingly/quite rare
  a rare **breed/species/bird/plant**
  a rare **condition/disease/disorder**
  a rare **occasion/instance/exception**
▸ **SYNONYMS:** scarce, exceptional, uncommon
▸ **ANTONYMS:** common, commonplace, ordinary
▸ **RELATED WORD:** unique

rare|ly /ˈreəli/

ADVERB If something **rarely** happens, it does not happen very often. ○ *They battled against other Indian tribes, but rarely fought with the whites.* ○ *Money was plentiful, and rarely did anyone seem very bothered about levels of expenditure.* ○ *Adolescent suicide is rarely an impulsive reaction to immediate distress.*

▶ **COLLOCATION:** rarely **see/mention/use** something
▶ **PHRASE:** only rarely
▶ **SYNONYMS:** seldom, hardly ever
▶ **ANTONYMS:** often, frequently

---

reach /riːtʃ/ (reaches, reaching, reached)

VERB If someone or something has **reached** a certain stage, level, or amount, they are at that stage, level, or amount. ○ *The process of political change in South Africa has reached the stage where it is irreversible.* ○ *We're told the figure could reach 100,000 next year.*

▶ **COLLOCATIONS:**
  reach a **stage/level/point**
  reach **agreement**
  reach a **conclusion/settlement/decision**
  reach a **temperature/age**
  finally/eventually/easily reach *something*
  already/almost/never reach *something*
▶ **SYNONYMS:** attain, arrive at

---

rea|son /ˈriːzən/ (reasons)

NOUN The **reason for** something is a fact or situation which explains why it happens or what causes it to happen. ○ [+ *for*] *There is a reason for every important thing that happens.* ○ *Who would have a reason to want to kill her?* ○ *the reason why Italian tomatoes have so much flavour* ○ *My parents came to Germany for business reasons.*

▶ **COLLOCATIONS:**
  a reason **for** *something*
  for a reason
  give/find/have a reason
  the **main/obvious/real/only** reason
  a **major/good/wrong/simple** reason
  for **personal/family/tax/health** reasons
  for **safety/security** reasons
▶ **PHRASES:**
  for no reason (at all)
  for some reason

r

see no reason why (not)
▶ **SYNONYMS:** grounds, cause, excuse, motive, justification

---

re|ceive /rɪˈsiːv/ (receives, receiving, received)

VERB When you **receive** something, you get it after someone gives it to you or sends it to you. ○ *They will receive their awards at a ceremony in Stockholm.* ○ *I received your letter of November 7.*
▶ **COLLOCATIONS:**
receive *something* **from** *someone*
receive a **letter/call/complaint/payment/message**
receive **treatment/attention/support/information**
receive a **gift/award/benefit**
receive **compensation/funding**
▶ **ANTONYMS:** give, present

> **EXTEND YOUR VOCABULARY**
>
> **Get** is a very common verb in everyday English and can be rather informal. In academic English, you often use more specific verbs. You use **receive** when you get something because someone gives it to you. ○ *Users receive text messages with regular updates.*
>
> You can use **obtain** when you get something, especially by searching for it or trying to get it. ○ *Researchers obtained information using detailed questionnaires.*

---

re|cent /ˈriːsənt/

ADJECTIVE A **recent** event or period of time happened only a short while ago. ○ *In the most recent attack one man was shot dead and two others were wounded.* ○ *Sales have fallen by more than 75 percent in recent years.*
▶ **COLLOCATIONS:**
recent **days/weeks/months/years**
a recent **survey/study/report**
recent **history**
fairly/relatively/comparatively recent

re|cent|ly /ˈriːsəntli/

ADVERB ○ *The bank recently opened a branch in Germany.* ○ *He was until very recently the most powerful banker in the city.*
▶ **COLLOCATIONS:**
until recently
recently **announced/released/published/completed**
recently **deceased**
fairly/relatively/comparatively recently

rec|om|mend /ˌrekə'mend/
(recommends, recommending, recommended)

1 VERB If someone **recommends** a person or thing to you, they suggest that you would find that person or thing good or useful. ○ [+ for] *foods that are recommended for diabetics* ○ *Ask your doctor to recommend a suitable therapist.* ○ [+ as] *Brenda came highly recommended as a hard-working manager.*

2 VERB If you **recommend** that something is done, you suggest that it should be done. ○ [+ that] *The judge recommended that he serve 20 years in prison.* ○ [+ v-ing] *We strongly recommend reporting the incident to the police.*

▶ COLLOCATIONS:
recommend *something* **to** *someone*
recommend *something/someone* **for/as** *something*
recommend for **use/children**
highly/strongly recommended
a **doctor/expert/report/committee** recommends *something*
guidelines recommend *something*

▶ SYNONYMS: put forward, suggest, commend, advise, advocate

rec|om|men|da|tion /ˌrekəme'ndeɪʃən/ (recommendations)

NOUN ○ *The committee's recommendations are unlikely to be made public.*
○ [+ of] *The decision was made on the recommendation of the Interior Minister.*

▶ COLLOCATIONS:
the recommendation **of** *someone*
on *someone's* recommendation

▶ SYNONYMS: suggestion, advice

rec|ord (records, recording, recorded)

The noun is pronounced /'rekɔːd, AM -kərd/. The verb is pronounced /rɪ'kɔːd/.

1 NOUN If you keep a **record of** something, you keep a written account or photographs of it so that it can be referred to later. ○ [+ of] *Keep a record of all the payments.* ○ *There's no record of any marriage or children.* ○ *The result will go on your medical records.*

▶ COLLOCATIONS:
a record **of** *something*
keep/check/enter a record
medical/dental/criminal/military records
a **written/historical/official** record

▶ PHRASES:
for the record

off the record
on record
set/put the record straight
▶ **SYNONYMS:** document, journal, database, register, file

2 VERB If you **record** a piece of information or an event, you write it down, photograph it, or put it into a computer so that in the future people can refer to it. ○ *Up to five wives, and sometimes in excess of twenty, are recorded in some tribes.* ○ *a place which has rarely suffered a famine in its recorded history*
▶ **COLLOCATIONS:**
record a **verdict/conviction**
record a **victory/gain/profit/loss**
faithfully/accurately/dutifully/duly record *something*
automatically/officially record *something*
▶ **SYNONYMS:** document, report
▶ **RELATED WORD:** transcribe

---

rec|tan|gle /ˈrektæŋgəl/ (rectangles)

NOUN A **rectangle** is a four-sided shape whose corners are all ninety degree angles. Each side of a rectangle is the same length as the one opposite to it. ○ *a long rectangle of grass* ○ *a number of regularly spaced rectangles*
▶ **COLLOCATION:** a rectangle **of** *something*
▶ **SYNONYM:** oblong
▶ **RELATED WORD:** square

rec|tan|gu|lar /rekˈtæŋgjʊlə/

ADJECTIVE Something that is **rectangular** is shaped like a rectangle.
○ *a rectangular table* ○ *a pattern of lines and rectangular shapes*
▶ **COLLOCATION:** a rectangular **shape/box/frame/block/table**
▶ **RELATED WORD:** square

---

re|cy|cle /ˌriːˈsaɪkəl/ (recycles, recycling, recycled)

VERB If you **recycle** things that have already been used, such as bottles or sheets of paper, you process them so that they can be used again. ○ *The objective is to recycle 98 per cent of domestic waste.* ○ *All glass bottles which can't be refilled can be recycled.* ○ *printed on recycled paper*
▶ **COLLOCATIONS:**
recycle **cans/glass/plastic/paper/packaging**
recycled **waste/rubbish/tyres/containers**
▶ **SYNONYM:** reuse
▶ **RELATED WORD:** compost

re|cy|cling

UNCOUNTABLE NOUN ○ *a recycling scheme* ○ *[+ of] a plan to increase recycling of household waste*

▸ **COLLOCATIONS:**
the recycling **of** *something*
the recycling of **paint/waste**
a recycling **bin/scheme**

▸ **PHRASE:** can be recycled

---

re|fer /rɪˈfɜː/ (refers, referring, referred)

1 VERB If you **refer to** a particular subject or person, you talk about them or mention them. ○ *[+ to] In his speech, he referred to a recent trip to Canada.* ○ *'What precisely is your interest in the patient referred to here?'*

▸ **COLLOCATIONS:**
refer **to** *something/someone*
refer to a **memo/paragraph/article/document**
refer to a **word/phrase/term/statistic**

▸ **SYNONYMS:** mention, cite

2 VERB If you **refer to** someone or something **as** a particular thing, you use a particular word, expression, or name to mention or describe them. ○ *[+ to] Marcia had referred to him as a dear friend.* ○ *Our economy is referred to as a free market.*

▸ **COLLOCATIONS:**
refer **to** *something/someone*
refer to *something/someone* **as** *something*
often/repeatedly/frequently/constantly referred to as *something*
commonly/jokingly/affectionately referred to as *something*

▸ **SYNONYMS:** allude, call, describe

3 VERB If a word **refers to** a particular thing, situation, or idea, it describes it in some way. ○ *[+ to] The term electronics refers to electrically-induced action.* ○ *English prefers nouns to verbs -- that is, words which refer to objects rather than words which refer to actions.*

▸ **COLLOCATION:** refer **to** *something/someone*

▸ **SYNONYMS:** describe, relate to, apply to

---

re|gion /ˈriːdʒən/ (regions) `ACADEMIC WORD` `GEOGRAPHY`

NOUN A **region** is a large area of land that is different from other areas of land, for example because it is one of the different parts of a country with its own customs and characteristics, or because it has a particular geographical feature. ○ *Barcelona, capital of the autonomous region of Catalonia* ○ *a remote mountain region*

▶ COLLOCATIONS:
tour/visit/explore a region
affect/destabilize/devastate/dominate a region
divide/surround a region
a **mountain/mountainous/industrial/mining** region
a **barren/icy/remote/coastal** region
a **disputed/autonomous/troubled** region
a **border/frontier/desert/farming** region
▶ SYNONYMS: area, province, country

re|gion|al /ˈriːdʒənəl/

ADJECTIVE ○ *the autonomous regional government of Andalucia* ○ *Many people in Minnesota and Tennessee have noticeable regional accents.*
▶ COLLOCATIONS:
a regional **assembly/government/council**
regional **authority/elections/issues**
regional **security/peace/conflicts**
regional **differences/variations**
a regional **dialect/accent**
a regional **centre/airport/airline/office**
a regional **director/co-ordinator/manager**
regional **conference/headquarters**
▶ SYNONYMS: local, district, provincial

---

regu|lar /ˈregjʊlə/

ADJECTIVE **Regular** events have equal amounts of time between them, so that they happen, for example, at the same time each day or each week.
○ *Take regular exercise.* ○ *We're going to be meeting there on a regular basis.*
○ *The cartridge must be replaced at regular intervals.*
▶ COLLOCATIONS:
regular **breathing/rhythm/exercise**
a regular **visitor/contributor/user/customer**
regular **intervals/updates**
regular **meetings/appointments/check-ups/visits**
a regular **occurrence/incident/feature/schedule**
▶ PHRASE: on a regular basis
▶ SYNONYM: frequent
▶ ANTONYM: irregular

regu|lar|ly

ADVERB ○ *Exercise regularly.* ○ *He also writes regularly for 'International Management' magazine.*

▶ COLLOCATIONS:
  happen/occur/meet/check/update/pause regularly
  exercise/appear/visit regularly
  ▶ SYNONYMS: frequently, routinely
  ▶ ANTONYM: occasionally

---

regu|la|tions /ˌregjʊ'leɪʃənz/ `ACADEMIC WORD` `BUSINESS`

PLURAL NOUN Regulations are rules made by an authority in order to control the way something is done or the way people behave. ○ [+ to-inf] *The European Union has proposed new regulations to control the hours worked by its employees.* ○ *Under pressure from the government, the manufacturers obeyed the new safety regulations.*
  ▶ COLLOCATIONS:
  introduce/adopt/impose/propose regulations
  enforce/tighten/observe/abide by regulations
  ignore/disregard/breach/violate regulations
  check/refer to regulations
  regulations **require/govern/cover/allow** *something*
  new/strict/stringent/tough/current regulations
  ▶ PHRASES:
  according to regulations
  rules and regulations
  ▶ SYNONYMS: rules, laws, guidelines, requirements

---

re|la|tion|ship /rɪ'leɪʃənʃɪp/ (relationships)

1 NOUN The **relationship** between two people or groups is the way in which they feel and behave towards each other. ○ *the friendly relationship between France and Britain* ○ *family relationships*
  ▶ COLLOCATIONS:
  a relationship **between** *people*
  personal relationships
  a **professional/working/strong** relationship
  a **good/healthy/close/intimate** relationship
  a **romantic/loving/sexual** relationship
  a **lesbian/homosexual/same-sex** relationship
  a **meaningful/abusive/love-hate** relationship
  a **stable/long-term/lasting/long-standing** relationship
  develop/start/form/establish a relationship
  build/maintain a relationship
  strengthen/improve/sustain a relationship
  ▶ SYNONYMS: bond, partnership

r

2 NOUN The **relationship** between two things is the way in which they are connected. ○ [+ between/of] *There is a relationship between diet and cancer.* ○ [+ to] *an analysis of market mechanisms and their relationship to state capitalism and political freedom*

▶ COLLOCATIONS:
a relationship **between** *things*
a relationship **to** *something*
analyse/understand a relationship
a **close/strong/important/complex** relationship
a **cause-and-effect** relationship

▶ SYNONYMS: connection, association, link

---

rela|tive /ˈrelətɪv/ (relatives)

NOUN Your **relatives** are the members of your family. ○ *We need to inform his relatives.* ○ *I was taken in by my mother's only relative.* ○ *a counselling service for relatives and friends as well as the drug abusers themselves*

▶ COLLOCATIONS:
a **close/near/distant/long-lost** relative
a **sick/elderly** relative
a **living/dead/surviving/blood** relative
grieving/bereaved relatives
visit/contact/trace relatives

▶ PHRASE: friends and relatives

▶ SYNONYM: relation

---

re|li|gion /rɪˈlɪdʒən/ (religions)　　SOCIAL SCIENCE

1 UNCOUNTABLE NOUN Religion is belief in a god or gods. ○ *his understanding of Indian philosophy and religion* ○ *Avoid subjects such as religion, sex or politics.*

2 NOUN A **religion** is a particular system of belief in a god or gods and the activities that are connected with this system. ○ *the Christian religion*

▶ COLLOCATIONS:
organised/comparative/orthodox religion
an **official/ancient/orthodox** religion
a **world/state/folk** religion
the **Christian/Islamic/Muslim/Jewish/Buddhist/Sikh** religion
practise/teach a religion

▶ PHRASES:
religion and spirituality
culture and religion

▶ SYNONYMS: faith, belief, creed

re|li|gious /rɪˈlɪdʒəs/

ADJECTIVE You use **religious** to describe things that are connected with religion or with one particular religion. ○ *religious groups* ○ *different religious beliefs*

▶ COLLOCATIONS:
religious **belief/faith/conviction/practice**
religious **fundamentalism/extremism**
religious **freedom/tolerance/hatred/persecution**
religious **leaders**
a religious **tradition/ceremony/symbol/institution/text**

---

re|mote /rɪˈməʊt/ (remoter, remotest) `GEOGRAPHY`

ADJECTIVE **Remote** areas are far away from cities and places where most people live, and are therefore difficult to get to. ○ *Landslides have cut off many villages in remote areas.* ○ *a remote farm in the Yorkshire dales*

▶ COLLOCATIONS:
a remote **location/community/part**
a remote **area/region/place/corner**
a remote **island/mountain/village/town**

▶ SYNONYMS: isolated, inaccessible

---

re|move /rɪˈmuːv/ (removes, removing, removed) `ACADEMIC WORD`

VERB If you **remove** something from a place, you take it away. [WRITTEN]
○ [+ from] *attempts to remove carbon dioxide from the atmosphere* ○ [+ from] *Three bullets were removed from his wounds.*

▶ COLLOCATIONS:
remove *something* **from** *somewhere*
surgically/forcibly/carefully/completely remove *something*
remove a **tumour/organ/layer/lump**
remove **tissue/skin/fat**
remove a **barrier/restriction/reference**

▶ SYNONYMS: take away, take out, extract

> **ACADEMIC WRITING: Phrasal verbs in academic writing**
>
> Phrasal verbs, like **take away** and **carry on**, are common in everyday English. However, they are often rather informal and are, therefore, less common in formal, academic writing. More specific, one-word verbs are used instead, like **remove** and **continue**.

re|mov|al /rɪˈmuːvəl/

UNCOUNTABLE NOUN ○ [+ of] *The removal of a small lump turned out to be major* surgery. ○ *The most common type of oxidation involves the removal of hydrogen atoms from a substance.*

▶ **COLLOCATIONS:**
removal **of** *something*
stain/rubbish/hair removal
surgical/immediate/complete removal
a removal **tool/system**
a removal **cost/process/centre**

▶ **PHRASE:** removal and replacement

▶ **SYNONYMS:** extraction, eradication

---

re|peat /rɪ'piːt/ (repeats, repeating, repeated)

1 VERB If you **repeat** something, you say or write it again. ○ [+ *that*] *He repeated that he had been mis-quoted.* ○ *The Libyan leader Colonel Gadaffi repeated his call for the release of hostages.*

▶ **COLLOCATIONS:**
repeat a **word/phrase/warning/allegation/accusation**
repeat *something* **verbatim**

▶ **SYNONYMS:** reiterate, restate

2 VERB If you **repeat** an action, you do it again. ○ *The next day I repeated the procedure.* ○ *He said Japan would never repeat its mistakes.* ○ *Hold this position for 30 seconds, release and repeat on the other side.*

▶ **COLLOCATIONS:**
repeat a **cycle/pattern**
repeat the **process/exercise/mistake/feat/success**
endlessly repeat

▶ **PHRASE:** history repeats itself

rep|eti|tion /ˌrepɪ'tɪʃən/ (repetitions)

1 NOUN If there is a **repetition of** an event, it happens again. ○ [+ *of*] *Today the city government has taken measures to prevent a repetition of last year's confrontation.* ○ *He wants to avoid repetition of the confusion that followed the discovery of the cystic fibrosis gene.*

2 UNCOUNTABLE NOUN **Repetition** means using the same words again.
○ *He could also have cut out much of the repetition and thus saved many pages.*
○ *Unnecessary repetition weakens sentences.*

▶ **COLLOCATIONS:**
repetition **of** *something*
avoid/prevent (a) repetition
endless/constant/sheer/relentless repetition
mere/frequent/unnecessary repetition

▶ **SYNONYMS:** duplication, reiteration, recurrence

re|peti|tive /rɪˈpetɪtɪv/

1 ADJECTIVE Something that is **repetitive** involves actions or elements that are repeated many times and is therefore boring. ○ *factory workers who do repetitive jobs* ○ *Suddenly music that seemed dull and repetitive comes alive.*

2 ADJECTIVE Repetitive movements or sounds are repeated many times. ○ *problems that occur as the result of repetitive movements* ○ *the repetitive nature of a chant*
▶ **COLLOCATIONS:**
a repetitive **movement/pattern/job/task**
highly repetitive
the repetitive **nature** of *something*

re|place /rɪˈpleɪs/ (replaces, replacing, replaced)

VERB To **replace** a person or thing means to put another person or thing in their place. ○ [+ *with*] *They were planning to pull down the building and replace it with shops and offices.* ○ *The council tax replaces the poll tax next April.* ○ [+ *as*] *A lawyer replaced Bob as chairman of the company.*
▶ **COLLOCATIONS:**
replace *someone* **as** *something*
replace *something/someone* **with** *something/someone*
be replaced **by** *something/someone*
be replaced by a **newcomer**
replace a **battery/bulb/window/pipe/system**
replace **equipment**
▶ **PHRASE:** remove and replace
▶ **SYNONYM:** substitute

re|place|ment /rɪˈpleɪsmənt/

UNCOUNTABLE NOUN ○ [+ *of*] *the replacement of damaged or lost books*
▶ **COLLOCATIONS:**
the replacement **of** *something*
require replacement
complete/partial replacement
hormone replacement
replacement **therapy/surgery/cost**
▶ **SYNONYMS:** substitution, exchange

re|port /rɪˈpɔːt/ (reports)

NOUN A **report** is an official document which a group of people issue after investigating a situation or event. ○ *After an inspection, the inspectors must* *publish a report.* ○ [+ by] *A report by the Association of University Teachers finds that only 22 per cent of lecturers in our universities are women.*

▶ **COLLOCATIONS:**
    a report **by** *someone*
    a report **on** *something*
    produce/present/publish/release a report
    commission/compile/prepare a report
    a report **suggests/concludes/recommends/says** *something*
    a report **shows/reveals/finds/claims** *something*
    a **recent/annual/special** report
    a **preliminary/quarterly/internal** report
    a **detailed/confidential/independent** report
    a **background/intelligence/progress/research** report
    a **police/financial** report

▶ **SYNONYMS:** analysis, account

---

rep|re|sent /ˌreprɪˈzent/ SOCIAL SCIENCE POLITICS
(represents, representing, represented)

VERB If someone such as a lawyer or a politician **represents** a person or group of people, they act on behalf of that person or group. ○ *the politicians we elect to represent us* ○ *The offer was accepted by the lawyers representing the victims.*

▶ **COLLOCATIONS:**
    a **lawyer/attorney/solicitor** represents *people*
    a **politician/MP/councillor** represents *people*
    a **group/body** represents *people*
    a **union/association/organization** represents *people*

rep|re|senta|tive /ˌreprɪˈzentətɪv/ **(representatives)**

NOUN A **representative** is a person who has been chosen to act or make decisions on behalf of another person or a group of people. ○ *trade union representatives* ○ *Employees from each department elect a representative.*

▶ **COLLOCATIONS:**
    a representative **from** *somewhere*
    elect/appoint/send/invite/meet a representative
    a **registered/elected/sole/legal/authorized** representative
    a **special/senior/official** representative
    a **union/sales/industry** representative
    a **community/state** representative

▶ **SYNONYM:** agent

repu|ta|tion /ˌrepjʊˈteɪʃən/ (reputations)

1 NOUN To have a **reputation** for something means to be known or remembered for it. ○ [+ for] *Alice Munro has a reputation for being a very depressing writer.* ○ *Barcelona's reputation as a design-conscious, artistic city*

2 NOUN Something's or someone's **reputation** is the opinion that people have about how good they are. If they have a good reputation, people think they are good. ○ *This college has a good academic reputation.* ○ *The stories ruined his reputation.*

▶ **COLLOCATIONS:**
a reputation **as/for** *something*
a reputation for **excellence/reliability/integrity**
a **good/bad/international** reputation
acquire/build/earn/establish/gain/have a reputation
ruin/damage/tarnish *someone's* reputation

▶ **SYNONYMS:** name, image, standing

re|search /rɪˈsɜːtʃ/ (researches, researching, researched) `ACADEMIC WORD`

1 UNCOUNTABLE NOUN **Research** is work that involves studying something and trying to discover facts about it. ○ *65 percent of the 1987 budget went for nuclear weapons research and production.* ○ *money spent on cancer research* ○ [+ into] *a centre which conducts animal research into brain diseases*

▶ **COLLOCATIONS:**
research **into/on** *something*
conduct/undertake/carry out research
fund/publish research
research **suggests/shows/reveals/indicates** *something*
market/cancer/animal research
scientific/biological/clinical/medical research
current/recent/experimental research
a research **facility/scientist/laboratory**
research **findings/results/methods**
a research **report/paper/project/fellow**

▶ **PHRASE:** research and development

▶ **SYNONYMS:** analysis, investigation

2 VERB If you **research** something, you try to discover facts about it. ○ *She spent two years in South Florida researching and filming her documentary.* ○ *So far we haven't been able to find anything, but we're still researching.* ○ *a meticulously researched study*

▶ **COLLOCATION: thoroughly/meticulously** research *something*

▶ **SYNONYMS:** investigate, examine, explore, study, analyze

r

re|search|er (researchers)

NOUN ○ *He chose to join the company as a market researcher.* ○ *Researchers have found that vitamin A can protect the lungs from cancer.*

▶ **COLLOCATIONS:**
  researchers **find/say/believe/report** something
  a **medical/senior/independent** researcher
  a **market/university/cancer/sex** researcher

▶ **SYNONYMS:** analyst, scientist

---

resi|dent /ˈrezɪdənt/ (residents)　　　ACADEMIC WORD

NOUN The **residents** of a house or area are the people who live there. ○ *The Archbishop called upon the government to build more low cost homes for local residents.* ○ *More than 10 percent of Munich residents live below the poverty line.*

▶ **COLLOCATIONS:**
  residents **of/in** somewhere
  evacuate/warn/advise residents
  residents **say/fear/complain about/want/report** something
  former/local/permanent/nearby/elderly residents

▶ **SYNONYMS:** inhabitant, citizen

---

re|spect /rɪˈspekt/ (respects, respecting, respected)

1 **VERB** If you **respect** someone's wishes, rights, or customs, you avoid doing things that they would dislike or regard as wrong. ○ *Finally, trying to respect her wishes, I said I'd leave.* ○ *It is our policy to respect the privacy of every customer.*

▶ **COLLOCATION:** respect someone's **wishes/rights/customs/privacy**
▶ **SYNONYM:** honour

2 **UNCOUNTABLE NOUN** If you show **respect for** someone's wishes, rights, or customs, you avoid doing anything they would dislike or regard as wrong. ○ [+ for] *They will campaign for the return of traditional lands and respect for aboriginal rights and customs.* ○ *showing no respect for the law*

▶ **COLLOCATIONS:**
  respect **for** something
  lack/show/treat with respect
▶ **PHRASE:** lack of respect
▶ **SYNONYM:** regard
▶ **ANTONYM:** disrespect

3 **VERB** If you **respect** a law or moral principle, you agree not to break it.
  ○ *It is about time tour operators respected the law and their own code of conduct.*
  ○ *pledges by both sides to respect the ceasefire*

▶ **COLLOCATIONS:**
respect a **law/rule/principle/tradition**
respect the **ceasefire/truce**
▶ **SYNONYMS:** recognise, honour, acknowledge
▶ **ANTONYMS:** break, breach

---

re|spon|sible /rɪˈspɒnsɪbəl/

1 ADJECTIVE If someone or something is **responsible for** a particular event or situation, they are the cause of it or they can be blamed for it. ○ [+ *for*] *He still felt responsible for her death.* ○ *I want you to do everything you can to find out who's responsible.*

▶ **COLLOCATIONS:**
responsible **for** *something*
be/feel responsible
hold *someone* responsible
the **person/individual/terrorist/gang/organisation** responsible
criminally responsible
▶ **SYNONYMS:** to blame, guilty
▶ **ANTONYM:** innocent

2 ADJECTIVE If you are **responsible for** something, it is your job or duty to deal with it and make decisions relating to it. ○ [+ *for*] *the minister responsible for the environment* ○ *The man responsible for finding the volunteers is Dr. Charles Weber.*

▶ **COLLOCATIONS:**
responsible **for** *something*
the **minister/organisation/agency/department/body** responsible
financially responsible
partly/solely/ultimately/largely/primarily/chiefly responsible
personally/indirectly/directly responsible
▶ **SYNONYM:** accountable

re|spon|sibil|ity /rɪˌspɒnsɪˈbɪlɪti/ (responsibilities)

1 UNCOUNTABLE NOUN If you have **responsibility** for something or someone, or if they are your **responsibility**, it is your job or duty to deal with them and to take decisions relating to them. ○ [+ *for*] *Each manager had responsibility for just under 600 properties.* ○ [+ *for*] *We need to take responsibility for looking after our own health.* ○ *'She's not your responsibility,' he said gently.*

▶ **COLLOCATIONS:**
responsibility **for** *something*
have/assume/be given/shoulder/carry responsibility
delegate/assign responsibility
financial/personal/moral/legal responsibility

parental/social/personal/corporate responsibility
▶ SYNONYMS: duty, obligation

2 UNCOUNTABLE NOUN If you accept **responsibility for** something that has happened, you agree that you were to blame for it or you caused it. ○ [+ for] *No one admitted responsibility for the attacks.* ○ [+ for] *Someone had to give orders and take responsibility for mistakes.*
▶ COLLOCATIONS:
responsibility **for** something
accept/claim/bear/share/take responsibility
deny/admit/acknowledge responsibility
diminished/collective/full/individual responsibility
▶ SYNONYMS: accountability, guilt, blame, fault, liability

3 PLURAL NOUN Your **responsibilities** are the duties that you have because of your job or position. ○ [+ as] *He handled his responsibilities as a counselor in an intelligent and caring fashion.* ○ *programmes to help employees balance work and family responsibilities*
▶ COLLOCATIONS:
responsibilities **as** something
family/community/adult responsibilities
share responsibilities
▶ SYNONYMS: duties, obligations

re|sult /rɪˈzʌlt/ (results)

1 NOUN A **result** is something that happens or exists because of something else that has happened. ○ [+ of] *Compensation is available for people who have developed asthma as a direct result of their work.* ○ *Cancer is the end result of a long degenerative process.*
▶ COLLOCATIONS:
a result **of** something
a **direct** result
the **end** result
▶ PHRASE: as a result
▶ SYNONYMS: by-product, consequence

2 NOUN A **result** is the number that you get when you do a calculation. ○ *They found their computers producing different results from exactly the same calculation.*
▶ SYNONYM: answer

3 NOUN A **result** is the information that you get when you carry out an experiment or some research. ○ *There were some experimental errors on my part, invalidating the results.* ○ [+ of] *Here he published the results of his meticulous research.*

▶ **COLLOCATIONS:**
the results **of** something
the results of a **study/survey/experiment/inquiry**
get/achieve/produce/yield results
await/expect results
report/announce/release/publish results
disappointing/surprising results
consistent/impressive/positive results
▶ **SYNONYM:** findings

---

re|tire /rɪˈtaɪə/ (retires, retiring, retired) `BUSINESS`

VERB When older people **retire**, they leave their job and usually stop working completely. ○ *At the age when most people retire, he is ready to face a new career.* ○ *Many said they plan to retire at 50.* ○ [+ *from*] *In 1974 he retired from the museum.*
▶ **COLLOCATIONS:**
retire **at** an age
retire **from/as** something
retire at the **age** of x
retire from **football/politics/teaching/the chairmanship**
retire as **chairman/president/manager/head**
▶ **SYNONYMS:** finish, leave, stop, quit
▶ **RELATED WORD:** resign

re|tire|ment /rɪˈtaɪəmənt/

UNCOUNTABLE NOUN ○ *the proportion of the population who are over retirement age* ○ *The Governor of the prison is to take early retirement.*
▶ **COLLOCATIONS:**
near retirement
early/mandatory/impending/premature retirement
contemplate/approach/consider retirement
announce someone's retirement
retirement **age/savings/income/benefits**
a retirement **home/pension/fund**
▶ **RELATED WORDS:** redundancy, resignation

---

re|ward /rɪˈwɔːd/ (rewards)

NOUN A **reward** is something that you are given, for example because you have behaved well, worked hard, or provided a service to the community. ○ [+ *for*] *He was given the job as a reward for running a successful leadership bid.*
▶ **COLLOCATIONS:**
a reward **for** something
a reward for **good behaviour/information**

a reward for **performance/achievement**
give/offer/get/receive/earn/deserve a reward
a **financial/just/fitting/tangible** reward
a **cash/material/million-dollar** reward
a reward **scheme/programme/system**
reward **money**

▶ PHRASES:
as a reward
risk and reward

▶ SYNONYMS: bonus, prize

▶ ANTONYM: punishment

---

rich /rɪtʃ/ (richer, richest)

1 ADJECTIVE A **rich** person has a lot of money or valuable possessions. ○ *Their one aim in life is to get rich.* ○ *the kind of treatment that only rich people could afford*

▶ COLLOCATIONS:
a rich **man/woman/family**
rich **people/kids**
get/become rich
extremely/incredibly/fabulously/immensely/newly rich

▶ PHRASES:
rich and beautiful
rich and famous
rich and powerful

▶ SYNONYMS: wealthy, well-off, affluent

▶ ANTONYM: poor

2 ADJECTIVE A **rich** country has a strong economy and produces a lot of wealth, so many people who live there have a high standard of living. ○ *There is hunger in many parts of the world, even in rich countries.* ○ *the means by which the rich nations dictate economic policy to the poor*

▶ COLLOCATIONS:
rich **in** something
a rich **country/nation**
rich in **natural resources/minerals**

▶ SYNONYM: developed

▶ ANTONYMS: poor, developing

---

right /raɪt/ (rights)

1 PLURAL NOUN Your **rights** are what you are morally or legally entitled to do or to have. ○ *They don't know their rights.* ○ *You must stand up for your rights.* ○ *voting rights*

▶ COLLOCATIONS:
protect/violate/respect/defend *someone's* rights
human/civil/constitutional rights
women's/workers'/gay rights
equal/basic/religious/democratic rights
rights **violation/abuse/legislation**
a rights **lawyer/activist/organisation/movement**
the rights of the **defendant/citizen/public/victim/patient**

▶ SYNONYM: entitlements
▶ ANTONYM: duties

2 NOUN If you have a **right to** do or to have something, you are morally or legally entitled to do it or to have it. ○ *a woman's right to choose* ○ *People have the right to read any kind of material they wish.*

▶ COLLOCATION: **have/earn/win/exercise** a right
▶ SYNONYM: entitlement
▶ ANTONYM: duty

---

rise /raɪz/ (rises, rising, rose, risen)

1 VERB If an amount **rises**, it increases. ○ [+ *from/to*] *Pre-tax profits rose from £842,000 to £1.82m.* ○ [+ *by*] *Tourist trips of all kinds in Britain rose by 10.5% between 1977 and 1987.* ○ *Exports in June rose 1.5% to a record $30.91 billion.* ○ *The number of business failures has risen.* ○ [V-ing] *rising costs*
→ see note at **raise**

▶ COLLOCATIONS:
rise **from** *x* **to** *y*
rise **by** *x*
costs/prices/rates/levels rise
unemployment/inflation rises
demand/tension/temperature/crime rises
sharply/steadily/dramatically/rapidly rise

▶ SYNONYM: increase
▶ ANTONYM: fall

2 NOUN A **rise in** the amount of something is an increase in it. ○ [+ *in*] *the prospect of another rise in interest rates* ○ *a sharp rise in violence*

▶ COLLOCATIONS:
a rise **in** *something*
a rise in **profits/prices/rates/costs/sales/value**
a rise in **unemployment/temperature/number/crime**
see/report/expect/predict/show a rise
a **sharp/rapid/further/recent/huge** rise
a **pay/price/tax/interest-rate** rise

r

▶ **PHRASE:** rise and fall
▶ **SYNONYM:** increase
▶ **ANTONYM:** fall

---

risk /rɪsk/ (risks)

1 NOUN If there is a **risk of** something unpleasant, there is a possibility that it will happen. ○ [+ of] *There is a small risk of brain damage from the procedure.* ○ [+ that] *In all the confusion, there's a serious risk that the main issues will be forgotten.* ○ *People do it because there is that element of danger and risk.*

2 NOUN If something that you do is a **risk**, it might have unpleasant or undesirable results. ○ *You're taking a big risk showing this to Kravis.* ○ *This was one risk that paid off.*

3 NOUN If you say that something or someone is a **risk**, you mean they are likely to cause harm. ○ *It's being overfat that constitutes a health risk.* ○ *The restaurant has been refurbished – it was found to be a fire risk.* ○ [+ to] *a risk to national security*

▶ **COLLOCATIONS:**
a risk **of** something
a risk **to** something/someone
a risk of **cancer/disease/injury**
a risk of **failure/attack**
a **serious/associated/high/low/great/potential** risk
pose/reduce/increase a risk
assess/involve/run/take a risk
a **health/fire/security** risk
risk **factor/assessment/management**

▶ **SYNONYMS:** gamble, danger, hazard

---

rock /rɒk/   `GEOGRAPHY`

UNCOUNTABLE NOUN Rock is the hard substance which the Earth is made of. ○ *The hills above the valley are bare rock.* ○ *A little way below the ridge was an outcrop of rock that made a rough shelter.*

▶ **COLLOCATIONS:**
solid/volcanic/sedimentary rock
a rock **formation/outcrop/ledge/pool**
rock **salt/sediment/ash**

▶ **SYNONYM:** stone

---

role /rəʊl/ (roles)   `ACADEMIC WORD`

NOUN If you have a **role** in a situation or in society, you have a particular position and function in it. ○ [+ in] *the drug's role in preventing more serious effects of infection* ○ [+ to-inf] *Both sides have roles to play.*

▶ **COLLOCATIONS:**
a role **in/as** *something*
the role **of** *something*
play/take/assume a role
a **key/lead/central/crucial/vital** role
a **major/active/important/significant** role
a **parental/positive/traditional/leadership** role
a role **model/play/reversal**

---

root /ruːt/ (roots)   `SCIENCE` `BIOLOGY`

NOUN The **roots** of a plant are the parts of it that grow under the ground.
○ *the twisted roots of an apple tree* ○ *Mint roots spread rapidly.*

▶ **COLLOCATIONS:**
a **tap/plant/tree** root
roots **grow/form/spread**
take root
a root **crop**

▶ **PHRASE:** root and branch

▶ **SYNONYMS:** tuber, rhizome

---

rough /rʌf/ (rougher, roughest)

ADJECTIVE A **rough** calculation or guess is approximately correct, but not exact. ○ *We were only able to make a rough estimate of how much fuel would be required.* ○ *As a rough guide, a horse needs 2.5 per cent of his body weight in food every day.*

▶ **COLLOCATIONS:**
a rough **estimate/guess/draft/sketch/guide**
a rough **outline/approximation/calculation**

▶ **SYNONYMS:** approximate, vague

▶ **ANTONYM:** exact

rough|ly

ADVERB ○ *Gambling and tourism pay roughly half the entire state budget.* ○ *The Ukraine is roughly equal to France in size and population.* ○ *a period of very roughly 30 million years*

▶ **COLLOCATIONS:**
roughly **half/quarter/one-third/double**
roughly **equal/equivalent**
roughly **translated/speaking**
correspond/coincide roughly

▶ SYNONYM: approximately
▶ ANTONYM: exactly

---

row /rəʊ/ (rows)

NOUN A **row of** things or people is a number of them arranged in a line.
   ○ [+ of] *a row of plants* ○ *Several men are pushing school desks and chairs into neat rows.*
   ▶ COLLOCATIONS:
   a row **of** *things*
   in/into a row
   put/place/arrange *things* in a row
   the **front/back/top/bottom** row
   a **single/double** row

---

rule /ruːl/ (rules)

NOUN The **rules of** something such as a language or a science are statements that describe the way that things usually happen in a particular situation. ○ [+ of] *according to the rules of quantum theory* ○ *Children often apply grammatical rules correctly in order to express what they want.*
   ▶ COLLOCATIONS:
   the rules **of** *something*
   apply/break a rule
   an **exception to** a rule

---

ru|ral /ˈrʊərəl/   GEOGRAPHY

ADJECTIVE **Rural** means relating to country areas as opposed to large towns. ○ *These plants have a tendency to grow in the more rural areas.* ○ *the closure of rural schools*
   ▶ COLLOCATIONS:
   a rural **area/community/population**
   a rural **economy/development/road**
   ▶ SYNONYM: country
   ▶ ANTONYM: urban

Ss

sala|ry /ˈsæləri/ (salaries)

BUSINESS

NOUN A **salary** is the money that someone is paid each month by their employer, especially when they are in a profession such as teaching, law, or medicine. ○ *the lawyer was paid a huge salary* ○ *The government has decided to increase salaries for all civil servants.* ○ [+ *of*] *IT directors can expect to earn average salaries of between £55,000 and £80,000.*

→ see note at **earn**

▶ COLLOCATIONS:
a salary **of** x
a **monthly/annual/average/£x** salary
earn a salary
be **paid** a salary
a salary **increase**

▶ SYNONYMS: wage, earnings, income

---

sat|is|fied /ˈsætɪsfaɪd/

1 ADJECTIVE If you are **satisfied with** something, you are happy because you have got what you wanted or needed. ○ [+ *with*] *We are not satisfied with these results.* ○ *asking for referrals from satisfied customers*

2 ADJECTIVE If you are **satisfied that** something is true or has been done properly, you are convinced about this after checking it. ○ [+ *that*] *People must be satisfied that the treatment is safe.*

▶ COLLOCATIONS:
satisfied **with** *something*
reasonably/completely/very satisfied
a satisfied **customer/user**

▶ SYNONYMS: pleased, contented
▶ ANTONYM: dissatisfied

---

save /seɪv/ (saves, saving, saved)

VERB If you **save** something such as time or money, you prevent the loss or waste of it. ○ *More cash will be saved by shutting studios and selling outside-broadcast vehicles.* ○ *New computers which will potentially save companies time and money.* ○ [+ *on*] *minimal use of packaging to save on paper*

▶ COLLOCATIONS:
save **on** *something*
save **money/time**
▶ ANTONYMS: waste, squander

---

scan /skæn/ (scans, scanning, scanned)　　ACADEMIC STUDY　MEDICINE

1 VERB When you **scan** written material, you look through it quickly in order to find important or interesting information. ○ *She scanned the advertisement pages of the newspapers.* ○ *[+ through] I haven't read much into it as yet. I've only just scanned through it.*

● **Scan** is also a noun. ○ *[+ through] I just had a quick scan through your book again.*
▶ COLLOCATION: scan **through** *something*
▶ SYNONYMS: skim, browse
▶ ANTONYMS: pore over, examine

2 NOUN A **scan** is a medical test in which a machine sends a beam of X-rays over a part of your body in order to check that it is healthy. ○ *He was rushed to hospital for a brain scan.* ○ *a scan revealed a bone injury in his back*
▶ COLLOCATIONS:
a **brain/bone/body** scan
a scan **reveals/shows** *something*
▶ SYNONYM: X-ray

---

scene /siːn/ (scenes)　　LITERATURE

NOUN A **scene** in a play, film, or book is part of it in which a series of events happen in the same place. ○ *I found the scene in which Percy proposed to Olive tremendously poignant.* ○ *[+ of] the opening scene of 'A Christmas Carol'* ○ *Act I, scene 1.*
▶ COLLOCATIONS:
a scene **of/in** a play
a **love** scene
the **opening/final** scene

---

sched|ule /ˈʃedjuːl, AM ˈskedʒuːl/ (schedules)　　ACADEMIC WORD

NOUN A **schedule** is a plan that gives a list of events or tasks and the times at which each one should happen or be done. ○ *He has been forced to adjust his schedule.* ○ *We both have such hectic schedules.*
▶ COLLOCATIONS:
a **busy/hectic/tight** schedule
a **punishing/gruelling/heavy** schedule
adjust/rearrange/disrupt a schedule
▶ SYNONYM: timetable

sci|ence /saɪəns/ (sciences) SCIENCE

1 UNCOUNTABLE NOUN Science is the study of the nature and behaviour of natural things and the knowledge that we obtain about them. ○ *The best discoveries in science are very simple.* ○ *one of the problems with the way we teach science*

2 NOUN A **science** is a particular branch of science such as physics, chemistry, or biology. ○ *Physics is the best example of a science which has developed strong, abstract theories.* ○ *the science of microbiology* ○ *recent innovations in medical science*

3 NOUN A **science** is the study of some aspect of human behaviour, for example sociology or anthropology. ○ *the modern science of psychology*

▶ COLLOCATIONS:
  applied/pure/basic/modern science
  biological/medical/computer/environmental science
  social/political science

▶ PHRASES:
  science and technology
  advances in science
  Master of Science

sci|en|tif|ic /ˌsaɪənˈtɪfɪk/

ADJECTIVE ○ *There has been a certain amount of scientific research into meditation* ○ *the use of animals in scientific experiments*

▶ COLLOCATIONS:
  scientific **research/evidence/discovery/study**
  the scientific **community**

sci|en|tist /ˈsaɪəntɪst/ (scientists)

NOUN ○ *Scientists have collected more data than expected.* ○ *a senior research scientist at the University of Maryland*

▶ COLLOCATIONS:
  a **leading/senior/chief** scientist
  a **computer/forensic/research/nuclear** scientist
  scientists **believe/say/claim** *things*
  scientists **find/discover/study/develop** *things*

sea|son /ˈsiːzən/ (seasons) GEOGRAPHY SCIENCE BIOLOGY

1 NOUN The **seasons** are the main periods into which a year can be divided and which each have their own typical weather conditions. ○ *the only region of Brazil where all four seasons are clearly defined* ○ *The climate is characterized by hot summers with a four-month rainy season.*

▶ COLLOCATION: a **rainy/dry** season

2 NOUN You can use **season** to refer to the period during each year when a particular activity or event takes place. ○ *birds arriving for the breeding season* ○ *For law students, autumn brings the recruiting season.*
  ▶ COLLOCATIONS:
    the **festive/holiday/shopping** season
    the **breeding/mating** season
  ▶ SYNONYMS: period, time

---

sec|ond|ary school /'sekəndri sku:l,   EDUCATION
AM 'sekənderi sku:l/ **(secondary schools)**

NOUN A **secondary school** is a school for pupils between the ages of 11 or 12 and 17 or 18. ○ *She taught history at a secondary school.* ○ *One in four pupils leaving secondary school can't read or write properly.*
  ▶ COLLOCATIONS:
    be **at** secondary school
    go to/attend secondary school
    secondary school **teaching**
    a secondary school **teacher/pupil/student**
  ▶ SYNONYM: high school
  ▶ RELATED WORD: primary school

---

sec|tion /'sekʃən/ **(sections)**   ACADEMIC WORD

NOUN A **section** of something is one of the parts into which it is divided or from which it is formed. ○ [+ *of*] *He said it was wrong to single out any section of society for Aids testing.* ○ *a large orchestra, with a vast percussion section* ○ *the Georgetown section of Washington, D.C.*
  ▶ COLLOCATIONS:
    a section **of** *something*
    a section of **society/the community/the population**
    a section of a **chapter**
    a **separate/entire/special** section
    the **relevant/preceding** section
    insert/amend a section
    a **percussion/brass/string** section
  ▶ SYNONYM: part
  ▶ ANTONYM: whole

---

se|cu|rity /sɪ'kjʊərɪti/   ACADEMIC WORD

UNCOUNTABLE NOUN **Security** refers to all the measures that are taken to protect a place, or to ensure that only people with permission enter it or leave it. ○ *They are now under a great deal of pressure to tighten their airport security.* ○ *Strict security measures are in force in the capital.*

▶ **COLLOCATIONS:**
national/airport/border security
tight/lax security
tighten/improve/increase security
security **measures**
a security **adviser/official/guard**

USAGE: safety or **security**?

You usually use **safety** to talk about keeping individuals away from physical harm. ○ *regulations on health and safety at work* ○ *concerns for their personal safety*

You use **security** to talk more generally about protecting a place or a group of people. ○ *tougher security measures to deal with terrorists*

---

seed /siːd/ (seeds)   SCIENCE BIOLOGY

NOUN A **seed** is the small, hard part of a plant from which a new plant grows. ○ *a packet of cabbage seed* ○ *I sow the seed in pots of soil-based compost.*

▶ **COLLOCATIONS:**
sow/plant a seed
a seed **germinates/sprouts**
sesame/sunflower seeds

---

seem /siːm/ (seems, seeming, seemed)

VERB You use **seem** to say that someone or something gives the impression of having a particular quality, or of happening in the way you describe. ○ [+ to-inf] *The study seemed to indicate that stimulating the brain can increase the number of brain cells.* ○ [+ that] *It seems likely that a calcium-rich diet may help prevent osteoporosis.* ○ *This phenomenon is not as outrageous as it seems.*

▶ **COLLOCATIONS:**
seem **like** *something*
seem **likely/certain/unlikely/strange/odd**
seem to **care/think/understand/know**
seem to **indicate/suggest/confirm**
▶ **PHRASE:** seem like a good/bad idea
▶ **SYNONYMS:** appear, look as if

S

sell /sel/ (sells, selling, sold) ╞ BUSINESS ╡

1 VERB If you **sell** something that you own, you let someone have it in return for money. ○ [+ to] *His heir sold the painting to the London art dealer Agnews.* ○ [+ for] *The directors sold the business for £14.8 million.* ○ *It's not a very good time to sell at the moment.*

▶ **COLLOCATIONS:**
sell something **to** someone
sell something **for** £x

▶ **ANTONYMS:** buy, purchase

2 VERB If a shop **sells** a particular thing, that thing is available for people to buy there. ○ *It sells everything from hair ribbons to oriental rugs.* ○ *Bean sprouts are also sold in cans.*

▶ **COLLOCATIONS:**
sell something **in** something
a **shop/store/supermarket/retailer/stall** sells something
products/goods are sold
be sold in a **shop/store/supermarket**
be sold in **bottles/cans/packets**

sale /seɪl/ (sales)

1 NOUN The **sale** of goods is the act of selling them for money. ○ [+ of] *Efforts were made to limit the sale of alcohol.* ○ [+ to] *a proposed arms sale to Saudi Arabia*

▶ **COLLOCATIONS:**
the sale **of** something **to** someone
the sale of **products/goods/equipment/alcohol/cigarettes**
an **arms** sale

▶ **ANTONYM:** purchase

2 PLURAL NOUN The **sales** of a product are the quantity of it that is sold. ○ [+ of] *The newspaper has sales of 1.72 million.* ○ *Retail sales rose by 3 per cent.* ○ *This year's sales figures are better than last.*

▶ **COLLOCATIONS:**
sales **of** something
ticket/record/retail sales
total/annual/net sales
sales **figures**
sales **rise/fall**

3 PLURAL NOUN The part of a company that deals with **sales** deals with selling the company's products. ○ *Until 1983 he worked in sales and marketing.* ○ *She was their Dusseldorf sales manager.*

▶ **COLLOCATIONS:**
work **in** sales

a sales **manager/representative**
the sales **department**
▶ **PHRASE:** sales and marketing

sen|ior /ˈsiːnjə/ `BUSINESS`

ADJECTIVE The **senior** people in an organization or profession have the highest and most important jobs. ○ *senior officials in the Israeli government* ○ *The budget was reviewed by senior management.* ○ *Television and radio needed many more women in senior jobs.*
▶ **COLLOCATIONS:**
a senior **official/executive/manager**
a senior **editor/analyst/politician**
senior **management**
a senior **job/position**
▶ **SYNONYMS:** chief, head
▶ **ANTONYM:** junior

sense /sens/ (senses) `SCIENCE` `BIOLOGY` `MEDICINE`

NOUN Your **senses** are the physical abilities of sight, smell, hearing, touch, and taste. ○ *She stared at him again, unable to believe the evidence of her senses.* ○ [+ of] *Sharks have a keen sense of smell.*
▶ **COLLOCATIONS:**
a sense **of** *something*
a sense of **smell/taste**

sepa|rate /ˈsepərət/

1 ADJECTIVE If one thing is **separate from** another, there is a barrier, space, or division between them, so that they are clearly two things.
○ *The financial review includes a separate section concerning exchange rates.*
○ *They are now making plans to form their own separate party.* ○ [+ from]
Business bank accounts were kept separate from personal ones.

2 ADJECTIVE If you refer to **separate** things, you mean several different things, rather than just one thing. ○ *They repeated the experiment on three separate occasions, with the same results.* ○ *Men and women have separate exercise rooms.*
○ *The authorities say six civilians have been killed in two separate attacks.*
▶ **COLLOCATIONS:**
separate **from** *something*
separate from **the rest of** *something*
a separate **section/unit**
a separate **room/bedroom/toilet/entrance**
a separate **incident/occasion/attack**

S

entirely/completely/totally separate
▶ **SYNONYMS:** distinct, different, discrete
▶ **ANTONYMS:** the same, merged

sepa|rate|ly /ˈsepərətli/

ADVERB If people or things are dealt with **separately** or do something **separately**, they are dealt with or do something at different times or places, rather than together. ○ *The software is sold separately.* ○ [+ *from*] *Acid fruits are best eaten separately from sweet fruits.*
▶ **COLLOCATIONS:**
  separately **from** *something*
  sold/bought/purchased separately
  calculated/analyzed separately
▶ **SYNONYM:** distinctly
▶ **ANTONYM:** together

---

se|ries /ˈsɪəriz/ (series)   `ACADEMIC WORD`

NOUN A **series of** things or events is a number of them that come one after the other. ○ [+ *of*] *a series of meetings with students and political leaders*
○ [+ *of*] *a series of explosions*
▶ **COLLOCATIONS:**
  a series **of** *things*
  a series of **events/meetings/interviews**
  a series of **attacks/bombings/explosions**
▶ **SYNONYMS:** succession, set, chain

---

se|ri|ous /ˈsɪəriəs/

ADJECTIVE **Serious** problems or situations are very bad and cause people to be worried or afraid. ○ *Crime is an increasingly serious problem in Russian society.* ○ *Doctors said his condition was serious but stable.*
▶ **COLLOCATIONS:**
  a serious **problem/difficulty/situation**
  a serious **accident/injury/illness/condition**
  a serious **crime/threat**
  potentially/extremely/increasingly serious

se|ri|ous|ly /ˈsɪəriəsli/

ADVERB ○ *If this ban was to come in it would seriously damage my business.*
○ *They are not thought to be seriously hurt.*
▶ **COLLOCATIONS:**
  seriously **injured/wounded/hurt/ill**
  seriously **damage/affect** *something*

ser|vice /'sɜːvɪs/ (services) BUSINESS

1 NOUN A **service** is an organization or system that provides something for the public. ○ *Britain still boasts the cheapest postal service.* ○ *We have started a campaign for better nursery and school services.* ○ *The authorities have said they will attempt to maintain essential services.*

2 NOUN If an organization or company provides a particular **service**, they can do a particular job or a type of work for you. ○ *The kitchen maintains a twenty-four-hour service and can be contacted via Reception.* ○ *The larger firm was capable of providing a better range of services.*

3 PLURAL NOUN Services are activities such as tourism, banking, and selling things which are part of a country's economy, but are not concerned with producing or manufacturing goods. ○ *Mining rose by 9.1%, manufacturing by 9.4% and services by 4.3%.* ○ *the doctrine that a highly developed service sector was the sign of a modern economy*

▶ **COLLOCATIONS:**
  health/social/public services
  a **financial/advisory/support** service
  a **telephone/online/mail-order** service
  an **essential/free** service
  provide/run/deliver/introduce/offer a service
  cut/disrupt/maintain/expand/improve services
  a service **provider/sector/industry**
  the service **sector**

▶ **PHRASES:**
  goods and services
  products and services

4 UNCOUNTABLE NOUN The level or standard of **service** provided by an organization or company is the amount or quality of the work it can do for you. ○ *Taking risks is the only way employees can provide effective and efficient customer service.* ○ *The current level of service will be maintained except that the evening 'Network Express' trains will be withdrawn.*

▶ **COLLOCATIONS:**
  customer service
  excellent/poor service

set|back /'setbæk/ (setbacks) also **set-back**

NOUN A **setback** is an event that delays your progress or reverses some of the progress that you have made. ○ [+ for/in/to] *The move represents a setback for the Middle East peace process.* ○ *He has suffered a serious setback in his political career.* ○ *The incident dealt a serious setback to reconciliation efforts.*

▶ COLLOCATIONS:
a setback **for/in/to** something
suffer/receive a setback
deal a setback to something
something **represents** a setback
a **temporary/minor** setback
a **severe/serious/major** setback
▶ SYNONYMS: upset, difficulty, hindrance
▶ ANTONYMS: advancement, progress

sev|er|al /'sevrəl/

DETERMINER **Several** is used to refer to an imprecise number of people or things that is not large but is greater than two. ○ *a period of several months* ○ *Jones cited several reasons for last year's slowdown.* ○ *Several hundred students gathered on campus.*

● **Several** is also a quantifier. ○ [+ *of*] *Several of the delays were caused by the new high-tech baggage system.*

● **Several** is also a pronoun. ○ *No one drug will suit or work for everyone and sometimes several may have to be tried.*

▶ COLLOCATIONS:
several **of** something
several **minutes/hours/days/months/years**
several **occasions/times**
several **reasons/factors**
▶ SYNONYMS: some, a few

show /ʃəʊ/ (shows, showing, showed, shown)

1 VERB If something **shows that** a state of affairs exists, it gives information that proves it or makes it clear to people. ○ [+ *that*] *Research shows that a high-fibre diet may protect you from bowel cancer.* ○ *These figures show an increase of over one million in unemployment.* ○ [+ *to-inf*] *It was only later that the drug was shown to be addictive.*

▶ COLLOCATIONS:
a **study/survey/report/poll/** shows something
research/evidence shows something
figures/statistics show something
show **clearly/conclusively**
▶ SYNONYMS: indicate, demonstrate

2 VERB If a picture, chart, film, or piece of writing **shows** something, it represents it or gives information about it. ○ *Figure 4.1 shows the respiratory system.* ○ *The cushions, shown left, measure 20 x 12 inches and cost $39.95.*

○ [+ v-ing] *Much of the film shows the painter simply going about his task.*
▶ **COLLOCATIONS:**
   shown **in** *something*
   shown in a **diagram/illustration/photograph**
   a **picture/photograph/video/chart/map** shows *something*
▶ **SYNONYMS:** present, represent
→ see note at **describe**

---

sight /saɪt/ (sights)   `MEDICINE`

1 UNCOUNTABLE NOUN Someone's **sight** is their ability to see. ○ *My sight is failing, and I can't see to read any more.* ○ *I use the sense of sound much more than the sense of sight.*
▶ **COLLOCATION: lose** your sight
▶ **SYNONYM:** vision

2 NOUN A **sight** is something that you see. ○ [+ of] *We encountered the pathetic sight of a family packing up its home.* ○ *Among the most spectacular sights are the great sea-bird colonies.*
▶ **COLLOCATIONS:**
   the sight **of** *something*
   a **familiar/common/rare** sight
   a **spectacular/amazing/welcome** sight

3 PLURAL NOUN **The sights** are the places that are interesting to see and that are often visited by tourists. ○ [+ of] *I am going to show you the sights of our wonderful city.* ○ *Once at Elgin day-trippers visit a number of local sights.*
▶ **COLLOCATIONS:**
   the sights **of** *somewhere*
   tourist sights
▶ **PHRASE:** see the sights

> **USAGE: sight or site?**
>
> A **sight** is something that you see or an interesting place that you visit to look at. ○ *Grey kangaroos are a common sight in the area.* ○ *the most popular tourist sights*
>
> A **site** is a place or a location, especially one where something happens or happened. ○ *Rescuers rushed to the crash site.* (the place where the crash happened) ○ *an ancient/archaeological site* ○ *a building/construction site*

S

---

sign /saɪn/ (signs)   `MATHS` `SCIENCE`

1 NOUN A **sign** is a mark or shape that always has a particular meaning, for example in mathematics or music. ○ *Equations are generally written with*

a two-bar equals sign.
▸ **COLLOCATION:** a **minus/equals/dollar/pound** sign
▸ **SYNONYM:** symbol

2 NOUN If there is a **sign of** something, there is something which shows that it exists or is happening. ○ [+ of] *They are prepared to hand back a hundred prisoners of war a day as a sign of good will.* ○ [+ of] *Your blood would have been checked for any sign of kidney failure.*
▸ **COLLOCATIONS:**
  a sign **of** *something*
  a sign of **life/recovery/improvement/progress**
  a sign of **disease/illness/trouble**
  a sign of a **problem**
  a **good/bad** sign
  no sign of *something*
▸ **SYNONYMS:** indication, symptom

---

sig|nifi|cant /sɪgˈnɪfɪkənt/

ADJECTIVE A **significant** amount or effect is large enough to be important or affect a situation to a noticeable degree. ○ *A small but significant number of 11-year-olds are illiterate.* ○ *foods that offer a significant amount of protein*
▸ **COLLOCATIONS:**
  a significant **amount/number/proportion/difference**
  a significant **improvement/change/increase/effect**
  highly/hugely/particularly/potentially significant
  statistically significant
▸ **SYNONYM:** important
▸ **ANTONYM:** insignificant

---

simi|lar /ˈsɪmɪlə/

ADJECTIVE If one thing is **similar to** another, or if two things are **similar**, they have features that are the same. ○ [+ to] *The accident was similar to one that happened in 1973.* ○ *a group of similar pictures*
▸ **COLLOCATIONS:**
  similar **to/in** *something*
  similar in **size/style**
  a similar **situation/incident/amount**
  similar **circumstances**
  strikingly/remarkably similar
▸ **SYNONYM:** alike
▸ **ANTONYM:** different

simi|lar|ly /ˈsɪmɪləli/

ADVERB ○ We tend to think and react similarly to people our own age. ○ Most of the men who now gathered round him again were similarly dressed.

▶ **COLLOCATIONS:**
  behave/react/respond similarly
  similarly **dressed/sized**
▶ **ANTONYM:** differently

simi|lar|ity /ˌsɪmɪˈlærɪti/ (similarities)

NOUN ○ [+ in] There was a very basic similarity in our philosophy. ○ The film bears some similarities to Spielberg's 'A.I.' ○ [+ between] The similarities between Mars and Earth were enough to keep alive hopes of some form of Martian life.

▶ **COLLOCATIONS:**
  similarity **to/in** something
  similarities **between** things
  bear a similarity to something
  share similarities
  a **striking/remarkable/uncanny/superficial** similarity
▶ **ANTONYM:** difference

---

sim|ple /ˈsɪmpəl/ (simpler, simplest)

1 ADJECTIVE If you describe something as **simple**, you mean that it is not complicated, and is therefore easy to understand. ○ a simple mathematical task ○ pages of simple advice on filling in your tax form ○ Buddhist ethics are simple but its practices are very complex to a western mind.

▶ **COLLOCATIONS:**
  a simple **question/answer/solution/explanation/fact/reason**
  a simple **task/method/procedure**
  simple **to use/understand/operate**
  fairly/relatively/comparatively simple
  deceptively/seemingly simple
  keep/make something simple
▶ **PHRASE:** plain and simple
▶ **SYNONYM:** straightforward
▶ **ANTONYM:** complicated

2 ADJECTIVE If you describe people or things as **simple**, you mean that they have all the basic or necessary things they require, but nothing extra. ○ He ate a simple dinner of rice and beans. ○ the simple pleasures of childhood ○ Nothing is simpler than a cool white shirt.

▶ **COLLOCATION:** a simple **life/pleasure**
▶ **SYNONYMS:** basic, plain
▶ **ANTONYMS:** ornate, elaborate

simp|ly /'sɪmpli/

ADVERB ○ *When applying for a visa, state simply and clearly the reasons why you need it.* ○ *The living room is furnished simply with wicker furniture.*

▶ **COLLOCATIONS:**
  reply/answer/explain simply
  state/say *something* simply
  live/dress simply
▶ **SYNONYM:** plainly

sim|plic|ity /sɪm'plɪsɪti/

UNCOUNTABLE NOUN ○ [+ *of*] *The apparent simplicity of his plot is deceptive.*
○ *Because of its simplicity, this test could be carried out easily by a family doctor.*

▶ **COLLOCATIONS:**
  the simplicity **of** *something*
  the simplicity of a **design/solution/approach**
  deceptive/rustic/stark/elegant simplicity
▶ **SYNONYMS:** clarity, straightforwardness
▶ **ANTONYMS:** complexity, difficulty

---

sin|gle /'sɪŋgəl/

1 ADJECTIVE You use **single** to emphasize that you are referring to one thing, and no more than one thing. ○ *A single shot rang out.* ○ *Over six hundred people were wounded in a single day.* ○ *She hadn't uttered a single word.*
▶ **COLLOCATION:** a single **shot/day/thing/word**

2 ADJECTIVE Someone who is **single** is not married. You can also use **single** to describe someone who does not have a girlfriend or boyfriend.
○ *financial support for single mothers* ○ *Gay men are now eligible to become foster parents whether they are single or have partners.*
▶ **COLLOCATION:** a single **parent/person/woman/mother**
▶ **ANTONYM:** married

---

site /saɪt/ (sites)

ACADEMIC WORD

1 NOUN A **site** is a piece of ground that is used for a particular purpose or where a particular thing happens. ○ *He became a hod carrier on a building site.* ○ *a bat sanctuary with special nesting sites*

▶ **COLLOCATIONS:**
  a **construction/building** site
  a **landfill/burial/caravan** site
  a **nesting/heritage** site

2 NOUN The **site of** an important event is the place where it happened.
○ [+ *of*] *Scientists have described the Aral sea as the site of the worst ecological*

disaster on Earth. ○ *Plymouth Hoe is renowned as the site where Drake played bowls before tackling the Spanish Armada.*

▶ **COLLOCATION:** the site **of** *something*
▶ **SYNONYMS:** position, spot, location
→ see note at **sight**

---

situa|tion /ˌsɪtʃʊ'eɪʃən/ (situations)

NOUN You use **situation** to refer generally to what is happening in a particular place at a particular time, or to refer to what is happening to you. ○ *Army officers said the situation was under control.* ○ *The local authority faced a difficult financial situation.* ○ *If you want to improve your situation you must adopt a positive mental attitude.*

▶ **COLLOCATIONS:**
   the **current/present** situation
   a **financial/economic/political** situation
   a **dangerous/difficult/tense** situation
   describe/discuss a situation
   handle/improve/understand a situation
   a situation **improves/changes/deteriorates**
▶ **SYNONYM:** circumstances

---

skill /skɪl/ (skills)

NOUN A **skill** is a type of work or activity which requires special training and knowledge. ○ *an opportunity to learn new computer skills* ○ *Trainees will be taught basic practical skills.*

▶ **COLLOCATIONS:**
   learn/acquire/develop/teach a skill
   a **basic/essential/technical/practical/transferable** skill
   communication/interpersonal/literacy/numeracy skills
   a skills **shortage/gap**
   skills **development/training**
▶ **SYNONYMS:** ability, technique

skilled /skɪld/

ADJECTIVE **Skilled** work can only be done by people who have had some training. ○ *New industries demanded skilled labour not available locally.* ○ *skilled workers, such as plumbers and electricians*

▶ **COLLOCATIONS:**
   skilled **labour**
   a skilled **job/worker**
   highly skilled
▶ **ANTONYM:** unskilled

S

skim /skɪm/ (skims, skimming, skimmed)

ACADEMIC WORD

VERB If you **skim** a piece of writing, you read through it quickly. ○ *He skimmed the pages quickly, then read them again more carefully.* ○ *[+ through] I only had time to skim through the script before I flew over here.*

- ▶ **COLLOCATION:** skim **through** *something*
- ▶ **SYNONYMS:** scan, browse
- ▶ **ANTONYMS:** pore over, examine
- ▶ **RELATED WORD:** scan

slight /slaɪt/ (slighter, slightest)

ADJECTIVE Something that is **slight** is very small in degree or quantity. ○ *Doctors say he has made a slight improvement.* ○ *a slight increase in the cost of a new car* ○ *He's not the slightest bit worried.*

- ▶ **COLLOCATIONS:**
  a slight **increase/decrease/variation**
  a slight **improvement**
  a slight **breeze/smile**
- ▶ **SYNONYM:** small
- ▶ **ANTONYM:** large

slight|ly /ˈslaɪtli/

ADVERB Slightly means to some degree but not to a very large degree. ○ *The pattern is slightly different each year.* ○ *The temperature is slightly above freezing.* ○ *Oil prices rose slightly.*

- ▶ **COLLOCATIONS:**
  slightly **above/below** *something*
  slightly **different/high/low**
  slightly **injured/wounded/hurt**
  rise/fall/differ slightly
- ▶ **ANTONYMS:** very, a lot

so|ci|ety /səˈsaɪɪti/ (societies)

SOCIAL SCIENCE

1 UNCOUNTABLE NOUN Society is people in general, thought of as a large organized group. ○ *This reflects attitudes and values prevailing in society.* ○ *He maintains Islam must adapt to modern society.*

2 NOUN A **society** is the people who live in a country or region, their organizations, and their way of life. ○ *Debate is fundamental to a democratic society.* ○ *those responsible for destroying our African heritage and the fabric of our society* ○ *the complexities of South African society*

- ▶ **COLLOCATIONS:**
  modern/contemporary society

a **democratic/capitalist/industrial** society
Western/American society
▶ SYNONYM: community

so|cial /ˈsəʊʃəl/

1 ADJECTIVE Social means relating to society or to the way society is organized. ○ *the worst effects of unemployment, low pay and other social problems* ○ *long-term social change* ○ *changing social attitudes* ○ *the tightly woven social fabric of small towns*
▶ COLLOCATIONS:
social **problems/issues/change**
social **policy/justice**
▶ PHRASE: social and economic

2 ADJECTIVE Social means relating to the status or rank that someone has in society. ○ *Higher education is unequally distributed across social classes.* ○ *The guests came from all social backgrounds.*
▶ COLLOCATION: social **class/background/circle**

so|cial|ly

ADVERB ○ *Gambling has become more socially acceptable.* ○ *one of the most socially deprived areas in Britain* ○ *socially disadvantaged children*
▶ COLLOCATIONS:
socially **acceptable/unacceptable**
socially **conscious/responsible/disadvantaged**
▶ PHRASES:
socially and economically
socially and culturally

---

soft|ware /ˈsɒftweə, AM ˈsɔːf-/ [IT]

UNCOUNTABLE NOUN Computer programs are referred to as **software**. ○ *the people who write the software for big computer projects* ○ *the latest software development technologies*
▶ COLLOCATIONS:
install/use/download software
design/develop software
computer/anti-virus software
software **development**
a software **developer/firm**
▶ RELATED WORD: hardware

soil /sɔɪl/ (soils)

NOUN **Soil** is the substance on the surface of the earth in which plants grow. ○ *We have the most fertile soil in Europe.* ○ *regions with sandy soils*

▶ COLLOCATIONS:
  fertile/well-drained/rich soil
  sandy/moist/acidic/chalky soil
  soil **erosion/moisture**
  a soil **sample**

solve /sɒlv/ (solves, solving, solved)

VERB If you **solve** a problem or a question, you find a solution or an answer to it. ○ *Their domestic reforms did nothing to solve the problem of unemployment.* ○ *We may now be able to get a much better idea of the true age of the universe, and solve one of the deepest questions of our origins.*

▶ COLLOCATIONS:
  solve a **problem/conflict/crisis**
  solve a **puzzle/riddle/equation**
  attempt/try to solve *something*
▶ SYNONYM: work out

so|lu|tion /sə'lu:ʃən/ (solutions)

NOUN A **solution to** a problem or difficult situation is a way of dealing with it so that the difficulty is removed. ○ *Although he has sought to find a peaceful solution, he is facing pressure to use greater military force.* ○ *[+ to] the ability to sort out simple, effective solutions to practical problems* ○ *The real solution lay in providing affordable accommodation.*

▶ COLLOCATIONS:
  a solution **to** a problem
  a **peaceful/diplomatic/political** solution
  a **simple/ideal/temporary** solution
  the **best** solution
  find/offer/provide a solution
  the solution **lies in** *something*
▶ SYNONYM: answer

south /saʊθ/ also South

1 UNCOUNTABLE NOUN **The south** is the direction which is on your right when you are looking towards the direction where the sun rises. ○ *[+ of] The town lies ten miles to the south of here.* ○ *All around him, from east to west, north to south, the stars glittered in the heavens.*

▶ RELATED WORDS: east, west, north

2 NOUN The south of a place, country, or region is the part which is in the south. ○ [+ of] *oil production in the south of Iraq*

▶ COLLOCATIONS:
  to/in the south
  south **of** *a place*
  south of a **border**
  lie to the south
  a **mile/kilometre** to the south

▶ RELATED WORDS: east, west, north

south|ern /ˈsʌðən/

ADJECTIVE **Southern** means in or from the south of a region, state, or country. ○ *The Everglades National Park stretches across the southern tip of Florida.* ○ *a place where you can sample southern cuisine*

▶ COLLOCATIONS:
  a southern **province/region/state/city**
  a southern **shore/coast/edge/border**

▶ PHRASE: the southern hemisphere

▶ RELATED WORDS: eastern, western, northern

space /speɪs/ GEOGRAPHY

UNCOUNTABLE NOUN **Space** is the area beyond the Earth's atmosphere, where the stars and planets are. ○ *The six astronauts on board will spend ten days in space.* ○ *launching satellites into space* ○ *pictures of the Earth from outer space*

▶ COLLOCATIONS:
  in/into/from space
  outer space
  a space **shuttle/station/probe/capsule**
  space **exploration/travel**

spe|cies /ˈspiːʃiz/ (species) SCIENCE BIOLOGY

NOUN A **species** is a class of plants or animals whose members have the same main characteristics and are able to breed with each other. ○ *Pandas are an endangered species.* ○ *There are several thousand species of trees here.*

▶ COLLOCATIONS:
  a species **of** *something*
  a species **of fish/bird/plant/animal**
  a **rare/endangered/threatened/protected** species
  the **human** species
  a **plant/fish/bird** species

▶ SYNONYM: breed

speed /spiːd/ **(speeds)**

1 NOUN The **speed** of something is the rate at which it moves or travels. ○ *He drove off at high speed.* ○ *An electrical pulse in a wire travels close to the speed of light.* ○ *Wind speeds reached force five.*

2 NOUN The **speed** of something is the rate at which it happens or is done. ○ *In the late 1850s the speed of technological change quickened.* ○ *Each learner can proceed at his own speed.*

▶ **COLLOCATIONS:**
the speed **of** *something*
at a speed of *x*
the speed of **light/sound**
top/high/cruising speed
wind speed
a speed **camera/limit**
gather speed
reach a speed of *x*

▶ **SYNONYMS:** rate, pace

spread /spred/ **(spreads, spreading, spread)**

1 VERB If something **spreads** or **is spread** by people, it gradually reaches or affects a larger and larger area or more and more people. ○ *The industrial revolution which started a couple of hundred years ago in Europe is now spreading across the world.* ○ *the sense of fear spreading in residential neighbourhoods* ○ *He was fed-up with the lies being spread about him.*

● **Spread** is also an uncountable noun. ○ *The greatest hope for reform is the gradual spread of information.* ○ *Thanks to the spread of modern technology, trained workers are now more vital than ever.*

2 VERB If something such as a liquid, gas, or smoke **spreads** or **is spread**, it moves outwards in all directions so that it covers a larger area. ○ *Fire spread rapidly after a chemical truck exploded.* ○ *A dark red stain was spreading across his shirt.* ○ *In Northern California, a wildfire has spread a haze of smoke over 200 miles.*

● **Spread** is also an uncountable noun. ○ *The situation was complicated by the spread of a serious forest fire.*

▶ **COLLOCATIONS:**
the spread **of** *something*
the spread of **disease**
spread **gossip/lies/the word**
spread a **rumour/virus/disease/infection**
a **virus/disease** spreads

word spreads that...
prevent/stop/halt the spread of *something*
wide/rapid/global spread
spread **evenly/thinly**
▶ SYNONYM: circulate
▶ ANTONYM: contain

---

square /skweə/ (squares)

1 NOUN A **square** is a shape with four sides that are all the same length and four corners that are all right angles. ○ *Serve the cake warm or at room temperature, cut in squares.* ○ *Most of the rugs are simple cotton squares.*

2 ADJECTIVE Something that is **square** has a shape the same as a square or similar to a square. ○ *Round tables seat more people in the same space as a square table.* ○ *His finger nails were square and cut neatly across.*

---

staff /stɑːf, stæf/   BUSINESS

NOUN The **staff** of an organization are the people who work for it. ○ *The staff were very good.* ○ *[+ of] the nursing staff of the hospital* ○ *It has 75 members of staff based at its London office.*

▶ COLLOCATIONS:
   the staff **of** *something*
   the staff of a **department/organization/office**
   the **medical/coaching/hospital/security** staff
   recruit/employ/hire/train/take on staff
   shed/cut/sack staff
▶ PHRASE: a member of staff
▶ SYNONYMS: employees, workforce, workers

> USAGE: Group noun
>
> **Staff** is a group noun (like 'team' and 'family') and it refers to a group of people who work somewhere. You use **the staff** to talk about all the people who work in a place or for an organization. ○ *the hotel's security staff*
>
> You can use a plural or singular verb after **staff**. The plural form is more common. ○ *The embassy staff was/were ordered to leave.*
>
> You also use **staff** to talk about some of the people who work somewhere. You do not say 'staffs' and you use a plural verb. ○ *A hundred extra staff were taken on.* ○ *Several senior staff have left.*
>
> You do not refer to an individual person as 'a staff'. You can say a **member of staff** or a **staff member**. ○ *Report any problems to a member of staff.* ○ *She was the only staff member at the station at the time.*

S

stage /steɪdʒ/ (stages)

NOUN A **stage of** an activity, process, or period is one part of it. ○ [+ of] *The way children talk about or express their feelings depends on their age and stage of development.* ○ *Mr Cook has arrived in Greece on the final stage of a tour which also included Egypt and Israel.*

▶ **COLLOCATIONS:**
a stage **of** *something*
a stage of **development/evolution/pregnancy**
a stage of a **competition/tournament**
a stage of a **cycle/process**

▶ **PHRASE:** in the early stages

▶ **SYNONYMS:** period, phase

state /steɪt/ (states)   GEOGRAPHY   SOCIAL SCIENCE

1 NOUN You can refer to countries as **states**, particularly when you are discussing politics. ○ *Mexico is a secular state and does not have diplomatic relations with the Vatican.* ○ *Some weeks ago I recommended to E.U. member states that we should have discussions with the Americans.*

→ see note at **country**

▶ **COLLOCATIONS:**
a **Palestinian/Arab/Jewish/Baltic/African** state
a **sovereign/communist/democratic/independent/rogue** state

▶ **SYNONYM:** country

2 NOUN Some large countries such as the USA are divided into smaller areas called **states**. ○ *Leaders of the Southern states are meeting in Louisville.* ○ *New York State*

▶ **COLLOCATIONS:**
state **legislature/law**
a state **attorney/department**
a **Democratic/Republican** state

sta|tis|tic /stəˈtɪstɪk/ (statistics)   ACADEMIC WORD   MATHS

NOUN **Statistics** are facts which are obtained from analysing information expressed in numbers, for example information about the number of times that something happens. ○ *Official statistics show real wages declining by 24%.* ○ [+ for] *There are no reliable statistics for the number of deaths in the battle.*

▶ **COLLOCATIONS:**
statistics **for** *something*
official statistics
economic/national statistics

statistics **show/indicate/reveal/suggest** *something*
compile/collect statistics
release/publish statistics
▶ SYNONYMS: figure, number

sta|tis|ti|cal /stə'tɪstɪkəl/

ADJECTIVE ○ *The report contains a great deal of statistical information.*
▶ COLLOCATIONS:
statistical **analysis**
statistical **data/evidence/figures/information**
statistical **significance/probability/correlation**
a statistical **method/technique**
▶ SYNONYM: numerical

stem /stem/ (stems)
`SCIENCE` `BIOLOGY`

NOUN The **stem** of a plant is the thin, upright part on which the flowers and leaves grow. ○ *He stooped down, cut the stem for her with his knife and handed her the flower.* ○ *Tansy has a tall leafy stem and ferny foliage.*
▶ COLLOCATIONS:
the stem **of** a plant
the **main** stem
a **thick/thorny/slender** stem
cut/remove a stem
▶ SYNONYMS: stalk, shoot

step /step/ (steps)

1 NOUN A **step** is one of a series of actions that you take in order to achieve something. ○ [+ towards] *He greeted the agreement as the first step towards peace.* ○ [+ to-inf] *She is not content with her present lot and wishes to take steps to improve it.* ○ *The elections were a step in the right direction, but there is a lot more to be done.*

2 NOUN A **step** in a process is one of a series of stages. ○ [+ to-inf] *The next step is to put the theory into practice.* ○ *Aristotle took the scientific approach a step further.*
▶ COLLOCATIONS:
a step **towards** *something*
take steps
a **logical/important/necessary/significant** step
the **first/next** step
a step **further**
▶ PHRASE: a step in the right direction
▶ SYNONYM: stage

store /stɔː/ (stores, storing, stored)   `IT`

VERB When you **store** information, you keep it in your memory, in a file, or in a computer. ○ *Where in the brain do we store information about colours?* ○ *chips for storing data in electronic equipment*

▶ COLLOCATIONS:
  store **data/information**
  store a **file/email/image**
  a **file/database/computer/brain** stores *things*

▶ SYNONYMS: save, keep
▶ ANTONYM: delete

stor|age /'stɔːrɪdʒ/

UNCOUNTABLE NOUN Storage is the process of storing data in a computer. ○ *[+ of] His task is to ensure the fair use and storage of personal information held on computer.* ○ *data-storage devices*

▶ COLLOCATIONS:
  storage **of** *something*
  storage of **data/information**
  data storage
  removable/built-in storage
  storage **capacity/space**

---

straight /streɪt/ (straighter, straightest)

ADJECTIVE A **straight** line or edge continues in the same direction and does not bend or curve. ○ *Using the straight edge as a guide, trim the cloth to size.* ○ *There wasn't a single straight wall in the building.*

● **Straight** is also an adverb. ○ *Stand straight and stretch the left hand to the right foot.*

▶ COLLOCATIONS:
  a straight **line/road/path/edge/wall**
  straight **hair**
  go/head/walk/stand straight

▶ ANTONYMS: curvy, curved, bent, wavy, twisted

straight|en /'streɪtən/ (straightens, straightening, straightened)

VERB If you **straighten** something, or it **straightens**, it becomes straight. ○ *Straighten both legs until they are fully extended.* ○ *The road straightened and we were on a plateau.*

▶ COLLOCATIONS:
  straighten **hair/teeth**
  straighten **legs/knees/arms**

a **road** straightens
▶ ANTONYMS: curve, bend, twist

---

strict /strɪkt/ (stricter, strictest)

ADJECTIVE A **strict** rule or order is very clear and precise or severe and must always be obeyed completely. ○ *The officials had issued strict instructions that we were not to get out of the jeep.* ○ *French privacy laws are very strict.* ○ *All your replies will be treated in the strictest confidence.*
▶ COLLOCATIONS:
   a strict **rule/instruction/law/guideline/regulation/limit**
   a strict **diet**
   strict **adherence** to *something*
▶ PHRASE: in strict confidence
▶ SYNONYMS: austere, severe
▶ ANTONYMS: lax, lenient

---

strike /straɪk/ (strikes, striking, struck)   BUSINESS   SOCIAL SCIENCE

1 NOUN When there is a **strike**, workers stop doing their work for a period of time, usually in order to try to get better pay or conditions for themselves. ○ *French air traffic controllers have begun a three-day strike in a dispute over pay.* ○ *Staff at the hospital went on strike in protest at the incidents.* ○ *a call for strike action*
▶ COLLOCATIONS:
   be **on** strike
   go/go out on strike
   call/stage a strike
   a **one-day/24-hour/48-hour** strike
   a **general/rail** strike
   a **miner's/firefighter's/teacher's** strike
   strike **action**
▶ SYNONYM: industrial action

2 VERB When workers **strike**, they go on strike. ○ *their recognition of the workers' right to strike* ○ [+ for] *They shouldn't be striking for more money.* ○ [V-ing] *The government agreed not to sack any of the striking workers.*
▶ COLLOCATIONS:
   strike **for** *something*
   strike for **higher pay/wages**
▶ SYNONYMS: go on strike, picket, protest

strik|er /ˈstraɪkə/ (strikers)

NOUN ○ *The strikers want higher wages, which state governments say they can't afford.*

▶ **SYNONYM:** protester

---

strong /strɒŋ, ᴀᴍ strɔːŋ/ (stronger, strongest)

1 ADJECTIVE Strong objects or materials are not easily broken and can support a lot of weight or resist a lot of strain. ○ *The vacuum flask has a strong casing, which won't crack or chip.* ○ *Glue the mirror in with a strong adhesive.*

▶ **SYNONYM:** sturdy
▶ **ANTONYMS:** weak, fragile

2 ADJECTIVE If you have **strong** opinions on something or express them using **strong** words, you have extreme or very definite opinions which you are willing to express or defend. ○ *She is known to hold strong views on Cuba.* ○ *There has been strong criticism of the military regime.* ○ *It condemned in extremely strong language what it called Britain's iniquitous campaign.*

▶ **COLLOCATIONS:**
strong **support/criticism/language/words**
a strong **supporter/view/feeling/position**
▶ **ANTONYM:** mild

strength /strɛŋθ/

1 UNCOUNTABLE NOUN The **strength** of an object or material is its ability to be treated roughly, or to carry heavy weights, without being damaged or destroyed. ○ [+ of] *He checked the strength of the cables.* ○ *the properties of a material, such as strength or electrical conductivity*

▶ **COLLOCATION:** the strength **of** something
▶ **ANTONYM:** weakness

2 UNCOUNTABLE NOUN The **strength** of a person, organization, or country is the power or influence that they have. ○ *America values its economic leadership, and the political and military strength that goes with it.* ○ *The Alliance in its first show of strength drew a hundred thousand-strong crowd to a rally.* ○ *They have their own independence movement which is gathering strength.*

▶ **COLLOCATIONS:**
a **show of** strength
military/economic/political strength
gather/gain strength
▶ **SYNONYM:** power

3 **UNCOUNTABLE NOUN** If you refer to the **strength of** a feeling, opinion, or belief, you are talking about how deeply it is felt or believed by people, or how much they are influenced by it. ○ [+ *of*] *He was surprised at the strength of his own feeling.* ○ [+ *of*] *What makes a mayor successful in Los Angeles is the strength of his public support.*
  ▶ **COLLOCATION:** the strength **of** *something*
  ▶ **SYNONYMS:** intensity, depth

---

struc|ture /ˈstrʌktʃə/ ACADEMIC WORD
(structures, structuring, structured)

1 **UNCOUNTABLE NOUN** The **structure of** something is the way in which it is made, built, or organized. ○ [+ *of*] *The typical family structure of Freud's patients involved two parents and two children.* ○ [+ *of*] *The chemical structure of this particular molecule is very unusual.*
  ▶ **COLLOCATIONS:**
    the structure **of** *something*
    the structure of a **molecule/protein/atom**
    organizational/hierarchical structure
    social/management structure
    the structure of **society**
  ▶ **SYNONYMS:** organization, arrangement

2 **VERB** If you **structure** something, you arrange it in a careful, organized pattern or system. ○ *By structuring the course this way, we're forced to produce something the companies think is valuable.*
  ▶ **COLLOCATIONS:**
    structure a **narrative/essay**
    structure a **course/examination/curriculum**
    society is structured
    tightly/rigidly/loosely/hierarchically structured
  ▶ **SYNONYM:** organize

struc|tur|al /ˈstrʌktʃərəl/

ADJECTIVE ○ *The explosion caused little structural damage to the office towers themselves.* ○ *structural reform such as privatisation*
  ▶ **COLLOCATIONS:**
    structural **change/reform/damage**
    structural **weakness/integrity**

---

study /ˈstʌdi/ **(studies, studying, studied)** EDUCATION ACADEMIC STUDY

1 **VERB** If you **study**, you spend time learning about a particular subject or subjects. ○ *a relaxed and happy atmosphere that will allow you to study to your* *full potential* ○ *He went to Hull University, where he studied History and Economics.* ○ [+ *for*] *The rehearsals make it difficult for her to study for law school exams.*

→ see note at **learn**

▶ **COLLOCATIONS:**
   study **for** *something*
   study for a **degree/doctorate/PhD/exam**
   study a **subject**
   study **medicine/engineering/psychology**
   study **part-time/full-time/abroad**

▶ **SYNONYMS:** learn, read

2 UNCOUNTABLE NOUN Study is the activity of studying. ○ *the use of maps and visual evidence in the study of local history* ○ *She gave up her studies to have Alexander.*

▶ **COLLOCATION:** the study **of** *something*

3 NOUN A **study** of a subject is a piece of research on it. ○ *Recent studies suggest that as many as 5 in 1000 new mothers are likely to have this problem.* ○ [+ *of*] *the first study of English children's attitudes*

▶ **COLLOCATIONS:**
   a study **of** *something*
   a study **shows/suggests/indicates** *something*
   a **recent/detailed study**
   a **scientific/clinical** study

▶ **SYNONYM:** analysis

4 VERB If you **study** something, you consider it or observe it carefully in order to be able to understand it fully. ○ *I know that you've been studying chimpanzees for thirty years now.* ○ *I invite every citizen to carefully study the document.*

▶ **COLLOCATIONS:**
   researchers/scientists/experts study *things*
   study *something* **carefully/intently**
   study the **effects of** *something*
   study a **document/map**

▶ **SYNONYMS:** analyze, examine

stu|dent /ˈstjuːdənt, ˈstuː-/ (students)

NOUN A **student** is a person who is studying at a university or college. ○ *Warren's eldest son is an art student, at St Martin's.* ○ *a 23-year-old medical student*

▶ **COLLOCATIONS:**
   a student **of** *something*

a **college/university/graduate/postgraduate/PhD** student
a **mature/foreign/overseas** student
a student **loan/grant**
student **accommodation**
▶ **RELATED WORD:** pupil

---

sub|ject /ˈsʌbdʒɪkt/ (subjects)   EDUCATION   ACADEMIC STUDY

1 NOUN The **subject** of something such as a conversation, letter, or book is the thing that is being discussed or written about. ○ [+ of] *It was I who first raised the subject of plastic surgery.* ○ *the president's own views on the subject* ○ *non-fiction books which covered subjects like handicrafts and leisure pursuits*

▶ **COLLOCATIONS:**
the subject **of** something
a subject of **debate/discussion**
broach/raise a subject
change the subject
cover a subject
a **taboo/sensitive/thorny/controversial** subject

▶ **SYNONYM:** topic

2 NOUN A **subject** is an area of knowledge or study, especially one that you study at school, college, or university. ○ *a tutor in maths and science subjects* ○ *Students must study six academic subjects over two years.*

▶ **COLLOCATIONS:**
teach/study a subject
an **academic/vocational/compulsory** subject
a **science/arts** subject

---

sub|stance /ˈsʌbstəns/ (substances)   SCIENCE   CHEMISTRY

NOUN A **substance** is a solid, powder, liquid, or gas with particular properties. ○ *There's absolutely no regulation of cigarettes to make sure that they don't include poisonous substances.* ○ *The substance that's causing the problem comes from the barley.*

▶ **COLLOCATIONS:**
a **toxic/hazardous/poisonous** substance
a **banned/illegal** substance
a **chemical/powdery/waxy/oily** substance

▶ **PHRASE:** substance abuse

---

sub|tract /səbˈtrækt/ (subtracts, subtracting, subtracted)   MATHS

VERB If you **subtract** one number **from** another, you do a calculation in which you take it away from the other number. For example, if you subtract 3 from 5, you get 2. ○ [+ *from*] *Mandy subtracted the date of birth from the date of death.* ○ *We have subtracted $25 per adult to arrive at a basic room rate.*

▶ **COLLOCATIONS:**
  subtract *something* **from** *something*
  subtract a **number/value/cost**
▶ **SYNONYM:** take away
▶ **ANTONYM:** add

sub|trac|tion /səb'trækʃən/ (subtractions)

NOUN ○ *She's ready to learn simple addition and subtraction.* ○ *I looked at what he'd given me and did a quick subtraction.*

▶ **COLLOCATION: do** a subtraction
▶ **PHRASE:** addition and subtraction
▶ **ANTONYM:** addition

suc|ceed /sək'siːd/ (succeeds, succeeding, succeeded)

1 VERB If you **succeed**, or if you **succeed in** doing something, you achieve the result that you wanted. ○ [+ *in*] *We have already succeeded in working out ground rules with the Department of Defense.* ○ [+ *in*] *Some people will succeed in their efforts to stop smoking.* ○ *the skills and qualities needed to succeed in small and medium-sized businesses*

2 VERB If something **succeeds**, it works in a satisfactory way or has the result that is intended. ○ *If marriage is to succeed in the 1990's, then people have to recognise the new pressures it is facing.* ○ *a move which would make any future talks even more unlikely to succeed*

▶ **COLLOCATIONS:**
  succeed **in/as** *something*
  a **bid/negotiation/experiment** succeeds
  succeed **admirably/brilliantly/academically**
  finally/eventually succeed
▶ **SYNONYMS:** accomplish, manage
▶ **ANTONYM:** fail

suc|cess /sək'ses/

UNCOUNTABLE NOUN Success is the achievement of something that you have been trying to do. ○ [+ *of*] *the success of European business in building a stronger partnership between management and workers* ○ *Nearly all of the young people interviewed believed that work was the key to success.*

▶ **COLLOCATIONS:**
  the success **of** *something*
  success **as** *something*

enjoy/achieve/taste success
success **depends on/lies in** *something*
huge/great success
the success **rate**

▶ PHRASES:
the key to success
success or failure

suc|cess|ful /sək'sesfʊl/

ADJECTIVE Someone or something that is **successful** achieves a desired result or performs in a satisfactory way. ○ *I am looking forward to a long and successful partnership with him.* ○ *[+ in] Women do not necessarily have to imitate men to be successful in business.* ○ *She is a successful lawyer.*

▶ COLLOCATIONS:
be successful **in/as** *something*
hugely/highly/enormously successful
commercially/financially successful
a successful **career/launch/campaign**
a successful **outcome/conclusion**
a successful **businessman/businesswoman/applicant**
prove/become successful

▶ ANTONYM: unsuccessful

---

suf|fer /'sʌfə/ (suffers, suffering, suffered)

1 VERB If you **suffer** pain or an illness, or if you **suffer from** a pain or illness, you are badly affected by it. ○ *Within a few days she had become seriously ill, suffering great pain and discomfort.* ○ *Can you assure me that my father is not suffering?* ○ *[+ from] He was eventually diagnosed as suffering from terminal cancer.*

▶ COLLOCATIONS:
suffer **from** *something*
suffer from a **disorder/illness/disease**
suffer from **depression/asthma/diabetes**
a **patient/victim** suffers
suffer **pain/damage**
suffer a **breakdown/attack/injury**
suffer **greatly/terribly/badly**

▶ SYNONYMS: be in pain, be affected

2 VERB If you **suffer** or **suffer** something bad, you are in a situation in which something harmful or very unpleasant happens to you. ○ *The peace process has suffered a serious blow now.* ○ *There are few who have not suffered.* ○ *[+ from] It is obvious that Syria will suffer most from this change of heart.*

▶ **COLLOCATIONS:**
suffer **from** *something*
suffer a **blow/setback**
a **reputation/economy** suffers
▶ **PHRASE:** suffer the same fate as something
▶ **SYNONYMS:** endure, experience

suf|fer|ing /ˈsʌfərɪŋ/

UNCOUNTABLE NOUN Suffering is serious pain which someone feels in their body or their mind. ○ *It has caused terrible suffering to animals.* ○ [+ *of*] *His many novels have portrayed the sufferings of his race.*

▶ **COLLOCATIONS:**
the suffering **of** *something*
the suffering of **people/civilians/animals**
cause/inflict suffering
alleviate/relieve/ease suffering
human/physical/mental suffering
unnecessary/untold/terrible suffering
▶ **PHRASES:**
long-suffering
pain and suffering
▶ **SYNONYMS:** pain, torment, agony

suf|fer|er /ˈsʌfərə/ **(sufferers)**

NOUN A **sufferer from** an illness or some other bad condition is a person who is affected by the illness or condition. ○ [+ *of*] *Frequently sufferers of this kind of allergy are also sufferers of asthma.* ○ *hay-fever sufferers*

▶ **COLLOCATIONS:**
a sufferer **of/from** *something*
a **migraine/asthma/cancer** sufferer
a **fellow** sufferer
▶ **SYNONYMS:** patient, victim

---

sug|gest /səˈdʒest, AM səɡˈdʒɜ-/ **(suggests, suggesting, suggested)**

VERB If you **suggest** something, you put forward a plan or idea for someone to think about. ○ *He suggested a link between class size and test results of seven-year-olds.* ○ [+ *to*] *I suggested to Mike that we go out for a meal with his colleagues.* ○ [+ *how*] *No one has suggested how this might occur.*

▶ **COLLOCATIONS:**
suggest *something* **to** *someone*
suggest a **possibility/solution/idea**

suggest a **compromise/alternative**
▶ SYNONYM: propose

sug|ges|tion /sə'dʒestʃən, AM səg'dʒ-/ (suggestions)

NOUN If you make a **suggestion**, you put forward an idea or plan for someone to think about. ○ *The dietitian was helpful, making suggestions as to how I could improve my diet.* ○ [+ of] *Perhaps he'd followed her suggestion of a stroll to the river.*

▶ COLLOCATIONS:
a suggestion **of/for** something
suggestions for **improvement**
make/have/offer/put forward a suggestion
dismiss/reject/welcome a suggestion
a **constructive/practical** suggestion

▶ SYNONYMS: proposal, recommendation, idea, plan

---

suit|able /'su:təbəl/

ADJECTIVE Someone or something that is **suitable for** a particular purpose or occasion is right or acceptable for it. ○ [+ for] *Employers usually decide within five minutes whether someone is suitable for the job.* ○ *The authority must make suitable accommodation available to the family.*

▶ COLLOCATIONS:
suitable **for** something
eminently/perfectly/particularly suitable
a suitable **candidate/applicant**
a suitable **location/venue/site**
a suitable **alternative/substitute**

▶ SYNONYMS: appropriate, right
▶ ANTONYMS: unsuitable, inappropriate, inappropriate

suit|ably /'su:təbli/

ADVERB ○ *There are problems in recruiting suitably qualified scientific officers for NHS laboratories.* ○ *Unfortunately I'm not suitably dressed for gardening.*

▶ COLLOCATION: suitably **qualified/equipped/dressed**
▶ SYNONYM: appropriately
▶ ANTONYMS: unsuitably, inappropriately

suit|abil|ity /ˌsu:tə'bɪlɪti/

UNCOUNTABLE NOUN ○ [+ of] *information on the suitability of a product for use in the home* ○ [+ for] *There are some who doubt his suitability for the job.*

▶ COLLOCATIONS:
the suitability **of** something

something's suitability **for** something

assess/question the suitability of something

▶ SYNONYM: fitness

▶ ANTONYM: unsuitability

---

super|vise /ˈsuːpəvaɪz/ (supervises, supervising, supervised) `BUSINESS`

1 VERB If you **supervise** an activity or a person, you make sure that the activity is done correctly or that the person is doing a task or behaving correctly. ○ University teachers have refused to supervise students' examinations. ○ He supervised and trained more than 400 volunteers.

2 VERB If you **supervise** a place where work is done, you ensure that the work there is done properly. ○ He makes the wines and supervises the vineyards.

▶ COLLOCATIONS:

supervise the **installation/construction/preparation** of something

supervise a **transition/operation**

supervise **properly/adequately**

be supervised by a **teacher/manager/coach/adult**

▶ SYNONYMS: oversee, direct

super|vi|sion /ˌsuːpəˈvɪʒən/

UNCOUNTABLE NOUN ○ A toddler requires close supervision and firm control at all times. ○ [+ of] The plan calls for a cease-fire and U.N. supervision of the country. ○ First-time licence holders have to work under supervision.

▶ COLLOCATIONS:

the supervision **of** something

be **under** supervision

parental/medical/adult supervision

close/strict/constant/proper supervision

exercise/provide/receive/need supervision

▶ SYNONYMS: control, management

super|vi|sor /ˈsuːpəvaɪzə/ (supervisors)

NOUN A **supervisor** is a person who supervises activities or people, especially workers or students. ○ a full-time job as a supervisor at a factory ○ Each student has a supervisor to advise on the writing of the dissertation.

---

sup|port /səˈpɔːt/ (supports, supporting, supported)

1 VERB If you **support** someone or their ideas or aims, you agree with them, and perhaps help them because you want them to succeed. ○ The vice president insisted that he supported the hard-working people of New York.

○ *The National Union of Mineworkers pressed the party to support a total ban on imported coal.*

▶ COLLOCATIONS:
  support a **proposal/effort/idea/war/ban**
  support **legislation**
  strongly/actively/fully/wholeheartedly support

▶ SYNONYMS: back, endorse

▶ ANTONYM: oppose

● **Support** is also an uncountable noun. ○ *The prime minister gave his full support to the government's reforms.* ○ *They are prepared to resort to violence in support of their beliefs.*

▶ COLLOCATIONS:
  support **for** something
  give/offer support
  full/strong/public support

▶ PHRASE: in support of

▶ SYNONYMS: backing, endorsement

▶ ANTONYM: opposition

2 UNCOUNTABLE NOUN Financial **support** is money provided to enable an organization to continue. This money is usually provided by the government. ○ *the government's proposal to cut agricultural support by only about 15%*

▶ COLLOCATIONS:
  support **for** something/someone
  financial/material support
  provide/withdraw support

▶ SYNONYM: funding

3 VERB If you **support** someone, you provide them with money or the things that they need. ○ *I have children to support, money to be earned, and a home to be maintained.* ○ *She sold everything she'd ever bought in order to support herself through art school.*

▶ COLLOCATION: support **children/a family**

▶ SYNONYMS: finance, fund

sup|port|er /sə'pɔːtə/ (supporters)

NOUN Supporters are people who support someone or something, for example a political leader or a sports team. ○ *The fourth night of violence in the German city of Rostock was triggered by football supporters.* ○ *Bradley was a major supporter of the 1986 tax reform plan.*

▸ COLLOCATIONS:
a supporter **of** something
a **major/staunch/keen/loyal** supporter
▸ SYNONYMS: proponent, fan
▸ ANTONYM: opponent

---

sur|round /sə'raʊnd/ (surrounds, surrounding, surrounded)

VERB If a person or thing **is surrounded** by something, that thing is situated all around them. ○ *The small churchyard was surrounded by a rusted wrought-iron fence.* ○ *The shell surrounding the egg has many important functions.* ○ *[V-ing] the snipers and artillerymen in the surrounding hills*
▸ COLLOCATIONS:
the surrounding **area/countryside/hills**
surrounded by a **fence/wall/forest**
surrounded by **buildings/trees/gardens**
completely/entirely/partially surrounded
▸ SYNONYMS: enclose, encompass

---

sur|vive /sə'vaɪv/ (survives, surviving, survived)   `ACADEMIC WORD`

1 VERB If a person or living thing **survives** in a dangerous situation such as an accident or an illness, they do not die. ○ *Those organisms that are that are most suited to the environment will be those that will survive.* ○ *Drugs that dissolve blood clots can help people survive heart attacks.*

2 VERB If something **survives**, it continues to exist even after being in a dangerous situation or existing for a long time. ○ *When the market economy is introduced, many factories will not survive.* ○ *The chances of a planet surviving a supernova always looked terribly slim.*
▸ COLLOCATIONS:
manage to survive
survive a **crash/war/illness/ordeal/cancer**
survive the **winter**
survive a **challenge/recession**
miraculously/narrowly/somehow survive
survive **intact/unscathed**
▸ PHRASE: survive and prosper
▸ SYNONYM: live
▸ ANTONYM: die

sur|viv|al /sə'vaɪvəl/

UNCOUNTABLE NOUN ○ *companies which have been struggling for survival in the advancing recession* ○ *If cancers are spotted early there's a high chance of survival.*

S

▶ **COLLOCATIONS:**
the survival **of** something
survival **depends on** something
a **chance of/struggle for** survival
ensure/threaten survival
one's **own** survival
political/economic/long-term survival
survival **rate/instinct**

sur|vi|vor /sə'vaɪvə/ **(survivors)**

NOUN A **survivor of** a disaster, accident, or illness is someone who continues to live afterwards in spite of coming close to death. ○ [+ of] *Officials said there were no survivors of the plane crash.*

▶ **COLLOCATIONS:**
a survivor **of** something
a survivor of a **crash/massacre**
a **holocaust/cancer/crash** survivor
search for/rescue survivors
the **sole/only** survivor

symp|tom /'sɪmptəm/ **(symptoms)**   `MEDICINE`

NOUN A **symptom** of an illness is something wrong with your body or mind that is a sign of the illness. ○ [+ of] *One of the most common symptoms of schizophrenia is hearing imaginary voices.* ○ *patients with flu symptoms*

▶ **COLLOCATIONS:**
a symptom **of** something
a symptom of **flu/depression/stress**
experience/display/show symptoms
relieve/alleviate symptoms
symptoms **appear/disappear/persist**
physical/mild/severe/flu/flu-like symptoms

▶ **SYNONYM:** indication

sys|tem /'sɪstəm/ **(systems)**

1 NOUN A **system** is a way of working, organizing, or doing something which follows a fixed plan or set of rules. You can use **system** to refer to an organization or institution that is organized in this way. ○ *a flexible and relatively efficient filing system* ○ [+ of] *a multi-party system of government*

▶ **COLLOCATIONS:**
a system **of** something
a system of **government/education**

a **health/education/management/justice/banking** system
a **filing/storage** system
design/develop/implement/use a system
a system **works/operates/fails**
▶ **SYNONYMS:** arrangement, organization

2 NOUN A **system** is a set of devices powered by electricity, for example a computer or an alarm. ○ *Viruses tend to be good at surviving when a computer system crashes.*
▶ **COLLOCATIONS:**
install a system
a **computer/alarm/electronic** system

Tt

ta|ble /ˈteɪbəl/ (tables) ACADEMIC STUDY

NOUN A **table** is a written set of facts and figures arranged in columns and rows. ○ *Consult the table on page 104.* ○ *Other research supports the figures in Table 3.3.*

▶ **COLLOCATIONS:**
a table **of** something
a table of **results/data/statistics/contents**
a table **illustrates/shows/summarizes** something
▶ **SYNONYMS:** chart, figure

tack|le /ˈtækəl/ (tackles, tackling, tackled)

VERB If you **tackle** a difficult problem or task, you deal with it in a very determined or efficient way. ○ *The first reason to tackle these problems is to save children's lives.* ○ *the government's latest scheme to tackle crime*

▶ **COLLOCATIONS:**
tackle a **problem/issue/task/crisis**
tackle **crime/poverty/corruption**
▶ **SYNONYMS:** deal with, confront
▶ **ANTONYM:** ignore

tail /teɪl/ (tails) SCIENCE BIOLOGY

NOUN The **tail** of an animal, bird, or fish is the part extending beyond the end of its body. ○ *The cattle were swinging their tails to disperse the flies.* ○ *a black dog with a long tail*

▶ **COLLOCATIONS:**
an animal **wags/swings/swishes** its tail
a **bushy/curly/furry** tail

t

task /tɑːsk, tæsk/ (tasks) ACADEMIC WORD

NOUN A **task** is an activity or piece of work which you have to do, usually as part of a larger project. ○ [+ *of*] *the massive task of reconstruction after the war* ○ *She used the day to catch up with administrative tasks.*

▶ **COLLOCATIONS:**
the task **of** something
the task of **management/leadership/reconstruction**

face/undertake/accomplish/perform a task
assign/give *someone* a task
a daunting/difficult/unenviable/thankless/easy task
a household/administrative/computing task
the task ahead
▶ SYNONYMS: chore, job, assignment, duty, responsibility

---

tax /tæks/ (taxes, taxing, taxed)   BUSINESS ECONOMICS

1 NOUN **Tax** is an amount of money that you have to pay to the
government so that it can pay for public services. ○ *They are calling for large
spending cuts and tax increases.* ○ [+ on] *a cut in tax on new cars* ○ *His decision
to return to a form of property tax is the right one.*
▶ COLLOCATIONS:
a tax **on** *something*
a tax on **profits/savings/fuel/petrol/cigarettes**
income/council/poll/property/capital gains/value added tax
pay/avoid/reclaim/owe tax
impose/introduce/levy/raise/cut taxes
tax **deductible/free**
a tax **cut/break/bill/return**
tax **relief/evasion**
▶ SYNONYMS: duty, custom
▶ RELATED WORD: VAT

2 VERB When a person or company **is taxed**, they have to pay a part of
their income or profits to the government. When goods **are taxed**, a
percentage of their price has to be paid to the government. ○ *Husband and
wife are now taxed separately on their incomes.* ○ *The Bonn government taxes
profits of corporations at a rate that is among the highest in Europe.*
▶ COLLOCATIONS:
tax **income/earnings**
tax **heavily/lightly/unfairly**
taxed by the **government/state**

taxa|tion /tæk'seɪʃən/

UNCOUNTABLE NOUN **Taxation** is the system by which a government
takes money from people and spends it on things such as education,
health, and defence. ○ [+ on] *a proposal to increase taxation on fuel*
▶ COLLOCATIONS:
taxation **of/on** *something*
taxation of/on **income/dividends**
increase/raise/introduce taxation
reduce/avoid taxation

a taxation **system/policy**
income/interest/business/personal taxation
general/indirect/double taxation

teach /tiːtʃ/ (teaches, teaching, taught)   `EDUCATION`

1 **VERB** If you **teach** someone something, you give them instructions so that they know about it or how to do it. ○ *The trainers have a programme to teach them vocational skills.* ○ [+ to-inf] *the way that children are taught to read* ○ [+ to] *The computer has simplified the difficult task of teaching reading to the deaf.*

2 **VERB** If you **teach** or **teach** a subject, you help students to learn about it by explaining it or showing them how to do it, usually as a job at a school, college, or university. ○ *Ingrid is currently teaching Mathematics at Shimla Public School.* ○ [+ to] *She taught English to Japanese business people.* ○ *She has taught for 34 years.* ○ *a twelve month taught course*
→ see note at **learn**
▶ COLLOCATIONS:
teach **at/in** somewhere
teach at/in **university/college/school**
teach a **lesson/class/course/subject/skill/technique**
teach a **student/pupil/child**
teach **maths/literature/science/English/French**
teach **part-time/full-time**
▶ PHRASE: teach someone how to do something
▶ SYNONYMS: educate, instruct
▶ ANTONYM: learn

teach|er /ˈtiːtʃə/ (teachers)

NOUN A **teacher** is a person who teaches, usually as a job at a school or similar institution. ○ *a teacher with 21 years' experience* ○ *The shortage of maths teachers is a problem.*
▶ COLLOCATIONS:
a teacher **of** something
a teacher **at/in** somewhere
a teacher of **maths/literature/language**
a teacher at/in **university/college/school**
a **trained/qualified/experienced/retired** teacher
a **school/primary school/secondary school/kindergarten** teacher
a **maths/science/English/piano** teacher
a **head/principal** teacher
a **supply/substitute/full-time/part-time** teacher
teacher **training/recruitment**

a teacher **strike/shortage**
- ▶ SYNONYMS: tutor, trainer
- ▶ ANTONYMS: pupil, student

teach|ing /ˈtiːtʃɪŋ/

UNCOUNTABLE NOUN Teaching is the work that a teacher does in helping students to learn. ○ *The Government funds university teaching.* ○ [+ of] *the teaching of English in schools*
- ▶ COLLOCATIONS:
  the teaching **of** something
  the teaching of **maths/grammar/reading**
  school/classroom/college/university teaching
  maths/language teaching
  one-to-one/interactive/traditional teaching
  a teaching **method/assistant/career**
  teaching **staff**
- ▶ SYNONYM: education
- ▶ ANTONYM: learning

---

team /tiːm/ (teams) `ACADEMIC WORD`

NOUN You can refer to any group of people who work together as a **team**. ○ [+ of] *Each specialist consultant has a team of doctors under him.* ○ *The governors were joined by Mr Hunter and his management team.*
- ▶ COLLOCATIONS:
  a team **of** people
  a team of **researchers/scientists/experts/engineers**
  a **management/research/medical/professional** team
  a team **member/manager/leader**
  lead/head/join/form a team
- ▶ SYNONYMS: group, squad
- ▶ ANTONYM: individual

---

tech|ni|cal /ˈteknɪkəl/ `ACADEMIC WORD`

1 **ADJECTIVE Technical** means involving the sorts of machines, processes, and materials that are used in industry, transport, and communications. ○ *In order to reach this limit a number of technical problems will have to be solved.* ○ *jobs that require technical knowledge*
- ▶ COLLOCATIONS:
  technical **assistance/knowledge/expertise**
  a technical **problem/glitch/fault**
  highly technical
- ▶ SYNONYMS: high-tech, technological, mechanical

2 ADJECTIVE **Technical** language involves using special words to describe the details of a specialized activity. ○ *The technical term for sunburn is erythema.* ○ *He's just written a book: large format, nicely illustrated and not too technical.*

▶ COLLOCATIONS:
a technical **term/word**
technical **jargon**
→ see note at **technique**

tech|ni|cal|ly /ˈteknɪkəli/

1 ADVERB **Technically** means in a way that involves machines and processes that are used in industry. ○ *the largest and most technically advanced furnace company in the world*
▶ COLLOCATION: technically **advanced/sophisticated/skilled/proficient**
▶ SYNONYM: technologically

2 ADVERB If something is **technically** the case, it is the case according to a strict interpretation of facts, laws, or rules, but may not be important or relevant in a particular situation. ○ *Nude bathing is technically illegal but there are plenty of unspoilt beaches where no one would ever know.* ○ *Technically, the two sides have been in a state of war ever since 1949.*
▶ COLLOCATION: technically **illegal/possible/feasible/correct**
▶ SYNONYM: theoretically

---

tech|nique /tekˈniːk/ (techniques)　ACADEMIC WORD

NOUN A **technique** is a particular method of doing an activity, usually a method that involves practical skills. ○ *tests performed using a new technique* ○ *developments in the surgical techniques employed*
▶ COLLOCATIONS:
a technique **of** *something*
a technique of **analysis/management/production**
a **sophisticated/modern/innovative/traditional** technique
a **surgical/mathematical/investigative** technique
a **breathing/relaxation/survival** technique
develop/perfect/master/learn a technique
employ/use/apply a technique
▶ SYNONYMS: method, style, system, way

> **USAGE: technique, technology** or **technical**?
> A **technique** is a practical way of doing something. **Technique** is a countable noun. ○ *traditional breadmaking techniques*

Technology refers to systems, devices and methods that make use of scientific knowledge. You can use **technology** as an uncountable noun to talk about the uses of science generally. ○ *Thanks to modern technology, many people are able to work from home.*

You can also use **technology** as a countable noun to talk about particular systems and devices. ○ *the development of new technologies to produce cleaner energy*

Technological is an adjective to describe things that involve the use of new scientific ideas. ○ *the latest technological advances*

You can also use the adjective **technical** to describe things that more generally involve machines or specialist knowledge. ○ *The flight was delayed by a technical fault.* ○ *his technical skill as a painter*

tech|nol|ogy /tekˈnɒlədʒi/   ACADEMIC WORD   SCIENCE   IT
(technologies)

NOUN Technology refers to methods, systems, and devices which are the result of scientific knowledge being used for practical purposes.
○ *Technology is changing fast.* ○ *They should be allowed to wait for cheaper technologies to be developed.* ○ *nuclear weapons technology*
→ see note at **technique**
▶ COLLOCATIONS:
  develop/use/embrace technology
  advanced/modern/new technology
  the **latest** technology
  digital/wireless/mobile/nuclear technology
  information/computer technology
  technology **advances/changes/improves**
  technology **enables/allows** *something*
  the technology **sector**
▶ PHRASE: science and technology
▶ SYNONYMS: electronics, mechanization

tech|no|logi|cal /ˌteknəˈlɒdʒɪkəl/

ADJECTIVE ○ *an era of very rapid technological change* ○ *workers with technological expertise*
▶ COLLOCATIONS:
  technological **change/progress**
  a technological **advance/development/innovation/breakthrough**
  technological **expertise/know-how/capability**
▶ SYNONYM: technical

tech|no|logi|cal|ly /ˌteknəˈlɒdʒɪkli/

ADVERB ○ *technologically advanced aircraft*
  ▶ COLLOCATION: technologically **advanced/sophisticated/complex**
  ▶ SYNONYM: technically

---

tem|pera|ture /ˈtemprətʃə/ (temperatures)　[SCIENCE] [MEDICINE]

1 NOUN The **temperature** of something is a measure of how hot or cold it is. ○ *The temperature soared to above 100 degrees in the shade.* ○ *Coping with severe drops in temperature can be very difficult.*

2 NOUN Your **temperature** is the temperature of your body. A normal temperature is about 37° centigrade. ○ *His temperature continued to rise alarmingly.*
  ▶ COLLOCATIONS:
    a temperature **of** $x°$
    the temperature **reaches** $x°$
    temperatures **soar/rise/drop/plummet/plunge**
    measure/record a temperature
    sub-zero/freezing temperatures
    a **high/average/mean/maximum** temperature
    ocean/body/room temperature
  ▶ SYNONYM: heat

---

tem|po|rary /ˈtempərəri, AM -reri/　[ACADEMIC WORD] [BUSINESS]

ADJECTIVE Something that is **temporary** lasts for only a limited time. ○ *His job here is only temporary.* ○ *a temporary loss of memory*
  ▶ COLLOCATIONS:
    temporary **accommodation/shelter**
    a temporary **injunction/ban**
    a temporary **measure/reprieve/setback**
    a temporary **visa/permit**
  ▶ PHRASE: on a temporary basis
  ▶ SYNONYM: short-term
  ▶ ANTONYMS: permanent, long-term

tem|po|rari|ly /ˌtempəˈreərɪli/

ADVERB ○ *The peace agreement has at least temporarily halted the civil war.* ○ *Checkpoints between the two zones were temporarily closed.*
  ▶ COLLOCATIONS:
    temporarily **suspended/halted/closed/blocked/shut/unavailable**
    temporarily **insane/homeless/unemployed/blind**
  ▶ ANTONYM: permanently

t

tend /tend/ (tends, tending, tended)

VERB If something **tends to** happen, it usually happens or it often happens. ○ [+ to-inf] *A problem for manufacturers is that lighter cars tend to be noisy.* ○ [+ to-inf] *In older age groups women predominate because men tend to die younger.*

→ see note at **appear**

▶ **COLLOCATIONS:**
  tend to **forget/ignore/assume/think** *something*
  tend to **prefer/favour** *something*
  tend to **focus/concentrate** on *something*
▶ **SYNONYM:** be likely to

ten|den|cy /'tendənsi/ (tendencies)

NOUN A **tendency** is a worrying or unpleasant habit or action that keeps occurring. ○ [+ towards] *the government's tendency towards secrecy in recent years*

▶ **COLLOCATIONS:**
  a tendency **towards** *something*
  exhibit/display/curb/increase a tendency
▶ **SYNONYMS:** trend, habit, disposition

term /tɜːm/ (terms)   ACADEMIC STUDY LANGUAGE

NOUN A **term** is a word or expression with a specific meaning, especially one which is used in relation to a particular subject. ○ [+ for] *Myocardial infarction is the medical term for a heart attack.*

▶ **COLLOCATIONS:**
  a term **for** *something*
  a **medical/technical/legal** term
  a terms **refers to/means** *something*
▶ **SYNONYMS:** name, word, terminology

test /test/ (tests, testing, tested)

1 VERB When you **test** something, you try it, for example by touching it or using it for a short time, in order to find out what it is, what condition it is in, or how well it works. ○ *Here the army has its ranges where Rapier missiles and other weaponry are tested.* ○ *The drug must first be tested in clinical trials to see if it works on other cancers.*

▶ **COLLOCATIONS:**
  test a **sample/vaccine/drug/weapon**
  test a **hypothesis/method/theory**
  routinely/thoroughly/rigorously/properly tested

scientifically/clinically tested
researchers/scientists **test** things
▶ SYNONYMS: check, inspect

2 NOUN A **test** is a deliberate action or experiment to find out how well
something works. ○ the banning of nuclear tests
▶ COLLOCATIONS:
conduct/administer/perform a test
a **nuclear** test
▶ SYNONYMS: experiment, inspection

---

text /tekst/   `ACADEMIC WORD` `LITERATURE`

UNCOUNTABLE NOUN Text is any written material. ○ The machine can
recognise hand-written characters and turn them into printed text. ○ A CD-ROM
can store more than 250,000 pages of typed text.
▶ COLLOCATION: **plain/written/typed** text
▶ PHRASES:
text and graphics
text and illustrations
▶ SYNONYM: writing

---

text|book /'tekstbʊk/ **(textbooks)**   `EDUCATION` `ACADEMIC STUDY`
also **text book**

NOUN A **textbook** is a book containing facts about a particular subject
that is used by people studying that subject. ○ a standard textbook on
international law ○ a chemistry textbook
▶ COLLOCATIONS:
a textbook **on** something
a **standard/classic/introductory/elementary/advanced** textbook
a **school/college** textbook
a **biology/chemistry/maths** textbook
▶ SYNONYM: course book

---

thea|tre /'θiːətə/ **(theatres)**   `ARTS`

1 NOUN A **theatre** is a building with a stage in it, on which plays, shows,
and other performances take place. [in AM, use **theater**] ○ If we went to
the theatre it was a very big event. ○ I worked at the Grand Theatre.
▶ COLLOCATIONS:
go to the theatre
a **packed/outdoor/open-air** theatre

2 NOUN You can refer to work in the theatre such as acting or writing plays as **the theatre**. [in AM, use **theater**] ○ *You can move up to work in films and the theatre.*
  ▶ **PHRASE:** theatre and cinema
  ▶ **SYNONYM:** drama

third /θɜːd/ (thirds)　　`MATHS`

NOUN A **third** is one of three equal parts of something. ○ *A third of the cost went into technology and services.* ○ *Only one third get financial help from their fathers.*
  ▶ **COLLOCATIONS:**
    a third **of** something
    a third of **respondents/voters/pupils/households**
    a third of the **population/electorate**
  ▶ **RELATED WORDS:** half, quarter

thor|ough /ˈθʌrə, AM ˈθɜːrəʊ/

ADJECTIVE A **thorough** action or activity is one that is done very carefully and in a detailed way so that nothing is forgotten. ○ *We are making a thorough investigation.* ○ *This very thorough survey goes back to 1784.* ○ *How thorough is the assessment?*
  ▶ **COLLOCATIONS:**
    a thorough **investigation/review/examination/search/analysis**
    a thorough **job**
    thorough **understanding/knowledge**
    painstakingly/exceedingly thorough
  ▶ **SYNONYMS:** careful, detailed, exhaustive
  ▶ **ANTONYMS:** partial, superficial

thor|ough|ly

ADVERB ○ *Food that is being offered hot must be reheated thoroughly.*
  ○ *a thoroughly researched and illuminating biography*
  ▶ **COLLOCATIONS:**
    thoroughly **researched/investigated/checked**
    wash/dry/mix/cook/clean thoroughly
  ▶ **SYNONYM:** carefully
  ▶ **ANTONYMS:** partially, superficially

thou|sand /ˈθaʊzənd/ (thousands)　　`MATHS`

1 NUMBER A **thousand** or **one thousand** is the number 1,000. ○ *five thousand acres* ○ *Visitors can expect to pay about a thousand pounds a day.*

2 QUANTIFIER If you refer to **thousands of** things or people, you are emphasizing that there are very many of them. ○ [+ of] *Thousands of refugees are packed into over-crowded towns and villages.*

• You can also use **thousands** as a pronoun. ○ *Hundreds have been killed in the fighting and thousands made homeless.*

▶ COLLOCATIONS:
thousands **of** *things*
thousands of **dollars/pounds/miles/people/troops/refugees**
cost/save/spend thousands
untold/countless/many thousands
▶ PHRASE: tens of thousands
▶ RELATED WORD: million
→ see note at **billion**

---

threat /θret/ **(threats)**

NOUN A **threat** is a statement by someone that they will do something unpleasant, especially if you do not do what they want. ○ [+ to-inf] *He may be forced to carry out his threat to resign.* ○ [+ by] *The priest remains in hiding after threats by former officials of the ousted dictatorship.*

▶ COLLOCATIONS:
a threat **by/from** *someone*
be **under** threat
make/issue/drop/carry out/receive a threat
a **veiled** threat
a **death/bomb** threat

threat|en /ˈθretən/ **(threatens, threatening, threatened)**

VERB If something or someone **threatens** a person or thing, they are likely to harm that person or thing. ○ *The newcomers directly threaten the livelihood of the established workers.* ○ [+ with] *30 percent of reptiles, birds, and fish are currently threatened with extinction.*

▶ COLLOCATIONS:
be threatened **with** *something*
be threatened with **extinction/eviction/closure/dismissal**
threaten **stability/security/safety**
threaten *someone's* **interests**
threaten a **species**
▶ SYNONYM: endanger

through|out /θruːˈaʊt/

1 PREPOSITION If you say that something happens **throughout** a particular period of time, you mean that it happens during the whole of that period. ○ *The national tragedy of rival groups killing each other continued throughout 1990.* ○ *Movie music can be made memorable because its themes are repeated throughout the film.*

• **Throughout** is also an adverb. ○ *The first song, 'Blue Moon', didn't go too badly except that everyone talked throughout.*
▶ SYNONYM: during

2 PREPOSITION If you say that something happens or exists **throughout** a place, you mean that it happens or exists in all parts of that place. ○ *'Sight Savers', founded in 1950, now runs projects throughout Africa, the Caribbean and South East Asia.* ○ *As we have tried to show throughout this book, companies that provide outstanding service don't do it by luck.*

• **Throughout** is also an adverb. ○ *The route is well sign-posted throughout.*

time|table /ˈtaɪmteɪbəl/ (timetables)   `EDUCATION`

1 NOUN A **timetable** is a plan of the times when particular events are to take place. ○ *Don't you realize we're working to a timetable? We have to have results.* ○ *[+ for] The two countries are to try to agree a timetable for formal talks.*
▶ COLLOCATIONS:
  a timetable **for** something
  a timetable for **disarmament/withdrawal/implementation**
  set/outline/propose/fix/agree a timetable
  a **strict/tight/realistic/ambitious** timetable
▶ SYNONYMS: schedule, agenda, plan

2 NOUN In a school or college, a **timetable** is a list that shows the times in the week at which particular subjects are taught. You can also refer to the range of subjects that a student learns or the classes that a teacher teaches as their **timetable**. [BRIT; in AM, usually use **class schedule**] ○ *Options are offered subject to staff availability and the constraints of the timetable.* ○ *Members of the union will continue to teach their full timetables.*

ti|tle /ˈtaɪtəl/ (titles)   `ACADEMIC STUDY` `LANGUAGE`

NOUN The **title** of a book, play, film, or piece of music is its name. ○ *'Patience and Sarah' was first published in 1969 under the title 'A Place for Us'.*
▶ COLLOCATIONS:
  the title **of** something
  the title of a **book/novel/article/essay**

tonne /tʌn/ (tonnes)

NOUN A **tonne** is a metric unit of weight that is equal to 1000 kilograms.

○ [+ of] *65.5 million tonnes of coal* ○ *Top quality Thai rice fetched $340 a tonne.*

▸ **COLLOCATIONS:**
a tonne **of** *something*
a tonne of **ore/coal/wheat/waste**
weigh *x* tonnes
import/export/produce *x* tonnes of *something*

top|ic /ˈtɒpɪk/ (topics)   `ACADEMIC WORD`

NOUN A **topic** is a particular subject that you discuss or write about.

○ [+ of] *The weather is a constant topic of conversation in Britain.* ○ [+ for] *The main topic for discussion is political union.* ○ *This topic is explored more fully in chapter 5.*

▸ **COLLOCATIONS:**
the topic **of** *something*
a topic **of/for** *something*
a topic of **conversation**
a topic for **debate/discussion**
the **main/key/specific/related** topic
a **taboo/controversial/contentious/sensitive** topic
a **thesis/essay/conversation** topic
broach/discuss/cover/research/explore a topic

▸ **SYNONYMS:** subject, matter, theme

to|tal /ˈtəʊtəl/ (totals)   `MATHS`

1 NOUN A **total** is the number that you get when you add several numbers together or when you count how many things there are in a group.

○ [+ of] *The companies have a total of 1,776 employees.*

▸ **COLLOCATIONS:**
a total **of** *x*
a **sum/grand/combined** total
cost/score/amass/raise at total of *x*
exceed a total

▸ **SYNONYM:** sum

2 ADJECTIVE The **total** number or cost of something is the number or cost that you get when you add together or count all the parts in it. ○ *They said that the total number of cows dying from BSE would be twenty thousand.* ○ *The total cost of the project would be more than $240 million.*

▶ **COLLOCATIONS:**
the total **number/cost/amount/value**
total **spending**
▶ **SYNONYMS:** whole, aggregate
▶ **ANTONYM:** partial

---

tour|ist /ˈtʊərɪst/ (tourists)

NOUN A **tourist** is a person who is visiting a place for pleasure and interest, especially when they are on holiday. ○ *places frequented by foreign tourists* ○ *Blackpool is the top tourist attraction in England.* ○ *a heritage site which attracts 300,000 tourists each year*
▶ **COLLOCATIONS:**
tourists **flock to/visit/travel to/frequent** *somewhere*
a tourist **attraction/destination/resort/spot**
the tourist **industry/trade/season**
something **attracts/lures** tourists
foreign/overseas/Japanese/German/British tourists
▶ **SYNONYM:** traveller
▶ **ANTONYMS:** local, native

tour|ism /ˈtʊərɪzəm/

UNCOUNTABLE NOUN **Tourism** is the business of providing services for people on holiday, for example hotels, restaurants, and trips. ○ *Tourism is vital for the Spanish economy.*
▶ **COLLOCATIONS:**
boost/promote/encourage/revive/discourage tourism
mass/domestic/responsible tourism
the tourism **industry**
▶ **PHRASES:**
leisure and tourism
travel and tourism

---

tra|di|tion /trəˈdɪʃən/ (traditions) `ACADEMIC WORD` `SOCIAL SCIENCE`

NOUN A **tradition** is a custom or belief that has existed for a long time. ○ [+ *of*] *the rich traditions of Afro-Cuban music, and dance* ○ [+ *of*] *Mary has carried on the family tradition of giving away plants.* ○ *The story of King Arthur became part of oral tradition.*
▶ **COLLOCATIONS:**
a tradition **of** *something*
a tradition of **tolerance/storytelling/poetry/worship**
uphold/maintain/preserve/continue a tradition
keep a tradition **alive**

a **long/proud/ancient/oral** tradition
a **family/folk/religious/Christian** tradition
tradition **dictates** something
▶ **SYNONYMS:** custom, heritage, culture, practice, ritual

tra|di|tion|al /trə'dɪʃənəl/

ADJECTIVE Traditional customs, beliefs, or methods are ones that have existed for a long time without changing. ○ *traditional teaching methods* ○ *traditional Indian music* ○ *pipers in traditional highland dress*
▶ **COLLOCATIONS:**
traditional **music/medicine/dress**
traditional **values/beliefs/culture**
a traditional **method/dish/style/marriage**
fairly/deeply/strictly traditional
▶ **SYNONYMS:** old-fashioned, conventional
▶ **ANTONYMS:** modern, contemporary

tra|di|tion|al|ly

ADVERB ○ *Married women have traditionally been treated as dependent on their husbands.* ○ *Some jobs, such as nursing, are traditionally associated with women.* ○ *Traditionally, election campaigns start on Labor Day.*
▶ **COLLOCATION:** traditionally **associated/viewed/favoured**
▶ **SYNONYMS:** conventionally, usually, generally

traf|fic /'træfɪk/

UNCOUNTABLE NOUN Traffic refers to all the vehicles that are moving along the roads in a particular area. ○ *There was heavy traffic on the roads.* ○ *the problems of city life, such as traffic congestion*
→ see note at **vehicle**
▶ **COLLOCATIONS:**
a traffic **jam/warden**
heavy/light traffic
block/divert/disrupt/slow/halt traffic
traffic **congestion/control/lights**
road/city/rush-hour traffic
▶ **SYNONYM:** vehicles

train /treɪn/ (trains, training, trained)   EDUCATION BUSINESS

VERB If someone **trains** you **to** do something, they teach you the skills that you need in order to do it. If you **train to** do something, you learn the skills that you need in order to do it. ○ [+ to-inf] *The U.S. was ready to train its troops to participate.* ○ [+ as] *Psychiatrists initially train as doctors.*

○ [+ *in*] *We don't train them only in bricklaying, but also in other building techniques.* ○ *I'm a trained nurse.*

▶ **COLLOCATIONS:**
train **as/in** something
train as a **nurse/architect/accountant**
train **staff/personnel/teachers/doctors**
classically/specially/properly trained

▶ **SYNONYMS:** educate, teach, prepare

train|ing /ˈtreɪnɪŋ/

UNCOUNTABLE NOUN Training is the process of learning the skills that you need for a particular job or activity. ○ *He called for much higher spending on education and training.* ○ [+ *as*] *Kennedy had no formal training as a decorator.*

▶ **COLLOCATIONS:**
training **in/as** something
basic/intensive/formal/vocational training
medical/military/teacher/staff training
undergo/receive/provide training
a training **session/course/programme/centre**

▶ **PHRASES:**
training and recruitment
education and training

▶ **SYNONYMS:** education, instruction, teaching, preparation

> **USAGE:** Uncountable noun
>
> Remember that **training** is an uncountable noun. You do not talk about 'a training' or 'trainings'. ○ *Supervisors receive formal training in health and safety.*
>
> You can talk about a **training session** or a **training course**. ○ *They attend two one-hour training sessions.*

trainee /treɪˈniː/ **(trainees)**

NOUN A trainee is someone who is employed at a low level in a particular job in order to learn the skills needed for that job. ○ *He is a 24-year-old trainee reporter.*

▶ **COLLOCATIONS:**
a **graduate/management** trainee
a trainee **teacher/solicitor/nurse/pilot**

▶ **SYNONYMS:** apprentice, learner

trans|late /trænz'leɪt/ (translates, translating, translated) `LANGUAGE`

VERB If something that someone has said or written **is translated from** one language **into** another, it is said or written again in the second language. ○ [+ into/from] *Only a small number of Kadare's books have been translated into English.* ○ [+ into/from] *Martin Luther translated the Bible into German.* ○ [+ as] *The Celtic word 'geis' is usually translated as 'taboo'.*

▶ COLLOCATIONS:
  translate *something* **from/into** a language
  translate *something* **as** *something*
  translate a **word/text/poem/passage**
  translate **loosely/roughly/literally**

▶ SYNONYMS: interpret, gloss, render

trans|la|tion /trænz'leɪʃən/

UNCOUNTABLE NOUN ○ *The papers have been sent to Saudi Arabia for translation.* ○ [+ of] *MacNiece's excellent English translation of 'Faust'* ○ *I've only read Solzhenitsyn in translation.*

▶ COLLOCATIONS:
  a translation **of** something
  read *something* **in** translation
  a translation of a **poem/novel/article/word/phrase**
  a **literal/faithful/accurate/rough** translation
  a **French/English/Russian** translation

▶ PHRASE: lose something/be lost in (the) translation

trans|la|tor /trænz'leɪtə/ (translators)

NOUN A **translator** is a person whose job is translating writing or speech from one language to another. ○ *He works as a Russian translator.*

▶ SYNONYM: interpreter

trans|port (transports, transporting, transported) `ACADEMIC WORD`

> The noun is pronounced /'trænspɔːt/. The verb is pronounced /træns'pɔːt/.

1 UNCOUNTABLE NOUN Transport is the moving of people or goods from one place to another, for example using buses or trains. [mainly BRIT; in AM, usually use **transportation**] ○ *The extra money could be spent on improving public transport.* ○ *An efficient transport system is critical to the long-term future of London.* ○ *Local production virtually eliminates transport costs.*

▶ COLLOCATIONS:
  public/rail/air/road/passenger transport

improve/provide/use transport
a transport **system/link/infrastructure**

▶ SYNONYMS: transportation, carriage

2 VERB To **transport** people or goods somewhere is to take them from one place to another in a vehicle. ○ *There's no petrol, so it's very difficult to transport goods.* ○ *They use tankers to transport the oil to Los Angeles.*

▶ COLLOCATIONS:
transport something **by** something
transport something by **aeroplane/helicopter/rail**
transport **freight/cargo/goods**
ferries/ships/trucks transport things

▶ SYNONYMS: move, ship

---

treat /triːt/ (treats, treating, treated)   MEDICINE

1 VERB If you **treat** someone or something in a particular way, you behave towards them or deal with them in that way. ○ [+ with] *The information should be treated with caution.* ○ [+ as] *Police are treating it as a case of attempted murder.* ○ *The issues should be treated separately.*

▶ COLLOCATIONS:
treat someone/something **with/as/like** something
treat someone/something with **contempt/caution/respect/dignity**
treat someone like/as a **criminal/slave/queen/king**
treat someone **unfairly/harshly/badly/humanely**
treat someone/something **differently/separately/accordingly**

▶ SYNONYMS: handle, deal with, behave towards

2 VERB When a doctor or nurse **treats** a patient or an illness, he or she tries to make the patient well again. ○ [+ with] *Doctors treated her with aspirin.* ○ [+ for] *The boy was treated for a minor head wound.* ○ *An experienced nurse treats all minor injuries.*

▶ COLLOCATIONS:
treat someone/something **with** something
treat someone **for** something
treat someone with **antibiotics/chemotherapy/medication**
treat someone for a **burn/injury/wound**
treat someone for **shock/dehydration/cancer**
treat a **patient/disease/illness/condition/symptom**
treat **cancer/depression/diabetes**

▶ SYNONYMS: heal, cure
▶ ANTONYM: harm

treat|ment /ˈtriːtmənt/ (treatments)

1 NOUN Treatment is medical attention given to a sick or injured person
or animal. ○ *Many patients are not getting the medical treatment they need.*
○ [+ of] *a veterinary surgeon who specialises in the treatment of cage birds*
○ [+ for] *an effective treatment for eczema*

▶ COLLOCATIONS:
   treatment **for** *something*
   the treatment **of** *something*
   treatment for **addiction/cancer/depression**
   the treatment of a **disease/disorder**
   medical/dental/fertility/hospital treatment
   an **effective** treatment
   successful/unsuccessful treatment
   AIDS/cancer treatment
   give/get/undergo/receive/prescribe treatment

▶ SYNONYMS: cure, medicine, therapy

2 UNCOUNTABLE NOUN Your **treatment** of someone is the way you behave
towards them or deal with them. ○ *We don't want any special treatment.*
○ [+ of] *the government's responsibility for the humane treatment of prisoners*

▶ COLLOCATIONS:
   the treatment **of** *someone*
   the treatment of **prisoners/offenders/asylum seekers**
   special/preferential/equal/fair/unfair treatment
   harsh/humane treatment

▶ SYNONYM: behaviour

---

tri|al /traɪəl/ (trials)   LAW

NOUN A **trial** is a formal meeting in a law court, at which a judge and jury
listen to evidence and decide whether a person is guilty of a crime. ○ *New
evidence showed the police lied at the trial.* ○ *He's awaiting trial in a military
court on charges of plotting against the state.* ○ *They believed that his case
would never come to trial.*

▶ COLLOCATIONS:
   be **on** trial
   be on trial **for** *something*
   go on/await/face/stand trial
   come to trial
   bring *someone* **to** trial
   put *someone* on trial
   be on trial for **murder/manslaughter/fraud**
   a trial **date/judge/lawyer**

a **murder/rape/perjury** trial
a **fair/speedy/upcoming/criminal** trial
▶ **PHRASE:** trial by jury
▶ **SYNONYMS:** case, prosecution, hearing, lawsuit

tri|an|gle /ˈtraɪæŋɡəl/ (triangles)

NOUN A **triangle** is an object, arrangement, or flat shape with three straight sides and three angles. ○ *Its outline roughly forms an equilateral triangle.* ○ [+ *of*] *triangles of fried bread*
▶ **COLLOCATIONS:**
a triangle **of** something
a triangle of **toast/bread/cheese/cloth**
a **right-angled/equilateral** triangle
▶ **RELATED WORDS:** square, rectangle, circle

tri|an|gu|lar /traɪˈæŋɡjʊlə/

ADJECTIVE Something that is **triangular** is in the shape of a triangle. ○ *cottages around a triangular green* ○ *triangular bandages to make slings*
▶ **COLLOCATION:** a triangular **shape/section**
▶ **RELATED WORDS:** square, rectangular, circular

true /truː/ (truer, truest)

ADJECTIVE If something is **true**, it is based on facts rather than being invented or imagined, and is accurate and reliable. ○ *Everything I had heard about him was true.* ○ [+ *that*] *He said it was true that a collision had happened.* ○ *The film tells the true story of a group who survived in the Andes in sub-zero temperatures.*
▶ **COLLOCATIONS:**
a true **story/tale**
perfectly/literally/absolutely true
▶ **SYNONYMS:** correct, accurate
▶ **ANTONYMS:** false, invented, untrue

truth /truːθ/

UNCOUNTABLE NOUN **The truth** about something is all the facts about it, rather than things that are imagined or invented. ○ [+ *about*] *I must tell you the truth about this business.* ○ [+ *of*] *The truth of the matter is that we had no other choice.* ○ *In the town very few know the whole truth.*
▶ **COLLOCATIONS:**
the truth **of/about** something
tell/know/speak the truth
uncover/discover/reveal/learn/find out/expose the truth

conceal/hide/cover up the truth
the truth of the **matter**
the **whole/absolute/shocking/simple/sad** truth
▶ **PHRASE:** the truth hurts
▶ **SYNONYMS:** facts, accuracy
▶ **ANTONYMS:** falsity, falsehood, lies, fiction

twice /twaɪs/   `MATHS`

1 ADVERB If something happens **twice**, there are two actions or events of the same kind. ○ *The government has twice declined to back the scheme.* ○ *Thoroughly brush teeth and gums twice daily.*
▶ **SYNONYM:** two times
▶ **RELATED WORD:** once

2 ADVERB If one thing is, for example, **twice as** big or old **as** another, the first thing is two times as big or old as the second. ○ *The figure of seventy-million pounds was twice as big as expected.* ○ *a report claiming that teachers could be twice as effective if they returned to traditional classroom methods*

• **Twice** is also a predeterminer. ○ *Unemployment in Northern Ireland is twice the national average.*
▶ **COLLOCATION:**
twice **as** *much*
twice as **much/big/old/effective**
▶ **SYNONYM:** double
▶ **ANTONYM:** half

type /taɪp/ (types)

NOUN A **type of** something is a group of those things that have particular features in common. ○ *[+ of] There are various types of the disease.* ○ *In 1990, 25% of households were of this type.*
→ see note at **kind**
▶ **COLLOCATIONS:**
a type **of** *something*
a type of **person/thing/behaviour/music/cancer/vehicle**
a **different/certain/particular/specific/new** type
various/other types
a **skin/blood/personality/soil** type
▶ **SYNONYMS:** sort, kind, class

typi|cal /'tɪpɪkəl/

1 **ADJECTIVE** You use **typical** to describe someone or something that shows the most usual characteristics of a particular type of person or thing, and is therefore a good example of that type. ○ *Cheney is everyone's image of a typical cop: a big white guy, six foot, 220 pounds.* ○ *A typical soil sample contains the following components.*

2 **ADJECTIVE** If a particular action or feature is **typical of** someone or something, it shows their usual qualities or characteristics. ○ [+ *of*] *This reluctance to move towards a democratic state is typical of totalitarian regimes.* ○ *With typical energy he found new journalistic outlets.*

▶ **COLLOCATIONS:**
typical **of** *someone/something*
typical of a **kind/sort** of *something*
typical of an **era/generation/region**
a typical **example/pattern/scenario**

▶ **SYNONYM:** characteristic

▶ **ANTONYM:** atypical

typi|cal|ly /'tɪpɪkəli/

1 **ADVERB** You use **typically** to say that something usually happens in the way that you are describing. ○ *Typically, parents apply to several schools and settle, if need be, for their fourth or fifth choice.* ○ *Female migrants are typically very young.*

▶ **SYNONYMS:** normally, usually

▶ **ANTONYM:** rarely

2 **ADVERB** You use **typically** to say that something shows all the most usual characteristics of a particular type of person or thing. ○ *The main course was typically Swiss.* ○ *Philip paced the floor, a typically nervous expectant father.*

▶ **COLLOCATIONS:**
typically **cost/involve/contain** *something*
typically **associated** with *something*

▶ **SYNONYMS:** normally, usually, characteristically

▶ **ANTONYM:** rarely

Uu

under|stand /ˌʌndəˈstænd/ (understands, understanding, understood)

VERB You say that you **understand** something when you know why or
how it happens. ○ [+ what] *They are too young to understand what is going on.*
○ *In the effort to understand AIDS, attention is moving from the virus to the
immune system.*

> ► **COLLOCATIONS:**
> **fully/really** understand
> understand the **importance/implication** of *something*
> understand the **significance/meaning** of *something*
> understand a **reason/difference**
> understand a **language/situation**
> ► **SYNONYMS:** appreciate, comprehend, grasp
> ► **ANTONYM:** misunderstand

under|stand|ing /ˌʌndəˈstændɪŋ/ (understandings)

NOUN If you have an **understanding of** something, you know how it
works or know what it means. ○ [+ of] *They have to have a basic
understanding of computers in order to use the advanced technology.* ○ [+ of]
testing students' understanding of difficult concepts

> ► **COLLOCATIONS:**
> an understanding **of** *something*
> an understanding of **nature/science/culture**
> a **good/clear/thorough/deep/basic** understanding
> **mutual/complete** understanding
> **gain/develop/reach** an understanding
> **promote/improve/share/increase/require** understanding
> ► **SYNONYMS:** grasp, appreciation, awareness
> ► **ANTONYM:** ignorance

u

un|em|ploy|ment /ˌʌnɪmˈplɔɪmənt/ `BUSINESS` `SOCIAL SCIENCE`

UNCOUNTABLE NOUN **Unemployment** is the fact that people who want
jobs cannot get them. ○ *an area that had the highest unemployment rate in
Western Europe* ○ *Unemployment is damaging both to individuals and to
communities.*

> ▶ COLLOCATIONS:
> a **rise/fall** in unemployment
> **reduce/increase/tackle** unemployment
> **high/low/mass/long-term/widespread** unemployment
> **youth/graduate** unemployment
> unemployment **benefit/figures/levels**
> the unemployment **rate**
> ▶ ANTONYM: employment

un|em|ployed /ˌʌnɪmˈplɔɪd/

ADJECTIVE Someone who is **unemployed** does not have a job. ○ *Millions of people are unemployed.* ○ *This workshop helps young unemployed people in Grimsby.* ○ [+ for] *Have you been unemployed for over six months?*

> ▶ COLLOCATIONS:
> unemployed **for** *a time*
> **become/remain** unemployed
> unemployed **workforce/population/workers/youth**
> **currently/newly/temporarily** unemployed
> ▶ SYNONYM: out of work
> ▶ ANTONYM: employed

un|for|tu|nate /ʌnˈfɔːtʃʊnət/

ADJECTIVE If you describe someone as **unfortunate**, you mean that something unpleasant or unlucky has happened to them. You can also describe the unpleasant things that happen to them as **unfortunate**. ○ *A few unfortunate individuals will develop the disease.* ○ *Through some unfortunate accident, the information reached me a day late.* ○ [+ for] *The situation was unfortunate for all concerned.*

> ▶ COLLOCATIONS:
> unfortunate **for** *someone*
> an unfortunate **incident/accident/event/situation/decision**
> an unfortunate **circumstance/mistake/misunderstanding**
> **doubly/particularly/desperately** unfortunate
> ▶ SYNONYMS: unlucky, regrettable
> ▶ ANTONYMS: fortunate, lucky

un|for|tu|nate|ly /ʌnˈfɔːtʃʊnətli/

ADVERB You can use **unfortunately** to express regret, sadness, or disappointment about what you are saying. ○ *Unfortunately, my time is limited.* ○ [+ for] *Unfortunately for the Prince, his title brought obligations as well as privileges.* ○ *The enclosed photograph is unfortunately not good enough to reproduce.*

▶ **COLLOCATION:** unfortunately **for** *someone*
▶ **SYNONYM:** regrettably
▶ **ANTONYM:** fortunately

---

uni|verse /ˈjuːnɪvɜːs/ (universes)　　GEOGRAPHY

NOUN **The universe** is the whole of space and all the stars, planets, and other forms of matter and energy in it. ○ *Einstein's equations showed the Universe to be expanding.* ○ *Early astronomers thought that our planet was the centre of the universe.*

▶ **COLLOCATIONS:**
inhabit/populate/create the universe
a **parallel/alternative/virtual/expanding** universe
the **entire/whole/observable/visible/physical** universe

▶ **RELATED WORDS:** galaxy, solar system

---

uni|ver|sity /ˌjuːnɪˈvɜːsɪti/ (universities)　　EDUCATION

NOUN A **university** is an institution where students study for degrees and where academic research is done. ○ *Patrick is now at London University.* ○ *exams required to attend university* ○ *a national conference convened by a major research university*

▶ **COLLOCATIONS:**
attend/enter/leave/apply for/graduate from a university
a **top/elite/prestigious** university
a university **student/graduate/lecturer/professor**
a university **education/degree/course/campus**
university **entrance/admissions**
university **research/funding/tuition**
a university **department/researcher**

▶ **PHRASE:** colleges and universities

▶ **SYNONYM:** college

---

un|like|ly /ʌnˈlaɪkli/ (unlikelier, unlikeliest)

ADJECTIVE If you say that something is **unlikely** to happen or **unlikely** to be true, you believe that it will not happen or that it is not true, although you are not completely sure. ○ *A military coup seems unlikely.* ○ [+ to-inf] *As with many technological revolutions, you are unlikely to be aware of it.* ○ [+ that] *It's now unlikely that future parliaments will bring back the death penalty.*

→ see note at **possible**

▶ **COLLOCATIONS:**
seem/look unlikely
highly/most/increasingly/very unlikely

u

an unlikely **event/breakthrough/move/combination**
an unlikely **scenario/setting/source**
▶ ANTONYM: likely

ACADEMIC WRITING: Avoiding negatives

In formal, academic writing, you need to be as clear and accurate as possible. Sometimes, it is better to avoid complicated negative constructions by using words like **unlikely** and **unnecessary** that have a negative meaning. For example, the sentence: ○ *The situation seems unlikely to change in the short term.* is simpler and clearer than: ○ *The situation does not seem likely to change in the short term.*

Try to use the antonyms in this book to learn negative words which you might be able to use to express your ideas more simply.

---

un|nec|es|sary /ʌnˈnesəsri, AM -seri/

ADJECTIVE If you describe something as **unnecessary**, you mean that it is not needed or does not have to be done, and is undesirable. ○ [+ to-inf] *She explained that it is quite unnecessary to hurt a patient.* ○ *The slaughter of whales is unnecessary.* ○ *Don't take any unnecessary risks.*
→ see note at **unlikely**
▶ COLLOCATIONS:
unnecessary **suffering/risk/expense**
unnecessary **legislation/regulation/treatment**
totally/completely/quite unnecessary
▶ SYNONYM: needless
▶ ANTONYM: necessary

un|nec|es|sari|ly /ʌnnesəˈserɪli/

ADVERB ○ *We spend millions and millions a year unnecessarily.* ○ *It works, but it's unnecessarily difficult.*
▶ COLLOCATIONS:
unnecessarily **cruel/complex/harsh/complicated**
unnecessarily **restrictive/intrusive/provocative**
▶ SYNONYM: needlessly

---

up|date /ʌpˈdeɪt/ (updates, updating, updated)

VERB If you **update** something, you make it more modern, usually by adding new parts to it or giving new information. ○ *He was back in the office, updating the work schedule on the computer.* ○ *The guide was updated last year.* ○ *an updated edition of the book*

▶ **COLLOCATIONS:**
an updated **version/edition/database/list/forecast**
updated **information/software/guidelines**
regularly/constantly/automatically updated
▶ **PHRASE:** revised and updated
▶ **SYNONYM:** modernize

up|per /ˈʌpə/

1 ADJECTIVE You use **upper** to describe something that is above something else. ○ *his upper lip* ○ *There is a restaurant on the upper floor.* ○ *Students travel on the cheap lower deck and tourists on the upper.*
▶ **COLLOCATION:** an upper **lip/deck/floor/limit/class/tier**
▶ **ANTONYM:** lower

2 ADJECTIVE You use **upper** to describe the higher part of something. ○ *the upper part of the foot* ○ *the muscles of the upper back and chest*
▶ **COLLOCATION:** the upper **arm/thigh/chest/body/torso**
▶ **ANTONYM:** lower

ur|ban /ˈɜːbən/ `GEOGRAPHY`

ADJECTIVE Urban means belonging to, or relating to, a town or city. ○ *Most of the population is an urban population.* ○ *Most urban areas are close to a park.* ○ *urban planning*
▶ **COLLOCATIONS:**
urban **sprawl/renewal/regeneration/planning**
an urban **neighbourhood/environment**
urban **warfare/poverty/living**
an urban **area/landscape/setting**
an urban **dweller/planner**
▶ **SYNONYM:** city
▶ **ANTONYM:** rural

us|age /ˈjuːsɪdʒ/ `LANGUAGE`

1 UNCOUNTABLE NOUN Usage is the way in which words are used, especially with regard to their meanings. ○ *The word 'undertaker' had long been in common usage.* ○ *the correct usage of English*
▶ **COLLOCATION:** **common/rare/everyday/linguistic** usage

2 UNCOUNTABLE NOUN Usage is the degree to which something is used or the way in which it is used. ○ *Parts of the motor wore out because of constant usage.* ○ *Your water usage may be very small.*

▶ **COLLOCATIONS:**
   increase/reduce/track/monitor/restrict usage
   boost/cut/encourage/limit usage
   Internet/power/water/energy usage
▶ **SYNONYM:** use

---

use (uses, using, used)

> The verb is pronounced /juːz/. The noun is pronounced /juːs/.

1 VERB If you **use** something, you do something with it in order to do a job or to achieve a particular result or effect. ○ *He had simply used a little imagination.* ○ [+ as] *using personal computers as teaching tools* ○ [+ to-inf] *Officials used microphones to call for calm.*
   ▶ **COLLOCATION:** use something **as** something

2 UNCOUNTABLE NOUN Your **use** of something is the action or fact of your using it. ○ [+ of] *The treatment does not involve the use of any artificial drugs.* ○ *research related to microcomputers and their use in classrooms* ○ [+ of] *He said he supported the use of force.*
   ▶ **COLLOCATIONS:**
      the use **of** something
      make use of something
      drug use
      use of **force/drugs/technology/weapons/words**
   ▶ **PHRASE:** for your own personal use

3 NOUN If something has a particular **use**, it is intended for a particular purpose. ○ *Infrared detectors have many uses.* ○ *It's an interesting scientific phenomenon, but of no practical use whatever.* ○ [+ for] *The report outlined possible uses for the new weapon.* ○ [+ of] *We need to recognize that certain uses of the land are simply wrong.*
   ▶ **COLLOCATIONS:**
      a use **for/of/in** something
      authorized/unauthorized/increased use
      recreational/personal/practical/commercial use
      regular/frequent/everyday use

user /ˈjuːzə/ (users)

NOUN A **user** is a person or thing that uses something such as a place, facility, product, or machine. ○ [+ of] *a regular user of Holland's health-care system* ○ [+ of] *a user of electric current, such as an electric motor, a lamp, or a toaster*

▶ **COLLOCATIONS:**
a user **of** *something*
a **regular/registered/heavy/average** user
a **drug/Internet/computer** user

use|ful /ˈjuːsfʊl/

ADJECTIVE If something is **useful**, you can use it to do something or to help you in some way. ○ *The data is useful for planning and scheduling.* ○ *[+ in] Hypnotherapy can be useful in helping you give up smoking.* ○ *The police gained a great deal of useful information about the organization.*

▶ **COLLOCATIONS:**
useful **for** *someone/something*
useful **in** *something*
useful **information/advice**
a useful **tool/tip/link/contribution/exercise**
prove/become useful
find *something* useful

▶ **SYNONYM:** helpful
▶ **ANTONYM:** useless

user-friendly /ˌjuːzəˈfrendli/

`ENGINEERING` `IT`

ADJECTIVE If you describe something such as a machine or system as **user-friendly**, you mean that it is well designed and easy to use. ○ *This is an entirely computer-operated system which is very user friendly.* ○ *user-friendly libraries*

▶ **COLLOCATIONS:**
a user-friendly **printer/display/site/guide**
a user-friendly **format/interface/application**
a user-friendly **feature/approach**
user-friendly **software/technology**

▶ **SYNONYM:** accessible

usu|al /ˈjuːʒʊəl/

ADJECTIVE **Usual** is used to describe what happens or what is done most often in a particular situation. ○ *all the usual inner-city problems* ○ *We've had more press coverage than usual in the last three weeks.* ○ *[+ to-inf] It is usual to tip waiters, porters, guides and drivers.*

▶ **COLLOCATIONS:**
a usual **routine/pattern/procedure/method**
a usual **route/practice/style**

▶ **PHRASE:** as usual

▶ **SYNONYMS:** normal, customary, typical

usu|al|ly /ˈjuːʒʊəli/

ADVERB If something **usually** happens, it is the thing that most often happens in a particular situation. ○ *The best information usually comes from friends and acquaintances.* ○ *Usually, the work is boring.* ○ *Offering only one loan, usually an installment loan, is part of the plan.*

▶ **COLLOCATION:** usually **reliable/harmless/sufficient/unnecessary**

▶ **SYNONYMS:** generally, normally, typically

Vv

value /ˈvæljuː/

BUSINESS ECONOMICS

UNCOUNTABLE NOUN The **value** of something is how much money it is worth. ○ [+ of] *The value of his investment has risen by more than $50,000.* ○ *The country's currency went down in value by 3.5 per cent.* ○ *It might contain something of value.*

▸ **COLLOCATIONS:**
the value **of** *something*
change **in** value
the **actual/present/current** value of *something*
of **equal/great/no** value
go up/increase/go down in value
something **of** value

▸ **PHRASE:** be of value

▸ **SYNONYMS:** cost, price, worth

valu|able /ˈvæljʊəbəl/

ADJECTIVE If you describe something or someone as **valuable**, you mean that they are very useful and helpful. ○ *Many of our teachers also have valuable academic links with Heidelberg University.* ○ *The experience was very valuable.*

▸ **COLLOCATIONS:**
extremely/less/very valuable
prove/become valuable
a valuable **asset/lesson/resource/experience**
a valuable **contribution/item**
valuable **property/information/advice**

▸ **SYNONYMS:** useful, helpful

va|ri|ety /vəˈraɪɪti/ (varieties)

NOUN A **variety of** things is a number of different kinds or examples of the same thing. ○ [+ of] *The island offers a wide variety of scenery and wildlife.* ○ [+ of] *People change their mind for a variety of reasons.*

▸ **COLLOCATIONS:**
a variety **of** *things*
a **wide/great** variety
offer/provide a variety

a variety of **reasons/activities/colours/problems**
a variety of **foods/issues/ways**
a variety of **products/sizes/styles**
▶ SYNONYM: range

var|ied /ˈveərid/

ADJECTIVE Something that is **varied** consists of things of different types, sizes, or qualities. ○ *It is essential that your diet is varied and balanced.* ○ *Before his election to the presidency, Mitterrand had enjoyed a long and varied career.*
▶ COLLOCATIONS:
extremely/richly varied
a varied **menu/diet/career**
a varied **landscape/coastline**
▶ SYNONYM: diverse

vari|ous /ˈveəriəs/

ADJECTIVE If you say that there are **various** things, you mean there are several different things of the type mentioned. ○ *He found various species of animals and plants, each slightly different.* ○ *The school has received various grants from the education department.*
▶ COLLOCATIONS:
various **artists/groups/locations**
various **types/forms/kinds/parts/species**
various **elements/components/categories**
▶ SYNONYM: different

ve|hi|cle /ˈviːɪkəl/ (vehicles) `ACADEMIC WORD`

NOUN A **vehicle** is a machine such as a car, bus, or truck which has an engine and is used to carry people from place to place. ○ *The vehicle would not be able to make the journey on one tank of fuel.* ○ *a vehicle which was somewhere between a tractor and a truck*
▶ COLLOCATIONS:
a **military/armoured/commercial** vehicle
a **motor/utility/sport/emergency** vehicle
a **stolen** vehicle

> **EXTEND YOUR VOCABULARY**
>
> In everyday English, you often use words that aren't 100% accurate. For example, you might say: ○ *There are too many cars on the city's roads.*
>
> When in fact, that might include vans, trucks and buses as well as cars.

In formal academic writing, it is important to be clear and accurate. Sometimes you need a general word to refer to a category of things. To talk about cars, buses etc. on the road generally, you can use **traffic**. ○ *recent increases in the city's road traffic*

Or to talk about the cars, buses etc individually, you can use **vehicles**. ○ *Almost 700,000 vehicles entered Central London each day, three-quarters of them cars.*

---

vic|tim /ˈvɪktɪm/ (victims)   `LAW`

NOUN A **victim** is someone who has suffered as a result of someone else's actions, or as a result of unpleasant circumstances. ○ *Not all the victims survived.* ○ [+ *of*] *Statistically, our chances of being the victims of violent crime are remote.* ○ *Infectious diseases are spreading among many of the flood victims.*

▶ **COLLOCATIONS:**
a victim **of** something
a victim of **crime/abuse/violence**
an **innocent** victim
a **murder/rape** victim
victim **support**

▶ **ANTONYM:** criminal

---

view /vjuː/ (views, viewing, viewed)

1 NOUN Your **views** on something are the beliefs or opinions that you have about it. ○ [+ *on*] *Washington and Moscow are believed to have similar views on Kashmir.* ○ *My own view is absolutely clear. What I did was right.* ○ *make your views known*

▶ **COLLOCATIONS:**
someone's views **on** something
reflect/express/share someone's views
hold/offer/take a view

▶ **SYNONYMS:** opinion, point of view, belief

2 VERB If you **view** something in a particular way, you think of it in that way. ○ [+ *as*] *First-generation Americans view the United States as a land of golden opportunity.* ○ *Sectors in the economy can be viewed in a variety of ways.* ○ *We would view favourably any sensible suggestion for maintaining the business.*

▶ **COLLOCATIONS:**
view *something* **as/with/in** *something*
view *something* with **caution/suspicion/scepticism/alarm**
view *something* **positively/favourably/negatively**

▶ **SYNONYM:** regard

v

vio|lent /ˈvaɪələnt/

1 ADJECTIVE If someone is **violent**, or if they do something which is **violent**, they use physical force or weapons to hurt, injure, or kill other people. ○ *A quarter of the prisoners have committed violent crimes.* ○ *violent anti-government demonstrations* ○ *Sometimes the men get violent.*

▶ COLLOCATIONS:
increasingly/sometimes violent
turn/become/get violent
a violent **husband/partner/father/individual**
a violent **criminal/offender/death**
a violent **demonstration/protest/incident**
a violent **clash/conflict/confrontation**
violent **acts/attacks/behaviour/conduct**

▶ SYNONYM: aggressive

▶ ANTONYMS: passive, peaceful

2 ADJECTIVE A **violent** film or television programme contains a lot of scenes which show violence. ○ *It was the most violent film that I have ever seen.*

▶ COLLOCATIONS:
a violent **film/movie/scene**
extremely violent

vio|lent|ly

ADVERB ○ *Some opposition activists have been violently attacked.* ○ *Even meek and mild people will sometimes react violently.*

▶ COLLOCATION: **behave/react/clash/quarrel** violently

▶ SYNONYM: aggressively

▶ ANTONYM: peacefully

vio|lence /ˈvaɪələns/

UNCOUNTABLE NOUN Violence is behaviour which is intended to hurt, injure, or kill people. ○ *Twenty people were killed in the violence.* ○ *They threaten them with violence.* ○ *domestic violence between husband and wife*

▶ COLLOCATIONS:
violence **against** someone
condemn/prevent/stop/resort to violence
violence **erupts**
a **victim/act/outbreak** of violence
gang/gun/street violence
domestic/physical/sexual violence
ethnic/racial/increasing/widespread violence

▶ SYNONYM: aggression

vo|cabu|lary /vəʊˈkæbjʊləri, AM -leri/ (vocabularies) `LANGUAGE`

1 NOUN Your **vocabulary** is the total number of words you know in a particular language. ○ *His speech is immature, his vocabulary limited.*
○ *Listen to the patient's vocabulary, which discloses what they think about their symptoms.*

2 NOUN The **vocabulary** of a language is all the words in it. ○ *a new word in the German vocabulary* ○ *[+ of] the grammar and vocabulary of the English language*

▶ **COLLOCATIONS:**
   the vocabulary **of** *something/someone*
   learn vocabulary
   a **basic/limited/extensive** vocabulary
   specialized/technical vocabulary
   vocabulary **development**

▶ **SYNONYMS:** lexicon, words, terminology

▶ **RELATED WORDS:** grammar, syntax

---

vote /vəʊt/ (votes) `SOCIAL SCIENCE` `POLITICS`

1 NOUN A **vote** is a choice made by a particular person or group in a meeting or an election. The **vote** is the total number of votes or voters in an election. ○ *He walked to the local polling centre to cast his vote.* ○ *The government got a massive majority – well over 400 votes.* ○ *Mr Reynolds was re-elected by 102 votes to 60.* ○ *The vote was strongly in favour of the Democratic Party.* ○ *a huge majority of the white male vote*

2 NOUN If you have **the vote** in an election, or have **a vote** in a meeting, you have the legal right to indicate your choice. ○ *Before that, women did not have a vote at all.*

▶ **COLLOCATIONS:**
   a vote **in** *an election*
   a vote **on** *something*
   a vote **for/against** *someone/something*
   a vote on a **proposal/resolution/matter/issue**
   a vote for a **candidate/president/party**
   cast a vote
   win/count votes
   a **parliamentary/presidential** vote
   a **wasted/protest/casting** vote

▶ **SYNONYM:** ballot

vot|er ./ˈvəʊtə/ (voters)

NOUN Voters are people who have the legal right to vote in elections, or people who are voting in a particular election. ○ *Austrian voters went to the polls this weekend to elect a successor to the President.* ○ *The voter turn-out was eighty-three per cent.*

▸ COLLOCATIONS:
   ask/remind/persuade voters
   attract/convince voters
   a **registered/eligible** voter
   a **floating/undecided** voter
   a **conservative/liberal** voter
   voter **turnout/registration/participation**
   voter **apathy/intimidation**
▸ SYNONYM: elector

Ww

wage /weɪdʒ/ (wages)

BUSINESS

NOUN Someone's **wages** are the amount of money that is regularly paid to them for the work that they do. ○ *His wages have gone up.* ○ *This may end efforts to set a minimum wage well above the poverty line.*

→ see note at **earn**

▶ **COLLOCATIONS:**
  earn/pay/raise/increase/cut wages
  a wage **rise/increase/cut**
  a **low/high/basic/minimum** wage
  a wage **demand/earner/packet**

▶ **SYNONYMS:** salary, pay, earnings, income

war /wɔː/ (wars)

NOUN A **war** is a period of fighting or conflict between countries or states. ○ *He spent part of the war in the National Guard.* ○ *matters of war and peace* ○ *They've been at war for the last fifteen years.*

▶ **COLLOCATIONS:**
  be **at** war
  go **to** war
  war **against/on** *something*
  war **between** *people*
  wage/make/declare/win a war
  start/fight/justify a war
  oppose/end/avert/avoid a war
  war **begins/breaks out/starts**
  a **civil/holy/cold/nuclear** war
  a **bloody/all-out/global** war

▶ **SYNONYM:** conflict
▶ **ANTONYM:** peace

W

warn /wɔːn/ (warns, warning, warned)

VERB If you **warn** someone about something such as a possible danger or problem, you tell them about it so that they are aware of it. ○ [+ *that*] *When I had my first baby friends warned me that children were expensive.* ○ [+ *of/about*] *They warned him of the dangers of sailing alone.* ○ [+ *that*]

Analysts warned that Europe's most powerful economy may be facing trouble.
○ [+ of] *He also warned of a possible anti-Western backlash.*
▶ **COLLOCATIONS:**
   warn *someone* **of/about/against** *something*
   experts/officials warn
▶ **SYNONYMS:** alert, caution

warn|ing /ˈwɔːnɪŋ/ (warnings)

NOUN A **warning** is something which is said or written to tell people of a
possible danger, problem, or other unpleasant thing that might happen.
○ [+ that] *The minister gave a warning that if war broke out, it would be
catastrophic.* ○ *The government has unveiled new health warnings for cigarette
packets.*
▶ **COLLOCATIONS:**
   a warning **of** *something*
   a warning of **danger**
   a **tsunami/flood/hurricane/storm** warning
   a **health/weather** warning
   a **severe/dire/stark/stern** warning
   an **advance/early/official** warning
   a warning **label/sign/signal**
   issue/give/send/receive/ignore a warning
▶ **SYNONYM:** alert

---

waste /weɪst/ (wastes, wasting, wasted)

1 VERB If you **waste** something such as time, money, or energy, you use
too much of it doing something that is not important or necessary, or is
unlikely to succeed. ○ [+ v-ing] *There could be many reasons and he was not
going to waste time speculating on them.* ○ [+ on] *I resolved not to waste money
on a hotel.* ○ *The system wastes a large amount of water.*
▶ **COLLOCATIONS:**
   waste *something* **on** *something*
   waste **energy/money/time/effort/water**
▶ **SYNONYMS:** misuse, squander
▶ **ANTONYM:** save

2 UNCOUNTABLE NOUN **Waste** is the use of money or other resources on
things that do not need it. ○ *The packets are measured to reduce waste.* ○ *The
department was criticised for inefficiency and waste.*
▶ **COLLOCATIONS:**
   reduce/eliminate waste
   complete/tragic/terrible waste

way of life /ˌweɪ əv ˈlaɪf, ᴀᴍ ˌweɪ ʌv ˈlaɪf/ (ways of life)

NOUN A **way of life** is the behaviour and habits that are typical of a particular person or group, or that are chosen by them. ○ *Mining activities have totally disrupted the traditional way of life of the Yanomami Indians.* ○ *Fighting among the boys was taken as a way of life.*
- ▶ **COLLOCATIONS:**
  a **normal/traditional/ancient/natural** way of life
  become a way of life
  part of *someone's* way of life
- ▶ **PHRASE:** just a way of life
- ▶ **SYNONYM:** lifestyle

wealth /welθ/

UNCOUNTABLE NOUN **Wealth** is the possession of a large amount of money, property, or other valuable things. You can also refer to a particular person's money or property as their **wealth**. ○ *Economic reform has brought relative wealth to peasant farmers.* ○ *His own wealth grew.*
- ▶ **COLLOCATIONS:**
  accumulate/amass/inherit/acquire wealth
  generate/create/share wealth
  vast/enormous/considerable/comparative wealth
  new-found/personal wealth
  wealth **management/creation**
- ▶ **PHRASES:**
  wealth and fame
  wealth and power
  wealth and beauty
- ▶ **SYNONYM:** affluence
- ▶ **ANTONYM:** poverty

wealthy /ˈwelθi/ (wealthier, wealthiest)

ADJECTIVE Someone who is **wealthy** has a large amount of money, property, or valuable possessions. ○ *a wealthy international businessman*
- ▶ **COLLOCATIONS:**
  fabulously/extremely/very/relatively wealthy
  a wealthy **businessman/individual/nation/family**
  a wealthy **landowner/donor/client**
- ▶ **SYNONYMS:** affluent, well-off, rich
- ▶ **ANTONYM:** poor

w

weight /weɪt/ (weights)

NOUN The **weight** of a person or thing is how heavy they are, measured in units such as kilograms, pounds, or tons. ○ *What is your height and weight?* ○ *This reduced the weight of the load.* ○ [+ *of*] *Turkeys can reach enormous weights of up to 50 pounds.*

▶ **COLLOCATIONS:**
   a weight **of** *an amount*
   lose/gain/put on weight
   weight **gain/loss**
   body weight
   excess/ideal/healthy/normal weight
▶ **PHRASE:** height and weight

weigh /weɪ/ (weighs, weighing, weighed)

1 VERB If someone or something **weighs** a particular amount, this amount is how heavy they are. ○ *It weighs nearly 27 kilos (about 65 pounds).* ○ *This little ball of gold weighs a quarter of an ounce.*

▶ **COLLOCATIONS:**
   weigh **exactly/roughly** *an amount*
   weigh **less than/more than** *an amount*
   weigh *x* **pounds/stone/grams/kilos/tons**

2 VERB If you **weigh** something or someone, you measure how heavy they are. ○ *The scales can be used to weigh other items such as parcels.* ○ *Each sample was accurately weighed.*

▶ **COLLOCATION:** weigh *something* **carefully/accurately**
▶ **SYNONYM:** measure

west /west/ also West   GEOGRAPHY

1 UNCOUNTABLE NOUN The **west** is the direction which you look towards in the evening in order to see the sun set. ○ *I pushed on towards Flagstaff, a hundred miles to the west.* ○ *The sun crosses the sky from east to west.*

2 NOUN The **west of** a place, country, or region is the part of it which is in the west. ○ [+ *of*] *physicists working at Bristol University in the west of England*

3 NOUN The **West** is used to refer to the United States, Canada, and the countries of Western, Northern, and Southern Europe. ○ *relations between Iran and the West* ○ *the leaders of the industrialized West*

▶ **COLLOCATIONS:**
   the west **of** *somewhere*
   west of the **border/city/capital**
   the west of a **country/city/region**

the **wild** west
the **capitalist/industrialised** West

▶ PHRASE: north, south, east, and west
▶ RELATED WORDS: north, south, east

west|ern /ˈwestən/

1 ADJECTIVE **Western** means in or from the west of a region, state, or country. ○ *hand-made rugs from Western and Central Asia* ○ *Moi University, in western Kenya*

2 ADJECTIVE **Western** is used to describe things, people, ideas, or ways of life that come from or are associated with the United States, Canada, and the countries of Western, Northern, and Southern Europe. ○ *Mexico had the support of the big western governments.* ○ *Those statements have never been reported in the Western media.*

▶ COLLOCATIONS:
western **governments/democracies/powers/leaders**
western **medicine/literature/music**
western **traditions/attitudes/dress**
▶ RELATED WORDS: northern, southern, eastern

west|ern|ized /ˈwestənaɪzd/

ADJECTIVE A **westernized** country, place, or person has adopted ideas and behaviour typical of Europe and North America, rather than preserving the ideas and behaviour that are traditional in their culture. [in BRIT, also use **westernised**] ○ [+ *in*] *Africans educated in Europe, and thoroughly Westernized in their thinking* ○ *But even in liberal, Westernized households, gender roles are strictly observed.*

▶ COLLOCATION: westernized **in** *something*
▶ SYNONYM: modernized
▶ ANTONYM: traditional

west|erni|za|tion /ˌwestənaɪˈzeɪʃən/

UNCOUNTABLE NOUN [in BRIT, also use **westernisation**] ○ [+ *of*] *fundamentalists unhappy with the westernization of Afghan culture* ○ *The explosive growth in casinos is one of the most conspicuous signs of Westernisation.*

▶ COLLOCATION: the westernization **of** *somewhere*
▶ SYNONYM: modernization

w

---

whole /həʊl/

1 QUANTIFIER If you refer to **the whole of** something, you mean all of it. ○ [+ *of*] *He has said he will make an apology to the whole of Asia for his country's*

past behaviour. ○ [+ of] I was cold throughout the whole of my body. ○ [+ of] the whole of August

▶ COLLOCATIONS:
the whole **of** something
the whole of **society/humanity/creation/history**

▶ SYNONYMS: entirety, all

2 PHRASE If you refer to something **as a whole**, you are referring to it generally and as a single unit. ○ He described the move as a victory for the people of South Africa as a whole. ○ As a whole we do not eat enough fibre in Britain.

▶ SYNONYMS: in general, generally

3 PHRASE You use **on the whole** to indicate that what you are saying is true in general but may not be true in every case, or that you are giving a general opinion or summary of something. ○ On the whole, this strategy works. ○ The wine towns encountered are, on the whole, quiet and modest.

▶ SYNONYMS: in general, generally, in the main

---

wide /waɪd/ (wider, widest)

ADJECTIVE You use **wide** to talk or ask about how much something measures from one side or edge to the other. ○ a corridor of land 10 kilometres wide ○ The road is only one track wide. ○ a desk that was almost as wide as the room

▶ COLLOCATIONS:
x **inches/feet/metres/miles** wide
wide **shoulders**
a wide **gap/space/expanse/berth**

▶ SYNONYMS: broad, large
▶ ANTONYM: narrow

width /wɪdθ/ (widths)

NOUN The **width** of something is the distance it measures from one side or edge to the other. ○ [+ of] Measure the full width of the window. ○ The road was reduced to 18ft in width by adding parking bays. ○ Saddles are made in a wide range of different widths.

▶ COLLOCATIONS:
the width **of** something
an amount **in** width
a width of x **feet/inches/metres/miles**
adjust/vary/decrease/increase/extend the width
the **full/overall/approximate/minimum/maximum** width
column/track/border/band width
hip/shoulder/trouser/foot width

▶ **PHRASES:**
  height and width
  length and width
  depth and width
▶ **SYNONYMS:** span, breadth
▶ **RELATED WORDS:** height, depth

---

wild /waɪld/ **(wilder, wildest)**   `SCIENCE` `BIOLOGY`

ADJECTIVE Wild animals or plants live or grow in natural surroundings and
are not looked after by people. ○ *The forests are home to rare birds and wild
animals.* ○ *The lane was lined with wild flowers.*
▶ **COLLOCATIONS:**
  a wild **animal/beast/boar/cat/dog/salmon**
  a wild **flower/mushroom/strawberry**
  wild **rice**
▶ **SYNONYMS:** feral, untamed
▶ **ANTONYMS:** tame, domestic

---

wild|life /ˈwaɪldlaɪf/   `SCIENCE` `BIOLOGY`

UNCOUNTABLE NOUN You can use **wildlife** to refer to the animals and other
living things that live in the wild. ○ *People were concerned that pets or wildlife
could be affected by the pesticides.* ○ *Opponents say drilling could threaten the
rich wildlife in the area.*
▶ **COLLOCATIONS:**
  conserve/protect/preserve/benefit/encourage wildlife
  harm/endanger/disturb/threaten wildlife
  endangered/abundant wildlife
  native/exotic/marine wildlife
  wildlife **conservation**
  a wildlife **refuge/sanctuary/habitat/reserve/park**
  a wildlife **biologist/photographer/enthusiast**
▶ **PHRASE:** scenery and wildlife
▶ **SYNONYMS:** animals, fauna

---

will|ing /ˈwɪlɪŋ/

ADJECTIVE If someone is **willing to** do something, they are fairly happy
about doing it and will do it if they are asked or required to do it.
  ○ [+ to-inf] *The military now say they're willing to hold talks with the political
parties.* ○ *There are, of course, questions which she will not be willing to answer.*
▶ **COLLOCATIONS:**
  a willing **accomplice/participant/partner/helper**
  a willing **volunteer/donor/victim**

▶ **PHRASES:**
willing and ready
able and willing
▶ **SYNONYM:** prepared
▶ **ANTONYMS:** unwilling, reluctant

wing /wɪŋ/ (wings)   `SCIENCE` `BIOLOGY`

NOUN The **wings** of a bird or insect are the two parts of its body that it uses for flying. ○ [+ of] *the outstretched wings of an eagle* ○ *the flapping of butterfly wings*
▶ **COLLOCATIONS:**
the wings **of** something
the wings of a **bird/butterfly/eagle/bat**
chicken/butterfly wings
outstretched/clipped wings
wings **flap/fold/flutter/beat/spread**

wire /waɪə/ (wires)

NOUN A **wire** is a long thin piece of metal that is used to fasten things or to carry electric current. ○ *fine copper wire* ○ *gadgets which detect electrical wires, pipes and timbers in walls*
▶ **COLLOCATIONS:**
electrical/electric/live/overhead wires
telephone/telegraph/high-voltage wires
fuse/steel/razor/fencing/perimeter wire
a wire **cutter/stripper**
a wire **brush/cage/basket/coil/fence**
wire **mesh**

wire|less /ˈwaɪələs/   `IT`

ADJECTIVE **Wireless** technology uses radio waves rather than electricity and therefore does not require any wires. ○ *the fast-growing wireless communication market* ○ *transmitting data across a wireless network* ○ *The company is going wireless.*
▶ **COLLOCATIONS:**
a wireless **phone/telephone/device**
a wireless **frequency/signal/zone**
a wireless **network/connection/infrastructure**
wireless **applications/equipment**
wireless **communications/systems/technology**
go wireless

wit|ness /'wɪtnəs/ (witnesses, witnessing, witnessed) `LAW`

1 **NOUN** A **witness to** an event such as an accident or crime is a person who saw it. ○ [+ to] *Witnesses to the crash say they saw an explosion just before the disaster.* ○ *No witnesses have come forward.*
   ▶ **COLLOCATION:** a witness **to** *something*
   ▶ **SYNONYM:** eye-witness

2 **VERB** If you **witness** something, you see it happen. ○ *Anyone who witnessed the attack should call the police.*
   ▶ **COLLOCATION:** witness *something* **firsthand**
   ▶ **SYNONYMS:** see, experience

3 **NOUN** A **witness** is someone who appears in a court of law to say what they know about a crime or other event. ○ *In the next three or four days, eleven witnesses will be called to testify.*
   ▶ **COLLOCATIONS:**
   a witness **for** *someone*
   a witness for the **defence/prosecution**
   a **defence/prosecution/material** witness
   a **character/surprise/mystery** witness
   question/interview/cross-examine a witness
   intimidate/discredit/protect a witness
   call/summon a witness
   a witness **testifies/reports/claims**
   a witness **swears/corroborates/alleges/identifies**
   a witness **stand/box**
   witness **intimidation/protection**
   a **reluctant/unreliable/credible** witness
   a **key/hostile/independent/expert** witness
   the witness's **testimony/statement/evidence**
   the witness's **description/account**

work /wɜːk/ (works) `ARTS`

NOUN A **work** is something such as a painting, book, or piece of music produced by an artist, writer, or composer. ○ *In my opinion, this is Rembrandt's greatest work.* ○ [+ of] *the complete works of Shakespeare* ○ [+ of] *The church has several valuable works of art.* ○ [+ for] *his first major work for orchestra*
   → see note at **job**
   ▶ **COLLOCATIONS:**
   a work **of/for** *something*
   a work of **art/fiction/non-fiction/literature/sculpture**
   a work of **genius**

W

a work for **orchestra/piano/theatre/dancers**
an **unfinished/complete/autobiographical** work
original/late/major/literary/new work
a **composer's/painter's/sculptor's/artist's/** work
a **playwright's/poet's/author's/writer's** work
▶ **PHRASE:** work in progress
▶ **SYNONYM:** piece
▶ **RELATED WORDS:** painting, sculpture

---

work|er /'wɜːkə/ (workers)   `BUSINESS`

1 NOUN A particular kind of **worker** does the kind of work mentioned. ○ *office workers* ○ *The society was looking for a capable research worker.* ○ *aid workers in Somalia*

2 NOUN Workers are people who are employed in industry or business and who are not managers. ○ *Wages have been frozen and workers laid off.* ○ *The agreement encourages worker participation in management decisions.*
▶ **COLLOCATIONS:**
  recruit/employ/pay workers
  unionize/represent/protect workers
  workers **earn/receive** *something*
  workers **fear/suffer/lose/face** *something*
  a **willing/skilled/unskilled** worker
  a **railway/postal/construction/factory** worker
  a **youth/charity/social/health/care** worker
  a **blue-collar/white-collar/manual/clerical** worker
  a **striking/full-time/part-time/temporary** worker
  a **foreign/migrant/low-paid** worker
  a **humanitarian/aid/rescue/emergency/relief** worker
  worker **safety/protection/productivity/output**
▶ **SYNONYMS:** employee, member of staff
▶ **ANTONYM:** employer

---

world|wide /ˌwɜːldˈwaɪd/ also **world-wide**

ADVERB If something exists or happens **worldwide**, it exists or happens throughout the world. ○ *His books have sold more than 20 million copies worldwide.* ○ *Worldwide, an enormous amount of research effort goes into military technology.*
▶ **SYNONYMS:** all over the world, around the world

wors|en /ˈwɜːsən/ (worsens, worsening, worsened)

VERB If a bad situation **worsens** or if something **worsens** it, it becomes more difficult, unpleasant, or unacceptable. ○ *The security forces had to intervene to prevent the situation worsening.* ○ [V-ing] *They remain in freezing weather and rapidly worsening conditions.*

▶ **COLLOCATIONS:**
  a worsening **situation/condition/crisis/problem**
  a worsening **economy/recession/shortage/deficit**
  worsening **relations/weather**
  steadily/dramatically/significantly worsen
  progressively/gradually/further worsen

▶ **SYNONYMS:** deteriorate, get worse

▶ **ANTONYM:** improve

worth|while /ˌwɜːθˈwaɪl/

ADJECTIVE If something is **worthwhile**, it is enjoyable or useful, and worth the time, money, or effort that is spent on it. ○ *The President's trip to Washington this week seems to have been worthwhile.* ○ *an interesting and worthwhile project* ○ [+ to-inf] *It might be worthwhile to consider an insurance policy.*

▶ **COLLOCATIONS:**
  the **sacrifice/effort/exercise/work** is worthwhile
  a worthwhile **endeavour/cause/project/initiative/exercise**
  a worthwhile **investment/contribution/addition/improvement**
  financially worthwhile

▶ **SYNONYMS:** useful, helpful, valuable

▶ **ANTONYMS:** useless, wasteful

w

Xx

X-ray /ˈeksreɪ/ (X-rays, X-raying, X-rayed) also **x-ray**   `MEDICINE`

1 NOUN X-rays are a type of radiation that can pass through most solid materials. X-rays are used by doctors to examine the bones or organs inside your body and are also used at airports to see inside people's luggage. ○ *X-rays are widely used in medicine to take pictures of bones.* ○ *Checked baggage is passed through X-ray machines.*

2 NOUN An **X-ray** is a picture made by sending X-rays through something, usually someone's body. ○ *She was advised to have an abdominal X-ray.* ○ *The X-ray revealed minor head injuries.*

▶ COLLOCATIONS:
  emit x-rays
  X-ray **diffraction/vision/equipment**
  take/have an X-ray
  a **precautionary/diagnostic** X-ray
  a **dental/chest** X-ray
  an X-ray **machine/telescope/image**
  an X-ray **reveals/shows** *something*

▶ SYNONYM: scan
▶ RELATED WORD: ultrasound

3 VERB If someone or something **is X-rayed**, an X-ray picture is taken of them. ○ *All hand baggage would be x-rayed.* ○ *They took my pulse, took my blood pressure, and X-rayed my jaw.*

▶ COLLOCATION: X-ray a **person/leg/joint**
▶ SYNONYM: scan

Yy

---

yard /jɑːd/ (yards)

NOUN A **yard** is a unit of length equal to thirty-six inches or approximately 91.4 centimetres. ○ [+ *from*] *The incident took place about 500 yards from where he was standing.* ○ *a long narrow strip of linen two or three yards long* ○ [+ *of*] *a yard of silk*

▶ **COLLOCATIONS:**
   x yards **from** *somewhere*
   x yards **of** *something*
   x yards of **fabric/cloth/silk/ribbon**
   x yards **deep/thick/wide/long**
   x yards **apart/ahead/behind/below**
   x **cubic/square** yards

▶ **RELATED WORDS:** meter, inch

---

young /jʌŋ/   SCIENCE   BIOLOGY

PLURAL NOUN The **young** of an animal are its babies. ○ *The hen may not be able to feed its young.* ○ *Its young are vulnerable to a range of predators.*

▶ **COLLOCATION:** **feed/suckle/protect/rear** young

▶ **SYNONYMS:** babies, family, litter, offspring, brood

Zz

zero /ˈzɪərəʊ/ (zeros)   MATHS

1 **NUMBER Zero** is the number 0. ○ *Visibility at the city's airport came down to zero, bringing air traffic to a standstill.* ○ *a scale ranging from zero to seven*

2 **UNCOUNTABLE NOUN Zero** is a temperature of 0°. It is freezing point on the Centigrade and Celsius scales, and 32° below freezing point on the Fahrenheit scale. ○ *It's a sunny late winter day, just a few degrees above zero.* ○ *That night the mercury fell to thirty degrees below zero.*

▶ **COLLOCATIONS:**
  above/below zero
  absolute zero
▶ **SYNONYMS:** nought, nothing

z